MY EXPERIENCES IN THE WORLD WAR

VOLUME II

MY EXPERIENCES IN THE WORLD WAR

VOLUME II

JOHN J. PERSHING

MILITARY CLASSICS SERIES

FIRST TAB EDITION
FIRST TAB PRINTING

My Experiences in the World War, Volume I, by John J. Pershing.
Published by arrangement with Harper & Row Publishers, Inc.
All rights reserved.

Library of Congress Cataloging in Publication Data

Pershing, John J. (John Joseph), 1860-1948.
    My experiences in the World War / by John J. Pershing.
        p.   cm.
    Reprint.
    Includes index.
    ISBN 0-8306-9407-2 (v. 2)
    1. Pershing, John J. (John Joseph) 1860-1948.   2. World
War, 1914-1918—Personal narratives, American.   3. World War,
1914-1918—United States.   4. Generals—United States—
Biography.   5. United
    States. Army—Biography.   I. Title.
    D640.P454   1989
    940.4'81'73—dc19   89-4261
                                                            CIP

TAB BOOKS Inc. offers software for sale. For information and
a catalog, please contact TAB Software Department, Blue Ridge
Summit, PA 17294-0850.

Questions regarding the content of this book
should be addressed to:

    Reader Inquiry Branch
    TAB BOOKS Inc.
    Blue Ridge Summit, PA 17294-0214

Cover photograph courtesy of U.S. Army

Military Classics Series

The U.S. military today is enjoying a renewed popularity with the American public. To help serve this burgeoning interest, TAB is proud to present the *Military Classics Series*.

This series will bring back into print quality, hardcover editions of many of the most famous books by or about key figures in U.S. military history. Whenever possible these will be firsthand accounts—the autobiographies of noted military figures or the memoirs of journalists who were at the front. Some will be biographies written by knowledgeable friends and associates of the subject. All will provide the closest possible insight into the events that have shaped our military history.

The series will span the length of American military history—from the Revolution to Vietnam. Although the series will be limited to the wars and conflicts in which the United States participated, it occasionally will include an outside perspective through the autobiographies of allies and enemies alike.

These books have long been unavailable in hardcover for both readers and collectors. The *Military Classics Series* will present them in an affordable personal-library format for military enthusiasts.

CONTENTS

VOLUME II

CHAPTER XXVII

CHAPTER XXXVI

CHAPTER XXXVII

CHAPTER XXXVIII

CHAPTER XXXIX

CHAPTER XL

CHAPTER XLV

CHAPTER XLVI

CHAPTER XLVII

CHAPTER XLVIII

CHAPTER XLIX

CHAPTER L

CHAPTER LI

MY EXPERIENCES IN THE
WORLD WAR

CHAPTER XXVII

Visit British Front—Inspection of 77th Division—Agreement on Training with British—Conference in England—London Agreement—Discussion with Foch on Shipment American Troops—Shipping Situation —Recommend Call for 1,500,000 Men—Seicheprey—French and British Propose Limiting our Production Airplanes—Italians and Unity of Command—Foch's Authority Extended to Include Italian Army.

(Diary) British G.H.Q., Saturday, April 20, 1918. Washington disturbed over German propaganda.[1] Came here yesterday at Sir Douglas Haig's invitation to discuss training of our troops and study operations in progress.

Stopped at our II Corps Headquarters at Fruges to-day and find organization well handled by Chief of Staff, Colonel G. S. Simonds. Saw some of 77th Division, now arriving in British area. Visited General Currie's headquarters at Chamblain l'Abbé.

WE were always made welcome at British headquarters. It so happened that on the day of our arrival Lord Derby, who had just been replaced as Minister of War by Lord Milner, was there en route to Paris as British Ambassador. During dinner the conversation ran along freely as though we were members of the official family. At length, Lord Derby and

[1] The following cable was sent on April 19th: "For Chief of Staff. With reference to your cablegram, German propaganda has used such stories persistently in effort to stir up distrust and dissension among Allies. In some cases facts have been distorted as, for example, the capture of unarmed American working parties being played up as capture of combat troops. In most cases stories are completely false. Following are examples from German wireless news: 'March 5th—The Americans recently captured had been placed with French troops in the front lines for training purposes. * * * They are strong young fellows but do not seem to have much desire to fight. They have no understanding of the war. To them it is an enterprise undertaken by New York financiers. They hate but respect the English. With the French they are on good terms. They have not the slightest idea of military operations and seem stupid and fatalistic in comparison with the war-accustomed Frenchmen. * * * They were glad

1

Sir Douglas drifted to the subject of British politicians. It would betray no confidence to say that during this conversation there was considerable criticism of some who held prominent places. The coalition Government came in for its share because of its attitude toward the military High Command. Lord Derby was well known to be a warm supporter of the British Commander-in-Chief, and from what I knew of the relations between the civil and the military authorities of Great Britain it is fair to presume that this might have been the reason he relinquished his post as Minister for War. He asked why all parties were not represented in our Cabinet, but I did not undertake to give any explanation, although I had often asked myself the same question. It need hardly be recalled that in so far as the Americans were concerned Lord Derby was always most helpful.

The operations on the Lys were still active and the Germans were showing their usual persistence. Marshal Haig spoke in high terms of the fine conduct of his divisions against the enemy's offensive. They deserved high praise, as they were not at all fresh, and generally occupied a much wider front than safety demanded. Sir Douglas seemed to be confident that the offensive would soon spend itself.

It was stimulating to morale to visit the headquarters of the Canadians, where one soon caught the fine spirit of that superb corps. We talked with the Corps Commander, Lieutenant General Sir Arthur Currie, his Chief of Staff, and others, and had tea with them. The alertness and confidence of these neighbors of ours were admirable, and the excellent record they had made and were still making gave us as much gratification as though they had been our own countrymen. I remember this visit with much pleasure and recall the prediction of the Canadians that Americans would soon play an important part in the war.

to escape further fighting. March 29th—French officers do not conceal their disillusionment over the value of the veteran American troops and are using them by battalions and larger units among the English and French infantry. They are entirely incapable of carrying out independent operations.' Distribution of propaganda is attempted by small balloons sent across with favoring wind; also printing of cleverly imitated Italian papers for distribution back of Italian front; also circulation of stories by enemy agents. These efforts having scant success."

General Currie deplored the fact that the British had so easily given up Passchendaele Ridge, which the year before he had been told must be taken at all cost, and for which the Canadians made the tremendous sacrifice of 16,000 casualties. His divisions were then holding 9,000 yards each, or a little over five miles of front, as compared with from 4,500 to 7,000 yards per division held by Gough's and Byng's armies in March. Currie considered that his extension would be excessive in the face of a determined and powerful offensive using shock tactics. Whatever the disadvantages were, it did show the British Commander-in-Chief's confidence in the Canadians.

I took advantage of the opportunity while on the British front to visit the Nordausques area to inspect the advance elements of the 77th Division, which was one of the divisions selected for training with the British. We took luncheon with Brigadier General Evan M. Johnson, then temporarily in command, and his staff officers. He praised the soldierly qualities of the men, but said they were very much behind in their training. This division had suffered severely from the practice followed by the War Department of taking men who had been under training for some time and sending them elsewhere for special purposes. A total of 30,000 men had been selected from time to time from this division and their places filled with recruits, with the result that the infantry and machine gun units, numbering about 17,000 men, that reported in France were composed largely of untrained or partially trained troops.

While at Sir Douglas' headquarters, he and I reached an understanding as to the training and administration of American troops that were to be temporarily with the British. In the first place, they were to be allocated by regiments to British skeleton divisions under such a schedule as might be agreed upon. The training staffs of British divisions were to be at the disposal of these regiments, especially for instruction in the use of the rifle and machine gun, and in the handling of gas. After that, and with the approval of their American division commander, each regiment was to be attached to a British division in line, so that each of its three battalions would have the opportunity of serving with one of the British brigades. Our battalions were to be commanded by our own officers, and our regimental staffs were to be attached to those of British brigades. In the next stage, each of our regiments, with its three battalions united under the regimental commander, was to act as a brigade in a British division. The final stage would find the four American regiments reunited to form the division under its own officers, with British artillery until the arrival of its own artillery brigade.

In carrying out this scheme, the tendency at first was for British officers actually to assume command of our units in training. Our officers in most cases permitted this to be done until it was checked by my orders, which directed that "American units must be commanded in training by the officers and noncommissioned officers who are to command them in battle," and, further, that American troops would in all cases be commanded in battle only by Americans.

The program probably expedited preparation in some respects, but questions of food, transport, and methods of instruction arose which demonstrated that any attempt at permanent amalgamation would have surely led to friction and inefficiency. Because they were needed elsewhere, none of the divisions sent to train with the British, except the 27th and 30th, remained long enough to carry out the prescribed course.

The subject of coördination of the supply systems of the armies on the Western Front was also taken up with Sir Douglas. I explained my idea of pooling supplies, and pointed out that he was already committed to the principle, as illustrated by his providing certain equipment and transportation for our divisions that were to serve behind his lines for training. But the proposition of relinquishing control of his supplies, even partially, did not appeal to him. He was afraid that if it should be given general application it would be a one-sided affair. To a certain extent this might have been the result, as we would probably have been the greatest beneficiaries. But if by pooling certain things common to all armies, more tonnage could have been saved to transport our troops and supplies, it would have meant that much more aid to the Allied cause.

(Diary) London, Wednesday, April 24, 1918. Left British G.H.Q. for London on Sunday, with Harbord, Boyd, and Adamson. Were met at Folkestone by Biddle and Rethers.[1] Also met Stevens and L. H. Shearman at Folkestone, both anxious about coal supply. Little evidence of food shortage at the Savoy Hotel, where we are stopping.

Called Monday on Ambassador Page, who said my offer to Foch had greatly pleased the British. Saw Admiral Sims and find he thinks decreased danger from submarines warrants sending troops by smaller ships. Started conference with Lord Milner and Sir Henry Wilson.

On Tuesday Winston Churchill told me that as the German attack was a month later than expected they had plenty of artillery and ammunition, notwithstanding recent losses. Called on Mr. Lloyd George and discussed Allied supply with him but got little encouragement.

Resumed conference this morning and agreed on details of troop shipments. Had luncheon with Major and Lady Astor. Dined informally at St. James' Palace with the Duke of Connaught, who does not share the gloomy outlook, although he deplores the severe losses.

Following the suggestion of Lord Milner, I went to London to consider further the shipment of American troops. At our first meeting there were present Lord Milner and General Sir Henry Wilson, who had succeeded General Robertson as the Chief of the General Staff, Harbord, and myself. The main point of difference that had developed in previous conferences as to just how far the Americans should be committed to serve in active operations was again considered. I stated that the principal thing was to get our units trained, and that while I was opposed to amalgamation, yet if during the period of instruction the British units with which they were serving should be attacked, or if another great emergency should arise, of course our men would go in. Naturally, the British wanted unlimited infantry and machine gun units, but I could not go further than to consider a limited extension of the six-division plan.

During the conference, a cable from Lord Reading to the Prime

---

[1] Maj. Gen. John Biddle was in command of the Base Section comprising England and Col. Harry Rethers was Chief Quartermaster of the section.

Minister was brought forth which stated that the President had agreed to the amalgamation of Americans with the British. I had nothing official at hand later than the President's conditional approval of Joint Note No. 18 as suggested by Mr. Baker, so I promptly said that it could not be possible that any such concession had been made, and that the classes of our troops to be shipped over and their disposition must be left to me. Of course, we knew that the British were pressing this point by constant appeals to the President and that they were insisting that he should agree to the shipment of 120,000 infantry and machine gun units per month for four months, to the exclusion of all other personnel. While the British conferees had concluded from Lord Reading's cable that their case was won, I took quite another view and declined to consider the information as conclusive.

As a result of these discussions, we reached an agreement which provided for the shipment in the month of May, by British and American tonnage, of the infantry, machine gun, engineer, and signal troops, together with the various unit headquarters, of six divisions for training with the British Army. It was provided that any shipping in excess of the amount required for this number of troops should be utilized to transport the artillery of these divisions, and that such personnel as might be required to build up corps organizations should then follow; it being understood that the artillery regiments would train with the French and join their proper divisions when the training of the infantry was completed.

In order to meet any emergency which might require an excess of infantry after the completion of this program, it was agreed that all the American and British shipping available for the transportation of troops was to be used under such arrangement as would insure immediate aid to the Allies, and thereafter as far as possible provide other units necessary to complete the organization of our divisions and corps. It was further agreed that the combatant troops mentioned in connection with May shipments should be followed by such service of supply troops and other contingents as we ourselves might consider necessary, inasmuch as the shipment of such troops had been postponed; and that all these troops should be utilized at my discretion, except that the six divisions which the British were to transport would be trained with them.

Upon reaching Chaumont, I found a cablegram, dated April 26th, transmitting a memorandum, dated April 19th, that had been sent by direction of the President to the British Ambassador at Washington in conformity with his approval of Joint Note No. 18 of the Supreme War Council. In this memorandum the shipment of only infantry and machine gun units for four months was conceded, and it was hoped and believed that the number would be 120,000 per month. Their assignment for training and use was to be left to my discretion. The memorandum went on to say that the United States, until the situation changed, had no intention of departing from as full compliance with the recommendation of the Permanent Military Representatives as the nature of the case would permit.

This was the first official information I had received that the Administration had agreed to send any specific numbers of infantry and machine units to France.

The following quotation is a continuation of the memorandum:

"It being also understood that this statement is not to be regarded as a commitment from which the Government of the United States is not free to depart when the exigencies no longer require it; and also that the preferential transportation of infantry and machine gun units here set forth as a policy and principle is not to be regarded as so exclusive as to prevent the Government of the United States from including in the troops carried by its own tonnage from time to time relatively small numbers of personnel of other arms as may be deemed wise by the United States as replacements and either to make possible the use of a maximum capacity of ships or the most efficient use of the infantry and machine gun units as such transported, or the maintenance of the services of supply already organized and in process of construction for the American Army already in France."

This concession went further than it was necessary to go and much further than I had expected. Realizing the complications that might arise from commitments so far in the future and the delay in forming an American army that would follow, I did not agree in later discussions at the Supreme War Council with all that the Allies now felt justified in demanding. I was opposed to the action of the Council in assuming the power to dispose of American troops under any circumstances. Moreover, it was not in any sense a prerogative of this body.

There can be little doubt that even before the President's memorandum was issued Lord Reading received the distinct impression that infantry and machine gun units would be sent to France at the rate of 120,000 men per month for four months, beginning with April. That the President agreed to this "in principle" is practically certain. It need not be further emphasized that such a concession, even though prompted by the most generous impulse, could only add to the difficulties of our task of building up an army of our own. It is probable that Lord Reading, skilled advocate that he was, did more while Ambassador at Washington to influence the Administration to grant Allied requests than any other individual.

The Secretary of War upon his return caused the Administration's position to be somewhat more clearly defined through the President's memorandum, but the statement still left much to be desired in the way of a positive declaration of our purpose to have our own army. It left a very definite notion in the minds of the Allies that the Administration at Washington was favorable to amalgamation and that the main obstacle to be overcome was the military head of the American forces in France. This is doubtless the reason why all the Allied verbal "heavy artillery" was often turned in my direction.

The agreement made in London, as actually drawn, while insuring the shipment of largely increased numbers of troops did not commit us to sending infantry and machine gun units exclusively beyond June 1st. It provided a reserve of the classes of troops that might be needed by the British until their new drafts should be available, and offered the possibility of our getting other classes of troops to complete our plans of organization for the auxiliary arms and Services of Supply. The British thought that this program could be very much exceeded and believed it might be possible to transport entire divisions besides a number of corps and S.O.S. troops. The concession we made for May was a radical departure from the wise policy of bringing over balanced forces in complete organizations, but the clamor was so great and the danger of the absolute defeat of the Allies seemed so imminent that it was thought to be warranted as a temporary expedient.

The question of applying conscription to Ireland was then under consideration by the British and it appeared probable, according to views expressed more or less guardedly, that British troops would be required to enforce it. Inasmuch as such a measure would more than likely have affected the attitude of American troops of Irish origin toward service with the British, our argument was strengthened regarding the desirability of keeping our own troops together and organizing them into an American army at the earliest possible date.

(Diary) Paris, Saturday, April 27, 1918. Left London Thursday by automobile, boarded a British destroyer at Folkestone, reaching Boulogne about four in the afternoon. Colonel Mott was there with request from General Foch for me to come to Sarcus. Held conference and went to Paris that night.

Yesterday morning met with Stevens, Morrow, Rublee, and Shearman of Allied Maritime Transport Council. Saw Colonel Percy L. Jones regarding relations with French of our ambulance companies under his supervision. Discussed coal situation with Loucheur, also heavy artillery and airplanes.

Cabled recommendation that call be made for 1,500,000 men.[1] Rumors thought reliable indicate that Germans contemplate building up armies with Russians. The enemy attacked the 26th Division at Seicheprey on the night of 20th-21st and inflicted considerable loss. 1st Division began entering line on the 24th and to-day assumed command of front opposite Cantigny.

[1] See page 381, volume I, for discussion of the subject of calling out men for training.

Arriving at General Foch's headquarters, we found Generals Bliss and Weygand, and after dinner we entered into a general discussion about American troop shipments:

Foch:
"On March 28th you came to offer the services of American troops. I have a vivid recollection of the occasion. As to the American divisions, in what order do you think they should be employed?"

Pershing:
"The order would be the 26th, 42d, 2d. (The 1st had already been sent to an active front near Amiens.) The regiments of the 32d will be ready by May 1st."

Foch:
"I do not think they can be used before May 5th, but the more we put into the line the better it will be. Your 77th Division has arrived, I see. What about the 3d and 5th?"

Pershing:
"The infantry of the 3d has arrived, and that of the 5th will soon follow."

Foch:
"What we need now is infantry, especially the British, on account of the present crisis. That is why the Supreme War Council at Versailles recommended that all tonnage be devoted to that purpose for the time being. I hope that America may send over as much infantry as possible during the next three months. The other arms to complete your divisions can come afterwards. What do you think of that plan?"

Pershing:
"I cannot commit myself to such a proposition. If nothing but infantry and machine gunners are brought over to the total of 360,000, it will be October or November before the artillery and auxiliary troops could arrive and we could not foresee the formation of an American army until next spring."

Foch:
"I think your calculation is rather pessimistic, for we could begin bringing your other troops in August, but, without considering that point, we can furnish you with artillery and its personnel, and you can have your divisions reconstituted beginning with October. What would you propose in this connection?"

Pershing:

"I think we should limit the transportation of infantry to the month of May, and that the artillery and auxiliary troops should come in June. They should not arrive more than a month later than the infantry."

General Foch then made some calculations based upon 100,000 men per month for three months and continued:

Foch:

"If we could bring 120,000 in May, that would still leave us 100,-000 below British losses."

Pershing:

"Under what conditions would you employ the American infantry units?"

Foch:

"What proposition have you to offer on that subject? To begin with, I would not split up your regiments."

Pershing:

"When would these regiments be grouped into brigades and the brigades into divisions?"

Foch:

"A final decision cannot be made on that subject. That will evidently depend upon the degree of instruction of the units. In the crisis that actually confronts the Allied armies, it is effectives that we lack. The method of employing these units is a question to be handled in due course and according to their efficiency."

Pershing:

"I would like to have the conditions under which these units are to be employed determined now and to fix the time during which the regiments and brigades will be used separately."

Foch:

"Make your proposition on that subject."

I then explained to him the details of the system that was being followed where our divisions were in training with the French, and the plan agreed upon with the British. I added that it was fully understood that if an emergency should arise while our troops were in training, they would go into battle as part of the divisions with which they were serving. He seemed to approve the method, but returned once more to the decision taken by the Supreme War Council with reference to the shipment of American infantry and machine gun units, upon which the following conversation ensued:

Foch:

"I do not doubt the excellency of the method, but in the crisis through which we are passing I return to the decision of the Supreme War Council and I ask you to transport during the months of May, June, and July, only infantry and machine gun units. Will you consent?"

Pershing:

"No, I do not consent. I propose for one month to ship nothing but infantry and machine gun units and after that the other arms and service of the rear troops to correspond."

Foch:

"If you adopt the plan I propose you would have by July 31st, 300,000 more American infantry."

Pershing:

"You said just now that you would furnish the artillery and even artillerymen, which would be joined with our infantry to complete our divisions. Then why not consent to transport our artillery personnel along with our infantry?"

Foch:

"I repeat that it is the infantry of which we have the greatest need at this time. I would like to have General Bliss tell us what were the considerations which led to the decision taken by the Supreme War Council at Versailles."

Bliss:

"The collective note recommended to the United States to send only infantry until the Supreme War Council should give instructions to the contrary. The Government of the United States in conformity with this note and with the recommendations of Mr. Baker consented to this plan. As far as the employment of the units on the front is concerned, the question should be decided by General Pershing according to agreement with the Commander-in-Chief to whose army they may be attached."

Pershing:

"I have been discussing this question of training our units for the last eight months, first with General Pétain and then with Marshal Haig. The method agreed upon leads naturally to the formation of constituted American divisions."

General Foch stated that he wished to see American divisions constituted and an American army formed as large as possible, but the policy he was advocating would have made it impossible to form an American army without serious delay, if ever. Continuing, he said:

"But do not forget that we are in the midst of a hard battle. If we do not take steps to prevent the disaster which is threatened at present the American Army may arrive in France to find the British pushed into the sea and the French driven back behind the Loire, while it tries in vain to organize on lost battlefields over the graves of Allied soldiers."

He was assured that it was fully understood that if an emergency should arise while our troops were in training with the British or French, they would go into the battle and do their part. I then gave him the numbers to be shipped during May and told him that it had been agreed between the British and ourselves to consider the question for June later. I informed him that the British shipping authorities now thought that it would be possible within the next three months to transport to France 750,000 men.

He was surprised to learn that enough shipping had been found to bring over so many, and, while insisting that we continue the May program into June, said that if it was possible to transport any such numbers he saw no reason why whole divisions should not soon be transported. Nevertheless, a few days later he made a still stronger demand for special shipments of infantry and machine gun units.

The shipping situation as brought out in conference with the American members of the Maritime Transport Council did not appear so favorable as we had been led to believe. Only two of our newly built vessels had been delivered and our shipbuilding program was not yet far enough along to count as an important factor, although prospects were that the rate would soon begin to increase. A full study made by our delegates to the Council of the demands to be made upon Allied and neutral tonnage for military, naval, and general needs showed an estimated shortage of nearly 2,000,000 tons. It was obvious that the program for strengthening the Western Front must be carried out if possible. Therefore, all practicable measures for the economical employment of every available ton of shipping, especially for freight, were given consideration at our conference.

It was thought, in the first place, that the Allied navies could reduce their requirements of merchant tonnage by a joint examination of the naval programs; second, that considerable shipping could be saved by suspending or reducing military and naval activities in theaters of war other than the Western Front; third, that further reductions in Allied civilian imports might be made temporarily; and, finally, that insistence upon the adoption of unified action in the supply services by the Allies on the Western Front, already suggested, would result in a material saving of tonnage.

I heartily approved of the above recommendations and sent a cable to Washington to that effect, of which the following is an extract:

"April 30, 1918.

"I therefore heartily approve the recommendation made by the Allied Maritime Transport Council (which, it is important to note, is a body upon which French and British ministers are sitting) that all of the military programs of the Allies be brought under joint review by the appropriate military authorities to the end that effort may be concentrated on the Western Front. While this is of vital importance to the common cause, it is of peculiar and of almost supreme importance to our own rapidly growing army. If programs are allowed to remain in effect which call for more tonnage than is in existence, the calls for diversion of our ships for food supplies, coal, nitrates, and other things essential to our Allies will become more and more insistent. They will tend to converge more and more upon our program because our program is rapidly expanding and the others are comparatively rigid. Therefore a cutting down of all military programs that do not directly contribute to the common cause and a greater unity in the prosecution of those plans that do contribute to the common cause are essential during the next few months if we are to avoid the disaster that will come from haphazard curtailments of absolute essentials at the eleventh hour."

Of course, certain agreements as to raw materials had to be maintained in order to keep production of ammunition and airplanes going and these required at least 30,000 tons monthly. In general, as with the question of unity of supply, to which all agreed in principle, so it was with sea transportation, but action in the latter case presented serious difficulties. As a matter of fact, in the broad sense the two were intimately connected. It seemed to me that the control of Allied supplies could well be vested in a board (with executive powers) consisting of a representative from each Government. It appeared logical that this board, in consultation with the Allied Maritime Council, should be authorized to allot Allied tonnage. This was fully stated in my cables, but Washington did not wholly accept my views.

Confronted as we were by the lack of trained men at this time, it was evident that we should within a few months find ourselves facing a still more serious situation unless increased numbers were put in training without delay. Supplementing the suggestion I had made verbally to the Secretary, a cable was sent on April 27th, which included also a reference to the numbers of partially trained men in divisions then arriving, as follows:

"Regard it most imperative that there be no delay in calling out a new draft and the entire summer season devoted to instruction and training so that new troops may be thoroughly and systematically trained without disturbing organizations when formed. Believe German offensive will be stopped but Allied aggressive must be undertaken as early as possible thereafter and American forces must be in position to throw in their full weight. Recommend that a call be issued at once for at least one million and a half men. Having in mind large replacements of losses that are sure to occur and the delays of organization and equipment of new drafts, this is the smallest number that should be considered."

In reply to this the following was received, dated May 7th:

"With reference to paragraph 1 your 990, troops sent you have been best available. Divisions became depleted during the winter on account large numbers being taken for staff corps and other unavoidable causes, and lack of equipment for replacements. Conditions will improve early in July so that eventually only those divisions with at least six months training will be sent. * * *

"With reference to paragraph 3 your 990, 643,198 white, and 73,326 colored men, total 716,524, have been drafted since January 1st, including May draft. Draft will be continued monthly to maximum capacity. Impracticable to draft one million and a half at one time. Draft already called will fill all divisions now organized and all other troops for second and third phases. Question of organizing new divisions under consideration. We now have troops of all classes under training in replacement camps."

On the night of April 20th-21st, the Germans made a raid on the 26th Division in the vicinity of Seicheprey. The attack covered a two-mile front extending west from the Bois de Remières. It came during a heavy fog and was a complete surprise to our troops, who were considerably outnumbered. The fighting in Seicheprey was violent, causing heavy losses on both sides. The town was taken by the enemy. The success of the raid may be attributed largely to the destruction by the German artillery of the divisional system of communications, which naturally resulted in some confusion in the division. Although coöperation among the units was difficult under the circumstances, it was finally established and the original front was reoccupied the following day.[1]

(Diary) Paris, Tuesday, April 30, 1918. Congress has wisely passed an act providing for indemnity to Allies for damage by our troops abroad.

On Sunday took up with Colonel H. B. Jordan, of the Ordnance, the subject of heavy guns from French, and with Foulois their production of airplanes. General Crozier, back from Italy, favors sending American troops there. Left for Chaumont that evening.

Generals John L. Hines and Brewster called yesterday, and Martin

[1] In this affair we lost 1 officer, 80 enlisted men, killed; 11 officers, 176 enlisted men, wounded; 3 officers, 211 enlisted men, gassed; and 5 officers, 182 enlisted men, missing and prisoners. The losses of the enemy in killed and wounded were reported as even greater.

Egan [1] came for confidential conference. General Liggett, I Corps,[2] reports good progress in his divisions. Censors of letters of French report very favorable comment on Americans in trenches. Returned to Paris to-day.

Under the provisions of the Act of Congress mentioned in the diary, authority was granted for the settlement of all claims "Of inhabitants of France or any other European country not an enemy or ally of an enemy" for injuries to persons or damage to property occasioned by our forces. The procedure followed was in accordance with the law and practice of the country in question. These claims were handled by the Renting, Requisition and Claims Service, which had been formed in March primarily to procure lands and buildings needed for our forces. The efficient administration of this Service in the prompt settlement of claims had an excellent effect upon the people of the European countries concerned.

We were never quite sure of obtaining airplanes from the Allies, as material and expert labor for their manufacture were never fully up to requirements. While advices from home and the frequent promises of the French kept us hopeful, the cancellation by the latter of our early contract for airplanes created an uncertainty that made it difficult to plan either for the training of our aviation personnel or their participation in operations. So far we had received no planes from home and none from the French except a few for training purposes.

My conference with General Foulois was to consider a proposition purporting to bring about closer coöperation with the French,

[1] Mr. Egan came to France about this time at my request and joined me as civilian aide. His experience in the newspaper and business worlds made him most valuable in this position. He was a keen observer and kept in touch with Allied sentiment and the attitude of the Allies toward Americans. The suggestions and advice he gave from time to time were of great assistance to me.

[2] This corps at the time of the report consisted of six divisions; the 1st (Bullard) with the French Fifth Army in line in vicinity of Gisors; the 2d (Bundy) with the French Tenth Army in line by small units between Verdun and St. Mihiel; the 26th (Edwards) in Toul Sector under French XXXII Corps; the 32d (Haan) in the 10th training area, headquarters at Prauthoy; the 42d (Menoher) in sector east of Baccarat under the French VII Corps; and the 41st (Alexander) depot division with headquarters at St. Aignan.

emanating from their Minister of Munitions, M. Loucheur. In a letter from the Undersecretary for Aeronautics, it was suggested that the French should increase their output of airplane bodies of various types and that we should confine ourselves to the production of Liberty engines, and possibly also undertake the manufacture of a particular type of engine which they recommended. Analysis of the proposal showed that, if adopted, we should have to abandon our plans for the manufacture of planes at home, and furnish the French additional raw material, and probably expert labor. We were always keen for coöperation that would advance the common cause, but production would not have been hastened under this plan. Our experience so far had not been such as to give confidence in their fulfillment of an agreement of this sort, so the suggestion was politely rejected.

A few days later a British air representative also sought joint coöperation with us. The proposal he made was that we should limit our construction, other than for training purposes, to long range strategic bombing aircraft and the manufacture of Liberty engines, and that the British would supply us aircraft for purely American operations. We were asked to send a small staff to London to coöperate along these lines and they would send a strong mission of experts to Washington. When the matter was presented to me along with a prepared telegram to be sent to Lord Reading stating that we and the French concurred, I inquired how it came that the French had agreed to this without consulting us, and it was found that the plan had not yet been taken up with them. I then told the British representative that when the air services of the Allied armies reached an agreement regarding this proposal I would consider it. This was the last we heard of it. Such incidents as these showed the tendency to gain particular advantage and caused us to doubt the sincerity of proposals for coöperation in such matters.

In discussing unity in general, the failure of the Italians to place their armies under the Supreme Command on the Western Front was frequently mentioned, and it was feared in high places that there might arise another dangerous situation similar to Caporetto, but all hesitated to take action. From the military standpoint the Western Front really extended to the Adriatic Sea, and support for the Italians in case of necessity would have to come, as before, from the armies in France.

The question was a delicate one, but it occurred to me to suggest to the Secretary of War that the President might intimate to the Italian Government the propriety of completing the unity of command by placing its armies under the same control as the others. It was believed that the Italian Cabinet might be willing to take the step if it could be done in such a way as to prevent hostile criticism among their own people. It was thought that if the suggestion should come from the British or the French, especially the latter, it would very likely be regarded with suspicion, whereas none could ascribe any but the highest motives to Mr. Wilson in making such a move. However, the question came up for discussion at the next meeting of the Supreme War Council, which was held at Abbeville, and the authority of General Foch was extended to include the Italian armies. This completed the unity of command from the North Sea to the Adriatic.

CHAPTER XXVIII

Conference at Abbeville—Allied Leaders Greatly Alarmed—Insistent on American Replacements—Infantry and Machine Gunners Urged—Heated Discussions—Lloyd George Makes More Tonnage Available—Agreement Reached—Some American Troops for Italy

(Diary) Paris, Thursday, May 2, 1918. Just returned with Colonel Le Roy Eltinge and Colonel Boyd from two-day conference of Supreme War Council at Abbeville.[1] Extreme pessimism prevailed regarding present crisis. Everybody at high tension. Allies persistent in urging unlimited shipment of our infantry and machine gun units. Discussion at times very lively. Have agreed to send a regiment to Italy. Informally discussed with Prime Ministers the pooling of supplies.

Swiss reported now favorable to us in view of allocation and shipment of wheat. War Department plans completion of shipment in May of infantry and machine gun units of twelve divisions.[2]

THE necessity for hastening the shipment of American troops was now fully realized and their allotment to the Allied armies had assumed great importance in the minds of the Allied leaders. They were urgently demanding that only infantry and machine gun units be sent to France as recommended by the Military Representatives of the Supreme War Council and approved with certain modifications by our Government. As we have seen, an agreement had just been concluded with the

[1] There were present for France, M. Clemenceau, General Foch, and General Pétain; for Great Britain, Mr. Lloyd George, Lord Milner, Marshal Haig, and General Lawrence; for Italy, Mr. Orlando and General di Robilant; while General Bliss and I represented the United States. Certain staff officers accompanied each group.

[2] These divisions were 77th (Johnson), 82d (Burnham), 35th (Wright), 28th (Muir), 4th (Cameron), 30th (Read), 3d (Dickman), 5th (McMahon), 27th (O'Ryan), 33d (Bell), 80th (Cronkhite), 78th (McRae).

NOTE: Total strength of the A.E.F. on April 30th, 23,548 officers, 406,111 enlisted men.

Divisional units arriving in April included elements of the 77th Division (National Army, New York), Brigadier General Evan M. Johnson, the first of the National Army divisions to reach France.

British for shipments in May, but, as foreshadowed in Foch's remarks during our recent conversation, the Council wanted that agreement extended to cover June. I was opposed to such commitment, as it was my expectation that in June we should bring over the artillery and auxiliary arms to correspond to the shipment of infantry in May. At this session of the Supreme War Council the discussion was prolonged and only the main points are given. M. Clemenceau, who presided, opened the meeting with the following statement:

"The military representatives expressed the opinion in their Joint Note Number 18 that only infantry and machine gun units should be sent to France for the present. Since then the agreement between Lord Milner and General Pershing, signed at London on April 24, 1918, has intervened. This agreement makes a change.

"It had been understood at Versailles [1] that America would send 120,000 men per month, which the French and British armies would share equally. Under the Milner-Pershing agreement, it appears none are to go to France. The French have not been consulted. We might suppose that in compensation the American troops arriving in June would be given to France. But it now appears they are also to join the British. I wish to protest that this is not satisfactory.

"I am not discussing the figure of 120,000 men; I am prepared to accept that these men go to the British in May. I am asking to receive the same number of troops in June. There are close to 400,000 Americans in France at present, but only five divisions, or about 125,000 men, can be considered as combatants. That is not a satisfactory proportion."

Lord Milner arose, much incensed at M. Clemenceau's statement, which he considered quite unjust. He said, in part:

"M. Clemenceau has intimated that there was something mysterious about the London agreement. I believe that an explanation is necessary. He appears to believe that the agreement we signed is a reversal of the Supreme War Council's decision. I know only of a Joint Note embodying the recommendations of the Military Representatives, but it is of no value without the approval of the Governments.

[1] This refers to the action of the Permanent Military Representatives on the Supreme War Council, who held their sessions at Versailles.

"Besides, M. Clemenceau seems to be under the impression that half of the American troops were to go to France and the other half to the British. I do not recollect any such decision. All that General Pershing and I have urged is that infantry and machine gunners should be sent to France. We had no intention of depriving France of any American troops. I do not know that anything has been said regarding their allotment on arrival in France. We simply wanted to hasten their coming."

I then said:

"In making the agreement with Lord Milner I had in mind bringing troops as rapidly as possible to meet the existing situation. Lord Milner is quite correct in stating that there was no agreement as to the allocation of American troops either to the British or French armies. There is no agreement between my Government and anybody else that a single American soldier shall be sent to either the British or French. There is in existence an agreement between Mr. Lloyd George and myself that six divisions should be brought to France. Mr. Clemenceau will remember that I spoke to him about going to London to arrange for the shipment of American troops to France and that he approved because it would expedite their arrival. I also spoke to General Pétain about it."

M. Clemenceau remembered my speaking of it, but disregarding his previous approval continued his objections, saying:

"We have been informed that nothing had been decided on at Versailles, but something has been decided on at London, and France was closely concerned in this. It was decided that six divisions should go to the British. Well, I will not argue about that. You announce to us that you want artillery for the month of June, but France is overflowing with it.

"Where four are in alliance, two of them cannot act independently. Nothing has been provided for France in June.

"The appointment of General Foch as Commander-in-Chief is not a mere decoration. * * * This post involves grave responsibilities; he must meet the present situation; he must provide for the future.

"I accept what has been done for May, but I want to know what is intended for June."

M. Clemenceau said further that the French had not received certain specialists they had asked for, and also quoted from the conversation I had held with General Foch with reference to sending over troops in May and June.

Mr. Lloyd George then spoke up and said:

"I am of M. Clemenceau's opinion. The interests of the Allies are identical; we must not lose sight of that, otherwise the unity of command has no meaning. We must consider what is best for the common cause.

"What is the situation to-day? The British Army has had heavy fighting and has suffered heavy losses. All available drafts have been sent to France and we shall send all who are available in May and June. This would be the case even if all the Americans who arrived in Europe during these months should be assigned to the British Army.

*　　　*　　　*　　　*　　　*　　　*　　　*

"At present certain British divisions have been so severely handled that they cannot be reconstituted. General Foch will remember the number."

General Foch:
"Yes, ten."

Lloyd George:
"As we cannot again put them in line, they must be replaced by new units. The Germans are now fighting with the object of using up our effectives. If they can do this without exhausting their own reserves they will, sometime, deal us a blow which we shall not be able to parry. In the meantime, I suggest that the decision for the allotment of the American troops for June be taken up when these troops arrive. In May, in fact, either of our two armies may be hard pressed. That is the one which should be reënforced. It is not desirable now to decide how troops arriving in June should be allotted."

Foch:
"It is undeniable that the British Army is now exhausted; so let it receive immediate reënforcement in May. But lately the French have had grave losses, notably at Montdidier, and both during the last few days have been fighting shoulder to shoulder. So American aid is now needed almost as much for France as for Great Britain. Above this question of aid to the French or to the British is aid to the Allies. We are agreed that the American Army is to reënforce the British Army at once; in June we too shall need infantry and machine gun units. So let us make the agreement for June at once by saying the same shipment of infantry and machine guns as for May. If there is

tonnage available, we shall devote it, after that, to the elements necessary for filling up the American divisions. I am sure that General
Pershing, with his generosity and his breadth of view, will grant the
fairness of this and will extend for June the agreement decided upon
for May."

Whereupon Mr. Lloyd George gave support to the declaration
of General Foch, saying that British recruits would not be available until August and he understood it was the same for France,
when both would be able to furnish their own recruits. He then
changed his previous suggestion and asked that the May program
be extended over June, a request in which M. Clemenceau joined.
Noting Foch's special plea for France, I said:

"I do not suppose that we are to understand that the American Army
is to be entirely at the disposal of the French and British commands."

M. Clemenceau:
"Of course this is not the intention."

Continuing I said:
"Speaking for my Government and myself, we must look forward to
the time when we shall have our own army. I must insist on its being
recognized. The principle of unity of command must prevail in our
army. It must be complete under its own command. I should like to
have a date fixed when this will be realized. I should like to make it
clear that all American troops are not to be with the British, as there
are five divisions with the French now and there will be two more in
a short time.
"As to the extension of the May agreement to June, I am not prepared to accept it. The troops arriving in June will not be available
for the front before the end of July or the middle of August. So we
have the whole month of May ahead of us before deciding whether
the emergency still exists. I have explained to Lord Milner and
General Foch why I do not wish to commit the American Army
so long in advance. If need be, I shall recommend the extension into
June. I can see no reason for it now."

Mr. Lloyd George spoke again and said that as a representative
of the British Government he fully approved of the principle of
an American army. He continued:

"It would not be reasonable or even honorable to consider the American Army as a reservoir from which we can draw. It is to our advantage to have a powerful American army as soon as possible to fight beside us, and as head of the British Government I accept the principle. However, at the present time, we are engaged in what is perhaps the decisive battle of the war. If we lose this battle, we shall need tonnage to take home what there is left of the British and American armies.

"What is our best hope of winning this battle?

"The decisive months will perhaps be those of September, October, perhaps later. If the American Army could intervene at that time, it would suit us all. I have no reason to believe that these two opinions are incompatible, but we should not wait until the end of May to decide, for questions of tonnage are involved which we must go into now."

He then proposed that the question of continuing the May program into June be held in abeyance for two weeks. He also brought up the question of the use of the slower ships for the transportation of troops and thought 30,000 or 40,000 more men a month might be transported in these ships. Both Admiral Sims and I had already pressed that point with our Government. Mr. Lloyd George calculated that the British would be able to transport 150,000 per month as a maximum, and that we could bring over 40,000 to 50,000, which he thought would allow us to include the auxiliary services required to complete our divisions and organize our own army. But he asked that priority in embarkation be given to the infantry and machine gun units.

I approved this request up to six divisions and stated that toward the end of May we could decide whether the program was to be continued into June.

Then General Foch announced that he, too, favored the formation of an American army, saying:

"Nobody is more for the constitution of an American army than I, for I know how much more an army is worth when fighting under its own commander and under its own flag. But now the needs are immediate; there is a battle to be won or a battle to be lost. I ask for the continuation of the May program. General Pershing asks that we transport the elements necessary for the constitution of his army; I am told that the tonnage will allow this; all the better; but in two weeks we shall all be dispersed, so we ought to decide to-day to continue in June what was decided on for May. I ask Lord Milner, as well as General Pershing, to join me after the meeting to sign an agreement."

Replying that I was glad to hear General Foch express himself so strongly in favor of an American army and that no one more fully than I appreciated the present situation, I said that it did not appear necessary for the Council to decide to-day. Foch then continued:

"I am Commander-in-Chief of the Allied Armies in France and my appointment has been sanctioned not only by the British and French Governments, but also by the President of the United States. Hence, I believe it my duty to insist on my point of view. There is a program signed by Lord Milner and General Pershing at London. I ask to be made a party to this arrangement. If the Supreme Commander has nothing to say regarding such conventions, I should not hold the position.

"So I ask that an agreement be made this evening between Lord Milner, General Pershing and myself, extending to June what has been decided on for May."

Of course, we all knew that no authority to dictate regarding such matters had been conferred upon General Foch and his remarks only showed that the Allies had put him forward to force the kind of agreement they wanted. They were ready to go to almost any length to carry their point.

M. Clemenceau then said that he agreed with General Foch and favored an American army, but that the Germans were at Villers-Bretonneux and if the lines were broken there they might quickly arrive under the walls of Paris and liaison between the Allied armies might have to be established on the Loire, or if the lines were pierced at Hazebrouck the enemy could reach the sea. "What is important for the morale of our soldiers," he said, "is not to tell them that the American soldiers are arriving, but to show them that they have arrived." In other words, he wanted smaller American units to be put in French divisions. He referred to the help the French were giving the British,[1] who had to break up ten divisions, he said, and added, "It is essential both in May and June when we shall be short of drafts that we should have men." Continuing, he said, "We have no right to order the American Government to do as we wish, but what we want is to attract its attention to the gravity of the situation," and he did not think I would refuse to listen.

In my opinion, the plan proposed was entirely unsound, and I thought that the best and quickest way to help the Allies would be to build up an American army. Moreover, the implied presumption that the Council might dictate to us either as a Council or through the Allied Commander-in-Chief in the arbitrary manner indicated, set me more firmly than ever against American units serving in Allied armies. The day's discussion made it quite clear that both Allies intended to obtain our commitment to the proposed schedule as far into the future as possible.[2]

At M. Clemenceau's suggestion, the meeting of the Council was

[1] There was no instance during the World War that I know of where small units such as battalions and companies of one nation served in the armies of another. As to regiments, we had four that were assigned, one to each of four French divisions. Entire divisions, under their own officers, were often sent in an emergency from the army of one country to that of another.

[2] As indicating the efforts made by the Allies to carry their point, the following extract from one of many cables on this subject sent by the British Secretary of State for Foreign Affairs to Lord Reading, British Ambassador at Washington, is pertinent. Referring to the conference held in Paris between General Hutchinson (British) on one side, and Mr. Baker and myself on the other, the cable read: "It is evident from this brief account of the conversation that General Pershing's views are absolutely inconsistent with the broad policy which we believe the President has accepted. The main difference, of course, is that we interpret the promise as meaning that 480,000 infantry and machine gunners are to be brigaded with French and British troops in the course of four months. General Pershing admits no such obligation and does not conceal the fact that he disapproves of the policy.

"A second and minor difference is that, while the British Government quite agrees as to the propriety of ultimately withdrawing American troops brigaded with the French and British so as to form an American army, they do not think this process could or ought to be attempted until the season for active operations this year draws to its close, say in October or November.

"I am unwilling to embarrass the President, who has shown such a firm grasp of the situation, with criticisms of his officers. But the difference of opinion * * * is so fundamental and touches so nearly the issues of the whole war, that we are bound to have the matter cleared up."—(See pp. 124-125, "It Might Have Been Lost," by Thomas Clement Lonergan, formerly Lieutenant Colonel, General Staff, U.S.A.)

adjourned at this point in order that Foch, Milner, and I might meet and examine the question, and see if some agreement could be reached. Whereupon we repaired to an adjacent room and went over the whole subject again.

Milner, and especially Foch, insisted that the war would be lost unless their program was carried out. I repeated the arguments presented to the Council and added that I fully realized the military emergency but did not think that the plan to bring over untrained units to fight under British and French commands would either relieve the situation or end the war.[1] I pointed out that, regardless of the depressing conditions and the very urgent need of men by the Allies, their plan was not practicable and that even if sound in principle there was not time enough to prepare our men as individuals for efficient service under a new system, with the strange surroundings to be found in a foreign army. The very lowest limit ever thought of for training recruits under the most favorable circumstances, even for trench warfare, had been nine weeks devoted to strenuous work. Counting out the time that would be consumed in travel, the untrained arrivals could not be ready before August, when the trained contingents of the Allies for 1918 would become available.

Here Foch said: "You are willing to risk our being driven back to the Loire?"

I said: "Yes, I am willing to take the risk. Moreover, the time may come when the American Army will have to stand the brunt of this war, and it is not wise to fritter away our resources in this manner. The morale of the British, French and Italian armies is low, while, as you know, that of the American Army is very high. It would be a grave mistake to give up the idea of building an American army in all its details as rapidly as possible."

Then Foch again said that the war might be over before we were ready.

I said that the war could not, in my opinion, be saved by feed-

---

[1] While our units were to be brought for training as a part of larger British or French units, it was thoroughly understood that they were there to fight, in case they were needed.

ing untrained American recruits into the Allied armies, but that we must build up an American army, and concessions for the time being to meet the present emergency were all that I would approve.

At about this juncture, Mr. Lloyd George, M. Clemenceau, and Mr. Orlando, evidently becoming impatient, walked into the room. Milner met Lloyd George at the door and said in a stage whisper behind his hand, "You can't budge him an inch." Lloyd George then said, "Well, how is the committee getting along?"

Whereupon we all sat down and Lloyd George said to me, "Can't you see that the war will be lost unless we get this support?" which statement was echoed in turn by Clemenceau and Orlando. In fact, all five of the party attacked me with all the force and prestige of their high positions.

But I had already yielded to their demands as far as possible without disrupting the plans toward which we had been striving for over a year, and a continuance of May shipments into June, without any provision for transporting artillery and auxiliary and service of supply troops, could not be granted without making it practically impossible in the future to have an American army. After going over the whole situation again and stating my position, they still insisted, whereupon I said with the greatest possible emphasis, "Gentlemen, I have thought this program over very deliberately and will not be coerced." This ended the discussion in committee and when the Council reconvened M. Clemenceau stated that the question of American troops would be taken up again on the following day.

The Council then examined a number of other matters. Among them was that of breaking up divisions in distant theaters of the war in order to obtain extra men for the Western Front and thus save the tonnage required for their supply. A resolution was adopted providing that "a French and a British general officer should be dispatched forthwith to Salonika, where, in association with the general officer commanding the Italian forces at Salonika, they will confer with General Guillaumat [1]

---

[1] General Guillaumat was the French Commander of Allied Forces at Salonika.

on this question in order if possible to arrange with him for the immediate withdrawal of Allied battalions."

Then some one suggested that with an Allied Commander-in-Chief there seemed to be no need of the Executive War Board of the Supreme War Council which had been created in February to handle the general reserve, and after considerable discussion, action was postponed until the following day, when a resolution dissolving the committee was adopted.

The next question taken up was that of Italian reënforcements for France. Mr. Orlando spoke at some length on the critical situation on the Italian front and declared that the Austrians were well prepared and were about to attack again, and that Italy could not spare any troops for service in France. This brought up the question of General Foch's authority over the Italian Army. Mr. Orlando said that the Italian Commander-in-Chief would have to be consulted before Italian troops could be taken to reënforce Allied armies elsewhere.

He failed to recall that it was the prompt action of the French and British in sending troops to Italy after Caporetto that probably saved the Italian Army. However, in further conversation on the following day, he agreed that the Western Front should be considered as extending from the North Sea to the Adriatic and accepted the principle of unity of command, but he specifically reserved the right of the Italian Commander to appeal to his Government in case any orders from Foch should be inimical to the general interests of Italy.

When the Council met for the afternoon session of the second day, the discussion of shipments of American personnel was at once resumed. General Foch spoke at length, repeating previous arguments and giving a rather grandiose dissertation on the Allied situation and the dire things that would happen unless the Americans agreed to the proposal of the Council. In the course of his remarks he said:

"I have been selected as Commander-in-Chief of the Allied armies by the Governments of the United States of America, France, and Great Britain, and my command has been extended to embrace the Italian

Army. In that capacity it is impossible at the most perilous stage of
the great battle of the war to withhold the expression of my views
on the question of disposal of American troops.

"That is why, feeling the very heavy responsibility that rests upon
me, at the time when the greatest German offensive is now threatening
Paris and our communication with Great Britain through Calais and
Boulogne, I expressly insist on each of the Governments taking, in its
turn, its portion of responsibility."

In a dramatic way, he went on to say that he thought it absolutely necessary that 120,000, or more, if tonnage permitted,
American infantrymen and machine gunners should reach
France monthly, by right of priority, at least during the months
of May, June, and July. Losses of the French and British had
been greater, he said, than in any previous offensive of the war
and could not be replaced, while on the other hand Germany
could furnish from 500,000 to 600,000 replacements for her
armies; and he most earnestly requested the Council to submit a statement to President Wilson on the subject. He fully
appreciated my remarks, he said, but the situation would not
warrant any delay, as the greatest of German armies was making
the most determined offensive of the war against Amiens and
Ypres and the issue of the war itself might depend upon the
success of the enemy before either of these objectives.

Mr. Lloyd George in turn spoke at some length. He asserted
that the Germans hoped to use up the British and French reserves
before their own were exhausted, and that the British had already
called up nearly 7,000,000 men for their army and navy and had
extended their age limits to all men between 18 and 50 years
of age. He continued:

"If the United States does not come to our aid, then perhaps the
enemy's calculations will be correct. If France and Great Britain
should have to yield, their defeat would be honorable, for they would
have fought to their last man, while the United States would have to
stop without having put into line more men than little Belgium."

Possibly realizing the unfairness of the comparison, he quickly
went on to say that he was sure that I was doing my best to meet
the emergency, and that:

"General Pershing desires that the aid brought to us by America should not be incompatible with the creation of the American army as rapidly as possible.

"I, too, am counting on the existence of that army, and I am counting on it this very year to deal the enemy the final blow. But to do that, the Allies will have to hold out until August."

He then took up my proposal that the May program, which called for 120,000 infantrymen and machine gunners, be extended into June, provided the British Government would furnish transportation for 130,000 men in May and 150,000 in June. After some further discussion, during which he offered to increase greatly the British tonnage, he said:

"I propose then that America give us 120,000 infantrymen and machine gunners in May—the same number in June, with a supplement of 50,000 infantrymen and machine gunners if we 'scrape together' the tonnage to transport them."

He further proposed that the situation be again examined in June before deciding whether there was reason to extend to July the program decided upon for May and June, and called on the Council for the acceptance of his plan.

I then made the following remarks:

"I am entirely in agreement with General Foch as to the gravity of the present situation. In fact, we are all agreed on that point.

"Speaking in the name of the American Army and in the name of the American people, I wish to express their earnest desire to take their full part in this battle, and to share the burden of the war to the fullest extent. We all desire the same thing, but our means of attaining it are different from yours.

"America declared war independently of the Allies and she must face it as soon as possible with a powerful army. There is one important point upon which I wish to lay stress, and that is that the morale of our soldiers depends upon their fighting under our own flag.

"America is already anxious to know where her army is. The Germans are once more circulating propaganda in the United States to the effect that the Allies have so little confidence in the American troops that they parcel them out among Allied divisions.

"The American soldier has his own pride, and the time will soon come when our troops, as well as our Government, will demand an autonomous army under the American High Command.

"I understand that in Mr. Lloyd George's proposal we shall have to examine the situation again in June before deciding for July.

"That is all I can agree to at present, and I think by this arrangement we are meeting the situation fairly and squarely."

My proposal contemplated a largely increased amount of British tonnage, which would permit the transportation of a greater number of artillery and auxiliary units, and a greater proportion of special troops for the Services of Supply than had been previously indicated. Upon consideration, it appeared that this would leave us with sufficient tonnage to provide at least 40,000 men by British shipping and all that could be transported by American shipping of the classes of troops we most desired. M. Clemenceau then read the resolution that I had submitted confirming the London agreement and including an understanding for June, which was agreed to substantially as set forth in the following cablegram to the Secretary of War:

"Following agreement adopted by Supreme War Council May 2d at Abbeville. Will cable more in detail later. It is the opinion of the Supreme War Council that, in order to carry the war to a successful conclusion, an American army should be formed as early as possible under its own commander and under its own flag.[1] In order to meet the present emergency it is agreed that American troops should be brought to France as rapidly as Allied transportation facilities will permit, and that, as far as consistent with the necessity of building up an American army, preference be given to infantry and machine gun units for training and service with French and British armies; with the understanding that such infantry and machine gun units are to be withdrawn and united with their own artillery and auxiliary troops into divisions and corps at the discretion of the American Commander-in-Chief after consultation with the Commander-in-Chief of the Allied Armies in France.

"Subparagraph A.

"It is also agreed that during the month of May preference should be given to the transportation of infantry and machine gun units of six divisions, and that any excess tonnage shall be devoted to bringing

[1] Then it was thought the war would continue to 1919.

over such troops as may be determined by the American Commander-in-Chief.

"Subparagraph B.

"It is further agreed that this program shall be continued during the month of June upon condition that the British Government shall furnish transportation for a minimum of 130,000 men in May and 150,000 men in June, with the understanding that the first six divisions of infantry shall go to the British for training and service, and that troops sent over in June shall be allocated for training and service as the American Commander-in-Chief may determine.

"Subparagraph C.

"It is also further agreed that if the British Government shall transport an excess of 150,000 men in June that such excess shall be infantry and machine gun units, and that early in June there shall be a new review of the situation to determine further action."

In his reply, the Secretary of War observed that this agreement provided less priority for infantry and machine gun units than was previously recommended by the Supreme War Council. This was true, as it was my intention to make it as favorable to the ultimate formation of an American army as possible, and it was more so than we had reason to expect in view of the recommendations contained in Joint Note No. 18 of the Military Representatives, which, as we have seen, had been practically approved by the President. The full purport of this commitment was not emphasized by the Allies during the discussion.

Nobody realized more than I that the military situation was most threatening. Following the powerful enemy offensive of March 21st had come that of April 9th, and another attack had been made by the enemy towards Amiens, while in the fighting farther east Villers-Bretonneux had been taken and retaken several times. As the British casualties since March 21st had been some 280,000, and those of the French 60,000 to 70,000, both Allies were prompted to make this urgent appeal for Americans to reconstitute their units not only physically but morally.

From the practical standpoint of increasing the efficiency of the Allied armies, the argument was against the unqualified acceptance of their proposals. The nationals of no country would willingly serve under a foreign flag in preference to their own.

The national sentiment involved was such that we could not possibly afford to enter into such an agreement, except in an extreme crisis. Moreover, the added strength of a distinct army would be much greater than to have its personnel parcelled out here and there. Another serious objection to our men serving in the Allied armies was the danger that the low morale and the pessimism in the Allied ranks would react adversely on our officers and men; in fact, this had already been the case to some extent, especially among our men with the British, where the contacts had been close.

As to personal relations, it was gratifying always to find that these discussions, though often heated, were largely regarded simply as official differences of opinion. There was at the same time a very distinct impression in my mind, and in the minds of many of our officers familiar with the arguments on both sides, that the Allies, while greatly in need of assistance, were especially inclined to press the plea for amalgamation as a means of keeping us in a subordinate rôle.

Yet, after these questions were settled, even temporarily, there was no ill-feeling in evidence, although, no doubt, at times each side thought the other difficult to deal with. Other proposals regarding the employment of American troops under Allied command were made from time to time, all of which I strongly opposed. Notwithstanding their attitude with respect to the use of our troops, I continued to maintain a high regard for my Allied associates, in consideration of their many acts of kindness and friendship.

After the decision at Abbeville, everybody seemed content, and General Foch, in parting with me, said, *"Mon Général, nous sommes toujours d'accord."* While this remark no doubt expressed satisfaction that an agreement had been reached, it did not mean that the Allies had at all given up their views as to how American troops should be trained or used.

The fact that neither the British nor French had trained their armies for open warfare, either offensive or defensive, was at least in part one cause of the tremendous success of the German drives with divisions trained expressly for that kind of warfare. That the French intended to impress their conception on us is indicated by a memorandum of instructions for the guidance of their officers on duty with American troops, emanating from the French General Headquarters, May 1st, that came to our attention. This memorandum shows also that the French still regarded the possibility of open warfare as more or less visionary. Speaking of Americans, it said:

"It should be borne in mind that they have an extremely highly developed sense of *amour-propre* based on their pride in belonging to one of the greatest nations of the world. Consequently an air of superiority over them should be assiduously avoided, a fact which in no way prevents the absolute subordination required by the service for carrying out the rules of hierarchy. * * * In case of necessity French officers should not hesitate to exercise their authority. * * * Americans dream of operating in open country after having broken through the front. This results in too much attention being devoted to this form of operations."

The attitude that the French assumed toward us in the World War was in marked contrast with the views held by them when their troops so generously came to America to aid us in the Revolution. The French Commander at that time received very explicit instructions from his Government on this subject, as the following sent to Rochambeau shortly before he sailed for America will show:

"It is His Majesty's desire and He hereby commands that, so far as circumstances will permit, the Count de Rochambeau shall maintain the integrity of the French troops which His Majesty has placed under his command, and that at the proper time he shall express to General Washington, Commander-in-Chief of the forces of the Congress, under whose orders the French troops are to serve, that it is the intention of the King that these shall not be dispersed in any manner, and that they shall serve at all times as a unit and under the French generals, except in the case of a temporary detachment which shall rejoin the main body without delay." [1]

[1] "Sa Majesté veut et ordonne au Sr. comte de Rochambeau de tenir, autant que les circonstances pourront le permettre, le corps des troupes françaises dont Sa Majesté lui a confié le commandement, rassemblé en un corps de troupes, et de représenter dans l'occasion au général Washington, généralissime des troupes du Congrès et aux ordres

After the sessions I spoke to M. Clemenceau and Mr. Lloyd George, suggesting that sending an American regiment might help to stimulate the Italian morale and asked their opinion. They both thought it would be a wise thing to do just at this time. I had opposed scattering our forces in this way, but the appeal of Italian officials and the recommendations of Americans who had visited Italy indicated that under the circumstances an exception could well be made for a small force.

When I told Mr. Orlando that this might be done, with the possibility of increasing the number up to a division later on, he was much pleased. Meanwhile, the President had been pressed by Italian representatives to send them troops, and word came by cable a few days later that he thought we might brigade some of our troops with the British and French divisions then in Italy. But to leave them independent was far preferable and the subject was not taken up with the Allies, my idea being that if we should find it necessary to send more troops to Italy it would be best to build up a division of our own.

Another matter taken up informally with the Prime Ministers after the conference was that of pooling Allied supplies. I explained its advantages and emphasized the saving in tonnage that would result. Mr. Lloyd George and Mr. Orlando did not commit themselves entirely, but accepted it in principle, as M. Clemenceau had done, and each of them agreed to designate an officer with business experience to meet with us at an early date to study the question. With this beginning, at least a step had been taken toward our objective, even though the principle might not be extended as far as we thought desirable. A few days later M. Clemenceau called a meeting of the representatives, in his office, General Sir Travers E. Clarke acting for the British, and Colonel Charles G. Dawes for the Americans.

duquel les troupes françaises doivent servir, que les intentions du Roi sont qu'il ne soit fait aucun dispersement des troupes françaises et qu'elles servent toujours en corps d'armée et sous les généraux français, sauf les cas de détachements momentanés et qui devront sous peu de jours rejoindre le corps principal. * * *

"Signé: Le Prince de Montbarey."

CHAPTER XXIX

Shipping Problems—British Request for Artillerymen—Venereal Question —British Object to Colored Troops—Résumé of Troops in France— Inspection of 2d Division—French and British Urging President for Further Priority Infantry and Machine Gun Units—Aviation—Duty at G.H.Q.

(Diary) Chaumont, Sunday, May 5, 1918. While in Paris saw Dwight Morrow and find prospects good for more shipping.

Returned to Chaumont yesterday. Have detailed Colonels Fox Conner, Nolan, Moseley, Fiske and Logan as Chiefs of Sections under revised General Staff organization. McAndrew appointed Chief of Staff to relieve Harbord, who will command Marine Brigade of the 2d Division. Regret my promise to let him serve with troops. Lieutenant Colonel Robert C. Davis made Adjutant General, succeeding Brigadier General Alvord, who has returned to States because of ill health. Branch of Judge Advocate General's office at Chaumont placed under Brigadier General E. A. Kreger.

OUR members of the Allied Maritime Transport Council were persistent in their search for additional tonnage. Mr. Dwight W. Morrow, of the Council's Executive Board of Shipping Control, had made an exhaustive study of shipping resources and was active in pointing out to his fellow members the urgency of our tonnage requirements. He reported to me prospects of some increase, besides calling attention to tonnage that was idle or not being used to the best advantage. The immense shipment of American troops contemplated the use of all available passenger-cargo carrying ships, British, American and neutral. As very little, if any, space would be left in such ships for freight, the demand would be greater than ever for cargo ships. Meanwhile, the amount of this class of Allied tonnage turned out during the preceding five months was scarcely equal to the losses, and the ships that we were building had only just begun to be available for service.[1]

It was at once evident that the large program of troop shipments would call for extraordinary concessions on the part of all concerned. Indeed there was some doubt in shipping circles whether enough cargo ships could be provided for us without neglecting the requirements of other nations for food and supplies. However, the prospects of increased tonnage from American yards within the next few months enabled the Shipping Control to take some chances and permit the use of the accumulated supplies in various countries in the hope of replacing them later.

As the need for shipping increased, the necessity of saving every possible ton became more urgent. Economy in the care of equipment and in the preparation of the ration was encouraged in every way. The troops were reminded of the severe restrictions and the sacrifices of the people at home in my instructions issued on the prevention of waste, and the response was fully in accord with the fine spirit exhibited by our men in all the exacting requirements made of them.

The salvage section of the Quartermaster Corps had grown to be an extensive institution for the rehabilitation of unserviceable equipment of every class and description that would otherwise have required replacement by shipments from home.[2] The economy in time, labor and transportation incident to the system was invaluable.

Labor procurement continued to be a difficult problem. The demand for labor in all armies always exceeded the supply, but when the great emergency increased the necessity for combat

[1] Although hundreds of millions of dollars and the most strenuous efforts were expended, the tonnage built after we entered the war and in the service of the army by months was only as follows: February, 1918, 8,571 tons; March, 17,092 tons; April, 17,092 tons; May, 32,822 tons; June, 85,833 tons; July, 126,834 tons; August, 165,107 tons; September, 219,515 tons; October, 266,833 tons; November, 273,846 tons.

[2] In this class came shoes, rubber boots, belts, haversacks, coats, trousers, hats, field glasses, underclothing, rifles, periscopes, motorcycles; in fact everything that could possibly be repaired. Artillery was salvaged by the Ordnance Department, and likewise the Signal Corps and the Medical Department each handled the salvage of its own special equipment.

troops we were able to prevail upon the Allies to furnish a considerable number of laborers, most of whom were French, to replace troops that we had previously been forced to detail as laborers. Through constant effort, the Labor Bureau had by this time obtained approximately 22,000 laborers, and an increase of 2,000 per week was expected.

The establishment of the European branch of the office of the Judge Advocate General expedited the final judicial review of records of trial in the expeditionary forces, as it saved the necessity of sending cases to the Judge Advocate General's office in Washington for review. The prompt action which resulted enabled commanding generals to carry into effect with the least possible delay all lawful sentences, thus preventing the detrimental effect that would have resulted had it been necessary to refer records of trial to the War Department prior to the execution of the sentences adjudged.

(Diary) Chaumont, Friday, May 10, 1918. Have had a very busy week in various conferences with staff, which is meeting new responsibilities in satisfactory manner. Majors Edward Bowditch, Jr., and John G. Quekemeyer have reported as aides. British object to taking colored troops for training.

Dr. John R. Mott and Mr. Carter, Y.M.C.A., came in Monday for conference on allotment of tonnage for canteens. Telegraphed all commanding officers about men writing home on Mother's Day, the 12th.[1]

Had request on Tuesday from Sir Douglas Haig for 10,000 artillerymen.

Several representatives of American Labor from home came to call yesterday.

Received letter from Foch to-day regarding early employment our divisions. Am sending committee to London for conference on venereal question. Marseille added to our ports; convoy in Mediterranean probably unnecessary.

[1] The following was my message to the command as indicated in the diary: "I wish that every officer and soldier of the American Expeditionary Forces would write a letter home on Mother's Day. This is a little thing for each one to do, but these letters will carry back our courage and our affection to the patriotic women whose love and prayers inspire us and cheer us on to victory."

On the heels of the clamor for nothing but infantry and machine gunners, I received a request from Marshal Haig for 10,000 artillerymen. The following are copies of letters from and to Marshal Haig:

"General Headquarters,
"British Armies in France.

"5 May, 1918.
"DEAR GENERAL PERSHING:
"I beg to enclose a note showing how I stand in the matter of Artillery Personnel. You will see that there is considerable shortage, and consequently if you could arrange to let me have 10,000 American Artillerymen, it would be of very great assistance to us.
"With kind regards,
"Believe me
"Yours very truly,
"D. HAIG."

"France, May 11, 1918.
"Confidential.
"MY DEAR SIR DOUGLAS:
"I am in receipt of your note of May 5th concerning the question of Artillery Personnel.
"Under the recent agreement the shipment from the United States of all Artillery Personnel other than that pertaining to divisions has been suspended, as you will recall, and infantry and machine gun units have a very considerable priority over even the divisional artillery.
"I regret to say that all divisional artillery units now in France have either joined their divisions at the front or are now on their way to do so, and, of course, will soon be in the line with their units to replace corresponding French divisions.
"As to heavy artillery, we have brought over only those units for which equipment was available at the time of embarkation or else promised for early delivery. But as the British War Office has been unable to deliver the heavy howitzers which had been promised for delivery in March and April, there are certain heavy artillery units which as yet I have been unable to equip or train.
"While under ordinary circumstances I would much prefer that the training be held at the usual centers, I would be glad to send a regiment of six batteries for temporary service, provided you have equipment available for them. In the event you desire these troops I should prefer that they be trained and employed by complete units.

I shall have the matter examined further and think I shall be able to increase this number.

"With high personal and official esteem, believe me
"Sincerely yours,
"JOHN J. PERSHING."

"General Headquarters,
"British Armies in France.
"15th May, 1918.

"MY DEAR GENERAL:

"I must express to you my sincere thanks for your kind offer of the services of a regiment of heavy artillery, conveyed in your letter of May 11th.

"I regret very much that no Field Artillery Personnel is available as my Heavy Artillery have not suffered to the same extent as the Field Artillery.

"I quite understand that you would of course prefer that the training of all your heavy batteries should be carried out at the usual centers, and I therefore appreciate all the more your generous readiness to assist me.

"Unfortunately, owing to our heavy expenditure of artillery material during the last two months' operations, I have only sufficient complete howitzer equipments to maintain British batteries in action and cannot hope to provide equipment for your six batteries under present conditions.

"I am, therefore, very sorry to say that I am unable to accept your kind offer.

"Yours very truly,
"D. HAIG."

The principle of coöperation among the Allies was being extended to many fields that affected the armies in common and it was now to be invoked for the promotion of morality. From the beginning, the prevention of social vices had given us serious concern, not only from the standpoint of effectives, but from that of morals. Large numbers of troops were soon to pass through England for service behind the British lines and it was deemed advisable that measures should be taken for collaboration in keeping our men clean. Bishop Brent was very active in this matter and had conferred with the Archbishop of Canterbury, who in turn suggested to the British War Office that a conference be held on the subject. Our representatives were Bishop Brent, Brigadier General Bethel and Colonel Ireland, who went with a definite plan of action to propose.

I wrote Lord Milner as follows:

"May 7, 1918.

"DEAR LORD MILNER:

"I am glad to respond to your call for the conference aimed at joint action by British and American authorities to handle the venereal situation as it affects the Allied troops in England and in France, and to our closer coöperation in measures that it may be deemed wise to take in the future. I am sending to represent the American Expeditionary Forces, General Walter A. Bethel, Judge Advocate of the Forces, Colonel Ireland, my Chief Medical Officer, and Bishop Brent, Senior G.H.Q. Chaplain, who are able to speak with authority on the general situation in America and France as regards the stand and measures our Government has taken to combat the venereal menace.

"The Allied military authorities have recognized the necessity of unity of purpose and coördination of effort in this fight in France. Three conferences on this matter have already been held between members of our medical corps and the French authorities with a very helpful outlook for concerted measures. The conference which you have called holds out the same promise as regards the coöperation of military and civil authorities in England, without which nothing we can say or do will help.

"I have heard also with great satisfaction of the recent decision of the British War Office that the licensed houses of prostitution are to be put out of bounds in the B.E.F. Many of us who have experimented with licensed prostitution or kindred measures, hoping thereby to minimize the physical evils, have been forced to the conclusion that they are really ineffective. Abraham Flexner has argued the case so convincingly that on the scientific side it seems to me there is no escape from the conclusion that what he terms 'abolition' as distinguished from 'regulation' is the only effective mode of combating this age-long evil.

"I have the greatest hope that the results of the conference which you have called will be far-reaching in their effect. This menace to the young manhood in the army forces and to the health and future well-being of our peoples cannot be met by the efforts of each Government working apart from the others. It is plain that every day it affects more and more all of the Allied nations now fighting on the Western Front in France. The question long since was an international one, and it is only by an internationalization of our aims and efforts that we can obtain the unity and coördination which will enable us to solve the problem.   The gravest responsibility rests on those to whom the parents of our soldiers have entrusted their sons for the battle, and we fail if we neglect any effort to safeguard them in every way.

"We have the common ground of humanity, we have the well-considered conclusions of the best scientific minds on our side, and from the fact that, in this war of nations-in-arms the soldier is merely a citizen on war service, we have all the elements which will force coöperation between military and civil authorities.   The army can do little unless the citizen at home plays his part in the big scheme.   With our nations coöperating hand-in-hand, both in France and at home, we have the brightest prospects of winning the victory.

"I remain with high personal and official esteem,

"Faithfully yours,

"JOHN J. PERSHING."

This conference did not meet with the success that had been anticipated and little came out of it that was of practical value to us.

In fulfilling our part in military coöperation, we had already gone far beyond the mere recognition of the principle of unity of command and had begun to bring over hundreds of thousands of men almost regardless of the organizations to which they belonged in order that they might be available in the event of extreme necessity.   This action was taken at the risk of our ever being able to form an American army.   In conversation with Foch I had also offered several divisions for use anywhere on the Western Front.   It was somewhat gratifying to realize that the Allies recognized our general attitude of coöperation, as indicated by the following extracts from a letter written by General Foch.

"During our conversation on April 25th you were most insistent that it was your desire that * * * American divisions should take part in the battle in which we are engaged, and you also suggested the order in which they should be employed.

"I am just as appreciative of this new evidence of your energetic and prompt coöperation as I was of the offer which you made with such generous impulse on March 28th."

A colored division, the 92d, had been selected by the War Department for temporary service and training with the British, armies, but their Military Attaché at Washington, acting under instructions from his Government, protested against it. I was surprised that they should take this attitude, inasmuch as the French were anxious to have colored troops assigned to their divisions, and, as has been mentioned, four regiments had been lent to them temporarily. In attempting to clear up the matter, I wrote to Marshal Haig, sending an identical letter to Lord Milner:

"May 5, 1918.

"My dear Sir Douglas:

"Some time ago, I received a cable from my Government to the effect that it was necessary to list one of our colored divisions for early shipment to France. As you know, all of our infantry and machine gun units to be embarked in the near future are destined for service, for the time being, with your forces. I accordingly replied to the cable * * * to the effect that the 92d (colored) Division could be included in the troops to be assigned to the forces under your command. It now appears, however, that the British Military Attaché in Washington has made a protest against including any colored battalions among the troops destined for service with your forces and that he has stated that this protest was made in behalf of your War Office.

"You will, of course, appreciate my position in this matter, which, in brief, is that these negroes are American citizens. My Government, for reasons which concern itself alone, has decided to organize colored combat divisions and now desires the early dispatch of one of these divisions to France. Naturally I cannot and will not discriminate against these soldiers.

"I am informed that the 92d Division is in a good state of training and I have no reason to believe that its employment under your command would be accompanied by any unusual difficulties.

"I am informing my Government of this letter to you. May I not hope that the inclusion of the 92d Division among the American troops to be placed under your command is acceptable to you and that you will be able to overcome the objections raised by your War Office?"

A few days later I received the following letter from Lord Milner, the British Minister of War:

"13 May, 1918.
"My dear General:
"Your letter of May 7th about the employment of colored Divisions with our British forces in France. I am rather hoping that this difficult question may not after all be going to trouble us, for I see, from a telegram received from General Wagstaff, that the Divisions so far arrived for training with the British do not include the 92d.
"I hope this is so, for, as a matter of fact, a good deal of administrative trouble would, I think, necessarily arise if the British Army had to undertake the training of a colored Division.
"Believe me,
"Yours very truly,
"Milner."

My cable to our War Department was to the effect that in the event the Secretary still desired to send this division to France I should adhere to my former recommendation that it be included among those to go to the British for training. However, the War Department evidently did not wish to insist upon it, as the division came over shortly afterwards and was not included among those assigned to the British.

(Diary) Chaumont, Tuesday, May 14, 1918. Report from Washington indicates that we have only limited number of trained men left. Spent three days last week inspecting units of the 2d Division, then under Major General Bundy. As division was just out of the trenches, the salvage dumps of this unit of about 25,000 men amounted to forty carloads of clothing and unserviceable equipment.
French and British Ambassadors are again asking the President for additional infantry and machine gun units. Washington cables that cavalry organized for A.E.F. now needed on Border.

To give a résumé of our strength on May 10th, it may be said that the number of men in the army at home and in Europe amounted approximately to 1,900,000, of whom more than 790,000 were volunteers. In France and England we had 488,224.[1]

[1] The 1st, 2d, 3d, 26th, 32d, 41st, 42d and 77th Divisions were complete—the 5th, 28th, 35th, 82d and 93d incomplete. There were also 3 brigades of heavy coast artillery, the 30th regiment of gas and flame engineers, 4 regiments of cavalry and certain special troops. All divisions not in line were in training. With the British we had the 77th Division, 4 regiments of railway engineers, 1 regiment of pioneer engi-

Of these, there were eight complete divisions in France and
five incomplete, which, with regiments and smaller units of
auxiliary troops, made a total of 290,765 combat troops.   Of the
complete units, the 1st Division was with the French in line near
Amiens, the 2d, 26th and 42d Divisions were occupying quiet

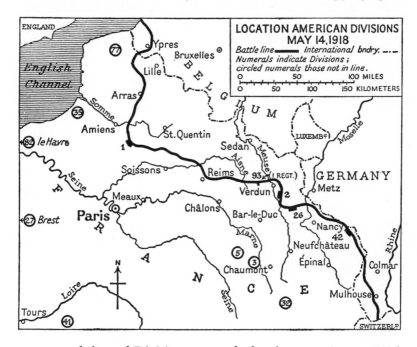

sectors, and the 32d Division was ready for that experience.   With
the troops then in line, we were holding an aggregate of thirty-
five miles of front, or more than double that held by the Belgians.
    Of those troops at home on May 10th, excluding three divisions
at ports of embarkation, 263,852 were infantrymen of sufficient

neers, 1 telegraph battalion and 6 base hospitals; also 9,826 officers and men of the
air service (4 squadrons being at the front).   With the French were 4 regiments of
colored troops in training, 5,500 motor mechanics, 6 machine shop truck units and
80 ambulance sections.
    To recapitulate: (1) In service: in line in American sectors, 103,089; S. O. S. troops,
140,049; combatant troops used in S. O. S., 16,885; serving with British, 11,410; serving with French, 12,234; total in service, 283,667.   (2) In training: in American training areas, 133,534; with British, 34,334; with French, 8,199; total, 176,067.   (3) En
route, 21,812; sick and detached, 6,678.

training for overseas service. It was therefore evident that the rapid rate at which they were being sent to France could not long continue without taking partially trained men.

It was my custom throughout the war, as both a duty and a pleasure, to visit the troops as frequently as possible in order to keep in touch with their state of efficiency and to help maintain the morale of officers and men. As Bundy's 2d Division was leaving the sector of the line south of Verdun where they had been for almost two months and was en route to the billeting and training area to finish preparation for battle, the moment was opportune to make an inspection.

I was pleased to find both infantry brigades, the regulars under Lewis and the marines commanded by Harbord and Cruikshank's artillery in very good shape. The trains of the division that were seen on the march did not look so well, due mainly to the appearance of the animals. This, however, was not entirely unexpected, as the care of animals is always difficult to teach and it was especially so in an army like ours in France. The entraining of that part of the division that I saw at Ancemont was being carried out in an orderly and systematic manner. I spent considerable time in talking with a number of different officers in command of smaller units and in discussing questions of supply with officers charged with that duty. On the whole my impression of the division was very favorable and this was soon to be confirmed on the battlefield, where it was to take its place among the best.

General Blondlat, in whose corps the 2d Division had been serving, spoke very highly of it, but, contrary to the view of most French officers, he thought that differences in language and temperament were serious handicaps to combined work and he was of the opinion that Americans should do their own training. It was exceptional to hear an expression from French sources that agreed so completely with our own.

Upon my return to Chaumont a cable from the Secretary of War was handed to me on the unwelcome subject of Allied demand for infantry and machine gun units. Extracts from it are given below.

"May 11, 1918.

"The President asked me to say to you that he has been very much impressed and disturbed by representations officially made to him by French and British Ambassadors showing the steady drain upon French and British replacements and the small number of replacement troops now available. He feels that you on the ground have full opportunity to know the situation and fully trusts your judgment as to how far we ought to give additional priority to infantry and machine gun units, in view of the fact that such troops seem to be the most immediately serviceable and urgently needed."

After saying that the Abbeville Agreement provided less priority than recommended by the Supreme War Council, it continued:

"It has been suggested to the President that General Foch may reopen this subject with you, and the President hopes you will approach any such interview as sympathetically as possible, particularly if the situation as to replacements which has been presented to him is as critical as it seems."

My reply set forth the principal arguments used at Abbeville against the unlimited shipment of the classes of troops the Allies requested. I pointed out that the statements made by Allied leaders at the conference indicated that possibly enough tonnage would be forthcoming to enable us to ship complete divisions, and that all concerned seemed to be satisfied with the concessions we made. I added further:

"I think we have fully and fairly met the situation. We have given the Supreme War Council all it asked at Abbeville. * * * It is believed that the action at Abbeville should be considered as the deliberate expression of the Supreme War Council's latest view. * * * Otherwise as long as there is the slightest hope of getting concessions there will be a continual clamor regardless of how it affects us. * * * Judging from what occurred at Abbeville and from the expressions of approval by General Foch, I think he cannot consistently reopen the subject until the question of July needs arises."

(Diary) Paris, Saturday, May 18, 1918. Saw a number of officers. Hamilton Holt and Judge Ben Lindsey came for luncheon and Irvin Cobb to dinner Wednesday at Chaumont.

Egan and Morrow called Thursday to talk over shipping. Talked with Eltinge, Deputy Chief of Staff, about reorganization of S.O.S. Headquarters. Left for Paris in evening.

Yesterday saw Patrick, who will be the new Chief of Air Service, and Foulois, and emphasized necessity for teamwork in aviation. Lunched with Ambassador Sharp, who says that Clemenceau, Cambon and others highly praise American troops.

Saw Foch at Versailles to-day and spoke again of building up an American sector, which he seems to approve. He expressed satisfaction with American aid and especially with the assignment of our aviators to the French. Had a talk with Bliss.

Brigadier General Foulois, at his own request and in order to assume charge of aviation in the First Army, was to be superseded by Brigadier General Patrick. Foulois' desire to secure general coöperation made him a valuable assistant and but for his experience and his efforts we might not have avoided so many of the pitfalls that lay in our way. In August he was relieved as Chief of Aviation First Army by Colonel Mitchell and became Assistant Chief of Air Service.

The demands of the Allies for material, for mechanics, for the adoption of this or that type of plane or engine, their efforts to secure preferential treatment from us or from each other, to say nothing of our own interior difficulties as to organization and manufacture, made accomplishment of definite results in preparation very difficult.

The Inter-Allied Aviation Committee, established in Paris in the fall of 1917 with the French Under-Secretary of Aeronautics as chairman, was presumably concerned with the requirements of the Allies in aircraft material, but it resulted in nothing practical in the way of coöperation. Meanwhile, in order to coördinate our own needs as well as assist the Allies, a Joint Army and Navy Aviation Committee in France was formed. Generally speaking, this committee did some effective work, but in the competition among the Allies for special advantage the interests of aviation as a whole were often overlooked. The French Aviation Control undertook, through the Inter-Allied Aviation Committee, to ignore the American Army and Navy Committee's action in allocating material by appealing to the Supreme War Council. As a consequence the Council established its own sub-committee, an outcome that really strengthened the American Army and Navy Committee and aided materially in bringing about better understanding among manufacturing interests.

Although conditions were unfavorable, training of aviators was being carried on, and our fliers were in demand for duty on the French front to fill their ranks. The services of these aviators were receiving commendation and General Foch seemed to be especially pleased with their work.

During the first few months at Chaumont I occupied quarters in the town, but later M. de Rouvre placed at my disposal his beautiful château some two miles away. My headquarters mess was limited to the few officers with whom I was most intimately associated and consisted of the Chief of Staff, the Adjutant General, my personal aides, and one or two others. Nearly always there were a few guests at meals invited from among the visitors, both French and American, who came to headquarters. Officers from French G.H.Q. were frequent guests and we were always glad to have them.

It was a welcome relief from the cares of the day when our dinner guests proved to be entertaining or interesting. If the guest was inclined to be more serious, he too was encouraged in his particular line. Irvin Cobb came along and in his inimitable character as an entertainer gave us an exceptional evening.

As a rule there was a ban on everything in the way of shop talk and the rule was rarely broken, and then only when we had special guests seeking enlightenment on some phase of the war, or information regarding our policies and activities. The members of the mess always looked forward to the occasion of meals as one of pleasure and relaxation. The mess was no place for one to pour out his woes or unnecessarily discuss the business of the day or the duties of the morrow.

There was one subject that would always start a discussion and that was the relative value of the different arms, each being represented by at least one officer, with an occasional guest from the staff to take sides according to his particular origin. The artilleryman would dispute honors with the infantryman, pointing out the helplessness of the foot-soldier without the support of the big guns, while the cavalryman would assert the superiority of his arm over either because he could fight on foot or on horseback and did not have to carry 110 pounds on his back over muddy roads day after day and night after night to get into battle.

Harbord and I were both from the cavalry and the member of the staff from that branch felt that he had at least a sympathetic audience. The infantry aide, however, with the support of Davis, who was originally a foot-soldier, always held his own in any discussion, for no matter how specious the arguments or perhaps the gibes at his expense we all knew that without the infantry the other arms would accomplish little. The associations of such a group are never forgotten and even a short period was enough to establish a permanent and affectionate relationship.

Rotation in office was early adopted as a principle to be applied to the staff in general and although it was never possible fully to carry it out, most of the officers of my staff got their chance at a tour with combat troops. Majors Collins and Shallenberger, two of the aides who went with me to France, were the first to go to other duty, being replaced by Majors Quekemeyer and Bowditch. Colonel Boyd, who joined me as aide shortly after my arrival in France, remained throughout the war. When General Harbord's turn came, his place as Chief of Staff was taken by General McAndrew. Several of the higher officers of the General Staff were given a tour with troops, not only that they might have the opportunity to serve at the front, which is every soldier's ambition, but because they would return to staff duty with a broader and more sympathetic understanding of the line officer's point of view and appreciate more fully the consideration that he deserves at the hands of the staff.

CHAPTER XXX

Visit Pétain at Chantilly—1st Division Preparing Offensive—Conference with S.O.S. Officials—Agreement Regarding Unified Supply—1st Division Attacks at Cantigny—Germans Drive French Beyond the Marne —2d and 3d Divisions Stop German Advance—Inspection of Divisions with British for Training—Call on Foch at Sarcus—Ragueneau on American Characteristics—Pétain's Instructions to French Liaison Officers

(Diary) Paris, Monday, May 20, 1918. Saw General Pétain at Chantilly yesterday. He says French must soon reduce twenty-five divisions to half strength and wants them filled up with American units. Went to 1st Division to discuss proposed offensive. Spent night with Bullard. To-day gave Bullard and his staff résumé of the general situation. Discussed tactical methods with Colonel George C. Marshall, Jr., Division Operations Officer. Saw Colonel B. T. Clayton, Division Quartermaster, on supply questions.

WHEN I called on General Pétain at Chantilly, he was found installed in a commodious private house hidden away in the forest, very near the residence that Marshal Joffre had occupied earlier in the war. The beauty and quiet of the surroundings on that Sunday morning seemed nature's protest against the horrors of other scenes and events of daily occurrence where the opposing armies were arrayed against each other.

The purpose of my visit was to discuss the possibility of assembling our divisions to form an American army. I recalled to Pétain that the earlier plans for their concentration in the vicinity of Toul had been postponed at my suggestion on account of the emergency that then confronted the Allies. He replied that he did not see how it could be done now, and that the matter of immediate concern to him was the reënforcement of his own divisions in such a way as to preserve both their number and

53

their strength. He was willing to accept our men by battalions, regiments, or brigades, but preferred the assignment of two American battalions to each of twenty-five divisions until October. Foch had asked for assignments of American troops only until August, when, it was said, the French 1919 class would be available for service. As fifty battalions of infantry would have been equivalent to that of at least four of our divisions, it would have compelled us to break up that number of incoming units, with little hope of reorganizing them. Of course, it was out of the question to consider such a possibility.

While his needs were appreciated, this was another request that could not be granted without yielding in my determination to bring about the formation of an American army. After some further discussion, we simply renewed the understanding previously reached that, for the present, American divisions with the French and not yet prepared for offensive action should occupy portions of the front in quiet sectors, relieving French divisions when the exigencies of the situation demanded that they should enter the battle. Thus for each partially trained division we would be able to free two French divisions. A few days later this arrangement received Foch's approval.

Although some weeks had passed since my offer of troops, so far none had been called upon to take part in active operations. The reason appeared to be that the Allies were skeptical as to the ability of our divisions, except for three or four of the best, to conduct an offensive. The opportunity soon came, however, to remove any reason for misgivings.

The 1st Division had now been in line for nearly a month opposite the town of Cantigny, near the point of farthest advance of the enemy in the Amiens salient. The French corps in which the 1st was serving had prepared a counterattack to be launched in that sector about the middle of May in case of another offensive by the enemy in Flanders, which it was believed would occur between May 15th and 20th. Since the enemy did not undertake the expected offensive, the proposed counterattack was not made.

It was then decided that the 1st Division should attempt to

improve its position. The Germans on its front continued to hold the advantage of higher ground, from which they were able to inflict constant losses on our troops while suffering little damage themselves. Another reason was that at this moment the morale of the Allies required that American troops make their appearance in battle. It was advisable also from the point of view that, if successful, it would demonstrate that we could best help the Allies by using our troops in larger units instead of adopting their plan of building up their forces. The high pitch of enthusiasm with which the 1st Division entered into the preparations for this attack gave us confidence that the result would be satisfactory.

(Diary) Chaumont, Thursday, May 23, 1918. Held a conference in Paris on Tuesday with Generals Kernan and Hagood on handling increase of men and supplies. Dr. Raymond Fosdick, under instructions from Mr. Baker, came to talk over welfare work.

Presented definite proposition yesterday to M. Clemenceau on Inter-Allied supply. Logan reported horse procurement more promising. Left for Chaumont in evening.

Went over aviation problems with Patrick and Foulois this morning and find organization difficulties are clearing up. Authority granted me to confer fifty Distinguished Service Medals on Allied officers. Local medical officers directed to assist mayors in carrying out law on epidemics. Have selected Grémévillers as casual advance headquarters because of its convenience to British front.

The matter of handling the rapidly growing business of the S.O.S. was one of constant concern. The expansion in shipments of men and material threw an increasing load on the inadequately manned system. Incoming freight was again accumulating at the ports somewhat faster than it could be removed. Still more berths had to be provided in order to prevent congestion. Although the submarine danger was passing, convoys were still necessary, and because they were composed of a larger number of ships, each individual vessel had to wait longer while the convoy was being assembled at ports of departure and before being docked at French ports. Therefore boats continued to be delayed at both ends of the voyage. Considerable new rolling stock was coming along and repairs were being made to the old, but yet the amount was not sufficient.

However, with anything like a normal or stable situation at the front and an economical allotment of railway resources, we should have been able to keep abreast of incoming tonnage. But conditions at the front were abnormal, as operations were in progress in several places at once. The constant shifting of troops from one end of France to the other to meet critical situations required an excess volume of rolling stock.[1] In order to be ready to move troops to meet emergencies, many trains had to be held in reserve behind the lines in the Zone of Operations, where they were beyond the control of the rail authorities in the rear. As we were dependent upon assignments from the French railway management, we were short of both engines and cars.

I called a joint conference of officials of the S.O.S., and the resulting improvement of methods relieved the congestion here and there and gave a more continuous flow of supplies toward the forward areas. The use of Marseille began to afford some relief to the port situation and although the voyage was longer it was offset by better accommodations for handling cargo. Moreover, as the railways from Marseille were not used in connection with operations, they could more easily carry the added burden. At all ports we had been able to obtain additional facilities, such as tugs, lighters, barges, troop tenders, and floating derricks, all of which increased our efficiency in unloading vessels, but we still lacked stevedores and other troops of the Services of Supply.

Coöperation in supply had been given a good start by the French and ourselves working together. As procurement abroad had a direct and important bearing on the tonnage question, efforts were renewed to extend organized coördination to Inter-Allied supply. At one period in our discussions, the control by a single authority had been proposed. But upon careful analysis, based upon the experience of the General Purchasing Board in negotiations with the French, it was concluded that an Inter-

---

[1] It required from twenty-five to thirty French trains to move one French division and twice as many for an American division.

Allied committee whose decisions should be unanimous would
be the best solution to this difficult problem.

In further conference with M. Clemenceau an agreement was
secured to broaden the scope of coöperation between our two
armies, in the hope that later the other Allies might be induced
to join. I presented the agreement given below, which became
the basis of our understanding:

"It is hereby agreed among the Allied Governments subscribing
hereto:

"1. That the principle of unification of military supplies and utilities for the use of the Allied armies is adopted.

"2. That in order to apply this principle and so far as possible
coördinate the use of utilities and the distribution of supplies among
the Allied armies a Board consisting of representatives of each of
the Allied armies is to be constituted at once.

"3. That the unanimous decision of the Board regarding the allotment of material and supplies shall have the force of orders and be
carried out by the respective supply agencies.

"4. That further details of the organization by which the above plan
is to be carried out shall be left to the Board, subject to such approval
by the respective Governments as may at any time seem advisable.

"We agree to the above and wish it to be submitted to the British
and Italian Governments.

"G. CLEMENCEAU,
"JOHN J. PERSHING."

At first glance at this very general agreement, one could readily
imagine many possible difficulties, such as indifference on the
part of the supply departments of the armies or governments concerned, their inherent jealousies, the question of credit adjustments, as well as those of joint storage and transportation. But
most of these were overcome in the actual application of the principles set forth and much duplication of effort was saved, with
consequent reduction in transportation and expense. Certain supplies, light railways, and truck transportation that would not
otherwise have been obtainable for our use, thus began to be
available from the common pool.

The agreement was immediately invoked in the hope of meeting the horse situation. M. Clemenceau, in compliance with my

request, and acting on information from his procurement agencies, promised to furnish us 100,000 horses, which was later reduced to 80,000. But the plan did not work out and our representative who was conducting the negotiations ran into several obstacles, the principal one being the disinclination of the French farmers to dispose of their horses. Only a limited number of owners could be tempted to present their serviceable animals for sale, even at the exorbitant prices offered, and the French Government so far had been loath to exert its powers of requisition. At times the difficulties would appear less formidable, yet, notwithstanding constant pressure, our expectations were only partially realized. The farmers in general simply would not sell, and one reason given us was that they had the idea that we would thus be compelled to make a large importation of horses, which would give them an opportunity to buy cheaply after the war.

(Diary) Grémévillers, Tuesday, May 28, 1918. Spent Saturday with 3d Division (Dickman) at maneuvers.

Next day visited 5th Division (McMahon) in Bar-sur-Aube region. Lunched with McMahon and his brigadiers, Walter H. Gordon and Joseph C. Castner. Reached Paris at 10 P.M. and had a talk with Atterbury, who was waiting to see me. Will make readjustments to give him greater independence. After year's delay, Department of Military Aeronautics has been established in the War Department.

Yesterday saw Major Lloyd C. Griscom,[1] who goes as Liaison Officer with Lord Milner. Strong German offensive began yesterday against French on Chemin des Dames, with "Big Bertha" firing on Paris.

Have recommended that the following new services be created by Executive Order: Transportation Service, Motor Transport Service, and Gas Service. Went to 1st Division (Bullard) and learned that attack on Cantigny to-day was completely successful.

The division maneuver in simulated attack, often repeated, such as that held by the 3d Division, was a valuable exercise in combat teamwork. It was a test of the efficiency of the unit, especially that of higher officers and their staffs. While the instruction of individual officers as leaders and the training of smaller units for open warfare were constantly stressed, particular emphasis was

---

[1] Lord Milner was anxious to have our relations work smoothly and suggested that I should send an officer to represent me at the British War Office.

given in the final preparation for line service to the importance of perfecting all means of communication throughout the division down to the smaller units in the trenches. No troops without considerable practice in this regard could be sent into battle with much hope of success.

The Cantigny sector at this time was very active, with artillery fire unusually heavy, and the preparations for the attack by the 1st Division were carried out under great difficulty. Many casualties occurred during the construction of jumping-off

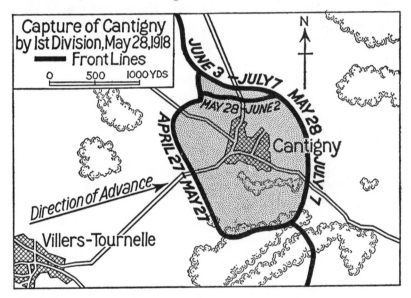

trenches, emplacements and advance command posts. The 28th Infantry, under Colonel Hanson E. Ely, designated for the assault, was reënforced by tanks, machine guns, engineers, and other special units. Additional French guns were sent to assist the artillery brigade of the division and particularly to suppress the hostile batteries that would attempt to interfere with the consolidation of the new position after it should be captured.

On the morning of May 28th, after a brief artillery preparation, the infantry advanced on a front of a mile and a quarter. The village of Cantigny and the adjacent heights were quickly taken, relatively heavy casualties inflicted on the enemy, and about 240 prisoners captured. Our troops behaved splendidly and suffered but slight loss in the actual attack.

Events then developing farther east, however, were seriously to complicate the success. The German assault in force against the French along the Chemin des Dames, between Soissons and Reims, began on the morning of the 27th and was making dangerous headway. By the morning of the 28th the gains of the enemy were such that the French High Command was compelled to relieve some of their artillery reënforcing the 1st Division and transfer it to the Chemin des Dames front. The enemy's artillery within range of Cantigny was increased soon after the assault and was thus able to concentrate a terrific fire on our troops in the captured position. His reaction against this attack was extremely violent as apparently he was determined at all cost to counteract the excellent effect the American success would produce upon the Allies.

Under cover of this bombardment, several counterattacks were made by the enemy, but our young infantrymen stood their ground and broke up every attempt to dislodge them. The 28th Infantry sustained severe casualties and had to be reënforced by a battalion each from the 18th and 26th Infantry regiments.

It was a matter of pride to the whole A.E.F. that the troops of this division, in their first battle, and in the unusually trying situation that followed, displayed the fortitude and courage of veterans, held their gains, and denied to the enemy the slightest advantage.[1]

(Diary) Paris, Friday, May 31, 1918. Went to British area Wednesday. Saw the 35th Division (Wright), its men above average size. Also the 82d (Burnham), which looks very promising. Took lunch with Wright and spent the night with Colonel Bacon, an admirable

[1] It is interesting to record that of the officers of the 1st Division to participate in this battle, Bullard was later to command an army; Summerall and Hines, corps; Buck, Ely, Parker and Bamford, divisions. Two members of the division staff, King and Marshall, were to become chiefs of staff of corps. Many other officers then with the division would have undoubtedly reached high positions of command had they not sacrificed their lives at Soissons and on other battle fields later on.

liaison officer. Our 2d and 3d Divisions ordered to reënforce the French.

Had breakfast yesterday with Sir Douglas Haig. He criticized the French and thought they should have foreseen this offensive, but added that his remarks were hardly warranted in view of recent British experience. Saw part of the 28th Division (Muir), the 77th (Duncan) and the 4th (Cameron) and am much pleased with them. All are apprehensive of being left with the British. Had luncheon with Muir and dined with General Foch at Sarcus.

Came to Paris to-day, held conference with McAndrew and Fox Conner, and saw M. Tardieu and Martin Egan. Have recommended training with British tanks at home. Tonnage allotments still short of requirements. Have cabled urgent request for trucks, also for 12,000 railway troops, badly needed.

The French situation is very serious. Our aviation doing well at the front.

The German attack of May 27th was made by thirty German divisions. It came as such a surprise that the French did not have time to destroy important bridges across the Aisne and the Vesle, over which their pursuers followed. By May 31st the enemy had captured Soissons and reached the Marne and Château-Thierry, a distance of thirty miles, driving the French in confusion toward Paris and inflicting upon them a loss of 60,000 prisoners, 650 guns, 2,000 machine guns, aviation material, and vast quantities of ammunition and other supplies.

I have heard this retirement referred to as a masterly, strategic retreat, but it was nothing of the kind and the French military authorities never made any such claim. The four French and three British divisions on the front of attack were completely overcome. The entire French reserve became engaged; in all, thirty-five French infantry and six cavalry divisions participating in the battle. In addition, two other British divisions which had been sent to that front to rest, two Italian, and two American divisions were called into action and suffered heavily.

Before the attack, it was the opinion of our Intelligence Section that the next blow would logically fall upon that part of the line and that view was expressed to the French by my Chief of Intelligence, Brigadier General Nolan. Yet on the day previous to the attack the French Army Headquarters on that front asserted that everything was quiet and that they did not expect an offensive there. This was indeed a compliment to the enemy as showing the secrecy with which his concentration was made, a precaution which we, ourselves, rather successfully followed later in preparing for both our major offensives.

The alarming situation had caused General Pétain to call on me on the 30th for American troops to be sent to the region

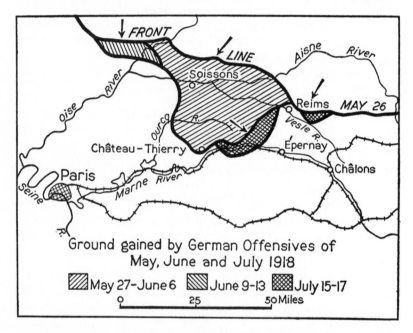

Ground gained by German Offensives of
May, June and July 1918

May 27–June 6   June 9–13   July 15–17

0   25   50 Miles

of Château-Thierry. The 3d Division (Dickman), then in training near Chaumont, being the only division within reach besides the 2d, was ordered to move north immediately. Dickman started his motorized machine gun battalion over the road on the afternoon of May 30th. The infantry and engineers entrained the same night and the division's supply trains marched overland.

The first element to reach Château-Thierry was the 7th Machine Gun Battalion, which arrived on the afternoon of May

31st and immediately went into action against the enemy, who then held the half of the town north of the Marne. By daylight on June 1st all available guns had been provided with cover and were in their positions, one company with eight guns defending the main wagon bridge and another with nine guns guarding the approaches to the railroad bridge. From these positions they repulsed all attempts by the Germans to cross the Marne. Meanwhile, as the infantry of the division came up on June 1st, its battalions were put into line to reënforce the French along the Marne for ten miles, from Château-Thierry east to Dormans. The conduct of the machine gun battalion in this operation was highly praised by General Pétain.

The 2d Division (Bundy) on May 30th was near Chaumont-en-Vexin and was preparing to move northward the next day for concentration near Beauvais to relieve the 1st Division at Cantigny. But its orders were changed late that night, and the division, moving by motor trucks, was rushed toward Meaux, which lies about twenty miles from Paris. On reaching there, the leading elements were hurried forward in the direction of Château-Thierry. The roads were crowded with French troops and refugees retreating in great confusion, many of the soldiers telling our men that all was lost. Definite information as to the location of the enemy and the disposition of the retiring French units in the vicinity was difficult to obtain.

The initial deployment of the infantry and marines of the division was made on June 1st, across the Paris highway near Lucy-le-Bocage, in support of two French divisions, which, however, had orders to fall back through the American lines. On June 4th, the French withdrew and that day the Germans began attacks against the American lines which were everywhere repulsed. On June 6th, the 2d Division began a series of local attacks which resulted in the retaking of important points from the enemy.

The sudden appearance and dramatic entrance of the 2d and 3d Divisions into the shattered and broken fighting lines and their dash and courage in battle produced a favorable effect upon the French *poilu*. Although in battle for the first time, our men maintained their positions and by their timely arrival effectively stopped the German advance on Paris. It must have been with a decided feeling of relief that the worn and tired French soldiers, retreating before vastly superior numbers, caught sight of Americans arriving in trucks at Meaux and marching thence on foot, hats off, eagerly hurrying forward to battle. And the Germans, who had been filled with propaganda depreciating the American effort and the quality of our training, must have been surprised and disconcerted by meeting strong resistance by Americans on different portions of this active battle front.

This defeat of the French furnished the second striking confirmation of the wisdom of training troops for open warfare. While the Germans had been practicing for a war of movement and concentrating their most aggressive personnel into shock divisions, preparatory to the spring campaign, the training of the Allies had been still limited generally to trench warfare. As our units were being trained for open warfare, this alone would have been sufficient reason why we could not allow them to be broken up and scattered among the Allies.

American divisions were arriving behind the British lines in increasing numbers without the artillery and other auxiliary components, but many of the infantry units were not up to strength and much of the personnel only partially trained. The late arrivals, like the earlier ones, complained of the vicious practice of the General Staff at home of frequently withdrawing large numbers of trained men and replacing them with recruits. It was, therefore, of the utmost importance to push their instruction, now fortunately beyond the possibility of such interruption. On visiting the new divisions, I impressed upon the officers the responsibility of putting their units in shape as quickly as possible and pointed out when practicable those features that should be especially stressed regardless of the type of instruction which the British might wish to undertake. There were many questions asked regarding their service with the British and all were given to understand that they were to be assembled as soon as possible to form an army of our own.

At British headquarters the officials were very anxious over the French situation and yet they expressed a feeling of relief that some of the adverse criticism which had been heaped upon them during the past few weeks could now perhaps be applied with the same force to their ally.

Returning from the British front, I stopped at Sarcus to see General Foch and took dinner with him and his staff. It would be difficult to imagine a more depressed group of officers. They sat through the meal scarcely speaking a word as they contemplated what was probably the most serious situation of the war. As we still had troops that were not actively engaged, I suggested personally to Foch, when we were alone after dinner, that an early counterattack be made against the new salient, offering him the use of these disengaged troops. Most confidentially, he said, that was what he had in mind. Speaking of the 2d and 3d Divisions, which had already been ordered to support the French, I told him that he could count on my doing everything possible in this crisis and that I was ready to exert the utmost effort to help meet it with all our forces then at hand, which he said of course he had never doubted. In further conversation, he seemed more than ever of the opinion that only infantry and machine gun units should be brought over from the States and still apparently could not see the advantage of having complete American combat units, or the urgency of bringing over men to relieve the extraordinary strain on our supply system.

After the success of our troops, we were in no mood to listen to unwarranted criticisms. Upon my return to Paris, M. Tardieu called and, no doubt with good intent, undertook to comment adversely on our staff and our organization. As these were subjects that he could not possibly know about, I replied that he had an entirely erroneous impression and that our General Staff was composed of men selected for their ability and efficiency. I intimated that we had had quite enough of this sort of thing from the French, either military or civilian, and suggested that if his people would cease troubling themselves so much about our affairs and attend more strictly to their own we should all get along much better. I fully appreciated M. Tardieu's ability and his eagerness to be helpful, and I really had a high regard for him, but the constant inclination on the part of a certain element among the French to assume a superiority that did not exist, then or at any later period, added to the attempts of some of them to dictate, had reached the limit of patience.

It must in fairness be said that a superior attitude was not assumed by the higher officers of the French Army and rarely by civilians, but was mainly noticeable among some bureau officials and others who, clothed with brief authority as instructors or otherwise, came in contact with our organizations. It is pertinent to mention here that the Chief of the French Mission made a full report to his superiors on the American characteristics, from which the following extracts are taken:

"The outstanding characteristics of Americans, taken as a people, are a highly developed national pride and a strong spirit of independence. * * * As a rule, these feelings of theirs are not openly expressed; they do not result in the slightest display of arrogance on their part in their dealings with us.

"* * * They have decided not to submit to any subordination whatsoever, and have made up their minds to be placed on a footing of complete equality.

"Now, we are sure to suffer a complete deception if we attempt to impose our opinions, or our advice, on Americans, even in matters of a strictly military nature. They are quite willing to recognize our true worth, and they appreciate our efforts. They are great admirers of France, of the achievements of her armies, and of the staunch bearing and the spirit of sacrifice displayed by her citizens. They are sincere in these feelings, but it does not follow that they are ready to take our advice blindly, or adopt our plans outright.

"* * * They argue that open warfare will regain all of its classic importance when the eventual break-through and its attendant exploitation takes place. This is bound to happen, in their opinion, when the American Army, as such, takes its place in line.

"Another consequence of this state of mind is that Americans are a unit in intending to organize an army which shall be wholly American and not have its components brigaded with the armies of the Allies. As to this point, they are unanimous, from their commander-in-chief down to the last officer who happens to give it any thought. The American officers will not listen to any talk of an amalgamation wherein the American Army would lose its distinctive character.

"At all events, it is my firm belief that, from now on, we should discard any idea of either systematically brigading entire American units with our own, or of systematically incorporating American soldiers with our troops.

"To sum up, we cannot flatter ourselves with the hope of forcing a complete and final adhesion to our way of thinking. The Americans are in the habit of listening to our views, and they often ask for them, when once we have gained their confidence; but they invariably reserve the right to make the final decision themselves, and they are accustomed, in the last analysis, to base their decision on their own reasoning.

" * * * It should not be forgotten that the leaders of the American forces actually in France enjoy President Wilson's entire confidence and that his powers are more extensive than those of any other ruler.

"Consequently, even if we cannot expect to realize all our aims, or secure the acceptance of all our views, this does not detract from the importance to us of American support, not only from the standpoint of financial backing and supplies of all kinds, but also with respect to military power. The first American troops to be organized as units are sturdy, eager, and well-disciplined, and have made rapid progress. Their officers, who are constantly subjected to a rigorous process of selection by elimination, already possess distinct qualities of character and leadership. The technical knowledge and the practical experience which they lack they can only acquire by degrees.

"We should therefore keep on working as we have begun. We should not indulge in pessimistic skepticism, nor should we pin our faith on results beyond reasonable expectation. By so doing, we can count on getting solid results. Our real and only danger lies in failure to make allowances for the spirit of the American people and for the idiosyncrasies of American mentality. In such case, we should proceed straight to defeat.

"I have reason to believe, on the contrary, that if we shall know how to give full play to the earnest craving of Americans to get into the fight with all of their resources, that we may then count implicitly on their joining hands with us in the spirit of utmost coöperation. * * * "

General Pétain himself was very particular in this regard and cautioned the French liaison officers in a letter of instructions which dwelt upon coöperation and friendly assistance:

"8 May, 1918.

"At the moment when the military assistance of our American allies assumes an importance which will make of it one of the decisive factors in the happy issue of the war, the General, Commander-in-Chief of the French Armies, believes it proper to recall to officers of every grade who are employed in connection with the American Army certain principles which should guide their action in the accomplishment of the important task which is confided to them.

"I. FRENCH OFFICERS SHOULD TAKE INTO CONSIDERATION THE IMPORTANCE OF THE MILITARY EFFORT MADE BY THE UNITED STATES.

"In April of 1917, at the moment of their entrance into the war, the United States did not have, properly speaking, an army.

"Within a year they have adopted universal and obligatory military service, raised, armed, equipped, and sent to France several hundred thousand men, and all of this is only the beginning. They have thus accomplished a task of military organization without precedent in history. They have accomplished and are now accomplishing within the interior of France various works of enormous importance (improvements of the ports of St. Nazaire and Bordeaux, storehouses and ice plants at Gièvres, etc.), which will remain after the war and will enable us to undertake the economic struggle under exceptionally favorable conditions as to equipment.

"The American Red Cross is placing at our disposition considerable sums, to relieve people who have met with all kinds of misfortunes.

"The General, Commander-in-Chief, desires that during their conversations with American officers the French officers prove to the American that the French fully appreciate the importance of the effort furnished by America and the grandeur of the service rendered to France.

"II. IN THEIR RELATIONS WITH AMERICAN OFFICERS THE FRENCH OFFICERS MUST ALWAYS USE THE GREATEST TACT.

"The Americans fully recognize the value of our military experience; for our part, we must not forget that America is a great nation, that the Americans have a national self-respect developed and justified by the breadth of vision which they bring to bear upon all the questions which they consider. French officers should treat the officers of their grade, or of a subordinate grade, as comrades who have arrived more recently than they upon the front, and should treat them as little as possible as a master does a scholar. As to officers who are of a higher grade than the French officers, the French should wait to give advice until such advice is requested.

"Finally, it is necessary, above all, to avoid giving advice, or to make criticisms in public.

"III. FRENCH OFFICERS SHOULD ENDEAVOR TO BE PERSONAL FRIENDS WITH AMERICAN OFFICERS.

"Between people who are living constantly side by side, official relations are necessarily very much influenced by personal relations.

"The French officers should, therefore, always endeavor to live with their American comrades under the best terms of friendship, and to gain their confidence by demonstrating to them that the advice which they give, and the criticisms which they make, have no other object than the general interest. Such relations are easily realized, for the American is by nature cordial and generous.

"It is important to ensure in the future as has been the case in the past close collaboration between the two Allied armies, a collaboration which constitutes the most certain guarantee of the final success of our common efforts.

"PÉTAIN."

CHAPTER XXXI

Animated Conference at Versailles—Allies Recommend 100 American Divisions—Allied Fear—Situation Reported to Washington—Refugees—British Partially Accept Principle of Coördination of Supply

(Diary) Paris, Sunday, June 2, 1918. Coördinated procurement established at home under principles in effect here since last August. Supreme War Council met yesterday afternoon and again to-day. Heated discussion with Allied leaders over shipment of American troops. French and British now insist on unlimited infantry and machine gun units. Haig wants to retain our divisions that are with British and French wish them to relieve their divisions in the Vosges. All much pleased with efficiency of 1st, 2d, and 3d Divisions. News from French front less pessimistic.

THE sixth session of the Supreme War Council convened June 1st, and one of the first subjects to receive attention was the further shipment of American troops. As already clearly indicated, it was my opinion that neither the character of the troops we should send to France nor their disposition was within the province of the Council to decide. I thought that these questions should be determined by ourselves according to circumstances, perhaps after consultation with the Allies if required to meet an emergency. So I objected to their consideration by the Council, as such, and suggested a meeting outside the Council, which was approved.

NOTE: Total strength of the A.E.F. on May 31st, 32,642 officers, 618,642 enlisted men. Divisional units arriving in May included elements of the following divisions: 4th Division (Regular Army), Maj. Gen. Geo. H. Cameron; 6th Division (Regular Army), Brig. Gen. James B. Erwin; 27th Division (National Guard, New York), Maj. Gen. John F. O'Ryan; 28th Division (National Guard, Pennsylvania), Maj. Gen. Chas. H. Muir; 30th Division (National Guard, Tennessee, North and South Carolina), Maj. Gen. Geo. W. Read; 33d Division (National Guard, Illinois), Maj. Gen. Geo. Bell, Jr.; 35th Division (National Guard, Missouri and Kansas), Maj. Gen. Wm. M. Wright; 80th Division (National Army, Virginia, West Virginia, and western Pennsylvania), Maj. Gen. Adelbert Cronkhite; 82d Division (National Army, Georgia, Alabama, and Tennessee), Maj. Gen. Wm. P. Burnham.

Accordingly, in the late afternoon, Lord Milner, General Foch, General Weygand and I, with Colonels Conner and Boyd, met in M. Clemenceau's office, the three Prime Ministers being, at the moment, engaged in closed session. General Foch began at once by stating the serious plight of the Allies and proposed the continued shipment from America of nothing but infantry and machine gun units in June and July, approximately 250,000 each month. Every one realized the gravity of the Allied situation, but there was a decided difference of opinion as to the best way to meet it. However, I was prepared to make some concessions, and stated them, with reasons for not entirely accepting Foch's view. But neither facts nor arguments seemed to make any impression. He was very positive and insistent and in fact became quite excited, waving his hands and repeating, "The battle, the battle, nothing else counts."

With equal emphasis I urged that we must build up our organization in order to carry on the battle to the end, and pointed out that our program had been seriously interrupted by the concessions already made. I called his attention to the fact that the railways all over France were breaking down for lack of efficient operators and of skilled workmen to repair rolling stock; that our ports would be hopelessly blocked unless we could improve the railways; that his plan would leave us 200,000 men short of enough to complete combat units and fill up special organizations that were absolutely necessary in the S.O.S.; and finally expressed the opinion that the restriction of our shipments to infantry and machine gun units would be a very dangerous and shortsighted policy. To much of this he paid little or no attention and replied that all these things could be postponed.

Mr. Graeme Thomson, the British expert on transportation and supply, came into the room at this point in company with Mr. Lloyd George and General Sir Henry Wilson and took part in the discussion. Mr. Thomson said with considerable emphasis that it would be a very serious mistake not to send over men to repair rolling stock and otherwise build up our rail transportation system and went on to describe the run-down condition of the railways. His views seemed to have no more effect on the French attitude than if they had not been uttered. This phase of the discussion further confirmed my opinion that none of the French officials had more than a vague conception of the tremendous difficulties of our problem.

At this point, I stated that it would be impossible for us to ship over as many infantry and machine gun troops as the Allies wished because on June 30th we should have left at home only 90,000 of such troops with the necessary training. General Foch used this as the basis for offhand criticism of our organization, asserting that we did not have enough infantry in proportion to other troops, failing entirely to appreciate our requirements for the services of supply and transportation, and for artillery, engineers, and other auxiliary arms.

It may be observed here that, notwithstanding my urgent recommendations for a large increase in the number of drafted men, the War Department had, up to May 1st, called out only an average of 116,000 men per month. Consequently, the supply of trained troops had run short in an emergency that required the shipment of 250,000 to 300,000 per month. During May, 373,000 men had been drafted, and of this number those who were being sent over had of course received but little training before their arrival in France, where it had to be completed oftentimes by costly experience in battle.

Continuing the conference, Mr. Lloyd George remarked that he thought President Wilson would be deeply interested to get General Foch's views. He then said that as America had no Prime Minister present he thought it would be inconvenient for us to make a decision, but that the question should be brought before the whole Council. I called attention to the cablegram from the Secretary of War, already quoted, showing that President Wilson had been very much embarrassed by representations made to him personally by the French and British Ambassadors and had suggested that the matter might be settled by a conference between General Foch and myself. I further pointed out that this cable did not mention the Supreme War Council and stated my opposition to making the subject one of general discussion by all Allied representatives and their staffs. I also mentioned the fact that the President was trusting to my judgment in this matter. As nothing was being accomplished, and hoping that the number of participants in the discussion might be limited, I proposed that we should adjourn until the following day.

The next afternoon, when we assembled, M. Clemenceau was waiting for the rest of us, and instead of there being fewer conferees the number had increased. Not unlike the situation at Abbeville a month before, everybody was keyed up, and, as we had anticipated, the battle had to be fought all over again. Foch, supported by Clemenceau and Lloyd George, reiterated his demand for exclusive shipments of infantry and machine gunners in June and in July. I was strongly opposed to this, and insisted that sufficient importance had not been attached to my reasons for the necessity of the auxiliary troops omitted in June. Foch resorted to his often-repeated question as to whether I was willing to take the risk, to which I replied very positively that I was ready to assume any responsibility that my proposal might entail, but that I must have a greater proportion of other troops to keep the American organization from going to smash.

Other objections, which the Allies apparently overlooked, and which I brought out, were that the drafts called in May could not possibly be ready for service until considerable time after arrival, and that neither the French nor the British could provide all the equipment and land transportation they would need. In accordance with my program, I was willing to agree to the reasonable shipments of fully trained infantry not needed for the instruction of recruits, but felt that this point should be left to the judgment of the Secretary of War.

Mr. Lloyd George then drew the conclusion that the month of July, as a consequence, would be a blank, and, in a rather dejected tone, said that the Allies were in a sense in the hands of the United States. He spoke of the generous and chivalrous attitude of President Wilson and said all they could do was to acquaint him with their needs and call upon him to come to their aid, more particularly to the aid of France at the period of the most terrible extremity that she had yet encountered. He proposed that we should bring over men that were partially instructed, as he thought they would learn faster in the atmosphere of war. I said we could not strip the country of every man with any sort of training as we should then be back where we had started in 1917, and argued that all men sent over should have at least three months' training if it were at all possible to give it. Whereupon M. Clemenceau asked what would become of the war in the interval.

I remarked that the discussion had become complicated, but that it was my hope that the greatest possible number of troops, including artillery and auxiliary combat troops and those required for railways and ports, should be transported. I tried to make our needs understood and appealed to Foch and Weygand, who, as soldiers, I said, could not fail to recognize the difficulties we had to surmount, not only in training our citizen army but in building up a complete system of supply in a foreign country. I well knew, however, that neither of them, in their extreme desire for American replacements, had given these questions serious thought, nor had they considered the deficiencies in our organization caused by concessions of the past few months. The British problems being similar to ours, though less difficult, the views of Mr. Thomson were more to the point. He had plainly said that it was impossible to assure the effective employment of our army without adequate rail and port facilities. Lord Milner agreed, and said he thought he fully understood our case.

M. Clemenceau reverted to the shortage of available men in the United States, saying he had thought our resources inexhaustible, and wanted to know when the shipments would be resumed. As he had evidently not followed the discussion, he was informed that in general they would of course be continued to the full capacity of tonnage and that the men we had called out in May would be available in August. He concurred with Mr. Lloyd George that President Wilson ought to be advised of the Allied situation.

Mr. Lloyd George then read a proposed message to the President suggesting that 170,000 infantry and machine gun units, without regard to training, be sent in each of the months of June and July out of a possible 250,000 in each month, leaving transportation for a total of 160,000 of the categories desired by me. Foch proposed that the message be sent and Lord Milner appealed for an agreement, but I objected to bringing troops with only one month's training. I called attention to the fact that we were being importuned on the one hand to send over nothing but replacements for Allied divisions to the utter neglect of our own military establishment and on the other hand we were being pressed to furnish thousands of men for their technical services. Moreover, I said, it had already been demonstrated by the experience of our units serving with them that the Allies were not prepared to supply our men with either equipment or accustomed food. I insisted that auxiliary and service troops be sent to build up our own organization in preference to the shipment of uninstructed men who would be of little use in the battle lines when they arrived. I suggested that the July program might be postponed until August. Clemenceau remarked that the German would not postpone his attacks, to which I replied that neither could we rely on untrained men in battle.

Here Mr. Lloyd George read a proposition which set forth the critical situation requiring the concentration of reserves in front of Paris and the urgent necessity of finding other troops to replace the French divisions taken from the British front. He drew attention particularly to the opinion expressed by General Foch that the Allies would be defeated unless the number of British divisions could be maintained. He then proposed that the British Commander-in-Chief should determine when the American troops with his armies had acquired sufficient training to be placed in the line. This meant that such troops would become replacements, and, of course, it was impossible for me to agree to that. I rather vigorously stated that this was a prerogative and a responsibility that I could not relinquish under any circumstances. I said that this was not the Allies' business, but that should an emergency arise requiring immediate action every consideration would be given by me to any request from General Foch for our troops, trained or untrained.

Reading from notes, and appealing to me, Foch then proposed that a request be made on the United States for a total of 100 combat divisions to be sent over at the rate of 300,000 men per month. I said that in my opinion we would send as many divisions as possible and that our people would not fail to raise an army of the necessary size.

Transferring his attention to the British for the moment, M. Clemenceau asked how many divisions it would be possible for them to maintain in France, to which Mr. Lloyd George replied with some sarcasm that it would be best to postpone the question until the return of the French expert whom M. Clemenceau had proposed to send to England.[1]

Then General Foch took the cue and went on to say that we found ourselves with 150 Allied divisions opposed to 204 German divisions, and if the number were reduced then we should fail, and that whatever might be the report of the expert there ought to be the strongest resolve on the part of the British Government to keep up its divisions. Disaster would be inevitable, he said, if they were unable to maintain the fifty-three British divisions, and that it would be impossible to continue the war in the name of the Allies against an enemy whose effectives increased while ours diminished.

The whole discussion was very erratic, as one of the Allies would take exception to nearly every statement made by the other. Mr. Lloyd George said here that he could not understand why all the losses fell to the Allies and none to the Germans. Then came a lively tilt between the British and the French, Lord Milner taking direct issue as to the figures. He showed that the Allies really had 169 divisions and not 150 as General

---

[1] At one of the meetings of the Supreme War Council, during a discussion of reserve manpower, M. Clemenceau had suggested that an investigation of that question as to England might be made by a French expert.

Foch had declared.[1] He said that measures had been taken to increase their effectives through the application of a law of extreme severity, but that it would not bring results until the month of August. Nevertheless, he continued, it was not the intention of the British to reduce the number of their divisions.

Foch again spoke of Allied inferiority and asked for definite information of the British Government as to the number of divisions they would maintain. During the dialogue that followed between Milner and Wilson, who differed as to the number, Foch quietly asked me about the agreement regarding our divisions serving with the British. I told him the understanding was that the British would be able to fill their divisions by July or August, thus relieving the Americans who might be in their units, and that the question as to where our divisions would be used was in his hands until they should be required for our own corps and armies. I told him that Haig hoped to keep them, but I did not wish them to become absorbed in either the British or French army and as a consequence be unavailable later for the formation of an American army.

Further conversation showed the feeling of uncertainty in the minds of the Allies. Mr. Lloyd George came back to the question of losses and said that before the great battle he was informed positively that the Germans had only 400,000 replacements left, and now, after the most violent fighting, in which it was reported that the Germans had suffered very heavy losses, they still had more than 300,000 replacements. The Allies also had 300,000, but it was now claimed, he said, that the British Army was on the decline while that of the enemy was not. He asked if that could be cleared up, to which Foch replied that it was because the enemy managed better, and he went on to say that Germany, with a population of 68,000,000 people, could maintain 204 divisions, while Great Britain, with 46,000,000 inhabitants,

[1] Of the 169 divisions on the Western Front at this time, Lord Milner pointed out, 101 were French, 2 Italian, 4 American, 11 Belgian and 51 British, besides 2 British that were reduced to mere skeletons. These numbers had been variously stated according to which side was speaking.

could keep up only forty-three.[1]   Then, in response to a further question by Mr. Lloyd George, he said he could not pretend to say where Germany procured her replacements, possibly it might be from prisoners returned from Russia, for example, but all he knew was that they had 204 divisions to the Allies' 169. Then Mr. Lloyd George said that probably the real reason was that Allied losses were greater than those of the enemy.

After some further argument on discrepancies of the various figures and insistence on the part of Foch that the number of divisions be maintained, the question of shipment of American troops in June and July was resumed.   The discussion having reached an impasse, it was suggested that Lord Milner, General Foch and I should undertake to draw up a program.   In the consideration of the matter by the three of us, the point of my contention was won when Weygand, who was Foch's principal adviser, came forward with the remark that it would be as well to leave the new drafts to be trained at home for a month or so longer.   Although my arguments had failed to make any impression on Foch, he at once approved Weygand's suggestion. With this out of the way we soon drew up the agreement embodied in the following cablegram sent to Washington on June 2d:

> "The following agreement has been concluded between General Foch, Lord Milner, and myself with reference to the transportation of American troops in the months of June and July. The following recommendations are made on the assumption that at least 250,000 men can be transported in each of the months of June and July by the employment of British and American tonnage. We recommend:
>
> "A. For the month of June: 1st, absolute priority shall be given to the transportation of 170,000 combatant troops (viz., six divisions without artillery, ammunition trains or supply trains, amounting to 126,000 men and 44,000 replacements for combat troops); 2d, 25,400 men for the service of railways, of which 13,400 have been asked for by the French Minister of Transportation; 3d, the remainder to be troops of categories to be determined by the Commander-in-Chief, American Expeditionary Forces.

---

[1] It had been stated that the British counted on keeping up fifty-three divisions but that ten of them would be practically American.

"B. For the month of July: 1st, absolute priority for the shipment of 140,000 combatant troops of the nature defined above (4 divisions minus artillery, etc., etc., amounting to 84,000 men plus 56,000 replacements); 2d, the balance of the 250,000 to consist of troops to be designated by the Commander-in-Chief, American Expeditionary Forces.

"C. It is agreed that if available tonnage in either month allows of the transportation of a larger number of men than 250,000 the excess tonnage will be employed in the transportation of combat troops as defined above.

"D. We recognize that the combatant troops to be dispatched in July may have to include troops with insufficient training, but we consider the present emergency is such as to justify a temporary and exceptional departure by the United States from sound principles of training especially as a similar course is being followed by France and Great Britain.

"Foch, Milner, Pershing."

The Prime Ministers at the same time sent a cable to the President expressing their "warmest thanks" for the remarkable promptness in sending American aid to meet the present emergency. They pointed out that General Foch had presented a statement of the "utmost gravity" showing the relative strength of the Allies and their adversaries with no possible increase in the number of Allied divisions in sight. While they declared that there was great danger of the war being lost unless the numerical inferiority of the Allies could soon be remedied by the addition of American replacements, their statement did not convey the extreme apprehension that prevailed. The cablegram as sent by the Prime Ministers is quoted in full, as follows:

"The Prime Ministers of France, Italy and Great Britain, now meeting at Versailles, desire to send the following message to the President of the United States:

"We desire to express our warmest thanks to President Wilson for the remarkable promptness with which American aid, in excess of what at one time seemed practicable, has been rendered to the Allies during the past month to meet a great emergency. The crisis, however, still continues. General Foch has presented to us a statement of the utmost gravity, which points out that the numerical superiority of the enemy in France, where 162 Allied divisions now oppose 200 German divisions, is very heavy, and that, as there is no possibility of the British and French increasing the number of their divisions (on the contrary, they are put to extreme straits to keep them up) there is a great danger of the war being lost unless the numerical inferiority of the Allies can be remedied as rapidly as possible by the advent of American troops.   He, therefore, urges with the utmost insistence that the maximum possible number of infantry and machine gunners, in which respect the shortage of men on the side of the Allies is most marked, should continue to be shipped from America in the months of June and July to avert the immediate danger of an Allied defeat in the present campaign owing to the Allied reserves being exhausted before those of the enemy.   In addition to this, and looking to the future, he represents that it is impossible to foresee ultimate victory in the war unless America is able to provide such an army as will enable the Allies ultimately to establish numerical superiority.   He places the total American force required for this at no less than 100 divisions, and urges the continuous raising of fresh American levies, which, in his opinion, should not be less than 300,000 a month, with a view to establishing a total American force of 100 divisions at as early a date as this can possibly be done.[1]

"We are satisfied that Gen. Foch, who is conducting the present campaign with consummate ability, and on whose military judgment we continue to place the most absolute reliance, is not overestimating the needs of the case, and we feel confident that the Government of the United States will do everything that can be done, both to meet the needs of the immediate situation and to proceed with the continuous raising of fresh levies, calculated to provide, as soon as possible, the numerical superiority which the Commander-in-Chief of the Allied Armies regards as essential to ultimate victory.

"A separate telegram contains the arrangements which Gen. Foch, Gen. Pershing, and Lord Milner have agreed to recommend to the United States Government with regard to the dispatch of American troops for the months of June and July.

"Clemenceau,
"D. Lloyd George,
"Orlando."

What a difference it would have made if the Allies had seen this a year or even six months earlier and had then given us as-

---

[1] In order to allow for a due proportion of corps and army troops, we roughly counted each combat division at 40,000 men. Thus 100 combat divisions would make 4,000,000 men in France.

sistance in shipping! Certainly, the situation had been clearly understood since the preceding August. It will be recalled that the commanders-in-chief and the chiefs of staff had at that time concluded that their dependence was upon America. The Governments, likewise, understood in August that the constitution of our army in France depended upon sea transportation, but they took no steps then to provide it. On the contrary their minds were centered on using America as a reservoir from which men could be drawn to serve under an alien flag. They failed to understand the psychology of the American people. They failed to foresee the results. They failed to do the only thing that good judgment dictated, and that was to assist by all possible means the organization of a powerful American army and to transport it to France at the earliest possible moment.

During this session of the Supreme War Council it was frequently asserted, and firmly believed in some circles, that there was real danger that Germany might recruit her manpower in Russia unless the Allied powers could counteract German influence. It was the opinion of several members of the Council that the Russians would look to the United States for advice and possible aid. But all believed that they would resent Japanese interference and might be inclined in this case to unite with the Germans. Apprehension of such a contingency possibly may have influenced the Supreme War Council to some extent in making such insistent demands on us, and no doubt prompted the Allies to send a mixed force into eastern Siberia.

It could not be questioned that the situation was decidedly serious, even though the German advance in the Marne salient had been held up for the time being. The French and British divisions which had occupied that front against the German attack had lost a large percentage of their personnel and practically all their matériel. Rested divisions had been sent to replace them, but the burden of aiding the British during the preceding two months had fallen heavily upon the French and their manpower was at a low ebb. The following cabled report, with recommendations, indicates the situation as seen at the time:

"June 3, 1918.

"Personal and confidential for the Chief of Staff and Secretary of War.

"Paragraph 1.

"Consider military situation very grave. The French line gave way before what was thought to be a secondary attack and the seven divisions that occupied that front have lost practically all their matériel and a large percentage of their personnel, although actual numbers of men and guns are yet unknown. The German advance seems to be stopped for the time being. The railroads in the area they have taken are not available for their use principally because of the destruction of the tunnel at Vauxaillon. As already reported, the infantry of our 3d Division is being used in Lorraine and the 5th along the Marne.[1] Our 2d Division entire is fighting north of Château-Thierry and has done exceedingly well. It is General Foch's plan to take the divisions from behind the British lines as needed and use them with French artillery in Lorraine to replace French divisions for the battle.

"Paragraph 2.

"The attitude of the Supreme War Council, which has been in session since Saturday, is one of depression. The Prime Ministers and General Foch appeal most urgently for trained or even untrained men, and notwithstanding my representations that the number of trained infantry in America would be practically exhausted by the middle of July, they still insisted on a program of infantry personnel. The agreement entered into, however, was not entirely satisfactory as to July, but instead of sending raw infantry troops it is believed wiser to send more of the classes we need for various services. I hope we shall be able to make heavy shipment of combat personnel in August and succeeding months.

"Paragraph 3.

"The utmost endeavor should be made to keep up a constant flow of personnel to the full capacity of tonnage, and I very strongly urge that divisions be organized as rapidly as possible and be sent over entire after July, and also that auxiliary troops of all kinds be shipped in due proportion. It should be most fully realized at home that the time has come for us to take up the brunt of the war and that France and England are not going to be able to keep their armies at present strength very much longer.

"Paragraph 4.

"I have pointed out to the Prime Ministers the necessity of both the French and British Governments utilizing every possible man at

[1] There was an error in the original cable. It should have read "Our 5th Division is being used in Lorraine and the 3d along the Marne."

this time, including 1919 drafts who still lack a month or so of completing their training. Attention is invited to general reference to this matter in the agreement which implies that both Governments are doing this, but I am not sure, however, that this is the fact. It might be wise to request the respective Ambassadors to urge their Governments to put in every available man to meet this crisis and hold on until our forces can be felt.

"Paragraph 5.

"In view of recent losses, the question of divisional artillery is also very serious. It is doubtful now whether the French will be able to supply us with the artillery we require. It is also reported that our program at home is very far behind. I most sincerely hope this is not so, as it is unlikely that France will be able to do more than meet her own requirements from now on. Will advise you more in detail later.

"Paragraph 6.

"The urgent cable sent by the three Prime Ministers giving General Foch's views as to Allied needs in troops and asking for an increased American program was read to me. I told them that America was fully alive to the necessity of doing everything possible and would do so. I can only add that our program should be laid out systematically and broadly, and men called out as fast as they can be handled.

"PERSHING."

This last request by the Allies for American troops was the climax of a succession of demands that must have created consternation at home. The first was based on my agreement with Mr. Lloyd George. Then came the one with Brigadier General Hutchinson, followed by that made in London. The Abbeville agreement came next and after that the one at Versailles. Each was an appeal to America for troops to build up the armies of the British and French, and each was greater and more pressing than the one before.

The difficulties that these successive demands presented can scarcely be imagined. Each of them made new calculations for shipment necessary. No sooner was one schedule determined upon than another had to be worked out. The selection of units, the transfers of available men from one unit to another, the movements of large bodies by rail to the seaports, and finally their embarkation, all constituted a task of tremendous proportions. In its execution as a whole, the achievement stands out as a lasting monument to our War Department, marred only by the lack of foresight that made it necessary to send over untrained men and units in such precipitate haste.[1]

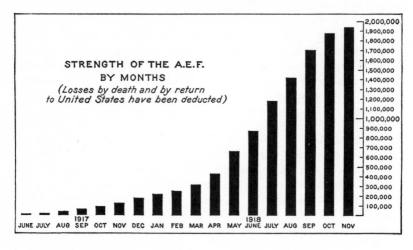

(Diary) Chaumont, Thursday, June 6, 1918.   Lord Milner lunched with me on Monday.   He thinks they have been let down because Foch has requested five of our divisions from the British Front for service with the French.

While en route here on Tuesday, with McAndrew and Boyd, visited 2d Division, talked with brigade commanders, Harbord and Lewis, and also visited Dickman's 3d Division.   Both divisions with excellent morale.   Each has made successful counterattack against enemy attempt to advance.

Urged Ragueneau yesterday to visit Paris in aid of horse procurement.   French hope to furnish us 15,000 monthly.

Received letter of appreciation from Pétain for sending divisions to French Front.   War Department requested to rush construction of tanks and 3,000 additional Liberty engines.   Approved Major George Walker's request for publication in orders of my letter to Lord Milner on the venereal question.   British only partially approve suggestion regarding coördination of supplies.

[1] Of the men that came to France, 46.25 per cent were carried in American ships, 51.25 per cent in British owned or controlled, and 2.5 per cent in others.

The 2d and 3d Divisions, facing the Germans near Château-Thierry, had made their places in line secure, giving heart to the French, who were trying to stabilize their own positions around the newly formed salient. We shall hear more of these two divisions later. Although fully taken for granted by all of us, it was none the less gratifying to see these divisions for the first time in the line acquit themselves so well.

En route to Chaumont, we motored through Montmirail, passing long columns of French refugees fleeing from their homes, many on foot, men and women with bundles on their backs, leading the smaller children, driving their stock before them, and hauling in various types of conveyances the few remaining worldly goods they were able to take with them in their flight. Almost indescribable were many similar scenes as reported by our troops as they came up to reënforce the retiring French. It seemed to me then that if this picture of civilization engaged in the persecution of innocent and unarmed noncombatants could be brought home to all peoples, reason would be forced upon rulers and governments where too often their passions and ambitions assume control.

Serious inconvenience resulted from the crowding of these unfortunate people in our billeting areas. We wished to do everything possible for their comfort and were able by readjustments to increase the accommodations in towns by about 15 per cent to make room for them.

Although our experience in coördination of supply between ourselves and the French had already proved that it was distinctly economical as compared with the separate and independent systems, the British were slow to accept it. However, with the help of Martin Egan, Dwight Morrow, and Paul Cravath, a conference was arranged in London between Dawes and the Chief Supply Officer of the British, Lieutenant General Cowans, representing the army, which resulted in the following letter from Lord Milner definitely committing the British to the principle:

"War Office, Whitehall, SW.
"29 May, 1918.

"MY DEAR GENERAL:

"Colonel Dawes has handed me the memorandum of May 22, 1918, signed by M. Clemenceau and yourself. We have all been in hearty accord with your aim to coördinate, so far as possible, the use of facilities and the distribution of supplies among the Allied Armies in France. Doubts, however, have been expressed by our Supply Departments as to the extent to which a unification of supplies and facilities would be practicable. I am glad to find that our hesitation, based on these doubts, has been due to a misunderstanding of the purpose and scope of your proposal.

"We now understand from your memorandum and Colonel Dawes' explanations:

"1. That your plan is intended to apply only to supplies and facilities of the Armies in France.

"2. That the avoidance of duplicate facilities in docks, warehouses, and railroads, and the proper distribution of labor supplies, are among the things of immediate importance. It is not intended that the Board shall interfere with the ration or with the distributing machinery of the respective armies, nor indeed with any other matters relating to their internal administration.

"3. That the requirement that the decision of the proposed Board shall be unanimous has been introduced in order to leave each army free to determine whether the principle of coördination is or is not applicable to any given case. For instance, your army might have what seemed like a surplus of foodstuffs on hand, but which was not a real surplus because of your distance from your base and the period that might elapse before further supplies arrive. The same might be true in the case of our army. The representative of each army on the proposed Board is therefore left free to exercise his own judgment in voting on such questions.

"4. That the decisions of the Board, when unanimous, are to be communicated, through proper military channels, to the Chiefs of the appropriate departments of the respective armies, and shall be given effect through them.

"If I am right in the above interpretation of your views, I shall be happy to give the proposed system an immediate trial and to nominate a representative on the Board. I assume that the Italians and the Belgians will also be invited to be represented on it.

"Yours sincerely,

"MILNER."

The sphere of coöperation as expressed in the letter from Lord Milner, while indicating acquiescence in our proposal, did not entirely reach our conception of the possibilities. We believed that consideration of the control of supplies at the source would become necessary eventually. Although now the principle was made applicable only to supplies actually in military hands, yet it had received distinct recognition and its larger application was open to further discussion and correspondence. The coördination of many facilities and supplies in common use under direct charge of the respective armies was soon to become an established fact.

CHAPTER XXXII

Fears for Safety of Paris—Belleau Wood Taken—Pétain's Appreciation
—Marne Counteroffensive Indicated—Visit Clemenceau and Foch—
French Advance in Counterattack—Anniversary of Arrival in France
—Discipline in Our Army—Italian Successes—Foch Requests Ameri-
can Regiments—Cables Regarding Promotions—Information to Press
—Letter to Secretary of War

(Diary) Paris, Sunday, June 9, 1918. Conferred with staff on
Friday regarding situation. The 2d Division is engaged in severe
fighting in Belleau Wood. General Foch desires to leave five of our
divisions with the British for the present. Hospital arrangements proceeding satisfactorily on 15 per cent bed status. Have recommended
privileges of War Risk Insurance for war correspondents.

Colonel Groome lunched with us yesterday; also Mr. Otto Kahn,
who referred to my position as embracing duties of the Secretaries
of War, Treasury, and State combined. General Pétain has agreed to
organization of American corps near Château-Thierry.

Arrived Paris last night; saw Clemenceau this morning. He spoke
of new threat on Paris by the German attack on Montdidier-Noyon
front. Went to Bombon for conference with General Foch. French
communiqué highly compliments Americans in Château-Thierry
region.[1]

M Y position in France required the consideration of many
questions of international importance, but as they all,
either directly or indirectly, affected the formation, maintenance, and use of our army in coöperation with the Allied
armies, it did not seem to me that the decisions involved could be
made by any authority in France not under my control. Moreover, I could always count on the loyal aid of Ambassador Sharp
when anything requiring his intervention came up, which was

[1] It said: "American infantry showed itself skilled in maneuvering. The courage
of officers and men approached recklessness. * * * The courage of the combatant
troops is equaled only by the superb coolness of some of their medical corps who, in
a perfect hail of bullets, gave first aid to the wounded."

frequently the case. He was very helpful in the procurement of supplies outside of Allied countries, especially Spain and Switzerland. General Bliss, our Military Representative on the Supreme War Council, sat in a civil capacity also, in that he transmitted to Washington those questions of Allied policy that required the President's approval.

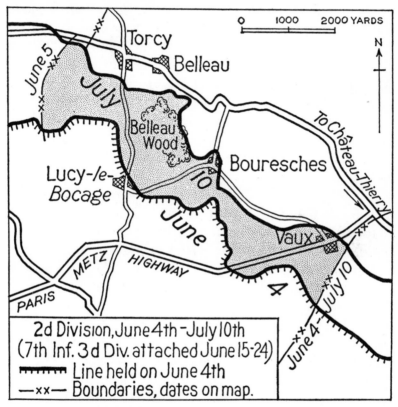

2d Division, June 4th – July 10th
(7th Inf. 3d Div. attached June 15-24)
▬▬▬ Line held on June 4th
—xx— Boundaries, dates on map.

As a result of the German successes against the French, something akin to a panic prevailed in Paris. Probably a million people left during the spring and there was grave apprehension among the officials lest the city be taken. Plans were made to remove the French government offices to Bordeaux and we were prepared to move those of our own that were in Paris. At the request of General Bliss, trucks were placed at his disposal for the removal, in case of necessity, of his offices and those of his British colleagues on the Supreme War Council. It was a matter of considerable satisfaction to feel that our base ports, lines of communication and supply areas were outside of the zone of the British armies and south of Paris, and hence comparatively safe.

The attacks begun on June 6th by the 2d Division culminated in the capture of the last German positions in Belleau Wood by its Marine Brigade and of Vaux by its Regular Infantry Brigade. The fighting during most of this period was intense. The German lines were favorably located on commanding ground and were made more formidable by the extensive use of machine guns, especially in Belleau Wood. The success of this division against an enemy determined to crush it was obtained with but little assistance from the tired French divisions on its flanks.

In the initial advance, the Marine Brigade (Harbord) captured Bouresches, and the Infantry Brigade (Lewis) made substantial gains. The progress during the next few days was slow but steady. On the 15th, the 7th Infantry, 3d Division, was attached to the 2d Division, relieving the Marines in the Wood, and holding the front there for a few days. The Marines then reëntered the line beginning on the night of the 21st. After an all-day artillery preparation on the 25th, they drove the enemy from his last position in Belleau Wood during the late afternoon and night. Meanwhile, the Infantry Brigade continued its attacks, and on July 1st, in a brilliantly executed operation, captured the village of Vaux. The division made no further advance. By July 9th, when it was relieved by the 26th Division, its lines had been consolidated on high ground captured from the enemy.[1]

Our first three divisions to participate in active operations had all distinguished themselves; the 1st at Cantigny, the 2d at Belleau Wood, and the 3d at Château-Thierry. Their achievements gave an indication of what trained American troops would do. Following, as it did, the crisis of May 27th, the conduct of these

[1] The casualties in the division were about 9,500. Over 1,600 prisoners were captured.

divisions was loudly acclaimed by the French, and, for the time being, it had a stimulating effect upon their morale.

With the transfer of activities to the French front northeast of Paris, our plan to build up an American corps near Amiens had become impracticable. It now appeared possible, however, to form at least a corps and perhaps an army somewhere along the Marne salient, preferably in the vicinity of Château-Thierry. I therefore suggested to General Pétain that we should bring other divisions to join with the 2d and 3d for that purpose, and accordingly the relief of the 26th and 42d from the inactive front was immediately ordered. The assembly of four American divisions on the Marne front would more than offset the recent French losses. General Pétain, in his letter accepting my offer, said in part:

"I must express my deep gratitude for the prompt and very important aid which you are bringing in the present crisis. The American troops already engaged in the battle have the unanimous admiration of the whole French Army. The power of the effort which your country is at present showing, as well as the resolute and generous spirit with which you enter the struggle are, for the Allies— and above all for France—a comfort in the grave times through which we are passing, and a pledge of hope for the future."

As the efficiency of certain units of our forces had been fully proved, it seemed to me that the time had arrived for us to utilize our troops to good advantage by combining them in an independent effort. It was a moment of depression for the Allies; but the large numbers of American troops arriving, and their success so far had helped Allied morale. The Germans had been stopped at the Marne, and their position in that salient was inherently weak. I felt that we should not give the enemy time to re-form and rest his forces, but should, if possible, take the initiative ourselves. It was with this thought especially in mind that I suggested to Pétain that we should assemble a number of American divisions in the Château-Thierry sector. I had already proposed to Foch that they should be utilized in a counterattack against the salient. It was obvious that a blow at the enemy's line south of Soissons, if successful, would compel him to retire. Such an attack would have the effect of threatening his rear, in so far as that part of his force in the vicinity of Château-Thierry was concerned. I was very eager that our troops should be allowed to undertake such an attack.

The German situation in the sector was set forth in my telegram to the War Department, as follows:

"JUNE 11, 1918.

"The arrival of the enemy's troops on the Marne and their establishment from the vicinity of Château-Thierry to Verneuil on the night of May 29th to 30th definitely marks the end of the first phase of the Aisne Offensive. The enemy had secured by the first stroke a tactically important objective—a defensive flank on the Marne—and possessed a strategically important objective, the control of our main line of lateral communication with Verdun. Thus in about two and one-half days from the time of the original attack the reason for directing the axis of the attack straight south ceased to exist.

"Since the night of May 29th to 30th, the direction of the attack has changed pronouncedly to the southwest. To this must be added the operations to the northwest of Soissons which began on the night of May 30th-31st, the general direction of which is also southwest. It seems clearly established that so long as the enemy is allowed to retain the initiative his future operations will be directed on Paris. The situation in the salient Noyon to Reims is important. The keys to the transportation systems of the salient are the rail and road centers, Soissons and Reims. Without these the enemy will be confronted with difficult transportation problems, involving the use of motor trucks on the sixteen roads, for the most part cross-country roads, now available to him. The possession of Soissons has proved an enormous relief to the enemy since by means of it, from Rethel to Laon, he can reach every other sector of his new lines. Nevertheless, the enemy's transportation situation cannot be satisfactorily adjusted until he has taken Reims; hence the recent heavy attack on this important center."

On the morning of my call on M. Clemenceau the fourth great German offensive of the year had started between Montdidier and the Oise and reports indicated that it was meeting with considerable success. In our conversation, I asked him what he thought would be the result if Paris should fall. He said that he and Mr. Lloyd George had discussed that possibility and had reached the conclusion that of course they would do everything in their power to save Paris, but if it should be lost they would go on fighting, as "above Paris is France, and above France is civilization."

He expressed himself satisfied with the agreement reached at the special conference at Versailles and I recall distinctly his more than usual graciousness that day as he said, "You need never make an appointment with me at any time, but just come whenever you wish and you shall always see me." As I was leaving, he came to the door with me, and I said, "Well, Mr. President, it may not look encouraging just now but we are certain to win in the end." He clung to my hand and in a tone that showed the utmost solicitude, he replied, "Do you really think that? I am glad to hear you say it." This was the first and only time that I ever sensed any misgivings in his mind. Notwithstanding our occasional rather heated discussions on the use to be made of American troops, I admired him greatly. It always seemed to me that he typified the true spirit of confidence and courage of the French people.

I then motored, with Boyd, to General Foch's headquarters at Bombon, arriving just in time for luncheon. We took up my proposal to form an American corps near Château-Thierry, and he at once agreed to it. He spoke especially of the fine work of our troops. I asked him how a German drive which threatened or perhaps captured Paris would affect the armies and the people. His reply was almost word for word like M. Clemenceau's, showing that they had considered it together. He, too, was certain that the armies would go on with the war. Foch spoke so positively and with such evident feeling that I was moved to get up and vigorously shake his hand. I said that his attitude was gratifying and that the French people could be certain that the American Government and people would be with them to the last. Everybody was in an agreeable mood, and as I departed Foch asked me to come to see him oftener and talk over matters in general and to continue to let him know when anything turned up that I did not like.

Looking back to those days, one must say that although the French regard their country as the very keystone of the arch of civilization it might have been difficult to keep them in the war if Paris had fallen. While no one could have openly suggested any such thought at that time, some French officers felt that the loss of Paris would cause the Ministry to fall; to be replaced by a Ministry in favor of peace.

(Diary) Chaumont, Thursday, June 13, 1918. Lunched with General Bliss on Monday at Versailles. Saw General di Robilant [1] there and discussed transportation of our regiment to Italy. Recommended adoption of wound chevron. Approved request from Foch that 4th and 28th Divisions should be held near Villers-Cotterêts.[2]

Visited 1st Division on Tuesday. French Third Army gained one and a quarter miles in counterattack south of Noyon.

Returned to Chaumont yesterday. Saw General Liggett to-day about I Corps affairs. M. Jules Cambon spending the night with us. Many messages received this first anniversary of my arrival in France.

While the Italian Government was anxious to have American troops, yet so far they had found no sea transportation available to bring them over. Mr. Orlando, the Italian Prime Minister, wanted them sent direct from the States in order that they might go through Italy by rail to show the people that Americans were actually there. Moreover, he wanted them to be other than naturalized Italians for fear the people might doubt their nationality. When we came to consider the details, General di Robilant proposed that they should be transported from New York by Italian shipping, and entered into a lengthy discussion of their plan to send over three or four ships, to which I readily agreed. But it turned out later that the vessels he counted on were already included in the list of those which the British were going to use for carrying our troops. After a delay of about a month, and acting under instructions from Washington, I directed that the 332d Infantry Regiment of the 83d Division, which had recently arrived, should go to Italy by rail.

[1] General di Robilant was at that time the Italian Military Representative on the Supreme War Council.

[2] Villers-Cotterêts is located southwest of Soissons, convenient to the western face of the Château-Thierry salient.

The 4th and 28th Divisions, en route from the British area to
the Vosges front, were halted in the vicinity of Villers-Cotterêts,
the object being to concentrate several of our divisions on the
west of the Marne salient, primarily as a precaution against another German movement toward Paris, but ultimately for possible use on the offensive. With the 2d, 3d, 26th, and 42d already
in that general region, the 4th and 28th gave us a force equivalent
to twelve French divisions, although the latter two were without
their artillery.

An encouraging circumstance at the moment was the success
of the French in holding von Hutier's attack on the Montdidier-
Noyon front. This German offensive was an effort not only to
widen the vulnerable Marne pocket but to secure the railway
between Compiègne and Soissons and open the way to Paris.
The French had anticipated this attack and fought desperately,
yielding only under great pressure until the 11th, when, using
tanks and quantities of mustard gas, they launched a series of
local counterattacks, by which they were able to advance more
than a mile on a seven-mile front. In view of their remarkable
success in the preceding offensives, the defeat of the Germans
and their heavy losses here materially encouraged the Allies. The
credit for this brilliant operation by the French must go to General Mangin, one of France's greatest generals.

The anniversary of the arrival of our advance contingent in
France was the occasion of many congratulations on the part of
the French. It seems worth while to record some of these
messages.

"The anniversary of your arrival in France furnishes a happy occasion to address my warmest congratulations to you and the valiant
troops which you command and who have so admirably conducted
themselves in the recent battles. I beg you to receive the assurance
of my best wishes for the continuation of their success.

"RAYMOND POINCARÉ."

"On the anniversary of your arrival in France to take command of
the American troops, I wish, my dear General, to express to you once
more the greatest admiration for the powerful aid brought by your
army to the cause of the Allies. With ever increasing numbers the

American troops cover themselves with glory under your orders in barring the route of the invader. The day is coming when, thanks to the support of your country and the valor of her sons, the enemy, losing the initiative of operations, will be forced to incline before the triumph of our ideals of justice and civilization.

"CLEMENCEAU."

"A year ago you brought us the American sword. To-day we have seen it strike. It is a pledge of certain victory. By it our hearts are more closely united than ever.

"FOCH."

"Your coming to French soil a year ago filled our country with enthusiasm and hope. Accept to-day the grateful homage of our soldiers for the daily increasing aid on the battlefield brought by their American brothers-in-arms. The last battles where the magnificent qualities of courage and military virtue of your troops were demonstrated in so brilliant a manner are a sure guarantee for the future. The day is not far off when the great American Army will play a decisive rôle, to which history calls this Army on the battlefields of Europe.

"Permit me, my dear General, to express to you on this anniversary my entire confidence and assure you of my feelings of affectionate comradeship.

"PÉTAIN."

(Diary) Chaumont, Monday, June 17, 1918. Frequent trench raids on our troops in quiet sectors indicate the enemy's anxiety. Our units, especially the 42d, which has been highly praised by French,[1] have made several successful raids.

[1] Although this division had so far served only in the quiet Baccarat sector, the Commanding General of the French VI Corps commended it highly in the following General Order, dated June 15th:

"GENERAL ORDER No. 50

"As the time has come when the 42d U.S.I.D. must leave the Lorraine front, the General commanding the VI Army Corps wishes to show his great appreciation of the excellent military qualities which this division has evidenced as well as the service which it has rendered in the Baccarat sector.

"Its fighting qualities, its ability to utilize and organize terrain, its appreciation of liaison, its systematic organization, the discipline shown by officers and men, and their initiative, all go to prove that this division will henceforth worthily fill its place on the new battle line.

"The General commanding the VI Army Corps wishes to express his sincere thanks to the 42d Division for its valuable coöperation. He especially expresses his gratitude to the distinguished Commander of this Division, General Menoher, to the General

On Saturday took up with General Bethel semi-monthly accumulation of court-martial cases. Brigadier General John A. Lejeune dined with us. Visited hostess house; found telephone girls comfortably situated.

Generals Foch and Weygand and Colonel Reboul lunched with us to-day. Foch had encouraging news from the Italian front, regarding attack begun on Saturday by Austrians on a twelve-mile front. Colonel William Hayward, 369th Regiment (colored),[1] called.

In a new army like ours, if discipline were lacking, the factor most essential to its efficiency would be missing. The army was composed of men representing every walk of life, from the educated professional and business men to those of the various trades and callings, and practically all were without military experience. In the beginning, our army was without the discipline that comes with training. The vast majority of both officers and men were unaccustomed to the restraints necessarily imposed, and unfamiliar with the rules and regulations required to insure good conduct and attention to duty. There existed, however, in general, a distinctly patriotic attitude of mind which made for self-discipline.

Yet, even after considerable military training, men were found in every command who, because of faulty bringing up or waywardness, could not be taught to realize the moral obligations of loyalty and obedience to constituted authority. It was from this class that usually came the offenders, relatively small in number, who gave the most trouble.

Officers under his orders, and to his Staff so brilliantly directed by Colonel MacArthur.

"It is with the deepest regret that the entire VI Army Corps views the departure of the 42d Division. But the affectionate bonds of comradeship which were formed here will not be broken. On our part, a faithful memory will be retained for both the living and the dead of the Rainbow Division; for those who are leaving to take part in other combats as well as for those who, having given their lives so nobly on the fields of the East, now remain there at rest, guarded with all sympathy by France.

"These expressions of highest esteem will surely be still further confirmed in coming battles, in which the future of the free people of the world will be decided.

"May our units, side by side, valiantly contribute to the triumph of Justice and Right.
"GENERAL DUPORT."

[1] Very naturally, the four infantry regiments of the 93d Division (colored), which had been assigned to four French divisions, were anxious to serve with our armies, and I made application for the organization and shipment of the rest of the division, but to no purpose and these regiments remained with the French to the end.

Minor delinquencies due to neglect or inexperience were handled by local commanders, but where moral turpitude and defiance of authority were in evidence trials by courts-martial were necessary. Such courts were ordered by division commanders and officers of that relative rank, who were also empowered in general to approve or disapprove the findings of the courts. Except in cases that originated in separate units not a part of a division or other similar organization, only those in which the penalty imposed was dismissal or death came to me for final action, or for recommendation before being forwarded to the President. In other words, as Commander-in-Chief of an army in the field, I was required to act personally upon, and was empowered to carry into execution, all sentences by courts-martial extending to the dismissal of any but general officers; and likewise, to take final action on all sentences of death adjudged after conviction for murder, rape, mutiny, desertion, and espionage.

At intervals of perhaps a week or two, the accumulated cases on which I had to act were brought before me by the Judge Advocate. There were forty-four sentences of death which reached me for confirmation and but eleven of these, all of them for murder or rape, were confirmed and executed. Of purely military offenses there were only four in which execution was recommended to the President, and none of these were approved by him.

When General Foch came to take luncheon with us on the 17th, he was much encouraged by the improved situation in Italy. The Austrians had attacked over a twelve-mile front on June 15th and succeeded in gaining certain crossings of the Piave, but in contrast to what had happened at Caporetto, the Italians had anticipated their opponents and vigorously confronted them with counter-artillery fire at each of the five main points of contact and had thus prevented more than small gains. Seizing the opportunity to counterattack, the Italians were able, by June 20th, to compel the Austrians to give up their gains. I sent General Diaz a cordial message of congratulations and it is presumed that he received many, as his success was very gratifying to the Allies, who were put at ease for the time being as to affairs on the Italian front.

In speaking of the numbers of Americans arriving, General Foch became a special pleader for the French and suggested that an American regiment be sent to each of their divisions. It would be especially desirable, he thought, thus to strengthen their exhausted units, at least during July. He said that many of the French soldiers had been asking where the Americans were, and this plan would have a beneficial effect on their morale. I could not see the question just as he did, as the effect on our troops would have been the other way, so I gave him no encouragement.

Evidently as an offset to this proposal, he said he was anxious to have an American army serving beside the French armies, to which I at once subscribed, saying that I hoped he would give us every assistance to this end. Due to previous concessions on our part regarding the shipments of infantry, we were already meeting with difficulty in providing auxiliary troops and armament necessary to complete even the more advanced divisions. These units were, nevertheless, rapidly increasing in efficiency, as shown by the complimentary orders and the general comment on their conduct after they had been tested in both quiet and active sectors.

In handling questions of policy it was not always easy to get my views before the Secretary of War in their proper light. This was especially true in attempting to cover important matters by cable. My experience led to the conclusion that the best way to reach him was through direct mail correspondence, as sometimes cabled requests were apparently acted on without his knowledge and in a manner adverse to our best interests. One of the questions involved was that of promotion to the grade of general officer. After frequent attempts to secure the promotion of several colonels whose abilities had been thoroughly tested in active service and having failed to get their names included in the list of promotions, I sent a cable asking for a reconsideration of my recommendations, suggesting that my cable be shown to the

Secretary in person. I also wrote him giving my point of view and explaining just what the promotion of tried officers with the armies would mean to the efficiency of my whole command. Referring to the matter in one of his letters, it was evident that he had not seen the full cable correspondence, as he replied in his usual cordial manner that it was his intention to give every consideration to the men of proved efficiency in France. Of course, this was all that I could ask but the principle was not altogether followed by his subordinates.

One subject that caused Secretary Baker some anxiety was that of giving the press news of our operations in a way that would meet the persistent demands, without disclosing the numbers or location of our forces, and which would "prevent the War Department from being regarded as suppressing and withholding news." Although necessarily never entirely satisfactory from either the news point of view or from that of morale building at home, this matter was adjusted as far as practicable through the distribution to the press by the War Department of material contained in the periodical communiqués published from my headquarters and cabled to the Secretary. These, and such information from my confidential cables on the situation as the War Department thought might be safely given out, furnished thereafter the basis of information to the press at home. It was, of course, fully recognized among the armies that communiqués rarely gave either fully or frankly all the facts. A complete statement in a communiqué might often have discouraged one's own people and encouraged the enemy. It was, therefore, natural that communiqués by opposing armies reporting the same engagement were often widely at variance.

A consideration of the question of supply for our forces, spread as they were over different parts of the battle line, led the Secretary of War to the same conclusion that I had reached. This was that there should be some coördination in the matter among the Allied armies. Mr. Baker wrote:

"* * * It looks as though an arrangement will ultimately have to be made either for a *common supply system* or else * * * the British will undertake to supply all the troops from the Channel up to a given point, the French from that point to another point, and the Americans the sector farthest east."

At that moment our forces were scattered all over France, some with the British and some with the French, the larger proportion being under our own command.

His inquiries and suggestions were taken up by letter, along with other matters uppermost at the time:

"June 18, 1918.

"Dear Mr. Secretary:

"Although I sent you a cablegram regarding the subjects discussed in your letter of May 13th, it does not seem to cover them quite fully enough, again illustrating the difficulties of expressing one's thoughts fully by cable.

"On the question of promotions, I feel sure that all concerned are prompted by the sole desire of selecting men who are best fitted for the work in hand. To make clear my purpose in writing you, permit me to say that in my recommendations of men in active service here it seemed to me that as their abilities to a certain extent have been tested in active service, we should be more likely to obtain efficiency in the new grades than if we should select men without such experience. I do not at all wish to intimate that promotions should be limited to men in France. Such a system would be manifestly impracticable and unfair, as well as discouraging to the hopes of good men still in the States. Yet, where you have men with experience available, it would be equally unfair to promote inexperienced men over their heads.

"As to establishing a 'Permanent Intelligence Department for the Signal Corps,' I quite agree with you that the difficulties of conducting aircraft construction by cable are well-nigh insuperable, and believe that the plan you suggest will help us over the difficulties. I need not assure you that any members of the aviation corps sent over by you for any purpose will always receive the very heartiest coöperation by their fellows on this side. I think the plan should enable us to speed up the aviation program, now very short of what was expected. A cable has just been received to-day regulating an exchange of officers for the very purpose of coördinating work between here and the States.

"With reference to the allotment of engines to the Navy, the correspondence between yourself and the Secretary of the Navy clears up my mind, as I cabled you a day or two ago, and we should be in a position to get harmonious coöperation between the Navy and Army Air Services from now on. General Patrick, the new head of our Air Service, is in London in conference with Admiral Sims regarding these questions and I have no doubt they will arrive at a satisfactory arrangement.

"In this connection, however, I wish to call attention to the fact that when the allotment of Liberty engines for the Navy was made, it was upon the theory that the production would reach certain estimates. We now find ourselves disappointed in that the supply of airplanes by the French has fallen off and we are face to face with a military crisis which demands the use of all airplanes possible. The enemy seems to have the advantage when he cares to use it and this adds to the odds he otherwise has over the Allies. We should meet this crisis on land as the success of the Allied Armies is at stake, and postpone the supply of engines for the Navy if necessary. The Naval program can have no effect upon the present emergency on the Western Front, and can only influence the final result. The situation is such as to warrant a reconsideration of the allotments, and I hope you may see your way to present the case to the Naval authorities and secure for us the Liberty engines we had expected.

"Regarding the distribution of news, I believe the matter has been placed on a satisfactory basis. Our newspaper men here have raised no protest against the plan of issuing our communiqué, as they understand that our cable is given out in Washington to the whole press.

"There have been requests here for the number of men we have in France, but I have in all cases declined to accede. The demands of the press at home are also insistent, and they are not so easy to decline. While we are exerting every possible effort to put trained men into action, there is indeed much to be said in favor of giving the people the facts. Just now it is very heartening to our Allies and has perhaps the opposite effect upon the enemy. But our Allies conceal their numbers and as our forces increase they will expect us to keep ours secret, and I think myself that, from a military standpoint, we must before long take the same view.

"I have taken up this matter of publication in the *Stars and Stripes* of certain military information and find that nothing has been published in that weekly recently that has not been either cabled home in our daily communiqués or by correspondents for publication in the daily press at home. The press men of course go much more into small details than we do in our cables. If any matter has escaped, it has been an oversight, as it is not the intention to publish in the

Stars and Stripes any exclusive matter or anything that has not been already published at home.

"As to the preferential shipment of infantry and machine gun units, I think that we have now reached the limit of those demands, although I thought the same thing last month. My reason for the conclusion is that both the French and British drafts will be available in August and September, so that after July they should not call upon us to supply infantry or machine gun units to fill up their divisions. I might add here on this subject that our men are almost universally against serving with the British or French and all clamor to serve under our own flag.

*   *   *   *   *   *   *

"With high esteem and warm personal regard, I remain, as always,
"Yours faithfully,
"JOHN J. PERSHING."

"P.S.

"With reference to sending over Mr. Stettinius as a member of the Munitions Board, the more I think of the proposal the more it appeals to me. Mr. Stettinius' broad acquaintance among Inter-Allied countries and his experience in handling just this line of work seems to me to fit him especially as your representative on the Munitions Board.

"This is a very broad subject which seems to me will become more and more complicated as time goes on. Board after board, and committee after committee are being piled one on top of the other and a state of confusion exists that only a man of Mr. Stettinius' abilities can straighten out, so far as we are concerned. I hope that you may send him over.

"His presence here would give great strength to our end of the program, which is destined to be a very important one. I have seen the telegrams sent by Mr. McFadden and Mr. Cravath, who were evidently brought into this by Mr. Loucheur. In the meantime, I have appointed General Wheeler as our representative until the question could be decided by you.
"Always sincerely,
"JOHN J. PERSHING."

CHAPTER XXXIII

Movements of Divisions—Allied Morale Dangerously Low—Sixty-six Division Program—Five Million Tons Shipping Required—Very Large Expansion Necessary—Progress of Services of Supply—Military Board of Allied Supply—Letter to Secretary of War on Urgency of Situation —Visit Troops in Vosges—Training with French and British of Slight Value—Physical Activity Required of General Officers—Colored Troops

(Diary) Chaumont, Tuesday, June 18, 1918. Called staff and supply officers together this morning and outlined plan to expand army to 3,000,000 men.

General Barnett, Chief of Marine Corps, recommends formation entire Marine division, but the 2d Division cannot be broken up after its fine record. The Navy will furnish a number of 14-inch guns, railway mounts and personnel. Shipment of 100 locomotives and 2,500 cars per month seems assured.

THE demands for American divisions were pressing. The 1st, 2d, and 3d had already become actively engaged, the 1st being slated to go to the reserve near the Château-Thierry salient when relieved from Cantigny. The 2d was still in line at Belleau Wood and the 3d south of the Marne. General Foch had asked for five of the recently arrived divisions that had been training with the British and I had agreed. While en route to the quiet Vosges sector to relieve French divisions, the 4th and 28th had been diverted to the reserve near the western face of the Marne salient. The 35th had moved to the vicinity of Épinal, and the 77th was about to enter the trenches in the Baccarat sector to replace the 42d, which was to reënforce Gouraud's Army east of Reims. The 82d was on its way to the Toul sector to relieve the 26th, which in turn was soon to replace the 2d. Thus there were three American divisions in quiet sectors and seven either in the battle line or held in readiness to meet any eventuality which might result from further activity of the Germans in the great wedge they had driven toward Paris.

The British were displeased at the transfer of our divisions from their area, claiming the right to retain them by reason of having brought them over. When Foch inquired of the conditions under which these troops were serving with the British, my reply made it clear that in the emergency he had entire authority to direct where they should go, as without it the supreme command would fail.

The rapid succession of German offensives had materially reduced the Allied powers of resistance, depressed their morale, and caused the darkest misgivings among them. They grew more and more fearful lest the enemy might still have untold reserves ready to swell his forces. Their low morale was shown in the conversation of many of their soldiers returning from the front to the rest areas. We have seen how the retiring French in the Marne sector expressed themselves concerning the situation. Reports from the British front were no better. Their troops continually told our men who were with them for training that we had come too late and that our entry into the battle would only postpone Allied defeat. This attitude seemed so alarming that I took steps to prevent such a spirit from affecting our army by promptly reporting the facts to Allied authorities. The prevalence of such sentiment was another important reason for opposition to any form of amalgamation.

We had fallen far short of the expectations of the preceding November when I had asked Foch and Robertson to join me in an appeal for twenty-four trained American divisions by the following June. It is small wonder that the Allies were now so insistent in urging increased and continuous shipments of men, trained or untrained. So serious was the Allied situation regarded that it was no longer a demand for twenty-four divisions but for one hundred. It is probable that the enormity of this request was not fully realized, or else the Allies had greatly exaggerated ideas of our power of accomplishment, surprising as it actually proved to be. A brief calculation of the demands of the Prime Ministers showed that they were asking for approximately 4,000,000 combatant troops by the following spring, which, augmented by those required for the Services of Supply, conservatively calculated for a well-balanced force campaigning in a foreign country under the circumstances that surrounded us, would increase the total to at least 5,000,000 men. The American combatant force would have equalled 200 divisions of the Allies, and their apprehension may be imagined when we realize that this was greater by one-fourth than the combined Allied army of 162 divisions then on the Western Front.

Although it is unlikely that this number could have been either transported, equipped, or supplied, it was imperative to lay plans for bringing over all we could. After giving the question careful study, it seemed to me that 3,000,000 men would be the limit we could hope to reach by the spring of 1919. Roughly speaking, this would provide at least sixty-six, or possibly seventy, combatant divisions. As we had hitherto made estimates for a total force of 2,000,000 men, it was necessary to make new calculations on the increased basis and begin the work of expansion everywhere in the A.E.F. accordingly.

In order to carry out such a program, the amount of passenger shipping then serving us would have to be retained and the cargo tonnage would have to be materially increased. Both Mr. Lloyd George and M. Clemenceau thought it would be possible to continue to aid us in shipping sufficiently to keep up the recent rate of troop arrivals, which was about 250,000 per month, and Mr. Graeme Thomson, the British shipping expert, also thought this could be done. In any event, the two Prime Ministers assured me that they would let us have all the shipping they could spare.

To supply the contemplated force of 3,000,000 men, the cargo tonnage would have to be augmented to at least 5,000,000 dead weight tons, and not less than 1,600,000 tons of cargo would have to be discharged monthly. At that moment there were only about 1,500,000 dead weight tons of American shipping in use, but our own yards were beginning to turn out ships more rapidly and it was presumed that construction would continue as long as necessary. However, it was certain that as much as possible of our cargo shipping engaged in commerce would have to be impressed.

The group of officers[1] to whom I outlined the enlarged program were those upon whom the additional burden would fall the heaviest. The spirit with which they accepted it was such as to inspire the utmost confidence in our ability to do our part. There was no word or hint of doubt expressed by any one present that it was excessive, but on the contrary every assurance was given by all that they could meet the new requirements. The ever-increasing demands made upon the various services of supply, transportation, and procurement in the A.E.F. had so far been taken care of in the most praiseworthy manner and the attitude of the entire personnel toward this vastly increased program was no exception. All staff and supply departments consequently instituted studies and investigations and at once began the preparation of new schedules for the guidance of the War Department and ourselves.

My cable sent three days later gave the reasons for fixing the program for the future definitely at 3,000,000 men as a minimum, and urged upon the War Department the utmost effort to meet our immediate needs for the expansion of port facilities and railroads. It also set forth in detail the numbers and classes of troops to be shipped each month from August, 1918, until May, 1919, inclusive. The situation as viewed at that time can perhaps be best shown by quoting part of my cable:

"June 21, 1918.

"The present state of the war under the continued German offensive makes it necessary to consider at once the largest possible military program for the United States. The morale of the French Government and of the High Command is believed to be good but it

---

[1] Those present at the conference were Maj. Gens. McAndrew, Chief of Staff; Kernan, Commanding Services of Supply; Langfitt, Chief of Utilities, S.O.S.; Brig. Gen. Atterbury, Chief of Transportation; Cols. and Assistant Chiefs of Staff Fox Conner, Operations; Logan, Administration; Moseley, Supply; Col. Dawes, General Purchasing Agent; and Mr. Shearman, Shipping Board.

is certain that the morale of the lower grades of the French Army is distinctly poor. Both the French and British people are extremely tired of the war and their troops are reflecting this attitude in their frequent inability to meet successfully the German attacks. It is the American soldiers now in France upon whom they rely. It is the moral as well as material aid given by the American soldier that is making the continuation of the war possible. Only the continual arrival of American troops and their judicious employment can restore the morale of our Allies and give them courage. The above represents the views of the Allied Military leaders as told me in person by General Foch himself, and I believe it is also the view of the civil leaders. We must start immediately on our plans for the future and be ready to strike this fall in order to tide us over till spring, when we should have a big army ready. The war can be brought to a successful conclusion next year if we only go at it now. From a purely military point of view it is essential that we make this effort, especially for the reasons above stated and on account of the grave possibility that the enemy will obtain supplies and men from Russia before next year.

"To meet the demands imposed by the above plan our minimum effort should be based on sending to France prior to May, 1919, a total force, including that already here, of 66 divisions (or better, if possible) together with the necessary corps and army troops, service of supply troops, and replacements. This plan would give an available force of about 3,000,000 soldiers for the summer campaign of 1919, and if this force were maintained, would in conjunction with our Allies give us every hope of concluding the war in 1919."

The organization of the S.O.S. was working at high pressure, the number of men in the various activities having grown from about 100,000 on March 1st to 175,000 on June 1st.[1] Every endeavor was being made to overcome the lack of men and material from which we constantly suffered. As to sea transport, we now had the exclusive use of thirty-nine berths at the most important ports, including ten of our own construction. An average of 244

---

[1] The chiefs of supply and transportation departments at this time were: Brig. Gens. Harry L. Rogers, Chief Quartermaster; Merritte W. Ireland, Chief Surgeon; Harry Taylor, Chief of Engineers; Charles B. Wheeler, Chief of Ordnance; Edgar Russel, Chief Signal Officer; Mason M. Patrick, Chief of Air Service; Maj. Gen. William C. Langfitt, Chief of Utilities; Brig. Gens. William W. Atterbury, Director General of Transportation; Edgar Jadwin, Director Construction and Forestry; Cols. Herbert Deakyne, Director Division of Light Railways and Roads; Francis H. Pope, Director Motor Transport Corps; Charles G. Dawes, General Purchasing Agent.

ships weekly were being discharged. The ports of St. Nazaire and Bordeaux were receiving 10,000 tons of supplies daily, principally consisting of armament, equipment, food, and some forage; while construction of trackage and shelter was slowly making progress.

The railways, employing the operators we had of our own both on the roads and in our principal railway shops at Tours and Nevers, were working with greater efficiency in conjunction with the French, although the demands for troop movements were creating an ever-increasing burden. The interior storage plants at Gièvres and Montierchaume had been expanded and were busy with the receipt and segregation of the accumulation of different classes of supplies provided by the Quartermaster Corps and Medical Department, not to mention the enormous quantities of Engineer and Signal Corps material.

Aviation had finally got started, though Liberty engines were not forthcoming in the numbers promised. Aviation centers at Romorantin and Issoudun, at the rear, and at Colombey-les-Belles, near the front, were busy places. Many of our aviators were in active service or ready for it and our mechanics were assembling and testing the D.H. planes that had begun to arrive in limited numbers from home.

The organization for the management of truck transportation was well under way, with main and subsidiary parks and extensive repair shops located at convenient points. Although only a small proportion of trucks, automobiles, and accessories had reached us, it was reported that the docks at Hoboken were crowded with them ready for shipment.

Some new construction and the adaptation of existing buildings for the Medical Department were gradually increasing hospital accommodations, about 40,000 beds then being available. The erection of great storehouses for the Ordnance Department was being hastened to meet the accumulation of ammunition of all calibers and extra equipment that would be necessary.

The activities of the Signal Corps were directed toward the extension and improvement of communications and the accumulation of material for use in our operations. The Forestry Department was extending its operations to almost every part of France, and even with the shortage of personnel was giving valuable aid in meeting our own and French requirements for heavy and light construction. The Chemical Warfare Service was energetically at work to discover new gases and to improve upon the British gas mask, which was never fully satisfactory. Its inadequate personnel was carrying on instruction throughout the A.E.F. in the use of gas, both in offensive and defensive operations.

In the establishment of the Military Board of Allied Supply, the principle of coöperation as to supplies in common use among the armies was recognized after prolonged debate and discussion. The Board consisted of one representative from each of the Allied armies. It was simply the representative body of the several supply departments of the respective armies and had nothing whatever to do with actual procurement. It was expected to study questions of supply and adopt proper measures for the coordination of Allied resources and utilities. Our supply officers were enjoined to utilize the services of the Board in seeking the equitable allotment of supplies and in coöperating with corresponding supply officers of the Allied armies. Colonel Dawes, who had charge in a more limited sphere of the coördination of our own supply departments, was detailed as the American member of the Board, and to him in coöperation with Colonel Payot, the French member, should largely go the credit for its success.

In order to emphasize further the urgency of beginning on the expanded plan and to put it before the Secretary of War directly, the following paragraphs were included in a letter which I wrote to him on June 18th:

"I now wish to take up a subject of very great importance. That is the burning one of getting troops over here and forming an army as rapidly as possible. I think it is imperative that our whole program for the next ten or twelve months be reconstructed. The Department's estimate of 91,000 men per month after August is not nearly as much as we must do. Mr. Secretary, I cannot emphasize this point too forcibly. We should have at least three million men in France by next April ready for the spring and summer campaign. To achieve this will involve the shipment of 250,000 men per month for the eight months ending April 1st. This is the smallest program that we should contemplate. The situation among our Allies is such that unless we can end the war next year we are likely to be left practically alone in the fight. If further serious reverses come to us this year it is going to be very difficult even to hold France in the war.

"The morale of both the French and British troops is not what it should be. The presence of our troops has braced them up very much but their staying powers are doubtful. Our 2d and 3d Divisions actually stopped the Germans. The French were not equal to it. I fear that I must put some of our regiments into the weaker French divisions, temporarily, to give them courage.

"After checking the German offensive, we must be prepared to strike as soon as possible. The German divisions are growing weaker and their manpower is running low. The German people would be inclined to make peace if they felt a few very heavy blows. We should be ready to give them. On the other hand, if we do not hasten, and the war is allowed to drag along during next year and the year after, we shall run a very great risk that Germany will recuperate by conscripting manpower from the Western Provinces of Russia. The British and French Governments are alarmed about this, as you know, and I consider it a real danger.

"Then, we must bear in mind the effect of a long war upon our own people. The idea seems prevalent at home that the war is going to be finished within a year and our people are wrought up and wish to see a big effort at once. But if we do not make ourselves strong enough on this front to assume the offensive and push the war to a finish, there is going to be criticism and dissatisfaction at home and a general letting down of our war spirit. Moreover, by using a large force and ending the war we shall avoid the large losses that have so dreadfully depleted our Allies. Let us take every advantage of the high tide of enthusiasm and win the war.

"I think that with proper representations as to the necessity for shipping, the British would do all they could to assist us. In fact, Sir Graeme Thomson said he thought the British would be able to continue the recent shipping schedule indefinitely. On our side, we should demand a greater amount of American tonnage than has hitherto been allotted to the army from the sum total of our available shipping, which is constantly increasing. Our shipping advisers here say that several hundred thousand tons can be added to the army allotment by proper paring.

"As to the preparation of this new army, may I not beg of you to consider a draft of 2,000,000 men by December 1st? My recent cable asking that 1,500,000 be called out should now be increased to 2,000,000. They should be called out, beginning now, at the rate of 400,000 per month for the next five months. We should not again be without trained men as we find ourselves now. Every possible means should be exhausted to train, clothe, and equip this force by the end of the year. These are strong words and the force looks large, but we are face to face with the most serious situation that has ever confronted a nation, and it must be met at any sacrifice and without any delay.

"I think we must bring women into our factories, transforming the whole country into an organization to push the war. The British could help on clothing. As to munitions, it matters little whether we have a particular kind of artillery; if we cannot get the French, we should take the British. The same can be said of small arms and personal equipment. If our ordnance cannot furnish them, the French and British have them. So in equipment and armament, there should be no delay.

"I am having a detailed study made of the supply and shipping questions involved, especially as to the amount of supplies that can be obtained in Europe. The pooling program will soon be in operation and I think we shall be able to obtain a greater amount of supplies here than we had anticipated. Spain is practically a virgin field for us which is as yet undeveloped and which, with diplomatic handling, should yield much more than she has hitherto yielded. I shall look into this further.

"The question of accommodations for our troops may have to be considered. If that stands in the way, then I am in favor of asking Congress to permit the billeting of troops. The French people are standing for it even by the forces of two foreign nations, why should not we at home be willing to billet our own troops among our own people?

"As to handling everything that must be sent over under this program, I stand ready now, without waiting for detailed study, to say that we can do it. The supply question will be less difficult as the pooling and the feeding of our troops by the Allies develop. The great port of Marseille is largely unused and will handle much additional tonnage. Our port construction and port facilities are progressing, the railroads are getting better and storage is becoming easier because the French are finding more and more room. The horse question will also probably be worked out here. So that there need be no hesitation in adopting the plan. We should do all that is humanly possible to carry it out.

"There is nothing so dreadfully important as winning this war and every possible resource should be made immediately available. Mr. Secretary, the question is so vital to our country, and the necessity of winning the war is so great, that there is no limit to which we should not go to carry out the plan I have outlined for the next ten months, and we must be prepared to carry it on still further after that at the same rate or maybe faster.

"I have outlined the plan as the least we should count upon to insure success, and I hope, with your strong support, that the President will approve it."

(Diary) Chaumont, Saturday, June 22, 1918. Recommendation for insurance privileges war correspondents disapproved. Orders published Thursday regarding Military Board of Allied Supply.

Have spent three days looking over divisions in the Vosges. 32d Division (Haan) is promising. Organization III Corps (Wright) going forward satisfactorily. Stopped at headquarters 42d Division (Menoher), at Châtel-sur-Moselle; also at Arches, headquarters of the 35th (McClure); and at Baccarat, 77th (Duncan). Found them making progress. Our officers insist that service with tired French divisions is of little benefit. Units now arriving much reduced in strength and deficient in training. Colored soldiers highly incensed that false stories of their mistreatment are being circulated at home.

The 32d, 35th, 42d, and 77th Divisions were engaged in training under the recently organized III Corps. Special effort was being made to hasten their preparation in both staff and line in anticipation of an early call for more serious service. My impressions of the troops inspected on this particular visit were favorable, although quite a number of officers were found unfamiliar with the principles of tactical leadership. In such hastily trained units this was hardly surprising, especially in view of the known defects of the instruction at home. Many were found with only slight appreciation of the natural defensive possibilities of a given position. Some battalion and even regimental commanders had not thought to ascertain the exact location of their front lines and of course had failed to work out the details of plans for defense.

My predilection for detailed instruction in minor tactics, growing out of my previous personal supervision of training in both small and large units, led me quickly to discover deficiencies. On all these visits, I emphasized the importance of understanding the basic principles of both offensive and defensive movements, laid emphasis on the question of mutual support among units, and above all stressed the importance of establishing every possible means of communication between the different elements of a command.

So much depends upon the leader of an organization that the process of selection of the more capable and the elimination of the unfit were constantly in operation. A competent leader can get efficient service from poor troops, while on the contrary an incapable leader can demoralize the best of troops.

Training in quiet sectors in association with French divisions, upon which the French laid so much stress, had proved disappointing during the past months, as their units coming out of the battle line, worn and weary, failed to set an example of the aggressiveness which we were striving to inculcate in our men. Of course our own officers were immediately responsible, but they were frequently handicapped by the lack of energy of tired French officers. After considerable experience, it was the inevitable conclusion that, except for the details of trench warfare, training under the French or British was of little value.

The adherence at home to the idea of concentrating on instruction in trench warfare, as advocated by the French instructors, placed practically the entire burden of training in open warfare upon us in France. This was not easy to accomplish under the circumstances in the brief time remaining after troops began to arrive in large numbers. In this regard the following extract from a cablegram sent to Washington seems pertinent:

"June 20, 1918.
"The reasons for sending men with insufficient instruction are fully appreciated in view of the large increase in number of troops sent over during past three months, and the inequalities in training are fully considered here. The plan of separating recently drafted

men from divisions and giving them special training for a longer period than the others before being put in the line has already been adopted. It will, however, considerably reduce the fighting strength of several divisions to be ordered into the line.

"This situation emphasizes the importance of establishing the rule at home of keeping divisions intact, both as to officers and enlisted men, from the time they are organized until they are sent to France. The plan of using divisions through which to pass large numbers of men for instruction is very detrimental to thorough training of the divisions. It need not be pointed out that it takes much time to consolidate a division into a homogeneous fighting unit and build up its esprit de corps. Almost without exception, division commanders complain of the methods that have been followed. I recommend that in future the training of replacements and of special troops of all kinds be kept distinct from that of divisions.

"Our inspections of divisions recently arrived show that the training is uneven and varies much in different divisions. It appears superficial in many cases and generally lacks spirit and aggressiveness. In most of these divisions little attention has been given to training in open warfare, and in this regard younger officers are especially deficient. The training appears to have been carried on in a perfunctory way and without efficient supervision. The general impression is that division officers have leaned too heavily on French instructors, whose ideas are not ordinarily in accordance with our own."

In response to my objections regarding the practice of the War Department of taking from organized divisions large groups of trained men and replacing them with recruits, the Department cabled in July that the policy of keeping divisions intact would be followed. However, serious harm had already been done, as most of the divisions that served abroad had departed by that time or were sent soon afterwards.

After visits to units that had lately joined, further attention was given to the physical qualifications necessary in our higher officers. The British and French both had commented unfavorably upon the evident inactivity of many of them and even upon the infirmities of some of the division commanders who had been sent over during the preceding months to observe and study conditions at the front. It had been proved over and over again by the Allies that only the strongest could stand the continuous and nerve-racking strain of actual battle. Many of the disasters that had come to the Allies were due in a large part to the lack of energy and alertness of older commanders, who often failed to exercise that eternal personal supervision and tactical direction necessary to success. M. Clemenceau himself, then seventy-six years of age, said that the French had made a serious error in the beginning in retaining old officers in the service, and that later they had to be retired in considerable numbers.

It was a question not merely of being able to pass a perfunctory medical examination, but vigor, stamina, and leadership were demanded. The physical requirements were not fully appreciated by inexperienced medical boards at home. Inactive officers only threw extra burdens upon their staffs. We had long been accustomed in our service to regard a general officer's position as one that did not require activity. Not a few of the older officers, upon being called to high command, had occupied themselves with minor matters, to the neglect of personal supervision of instruction of their commands in battle tactics. It was the exception to find such men equal to the active command of troops. The advisability of selecting younger men to command brigades and divisions was no longer a theory in our service.

Cables from the War Department about this time stated that the colored people were being told that negro soldiers in France were always placed in the most dangerous positions, were being sacrificed to save white troops, and were often left on the field to die without medical attention. It was not difficult to guess the origin of this sort of propaganda. As a matter of fact, none of these troops had been in line except in quiet sectors. Those I had recently seen were in fine spirits and seemed keen for active service. The only colored combat troops in France were those of the 92d Division, then in a quiet sector in the Vosges, and the four infantry regiments of the 93d, each of which was attached to a French division. Several individuals in these units serving with the French had already received the Croix de Guerre for conduct in raids.

My earlier service with colored troops in the Regular Army had left a favorable impression on my mind. In the field on the frontier and elsewhere they were reliable and courageous, and the old 10th Cavalry (colored), with which I served in Cuba, made an enviable record there. Under capable white officers and with sufficient training, negro soldiers have always acquitted themselves creditably.

When told of these rumors, the colored troops were indignant, and later they did everything possible to counteract such false reports. It was gratifying to learn shortly afterward that Congress had passed very positive legislation against that sort of propaganda. The following paragraph from a cable sent at the time is pertinent:

"June 20, 1918.

"Exploit of two colored infantrymen some weeks ago in repelling much larger German patrol, killing and wounding several Germans and winning Croix de Guerre by their gallantry, has roused fine spirit of emulation among colored troops, all of whom are looking forward to more active service. Only regret expressed by colored troops is that they are not given more dangerous work to do. They are especially amused at the stories being circulated that the American colored troops are placed in the most dangerous positions and all are desirous of having more active service than has been permitted them so far."

CHAPTER XXXIV

Conference with Clemenceau and Foch at Chaumont—Relative Allied and
Enemy Strength—Eighty to One Hundred Divisions Recommended—
Foch Again Asks for American Regiments—Not Always Impartial—
Naval Aviation—Progress of Aviation in A.E.F.—Twenty-two Divi-
sions in France—New Corps Completed—Hospitalization for our Cas-
ualties at Château-Thierry Inadequate

(Diary) Chaumont, Sunday, June 23, 1918. M. Clemenceau, General Foch, and M. Tardieu, with Generals Weygand and Mordacq,
came to Chaumont to-day for conference on increase of American manpower. General McAndrew and Colonels Fox Conner and Boyd
were with me. Took Clemenceau to see some of our troops. Foch asks
for our regiments to strengthen French divisions.

M. CLEMENCEAU'S popularity in France was probably
at its height at this time. As this was his first visit to
Chaumont, the people turned out en masse, crowded
into the plaza and gave him a rousing welcome. His reception
within the Hôtel de Ville by the officials, both civil and military,
was marked by eloquent speeches of tribute to his service for
France. In his remarks, M. Clemenceau expressed confidence in
the future and gave the people every encouragement, referring
especially to the increasing forces of Americans.

As we were leaving, a widowed mother of a missing soldier,
her only son, came up in great distress and told M. Clemenceau of
her sorrow. He spoke very tenderly of her patriotic sacrifice,
put his arm gently around her and kissed her cheeks, mingling
his tears with hers. The pathos of this scene touched every heart.

As General Foch and the others were not to arrive until later,
M. Clemenceau and I, driving together, accompanied by Generals
Wirbel and Ragueneau in a separate automobile, went to the
headquarters of the 83d Division, Major General E. F. Glenn
commanding, which was billeted at Montigny, not far from

Chaumont. We saw a battalion at Essey and one at Mandres, the headquarters of Brigadier General T. W. Darrah. During the inspection, M. Clemenceau found in the ranks several men of foreign birth from various countries, which interested him very much. He afterwards chatted with the officers and made a short speech to them and the inhabitants of the village, who had gathered around him.

It was one of those beautiful days that leave a lasting impression, and as we motored along through the rolling country that rose toward the foothills of the Vosges Mountains we fell to discussing the probable situation of the different Allied countries and their relative standing after the war. He went to some length in his conjectures. He said, "Great Britain is finished, and in my opinion she has seen the zenith of her glory." I said, "What makes you think so, Mr. Prime Minister?" He replied, "First of all, the immense drain of the war will make it impossible for her to retain commercial supremacy and, second, the experience of her Colonial troops in this war will make their people more independent and she will lose her control over them." I could not entirely agree with M. Clemenceau's view and said, "Mr. Prime Minister, I think you are mistaken about the British and believe we shall see them fully recover from the effects of the war."

Continuing, I said, "What about France's future?" "Ah! she will once more be the leading power in Europe," he replied. "But you do not mention Germany," said I. He replied, "The Germans are a great people, but Germany will not regain her prestige and her influence for generations." He spoke of the others only casually and made no predictions about them. I remember one expression he used regarding the United States. "Ah! General," he said, "yours is a wonderful country with unlimited possibilities."

His view of the future of France was and is without doubt the dominant one among Frenchmen, especially those of the educated classes. There is no denying the fact that the French as a whole regard themselves as a superior people in many respects. One striking evidence of this is that they lose no opportunity to extol the achievements of their great men. The thought naturally ran through my mind that this attitude of dominance on the part of the French might in some measure account for their inclination to keep the American Army in a subordinate rôle. In any event they never gave up the idea of regarding us as only an associated power, that had come into the war late, to be used as they might dictate.

M. Clemenceau and I went on to discuss the immediate military outlook. I gave him my views regarding the probable situation of the German armies in the Marne salient and pointed out the chance we had for a successful counterattack on its western face. I spoke especially of the strategical effect of a successful blow just south of Soissons and the material results it would have, to say nothing of its stimulating effect on Allied morale. I suggested that we had at least six divisions, and possibly eight, that could be used in such an offensive. The idea that we could strengthen the French with an attacking force of fresh troops equal to sixteen Allied divisions seemed to surprise him, and as the idea made an appeal to his common sense he said he would call Foch's attention to it at once.

Later in the day I reminded General Foch of the suggestion which I had made to him at Sarcus regarding a counteroffensive. He had given instructions, he said, to have a study made, although there was no intimation as to when, where, or whether, it would be undertaken. That part of the German position to which I have referred offered every advantage for the successful outcome of such a move. It will be evident to any one who will glance at the map that once the line there was pierced the German rear would be threatened and their position within the salient would be untenable. The Allies could not have asked for a better chance than the Germans gave them.

Shortly after our return to the château, Generals Foch and Weygand arrived, and after lunch we all went into conference. This meeting was arranged for Sunday to give us plenty of time to go over the whole question of troop requirements. Its particular purpose was to discuss in detail the rate of shipments that would be necessary in order to give the Allies unquestioned superiority the following year. The continuation of shipments up to one hundred divisions, as already recommended by the Prime Ministers—Lloyd George, Clemenceau, and Orlando—formed the basis of French argument. M. Tardieu's estimate of the American problem was accurate, and doubting the possibility of our being able to reach the greater program, he favored reducing the immediate demands, but Clemenceau and Foch were for the 100-division program.

I did not think it possible, from our experience, that we could accomplish so much and gave the opinion that even a force of eighty divisions, or a total combat force of about 3,200,000 men, would probably overtax our facilities of transportation and supply. It was also a question in my mind whether either M. Clemenceau or General Foch really thought that a program calling for one hundred divisions, or even eighty, could be carried out within a reasonable time. At any rate, it was my opinion that the 80-division plan would serve as a goal toward which effort could be directed.

Moreover, it was clearly evident that if the war should be prolonged for any length of time the burden would fall more and more upon us. Hence, there was no question but that we should make a supreme effort to increase our manpower on the Western Front sufficiently to give the Allies superiority under any probable contingency. I was willing to ask for the greater numbers, feeling, however, that the War Department would do wonders if it could carry out even the 66-division[1] plan. In the course of our discussion, M. Clemenceau gave assurance that every possible effort to meet our deficiencies, including those in munitions and aviation, would be made by the French Government.

Germany was believed to have 3,534,000 men on the Western Front at the time, while the combined forces of the Allies in

[1] These estimates were rather general and the numbers stated depended upon the method of calculation. 3,000,000 men would probably have given us seventy divisions, so there was little difference between that total and the total that would have been necessary for an 80-division program.

France, exclusive of Americans, were estimated at 2,909,000, of whom Great Britain had 1,239,000, and France 1,670,000 men. The Germans were supposed to be still bringing troops from the Russian front, but according to Allied information they would not be able to muster more than 340,000 replacements from their own population. The British claimed that in providing 130,000 replacements for June they had reached their limit and said they would not be able to furnish any more until October; and the French said that their units at the front were short 80,000 men, with a reservoir of only 60,000 men to draw upon until the class of 1919 should become available, which would not be until September.

This matter of finding replacements for the Allied armies was not at all clear and many different statements were made about it from time to time. Whenever it came up for consideration the British and French locked horns, so to speak, and the discussion often became very pointed, each apparently doubting whether the other was doing everything possible to keep up its armies. The French claimed unofficially that the British were holding an excessive number of men in England and Ireland for home defense, but the British denied this vigorously. Of course it was a matter of common knowledge that the draft had never been enforced in Ireland and it was something of a bombshell thrown into the British camp when, at one of the sessions of the Supreme War Council, during a discussion of the subject, M. Clemenceau asked Mr. Lloyd George why he did not draft the Irish. Not to be forced into an explanation, Mr. Lloyd George replied, after some hesitation, and to the amusement of all present, "Mr. Prime Minister, you evidently do not know the Irish."

This was the situation when the conference met at my headquarters. The whole subject was thoroughly thrashed out and, considering the shortage of manpower claimed by the French and the British, to say nothing of the possible increase of the German armies from Russian sources, the main thought was to get over as many Americans as we could. It was finally agreed that we should propose an 80-division program to be completed by April,

1919, and aim at the larger program of one hundred divisions for July, 1919. These conclusions were conveyed to the War Department in the following cable:

"Val des Écoliers, June 23, 1918.

"To win the victory in 1919, it is necessary to have a numerical superiority which can only be obtained by our having in France in April 80 American divisions and in July 100 divisions. At Versailles on the 2d of June, 1918, the three Prime Ministers, in order to obtain this result, requested President Wilson to draft 300,000 men per month. This draft should be made up as follows: *First:* For the creation of six new divisions per month with the corresponding troops for Corps, Army, and Service of the Rear, 250,000 per month beginning with the 1st of July, 1918. *Second:* For replacements, which we determine according to the experience of the French Army at 20 per cent per year of the total strength, a figure which will vary from month to month, but which for the whole period considered would bring the monthly figure of 250,000 men mentioned above to 300,000 men.

"Subparagraph. By the measures indicated above we will assure the existence and the replacements in France of an army of 46 divisions in October, 64 in January, 80 in April, and 100 in July.

"F. FOCH,
"JOHN J. PERSHING."

It was recommended that these numbers should replace those given in my dispatch of the 21st. The following paragraphs were included in the cable sent from Val des Écoliers:

"Paragraph 2. Recommend that above program be adopted in place of minimum outlined in our cable No. 1342. Am confident that with our tonnage liberally allotted for war purposes from now on, and augmented by available British and French shipping, we shall be able to handle both troops and supplies. M. Clemenceau, who was present at conference, gives assurance that every possible effort to supplement deficiencies in our supplies and equipment, including munitions and aviation, will be made by the French Government. No doubt British will do likewise.

"Paragraph 3. In working out details of cable No. 1342 we took into consideration our information regarding limited cantonment accommodations and lack of equipment, neither of which should enter as factors to delay immediate action on largest program possible. If cantonment facilities should be lacking, recommend that billeting be

given consideration. Will outline details of above extended plan
in a day or so.

"PERSHING."

As a number of our divisions had won recognition and praise
as offensive units, it was believed all concerned were convinced
that our views on building up entire units and eventually an army
were sound and that we should hear little more of amalgamation.
Indeed, M. Clemenceau had recently said that while he had been
opposed to the organization of a separate American army until
later, he was now in favor of its being formed at an early date,
as he thought it the best way to strengthen the Allied forces.

At this conference, consideration was given only to entire divisions and corps, and auxiliary combat and supply troops with
which to round out our forces into an American army. Yet after
the agreement had been reached and M. Clemenceau had departed General Foch remained and again brought up the question
of placing a few American regiments in French divisions. I very
frankly told him again that it could not be done. This was but
one of many suggestions made by Foch regarding the reënforcement of French divisions by American units. His general inclination to aid the French at the expense of the other armies in
France created the decided impression that he could not forget
that he was a Frenchman and that he did not always act with
the impartiality that the other Allies had a right to expect.

The visit of the party was in every way cordial and the discussions were carried on dispassionately, quite in contrast to some
that had gone before and others that came afterwards. M.
Clemenceau interposed a witty story now and then, but Foch
did not have that turn of mind. During this visit I was more
than ever impressed by M. Clemenceau's vitality and I asked him
how he kept himself so vigorous. He pointed out how little he
ate and said he drank no wine. He added that he took no violent
exercise but that he had an expert put him through a course of
bending and stretching exercises every morning followed by a
massage before he got out of bed.

(Diary) Chaumont, Thursday, June 27, 1918. Captain Cone, of the Navy, came on Monday at Admiral Sims' direction to discuss coöperation in aviation. Conferred with Ireland; if Medical Department fails us it will not be his fault. Nineteen lake steamers coming over for port and cross-Channel service.

Held further conferences Tuesday with Staff on organization. Have directed completion of three corps headquarters and staffs.

General Gillain, Belgian Chief of Staff, came yesterday for a visit. Cabled Secretary McAdoo appreciation Government's measures reference insurance.[1]

In the question of coöperation between Army and Navy aviation, the Secretary of War had decided that the use of aviation against U-boat bases was entirely a naval matter. The original allotment of Liberty engines to the Navy was confirmed, but the output was not so great as expected and the Allies and our army were then far short of the number of engines required. While the use of naval airplanes against the submarine would have been of value in the long run, they possessed no advantages over destroyers, and such use was certainly of no immediate aid in meeting the crisis that confronted us on the Western Front, and that was the most important consideration.

Our aviators were appearing in increasing numbers over the front lines, where they were badly needed to reënforce the French, who were as short of fliers as they were of mechanics. We had already furnished 4,200 mechanics and had agreed to send a still greater number, especially to assist in the manufacture of planes. While on April 1st we had only one aero squadron in action— my old squadron of the Mexican Punitive Expedition—the number on May 15th had increased to eight but these were all equipped with French airplanes.

The usefulness of our Air Service during this period could hardly be overestimated, as previously the enemy had seemed to

---

[1] Upon receipt of information from Secretary McAdoo that nineteen billion dollars of insurance had been taken by service men, I sent him the following cable: "All ranks of the A.E.F. appreciate deeply the generous measures the Government has taken to provide insurance for their families, in proof of which more than 90 per cent of the men have taken out insurance. This wise provision for their loved ones heartens our men and strengthens the bonds that unite the army and people in our strong determination to triumph in our most righteous cause."

have the superiority whenever he cared to use it. That its importance was duly recognized is shown by a letter of June 11th from General Foch in which he said that the results obtained by the direct use in battle of Allied pursuit and bombardment aviation in the recent offensive had been without precedent. He also suggested that still greater concentration of aviation would be an essential factor in future operations. It was, therefore, desirable that all available air forces under our control be prepared for active service, not only to aid Allied endeavor at the moment but to qualify our aviators for early service with our own armies. When the German offensive began on July 15th the number of our squadrons had increased to twenty-one out of a total of sixty that we had expected to have at the front by this time.

Twelve of our infantry divisions were then either in line or in reserve behind the French, five were in training in French areas, and five were in training in rear of the British Army. Of those with the French, six were concentrated in the vicinity of Villers-Cotterêts and Château-Thierry between the French front and Paris. The British seemed to think that the French were unduly nervous about the safety of Paris and felt that Foch was holding a greater proportion of American troops behind the French lines than was necessary. They believed that there was a strong probability of another attack against their front and thought that Foch was not paying enough attention to their situation. However, they probably did not realize that a counter-offensive was contemplated against the Marne salient should the occasion present itself.

The I Corps Headquarters, organized in January under Major General Hunter Liggett, with Colonel Malin Craig as Chief of Staff, had become a smoothly working machine ready for active service anywhere, but events had moved so swiftly that there had been no opportunity for the assembly of divisions. With the increasing size of our army, it was evident that a greater number of divisions would be available to take part in operations at earlier dates than we had hitherto thought possible. Consequently, the organization of the II, III, and IV Corps Headquarters was at once completed.

The II Corps, Major General George W. Read commanding, with Colonel George S. Simonds as Chief of Staff, and a limited number of staff officers, was charged with matters of administration and command pertaining to the divisions behind the British front. The III Corps, temporarily under command of Major General William M. Wright, with Colonel Alfred W. Bjornstad, Chief of Staff, continued to supervise the training of divisions serving in the Vosges area. The IV Corps was temporarily under the corps Chief of Staff, Colonel Stuart Heintzelman, with headquarters at Toul. By the actual constitution of these corps they were expected soon to become efficient enough to handle units in operations. It was our policy throughout the war to make the basic corps organizations as permanent as possible. The corps commander and his staff and certain corps troops such as heavy artillery, signal and engineer contingents, and supply units thus formed a team that grew in efficiency with experience. Divisions were assigned to corps according to circumstances but were not attached with any idea of permanency.

When our troops became suddenly engaged in the Château-Thierry region we had to rely largely upon the assistance of the French to care for our wounded. Although they had given us every assurance that hospital arrangements for those operations would be complete, and without question they did their best, yet it was only through the mobile hospitals which we had organized that we were able to give our casualties proper attention.

In extenuation of the French failure to take care of our casualties properly, it must be said that when the Germans swept over the Chemin des Dames to Château-Thierry the French lost 45,000 beds included in some of their best equipped hospitals. We had no hospitals on that front and with limited transportation found it difficult to supplement the scant French facilities. In fact, our situation there as to hospital accommodations was about to reach a critical stage.

In this connection, a cablegram, which was scathing in its denunciation of our Medical Department, was actually submitted by Mr. Casper Whitney for the New York *Tribune*. The censor immediately informed the medical representatives at my headquarters, and General Ireland, the Chief Surgeon, requested an investigation, which was at once carried out by General Brewster, my Inspector General. Mr. Whitney was asked to be present at all the hearings and when the actual facts were brought out, showing the efficiency of the Medical Department, he was most apologetic and thereafter became an enthusiastic supporter of the wisdom of the censorship.

Our experience during these operations showed that we must depend on our own resources for the kind of hospitalization and treatment that we expected our sick and wounded to receive. Mobile hospitals could not always take the place of more permanent installations needed after a great battle. The important question of enlarged hospitalization, with ample accommodations and attendants for the sick and wounded, was, therefore, receiving very earnest attention. Although new problems were encountered here and there as our troops were sent to different parts of the front, they were all met in such a way as to reflect credit upon our Medical Department.

CHAPTER XXXV

Allotment of Liberty Engines to Allies—Horse Procurement—Chaplains—
Meeting Supreme War Council—Belgians and Unity of Command—
Fourth of July—Troops of 33d Division Attack with British—Reor-
ganization of Services of Supply—American Troops Requested for
Balkan Front

(Diary) Paris, Tuesday, July 2, 1918. After busy days at Chaumont
came to Paris on Saturday, stopping at Orly to see new DH-4 with
Liberty engine. Saw General Langfitt on reorganization S.O.S., which
seems top-heavy.

On Sunday went to 1st Division and held first ceremony to confer
decorations. Camps in excellent condition. Motored to British
G.H.Q., stopping with Colonel Bacon. Called on Sir Douglas Haig.

Spent yesterday and to-day with General Read, II Corps, inspecting
new divisions, including the 80th, 78th, 30th, 33d, and 27th, and consider the personnel most promising.

Returned to Paris this evening. Have learned that French at last
have begun to enforce requisition for horses. Bishop Brent commis-
sioned Major, National Army. Brigade of Regulars, 2d Division,
stormed Vaux this afternoon, capturing 500 prisoners.

IT was encouraging to see our own airplanes, even in limited
numbers, coming over at last. While some defects in manufacture had been observed in both the DH-4 plane and in
the Liberty engine, these had been pointed out to the War Department and were in course of correction.

Note: Total strength of the A.E.F. on June 30th, 40,487 officers, 833,204 enlisted men.
Divisional units arriving in June included elements of the following divisions: 29th
Division (National Guard, New Jersey, Delaware, Virginia, Maryland, and District of
Columbia), Maj. Gen. Charles G. Morton; 37th Division (National Guard, Ohio),
Maj. Gen. Charles S. Farnsworth; 78th Division (National Army, western New York,
New Jersey and Delaware), Maj. Gen. James H. McRae; 83d Division (National
Army, Ohio and western Pennsylvania), Maj. Gen. Edwin F. Glenn; 89th Division
(National Army, Kansas, Missouri, South Dakota, Nebraska, Arizona, New Mexico,
and Colorado), Brig. Gen. Frank L. Winn; 90th Division (National Army, Texas and
Oklahoma), Maj. Gen. Henry T. Allen; 92d Division (National Army, colored), Maj.
Gen. Charles C. Ballou.

Although the French manufacturers made many suggestions that we should adopt this motor or that, and had none too mildly opposed the adoption of the Liberty engine, its success was instantaneous and the Inter-Allied Committee soon found itself swamped with requests for allotments. In addition to the requirements of our own Army and Navy Air Services both at home and abroad, the British wanted over 5,000, the French over 3,300, and the Italians nearly 2,000, to cover their new construction for the next six months. The tonnage situation considerably restricted the shipment of planes from home, but for the time being France and England could furnish them, provided we could supply the engines. At all times the demand for both planes and Liberty engines was greater than the supply.

The horse question was one that gave us trouble continuously. On account of the lack of shipping and the scarcity of forage in France, and in view of the promise of the French to purchase and deliver to us 15,000 animals per month from April to August, both inclusive, we had, in March, recommended to the War Department that shipments from home be discontinued. But, as has been stated, the French farmers were reluctant to sell animals, even at the increased prices offered, and the climax came on May 31st, when the French advised that due to military developments on the Western Front the Government had issued orders suspending the purchase of any additional animals for the American forces.

I immediately took the matter up with M. Tardieu, of the Franco-American Committee, calling his attention to the extent to which the French failure to supply animals would immobilize a considerable portion of our forces. As a result, the French agreed to adopt a system of enforced requisition throughout France, commencing on June 20th and extending to August 1st. It was estimated that there were in France not in military service approximately 3,000,000 animals, of which from 300,000 to 400,000 were thought to be of suitable types. We were promised 80,000 of the 160,000 to be obtained through the requisition and in addition counted on approximately 14,000 from the British, in accordance with their promise to supply horses for the divisions behind their lines. Negotiations were also reopened for obtaining animals in Spain and it was thought that 25,000 could be obtained from that source.

These numbers, however, would still leave us with a large shortage on August 1st and the War Department was therefore requested on June 30th to resume shipments at the rate of 8,000 per month. It was realized that this number would not meet requirements, but it was hoped that we might obtain still further assistance from the Allies and thus avoid a greater demand on our already inadequate tonnage.

A few days later the success of the French requisition began to appear dubious, less than half as many animals as expected having been obtained. The question was taken up with General Foch at a conference on July 10th and Weygand explained that the requisition committee had not taken advantage of the prices authorized, principally because they did not think the animals worth such prices. He said, however, that we could count on the full delivery of 80,000 horses, but he was very positive that this would be the limit they could furnish.

About this time M. Tardieu took the initiative and, without consulting any one, sent a cable to the French Ambassador at Washington requesting that our War Department begin the shipment of horses for our armies at the rate of 35,000 per month, to be increased progressively to 60,000 per month. The Department was naturally alarmed, as the cable indicated a situation entirely at variance with what I had reported. This is mentioned as one of many incidents that illustrate the sort of uncoördinated activity often exercised by the French. It will be recalled that exactly the same thing had occurred in the fall of 1917 in connection with the shipment of horses, except that then M. Tardieu was on the receiving end in Washington. When his attention was called to the importance of coöperation he was much embarrassed and said that no differences in the future need be feared. M. Tardieu was most efficient and in the position of Chief of the Franco-

American Committee he aided us materially in procurement and in many other ways.

From my conference with Foch and from M. Tardieu's cablegram, it was apparent that we could expect no assistance from the French after the 80,000 requisitioned horses had been delivered and that there must be a large increase in the number to be shipped from home, which we had been trying to avoid. Making every allowance for the possibility of substituting motor traction for horses, still we should need for the 80-division plan something over 200,000, or 25,000 a month for the following eight months, a number that seemed prohibitive in view of the already enormous amount of tonnage required for everything else. These numbers were never reached and we were always approximately 50 per cent short of our requirements. The question continued to give us concern to the end. As to forage, the French gave every assurance that they would be able to feed our animals and told us that it would be unnecessary to ship any more forage from the States until the following spring.[1]

The appointment of Bishop Brent as an officer of the Army, made in response to my request, assured me of his services in the important capacity as Chief of the Board of Chaplains, which was the controlling body in that service, at my headquarters. At the same time, provision was made by Congress, according to my recommendation of several months previous, for an increase in the number of chaplains to one for each 1,200 officers and men in the service. That the significance of this addition to our forces might be understood and appreciated, an order was issued placing chaplains of our forces on the same footing, as regards the performance of their duties, as other officers of the service. In part the order read:

"The importance in wartime of the chaplain's work can hardly be overestimated. The chaplain should be the moral and spiritual leader of his organization. His continued effort should be the maintenance of high standards of life and conduct among officers and men.

---

[1] In my cable on the subject of horses and forage I said: "Like many other assurances given us, this may not turn out to be altogether true," and it was not so long after the cable was sent that our horses were short of forage.

* * * Though holding a military commission, it is on the basis of the supreme performance of his ministerial duties that he fulfills his fundamental obligations to the army. A sympathetic recognition of the chaplain's duties and responsibilities is expected of every officer. It is only through their ready coöperation that he can reach the entire army."

(Diary) Chaumont, Saturday, July 6, 1918. Conferred with Lord Milner Wednesday morning in Paris and later with Haig, giving my objections to our troops in training being taken for an offensive. Attended meeting Supreme War Council in the afternoon.

Reached Chaumont at noon the 4th and participated in celebration at Hôtel de Ville. French Mission also gave an entertainment, with movies of 1st Division at Cantigny. General de Castelnau called, and General Pétain, General Ragueneau, and de Chambrun dined with us and attended a troop entertainment. Received many telegrams. As a compliment to the French, issued orders yesterday making July 14th a holiday.[1]

Part of the 33d Division made an attack with the Australians on the 4th.

Held detailed discussion to-day with McAndrew, Hagood, and Eltinge on S.O.S. reorganization.

Lord Milner came in from Versailles and together we went over the problems of troop shipments and especially the question of continuing the tonnage then being used for the increased American program. He assured me that their plans contemplated the same help they were giving us at that time. He spoke of

[1] France, July 5, 1918.

General Orders } No. 109 }

July 14 is hereby declared a holiday for all troops in this command not actually engaged with enemy. It will be their duty and privilege to celebrate French Independence Day, which appeals alike to every citizen and soldier in France and America, with all the sympathetic interest and purpose that France celebrated our Independence Day. Living among the French people and sharing the comradeship-in-arms of their soldiers, we have the deeper consciousness that the two anniversaries are linked together in common principles and a common cause.

By command of General Pershing:

JAMES W. McANDREW,
Chief of Staff.

General Pétain embodied the text in an order which he issued to the French Army.

the American divisions behind the British lines and was very anxious that they should remain there. Somehow I felt that his assurance as to shipping might depend upon the number of divisions that would be held for service with their armies. Marshal Haig, who called later, was also solicitous as to the retention of our troops and said that he would be very much weakened if any more divisions were taken away. I told him that for the moment the question as to where they should serve would naturally depend upon where they were needed most. The principal scene of action had changed from the British to the French front, so the stronger demands for our forces now came from the latter source.

The Supreme War Council was holding a session at this time, but it had not been my intention to attend, until a telephone message was received from Mr. Lloyd George asking me to come. Although I had already written him a note, my attendance gave me the opportunity to thank him in person for the fine spirit that prompted the British desire to celebrate the Fourth of July with us. He had sent word through Major Griscom that he wished to visit some of our units, and I took this occasion to tell him that I sincerely hoped he would do so.

At this session of the Council there was an absence of the tension that had prevailed at the last two meetings. The only question discussed while I was present was whether the Belgian Army would be under the Allied Commander-in-Chief. The Belgian Chief of Staff objected to Foch on the ground that a King could not be placed under the command of a Major General. It did not appear to me that the point was well taken, as Haig and Pétain and I were senior in rank to Foch, who, after all, held his place by common agreement. Although this technical question of rank was raised, the Belgian authorities, as represented by the King, were strongly in favor of coöperation.

Once the portion of the line to be held by each of the Allies was distinctly defined and the operations to be undertaken by each were agreed upon, Foch's duties might have been considered as those of a chief coördinator. Each Commander-in-Chief was supreme in his own army, as he had been before, and Foch's task was to coördinate the operations of the armies in such manner as to make it impracticable for the enemy to concentrate against any one of them. In effect, this was the rôle that he actually played under the provisions of his appointment.

The Fourth of July found me in Chaumont. The French people there never missed an opportunity to show their pleasure at having us in their midst and their appreciation of American aid to the cause. The principal ceremony of the day was a reception at the Hôtel de Ville tendered to the officers of my headquarters by the local French officials, both civil and military, and the prominent citizens. The program included a series of suitable speeches, and the spirit of fraternity that prevailed made it easy to respond. In fact, on this, as often on similar occasions, I found myself almost as enthusiastic as the French speakers, though perhaps less content with my effort.

Many Allied officials were kind enough to remember that it was our Independence Day, and messages came from Clemenceau, Foch, Haig, and others. In order to record the friendly attitude that existed at the moment, several of them are quoted below:

"General Headquarters,
"British Armies in France,
"2d July, 1918.

"DEAR GENERAL PERSHING:
"On behalf of myself and the whole British Army in France and Flanders, I beg you to accept for yourself and the troops under your command the warmest greetings on American Independence Day.

"On the 4th of July of this year, the soldiers of America, France, and Great Britain will stand side by side for the first time in history in the defense of the great principle of Liberty, which is the proudest inheritance and most cherished possession of their several nations.

"That Liberty which British, Americans, and French have won for themselves they will not fail to hold, not only for themselves but for the world.

"With heartfelt good wishes to you and your gallant army, believe me,
"Yours very truly,
"D. HAIG, F.M."

"Paris, July 5, 1918.
"General Pershing,
　"Commander-in-Chief of the
　　"American Forces in France.

"The American troops who took part in the Fourth of July ceremony on the Avenue President Wilson made a deep impression upon all Paris. On this holiday so wholeheartedly celebrated by all our Allies, the splendid appearance of your soldiers aroused not only our enthusiasm but our unbounded confidence as well. I beg that you transmit to your troops, with my compliments, the expression of my sincere admiration.

"CLEMENCEAU."

"July 3, 1918.
"General Pershing,
　"Commander-in-Chief of the
　　"American Forces in France.

"It is for independence that we all are fighting. With all our hearts we celebrate with you the anniversary of Independence Day.

"GENERAL FOCH."

"Trianon, Versailles, July 4, 1918.
"General Pershing, HAEF.

"On this day of national festivity for the United States tnat all Allied nations are solemnizing will you kindly accept the wishes which I send you in my name and in the name of all Italian soldiers present in France actually fighting or working for the great common cause for the triumph of civilization and of right.

"GENERAL ROBILANT."

"Belgian Army, July 4, 1918.
"General Pershing,
　"Commander-in-Chief, American Expeditionary Forces.

"On this memorable day, July 4, 1918, when the Army of the United States is celebrating Independence Day on the battlefield, I address to you the cordial greetings and the respectful sympathy of the Belgian Army which celebrates with you your national anniversary with the spirit and the fervor of troops who have been fighting almost four years without rest for the independence of their country. On this occasion detachments from every arm will march beneath the folds of the American Flag raised on the plain of Flanders. All our hearts are united in one prayer for the success of the Allied armies and in the expectation of that glorious day when your troops shall march in

their turn beneath the folds of our own Tricolor raised in our reconquered cities.

"De Ceuninck,
"Belgian Minister of War."

"Camp d'Auvours, July 4, 1918.
"Commander-in-Chief of the
"American Troops, H.A.E.F.

"At the moment when the Belgian troops at Camp d'Auvours,
Sarthe, have just filed before the United States flag giving honor to it
with all habitual ceremonies, I have the honor in the name of the officers and troops under my orders to transmit the expression of my
respect and admiration for the great and chivalrous America.

"Major General Commanding,
"Verbist."

"July 4, 1918.
"American Expeditionary Forces,
"HAEF.

"First Army send hearty greetings to their comrades of the American
Army. We are all one in sentiment and determination to-day.

"General Horne, B.E.F."

Regardless of the distinct understanding that our troops behind
the British front were there for training and were not to be used
except in an emergency, the British made constant efforts to get
them into their lines. They had planned an attack by the Australians on the Fourth of July and requested Major General
Read, Commander of the II Corps, to permit some of the troops
of the 33d Division (Bell), which was then still in training, to
take part. As the use of Americans at this time was directly
contrary to the arrangement, naturally it did not meet with my
approval, and on my visit to the II Corps on July 2d I advised
Read that our troops should not participate. I also spoke to
Marshal Haig about it when I saw him in Paris on the 3d, and he
entirely agreed with my point of view. In telephone conversation
with Read, further and positive instructions were given that our
troops should be withdrawn. It was, therefore, somewhat of a
surprise to learn on the following day that four companies of the
33d Division had taken part in the attack.

It seems that General Read, in accordance with my instructions, told General Rawlinson, Commander of the British Fourth Army, under whom the 33d was in training, that I did not want partially trained troops to participate. However, our units had become fully committed to the operation, and Rawlinson could make no change without instructions from his Commander-in-Chief. The Chief of Staff at British G.H.Q. then consented to leave our troops out, but when he learned from Rawlinson that it would compel the British to defer the operation he informed Read that no change could be made without orders from Marshal Haig, who, he said, could not be reached.

The incident, though relatively unimportant in itself, showed clearly the disposition of the British to assume control of our units, the very thing which I had made such strong efforts and had imposed so many conditions to prevent. Its immediate effect was to cause me to make the instructions so positive that nothing of the kind could occur again. It seems needless to add that the behavior of our troops in this operation was splendid. This division afterwards displayed the same eagerness to get at the enemy in several hard-fought engagements during the trying days of the Meuse-Argonne offensive.

(Diary) Chaumont, Tuesday, July 9, 1918. Have spent last few days on reorganization of Services of Supply, consulting with Generals Atterbury, McAndrew, and Hagood, and Colonel Eltinge.

Yesterday saw General Meriwether Walker, head of Motor Transport, and Colonel A. D. Andrews, Deputy Chief of Utilities. Melville E. Stone took luncheon with us yesterday and told me that the Associated Press, of which he is the head, was for America first, and if we needed its services to call upon him. Brigadier General Perelli arrived as Chief of Italian Mission. Had calls by Frederick Palmer and Casper Whitney.

To-day discussed corps and army organization and sector occupation with McAndrew, Fox Conner, and Fiske. Have recommended shipment of 120,000 tons of steel, besides copper, iron, lead, and lumber promised the British. Inefficient loading of transports and arrival of troops without equipment causing some confusion. Bulgarians reported tired of war. Allied Commander on Balkan Front telegraphs request for American troops. Received letter from General Bliss [1] concerning admiration of French for our troops.

In the month of June the amount of cargo discharged daily at all ports had increased to an average of 20,000 tons, including coal and oil, but due to continued shortage of rail facilities the corresponding transfers to depots and to the front were still falling short. This was a condition that we had been doing everything possible to overcome, but, having sown the wind, we were now about to harvest the whirlwind.

In order to meet what was considered by the Allies an extreme emergency, we had already devoted such a tremendous effort to the shipment of infantry and machine gun units, to the exclusion of the necessary personnel to keep the supply services abreast of requirements, that we were again facing a serious situation. Not only was personnel lacking, but there was need of material for completion of construction at ports, and for warehouses and railway improvement. Cargo ships were not being provided to increase supplies to a reasonable level. The shipment of locomotives, cars, and rails was behind and the railroads were not able to meet our demands. Instead of making the supreme effort during the preceding six or eight months in compliance with insistent and repeated cable demands for all these things, the War Department had been content to stand on an entirely inadequate program and had failed to live up to that.

As to the increase in the number of cargo vessels and shipments, it was feared by the War Department General Staff that the home ports, which were already congested, would not be able to handle the increased activity that would result. Concerning the situation at French ports, Washington again had expressed

[1] "From the time when your men began to do such fine work in the vicinity of Château-Thierry, I heard in all quarters the most enthusiastic expressions of admiration for them, accompanied in many cases by statements that the speaker believed that they had saved Paris. * * * It occurred to me that it would be a good thing to quietly put on record such statements, * * * so that when the history of the war comes to be written up these things will not be forgotten. There may be a tendency a year or so from now to minimize the credit which at the moment they gave to our troops. * * * "

doubt as to whether we should be able to handle a greater amount of cargo. The whole scheme of the War Department had been upset by the military crisis long since predicted. Yet the new demands of the situation required that an even higher rate of shipments should be carried out for several months to come.

Realizing that any expression of doubt on our part about handling cargo would probably cause a slowing down at home, from which it might be impossible later to recover, and which would cause far more embarrassment to us than any delay that might exist in the dispatch of freight, I continued to urge the War Department to send over cargo as rapidly as possible, giving no hint or statement which might be used later as a reason for not sending along everything they could.

It was a condition of affairs not entirely pleasing, but on the other hand not so gloomy as it appeared. It was merely a question of courage, persistence, and coöperation. Although difficult, it did not seem at all insuperable at the time.

It became necessary to examine the conditions in our Services of Supply very carefully in an effort to correct any defects in that organization which might be slowing us up. It appeared that the Transportation Department especially needed greater freedom of action. It was bound up with several other departments grouped under the Service of Utilities, which had been interposed in the organization in the belief that it would relieve the Commanding General of the S.O.S. of some of the details of administration. Unfortunately the scheme had not worked out that way. It would not be fair to say that there was any lack of inclination on the part of the personnel, which was straining every nerve to accomplish its task, but some unnecessary interference and faulty coöperation existed here and there for which it was difficult to fix the responsibility.

It was my idea to give the separate services as much independence of action as possible and yet have them linked up under the direction of the General Staff of the Commanding General, S.O.S., in such a way as to bring the activities into full coördination. After further consideration, it was decided to abolish the Service of Utilities, leaving the Transportation Department practically an independent agency. As such it was charged, as we have seen, with the operation and maintenance of railways and canals, of inland water transport and sea connection with England and other European countries, and of terminals, including unloading of ships. Its other obligations were the procurement of railway supplies, control of telegraph and telephone lines used by railways, and maintenance of all rolling stock. Construction was left with the Department of Construction and Forestry, while exclusive charge of motor vehicles with our forces was given to the Motor Transport Corps. All these services, including the Transportation Department, were to be directly under the Commanding General, Services of Supply, for proper coördination.

About this time the Allied Commander-in-Chief of the forces on the Bulgarian front sent a request through General Bartlett, our representative there, for American troops, as indicated by the following cablegram:

"July 8, 1918.
"Commander-in-Chief Allied forces on Balkan Front desires I report that Bulgarians are tired of war. Austria-Hungary is in unstable condition and her troops on this front are not the best. Line of least resistance to decisive victory is now through Balkan ways. With additional help of one American division without artillery Bulgaria can be defeated and Germany attacked through Austria-Hungary where Jugo-Slavs would aid Allies. American division should arrive with as little delay as possible for action before snow fall. All Greeks, Serbians and Slavs in the American Army should come to Balkan Front to encourage Greeks and Serbians and to discourage Bulgaria. Declaration of war by the United States against Bulgaria would greatly increase discouragement in latter country which now considers United States her friend on final peace congress. All British troops are now leaving Struma Section having been replaced by three Greek divisions. One of every four British infantry battalions are now leaving Balkans for another front."

Of course it was out of the question to send one of our divisions to the Balkan front, and the request was not seriously considered. It is quoted only to show how widely our troops would have been dispersed if we had not taken the firm stand that the Western Front was the place for our effort.

CHAPTER XXXVI

Conference with General Foch—Propose American Sector at Château-Thierry—Foch Declares for an American Army—Possible Operations Discussed—Kerensky and Intervention in Russia—French Independence Day—Postal Service—German Attack in Marne Salient Expected—Began on Fifteenth and Was Stopped—Our 3d and 42d Divisions Do Well—Situation Favorable for Allies

(Diary) Paris, Wednesday, July 10, 1918. Have issued orders commending the 1st and 2d Divisions. Went to Bombon to-day, taking Conner, Mott, and Boyd, for conference with Foch. Afterward went to 2d Division, northeast of La Ferté-sous-Jouarre, to bestow decorations. One of the men to receive the Distinguished Service Cross swam the river to be present.[1]

MY visits to General Foch were usually by appointment. I went this time to discuss the assembly and the employment of our troops as an army. The first question considered was the withdrawal of those that were with the British. I said that it had been my intention from the beginning to have them transferred to the American sector as soon as it could be decided just where that would be. It was important that they should be taken before they became engaged in operations on the British front because it would be difficult to get them after that without causing some inconvenience to the British. I asked General Foch to take up the question with Sir Douglas Haig, but he said he would prefer that I should handle it.

Confronting the Château-Thierry salient we had the 3d (Dickman) and the 26th (Edwards) Divisions in line, the latter being a part of our I Corps, and there seemed to be an opportunity of adding other divisions then in the vicinity and forming our army

---

[1] Marine Gunner (later Lieutenant) Henry L. Hulbert, 5th Regiment, U. S. Marines, afterward killed in action while his division was aiding the French in the Champagne, Oct. 4, 1918. This gallant soldier had also received the Croix de Guerre with Palm, and the Navy Cross; and in 1899, in Samoa, received the Medal of Honor.

there. This was suggested for consideration only as a temporary arrangement, and I stated to General Foch that, "We should look beyond and decide upon a permanent front without delay." His attention was called to my tentative agreement with Pétain that the American sector should include the St. Mihiel salient, and to the fact that we had done a great amount of work in that region, such as the construction of railway sidings, yards, depots, airdromes, and a regulating station which was nearing completion.

I went on to say that with American units scattered all along the Western Front, assigned to no particular zone for future operations, we were postponing the day when the American Army would be able to render its greatest help to the Allied cause. I stressed the point that we were thus dissipating our resources for lack of a plan and were not in position to utilize the full capacity of our facilities. Instead of thinking of the future, even the immediate future, we were merely temporizing. In short, if we were to do our part to the best advantage we should at once have a definite place on the front which could be served by our own lines of communication.

I again pointed out that the British were compelled to remain in the north and that the French were covering Paris and the area west of Verdun and that it seemed logical that we should hold to our original idea as to the location of an American sector. Also, that from a strategical point of view the new line resulting from the reduction of the St. Mihiel salient would afford a most favorable base for a later offensive toward the vital part of Germany which, if successful, would deprive her of a considerable part of her resources in iron and coal. I, therefore, strongly recommended to Foch that he approve the plan that Pétain and I had agreed upon for the reduction of the St. Mihiel salient as the first operation to be undertaken by the American Army.

In reply, he said that he was glad that our views on the situation were so nearly alike. He then said: "To-day, when there are a million Americans in France, I am going to be still more American than any of you. America must have her place in the war. America has the right to have her army organized as such. The American army must become an accomplished fact. Moreover, the cause of the Allies will be better served by an American army under its own chief than if its units are dispersed. Therefore, it is necessary at the earliest possible date to constitute an American army side by side with the French and British armies, and it should be as large as possible."

At one point in the conversation he dropped the remark that it might be possible by the end of July to constitute an American army with at least thirteen divisions. When asked about the artillery for some of our units whose artillery had not arrived, he said that Pétain would arrange that. He talked a great deal that day and went on to say that in order to bring victory to the Allies it would be necessary for them to have an incontestable numerical superiority. He laid particular stress on the view that the strength of the British and French divisions should be maintained and the number of American divisions increased as rapidly as possible. Temporarily, he said, as long as the present battle lasted he was going to ask the American Army to help the French Army by the loan of the divisions that had not yet received their artillery. He wanted them to be placed in quiet sectors or else be sent to complete their training in areas behind the lines where they would be available if necessary to assist the French troops in front of them. I agreed with the idea of putting newly arrived divisions in the inactive portions of the line and we left the details of assignment to be discussed by Weygand and Conner.[1]

With my objective always in mind, I again made the suggestion that the assembly of an American army as a temporary measure might take place in the vicinity of Château-Thierry, to which he promptly replied that this accorded with his plans. He then referred to a proposed attack that might occur between July 20th and 31st, and indicated that he expected the 1st and 2d Divisions

[1] According to the understanding, five of our new divisions were to go to the Vosges to relieve for active employment in case of necessity five which were there, provided certain artillery could be furnished them by the French. This involved sending the 29th (Morton) and 37th (Farnsworth) to relieve the 32d (Haan) and 77th (Duncan), and later the 90th (Allen), 89th (Winn), and 92d (Ballou) to relieve the 5th (McMahon), 82d (Burnham), and 35th (McClure), respectively.

to take part. He also said that an offensive would probably be made by the Allies in September to reduce the Marne salient, if it had not been reduced by that time. He mentioned the possibility of an operation in the region of Amiens for the purpose of freeing the railroads through that place. The impression this conference left on my mind was that although he had spoken of ar early date General Foch did not think the formation of an American army possible before September or October.

In their mental processes Foch and Weygand were somewhat alike.[1] It had been frequently noticed that when Weygand expressed himself on any question under discussion, Foch was quite certain to be of the same opinion. During the conference and afterwards they laid stress on the view, which we all held, that every effort should be made to win the war in 1919. Foch said that the French and British armies and peoples were tired of the war and the minimum result required of the campaign of 1919 would be to free northern France and at least a part of Belgium. This would demand that the three Allies should utilize all available divisions in continuous attack.

The thought was expressed, especially by Weygand, that a certain spirit of emulation among the Allied armies would be necessary to coördination and that the attacks should be launched in the same general region, with interdependent objectives, a conception which would accord with the principle of concentration of effort. They pointed out that with the British lines extending to the vicinity of Amiens, the French would probably cover the front from there to about Reims, while the Americans, on account of the ports and railroads serving them, would be to the east. Their opinion, however, at that time was that the proper coördination of Allied attacks would forbid our going farther east than the sector Reims—Argonne. This distribution, they both thought, would correspond to the forces that would be available in 1919 and also to the peculiar necessities that governed the location of troops of the various nations.

The objective, it was stated, other than the enemy forces would

[1] See Footnote page 323, Volume I.

naturally be the railroad net to include the lateral railway from Mézières via Cambrai toward Valenciennes and the north. If this line were cut, it would throw the bulk of the enemy's traffic on those lines through Liège and would force a considerable portion of the army back against the rocky and heavily wooded Ardennes. This would cause him much embarrassment and compel him to relinquish the territory in northern France and at least a part of Belgium. Both Foch and Weygand viewed the terrain of the Arras-Argonne Front as lending itself to offensive movements, whereas the railroad systems and fortresses of Metz and Saarburg would give a certain advantage to the German defense of Lorraine; also that an attack in the region of Nancy would be more in the nature of a diversion. I took the view that operations on different portions of the Western Front if coördinated as to time would be more confusing to the enemy than if the armies were fighting side by side. Moreover, an offensive to the northeast in Lorraine would directly threaten a region that was vital to Germany. The strongest reason advanced at the time in support of their general conception of an Allied offensive was that the spirit of rivalry would be aroused among the armies operating in one great zone. It was argued that this feature would be missed if the Americans should attack in Lorraine while the British and French attacked in the north.

As to the immediate future, it was evident that some further action on the part of the enemy in the Marne salient might be expected before very long. His position there was not comfortable and, furthermore, a drive from there seemed to offer him the best chance of success under the circumstances. But the Allies were watching for indications of his intentions in order to strike a counterblow. It was certain that our troops would be called upon to participate in any Allied activity in that vicinity.

While nothing definite was then decided, the exchange of views, although rather general in character, covering the probable operations to be undertaken during the fall and in the following year, did furnish several factors to be considered in the study regarding the employment of the American Army. General Foch asked me to come and let him know if at any time I had any suggestions to make and added that he expected very soon to call the Commanders-in-Chief together for a conference.

(Diary) Paris, Friday, July 12, 1918. Visited Liggett's headquarters (I Corps) at La Ferté-sous-Jouarre yesterday. Called on 4th Division (Cameron) at Lizy-sur-Ourcq. Inspected positions of its 7th Brigade, Brigadier General B. A. Poore, commanding. Returned to Liggett's for the night.

Saw the 28th (Muir) at La Houssière to-day and went to front in sector of Brigadier General Wm. Weigel's brigade. Took lunch with Harbord at Nanteuil-sur-Marne, where his brigade of the 2d Division is resting. He told of a marine who had captured seventy-five German prisoners single-handed, at which I remarked that if he told such stories as that it was little wonder that he was popular with the Marines.[1] Visited 26th Division (Edwards) at Genevrois Farm to bestow decorations. At Paris Miss Anne Morgan and Mrs. Dyke came to talk of the important work they are doing in the devastated regions. Building program for Medical Department falling behind. Number of alien laborers increasing. Serious situation as to motor transport cabled to Washington. An intelligence agent obtained Kerensky's views on Russian situation.

As we have seen, Russia had come to be regarded as a possible recruiting ground for the German armies and various suggestions of ways and means to counteract German influence had been made. Apropos of the apprehensions of the Allies, it was not without interest to get the views of Kerensky, who, in command of the Russian armies, had at one time met with considerable temporary success in attempting to stem the tide of revolution.

One of our intelligence officers who had known Kerensky met him in Paris and was told that Trotsky desired the intervention of American troops in Russia, to be landed in Vladivostok. He said that Trotsky was personally opposed to Allied intervention and that if the Japanese participated they would meet with opposition unless they should be preceded by American troops. If Americans were accompanied by British and French, he said, both Lenin and Trotsky would inform Russian peasants

---

[1] It appears that at 5:30 A.M. on June 26th, four German officers and seventy-eight men had surrendered to one of his men and were brought in as prisoners.

that Allied forces had landed to deprive them of their property and liberty. He characterized Lenin and Trotsky as being in the pay of the Germans and said the real governor of Russia was the German Ambassador. Kerensky advised propaganda in favor of American aid and said that all Cossacks and 100,000 Czecho-Slovaks would join them because the Russians believed in the disinterested motives of Americans in Europe. He suggested, however, that if we should intervene the entry should be by way of Archangel.

The question of sending troops there was also presented from another source. When our Ambassador to Russia, Mr. David R. Francis, was in Paris in June, 1918, he strongly advo-cated our intervention and thought 100,000 men would save the nation. He urged me to recommend it, but I was opposed in principle to any undertaking that would deplete our strength in France and thought that such a diversion would only lead to complications and would not affect the final result an iota. It was my belief that our task clearly lay on the Western Front and that we would have all we could do to beat the enemy there. But, as mentioned later, Allied forces were sent both to Arch-angel and Vladivostok.

The fact is that the tendency persisted on the part of the Allied Governments to send expeditions here and there in pursuit of political aims. They were prone to lose sight of the fundamental fact that the real objective was the German Army. Once that was beaten, the political and naval power of Germany would collapse.

(Diary) Chaumont, Sunday, July 14, 1918. Had interesting talk with Mr. John Bass in Paris yesterday on Italian situation. General Rogers reported many shortages in quartermaster supplies. Motored to Provins; had dinner with General Pétain, who expects German advance soon. Arrived at Chaumont late last night.

This morning presided at exercises of *lycée* and presented prizes. The children of the school gave me a beautiful volume, "Episodes from the History of France," for my son, which we shall long treasure. Held reception this afternoon for civil and military officials.

Our mail service improving under Davis. Have recently discussed possibilities of making purchases in Japan.

The celebration in Chaumont of the French national holiday and similar occasions in which French and Americans joined, served not only to relieve the strain of this period of the war but gave us a closer and clearer understanding of the French people and their hopes and fears. On this particular day their spirits were high. "Liberté, Fraternité, Egalité" are too often only empty words that fail to inspire, but when uttered by a people in the throes of war, with everything at stake, the cry carries a special appeal to patriotic instincts that only those who have witnessed its effect can fully realize. The genuine gratitude they felt toward us was manifest in a thousand ways and the fraternal spirit on both sides was dominant. I have often thought since that if nations could but be guided under all circumstances by the sincere and sympathetic sentiments that then so strongly united in common purpose those who fought side by side, how much it would mean to the people of the world.

The prompt dispatch and delivery of mail was difficult, yet its bearing on the morale of the army and the folks at home made it very important. As far back as June, 1917, the Postmaster General had offered to aid in establishing an organization to assist in handling the mail for our forces and had sent over a superintendent and several assistants. While our numbers were still limited, the mail service went reasonably well, but as they increased the problem became most difficult and a complete reorganization was necessary. Some of the things that caused confusion were that divisions were disrupted to provide the special troops needed in the great emergency and that other units had usually been reconstituted at the last moment before embarkation and records of assignments were not kept up to date. Moreover, the public did not understand the composition of units, and as a result letters were, in a vast number of cases, misdirected and often completely lost.

In May the Postal Service was placed under control of the Adjutant General, A.E.F., and reorganized under the direction of Brigadier General R. C. Davis, the Adjutant General. An officer of extended postal experience was sent to the States with

a full understanding of conditions to arrange for giving pub-
licity to instructions regarding the address of mail and to supervise shipment from points of embarkation. A military postal
organization was established at each port of debarkation where
it was expected to receive mail, and a railway mail service was
organized along our lines of communication. A central post
office in connection with the Central Records Office of the Adjutant General's Department, A.E.F., was established; corps and
divisions were directed to organize postal departments; and it was
arranged to forward mail to units at the front along with supplies from the regulating stations.

This is a matter that might have been simplified by previous
joint consideration by the General Staff and the Post Office
Department, with regulations laid down beforehand for the
guidance of all concerned. As a result of our efforts, there was
considerable improvement, but the mail service never became
entirely satisfactory.

> (Diary) Chaumont, Wednesday, July 17, 1918. Another German
> attack broke Monday. Our 42d, part of the 28th, and the 3d Divisions
> became engaged. The latter counterattacked and captured 600 pris-
> oners. Advised Foch that the 32d and 29th Divisions are available
> at once. Five other divisions have been placed at his disposal. Situation
> yesterday more favorable for Allies. General Bullard assigned to III
> Corps and General Wright to V Corps.

The battle lines in the Marne salient, with some local excep-
tions, had stood without material change since early in June. It
was evident, as stated in my cable to Washington, quoted in a
previous chapter,[1] that the question of interior transportation and
supply was troublesome and could not be regarded by the enemy
as satisfactory. His effort of June 9th to improve his exposed
position near Soissons and to make a further advance which
would possibly open the route to the French capital had met with
little success.

No further offensives of consequence against the British in
Flanders having been immediately undertaken, interest was cen-

[1] Chapter XXXII.

tered on the Champagne front as the most probable place to expect the next blow. The American and French divisions that had been quietly concentrated in reserve west of the Marne salient for use with either the French or British, as circumstances might require, most of them carefully hidden in the forest of Villers-Cotterêts and vicinity, were now about to get into the picture.

The intelligence services of all the Allied armies had been exerting every endeavor to discover the enemy's plans, with the result that for some days it appeared almost certain that his next move would be directed toward the southeast, on the right and left of Reims. On the evening of the 14th, a French raiding party from General Gouraud's Fourth Army, then holding that part of the line east of Reims, luckily secured prisoners who confirmed this belief and who gave the exact hour fixed for the attack, which they said was to take place on the following morning.

Our 3d Division, still in line south of the Marne, faced the enemy between Jaulgonne and Château-Thierry, and the 26th held a sector between Torcy and Vaux. Infantry elements of the 28th Division were south of the Marne, serving with the two French divisions on either side of the 3d; several companies of the 42d were in the main line of resistance and the rest occupied a support position behind Gouraud's front; the 4th went into line the night of the 16th; the 1st Division was in reserve north of Meaux, and the 2d near Château-Thierry.

The German offensive was launched on the early morning of the 15th, as expected, but at the very beginning their formations were more or less broken up and their forces seriously weakened by heavy Allied counter-artillery fire. The enemy concentrated his artillery on the French first line, from which practically all troops had been withdrawn to the second and main defensive line. The first position was taken by the enemy without difficulty, but as the barrage lifted for the attack on the second line he was met again with violent artillery fire and with unexpected infantry resistance and suffered further serious losses. By evening, thanks to the strong and skillful defense by the French and our 42d Division, which became engaged and sustained relatively heavy losses, the situation on General Gouraud's army front in Champagne was very satisfactory. The conduct of the 42d on this and succeeding days brought high praise from the French Army Commander.

Farther west, the enemy succeeded in crossing the Marne, penetrating in one place as far as five miles. In a determined attempt to force a crossing near Mézy he struck our 3d Division, which was posted along the river, and the fighting became intense, some units of the 30th and 38th Infantry Regiments which were holding the front lines being attacked from both the front and flanks. The brilliant conduct of these units, however, threw the enemy's effort into confusion and by noon of the next day he had nothing to show in most of the 3d Division sector for his careful preparations, except tremendous losses. The attacks against the division had stopped by noon of July 16th.

The Germans made but slight gains to the east of Reims, while to the southwest they got across the Marne and made some progress toward Épernay. The failure of their attack in Champagne and the relatively slight gains to which they were held to the west of Reims on the first day materially heartened the Allies. Although there were some ten divisions of the enemy remaining south of the Marne, the evident conclusion, judging from the results of the following two days and the losses he had suffered, was that he would be unable to continue the offensive.

Our I Corps, on the front from Château-Thierry to Belleau Wood, was in position to be expanded and there was the possibility of adding still another corps to that front. The original plan, which contemplated the first employment of this corps in the St. Mihiel region, with headquarters at Toul, like so many plans, had been upset temporarily by the changing situation caused by the successive German victories.

The Château-Thierry region now seemed to be further indicated as the sphere of activity for Americans for the time being. With one corps already in that vicinity, the first step had been

taken. In addition to the seven American divisions in line or near
the salient, there were nineteen others in France, five in quiet
sectors to the east, five behind the British lines, five in training
areas, two in depots, and two just arrived. So that we then had
in France at that moment the equivalent of fifty-two French or
average British divisions. Omitting the five in training areas, the
two in depots, and the two just arrived, there remained for service

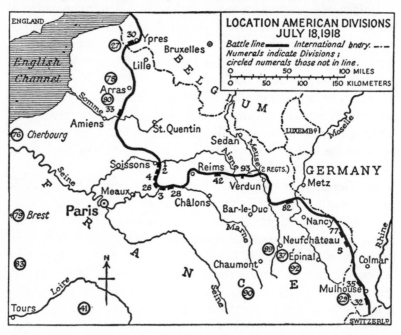

at the front a force of Americans equal in numbers to thirty-four
Allied divisions.

Thus at this time the American combat reënforcements to the
Allies more than offset the reënforcements which Germany had
been able to bring from the Eastern to the Western Front after
the collapse of Russia. Without the addition of the Americans
the Allies would have been outnumbered by nearly 400,000 men.

Now that the Allied armies were no longer in jeopardy, it
seemed opportune to push the formation of our own army near
Château-Thierry for use against the Marne salient in the counter-

offensive which I had frequently urged. The outlook for the
Allies had changed materially since the crisis of early June. The
enemy had been held in his most recent attacks and his losses
were presumably heavy. He was losing the advantage of numbers
and his superiority in every respect was passing.

CHAPTER XXXVII

American Forces Provide Superiority in Manpower—Counteroffensive Marne Salient—1st and 2d Divisions Arrowhead of Attack—Capture over 6,000 Prisoners—Germans Begin Retirement—Turning Point of War—Other American Divisions Take Part in Attack—Visit to Units Engaged—Confer with Pétain and Foch—American Sector Decided— Entertain Haig

(Diary) Provins, Saturday, July 20, 1918. The 1st and 2d Divisions, with Moroccan Division, pierced the Marne salient below Soissons on the 18th. The 4th and 26th Divisions also gained ground. Wrote M. Clemenceau protesting against French press publishing news of American activities.

Martin Egan back yesterday from visit to base ports impressed with improvement. Only 65 per cent of tonnage needed operating in our European service. Have requested 23,000 men qualified only for limited service to replace able men for combat.[1] Cabled War Department proposing four months' training program at home. Left for front after luncheon, accompanied by General Wright and Colonel Thomas H. Emerson. Spent the night at Montmirail.

To-day visited our troops in Marne sector.

WITH a preponderance of over 300,000 rifles, the Germans inflicted a crushing defeat on the British in March, followed by another in April, and in May achieved a striking victory against the French. Allied manpower rapidly dwindled to a dangerous degree and their morale almost reached the breaking point. In the supreme emergency, which, unfortunately, had not been wholly foreseen and only partially provided for, the necessity of greater effort by America had be-

[1] As showing the diversity of requirements, the following are some of the positions for which these men were needed: Forestry and general construction work, laborers, carpenters, chauffeurs, checkers for docks and depots, watchmen, kitchen helpers, cooks, mechanics, stenographers, storekeepers, telephone installers, telephone operators, typists, warehousemen, quartermaster clerks, engineer clerks, ambulance drivers, bakers, blacksmiths, canvas workers, cable splicers, draftsmen, electricians, finance men, harness workers, laundrymen, multiplex operators, photographers, punchers, sheetmetal workers, shoemakers, supervisors, tailors, toolmakers and wheelwrights.

come imperative. With the help of British shipping our troops, without which the Allied defeat would have been inevitable, had been pouring into France at a rate hitherto unbelievable.

Thanks to this unprecedented movement, Allied inferiority in March had been within three months transformed into Allied superiority of over 200,000 men. Biding their time, the Allies had waited until our arrivals should give them the preponderance.

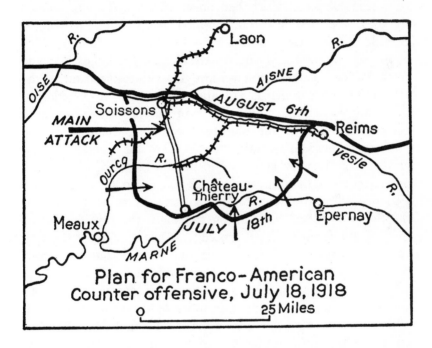

Plan for Franco-American
Counter offensive, July 18, 1918
25 Miles

When the Germans chose the front near Reims for their attack on July 15th, they played into the hands of the Allies. Plans already made provided for a counterattack against the base of the salient south of Soissons by the French Tenth Army, with our troops to pierce the line. Several French and American divisions had been held southwest of Soissons in readiness to participate. The youth and the enthusiasm of the vigorous young Americans, not yet war-weary, more than offset their lack of training and experience. With the German offensive suddenly frustrated, the moment had arrived for the counterblow that was destined to change the entire aspect of the war.

Our 1st (Summerall) and 2d (Harbord) Divisions were hastily assembled to form the American III Corps under General Bullard, but, as his corps staff had not yet been fully organized, these divisions became a part of the French XX Corps (Berdoulat). This corps, composed of these two divisions and the French 1st Moroccan Division, which had an excellent reputation, was assigned to the most important position on the left center of the French Tenth Army, commanded by General Mangin. The corps, which was four-fifths American, had the honor of being the spearhead of the thrust against this vulnerable flank of the salient, an honor which it gallantly sustained. The direction of the attack was eastward over the commanding plateau just south of Soissons and across the main road leading to Château-Thierry.

The 1st Division, recently relieved from the Cantigny sector and en route to a rest area, was north of Meaux when it received orders on the 13th to move by truck to the front. After a hurried departure, the advance troops early on the 16th reached the Forest of Retz[1] and during the night the division moved through the forest to its eastern edge. On the night of the 17th its columns marched forward over muddy and congested roads toward the front, where they arrived just in the nick of time.

The 2d Division was recuperating near Montreuil-aux-Lions when the order came on the 14th to move toward the lines south of Soissons. Starting by truck on the afternoon of the 16th, dawn on the 17th found the infantry and machine gun elements arriving at the Forest of Retz, the artillery and trains having gone before. That night the movement toward the front, through the dark forest, was made with extreme difficulty. The narrow roads had now become crowded, troops lost their direction and there was serious doubt whether they would be at their line of departure by the appointed hour of 4:35 A.M., on the 18th. With most commendable energy and initiative the officers led their commands

[1] This forest, which lay near the western face of the salient, was also known as the Forest of Villers-Cotterêts.

forward, winding in and out through the almost inextricable confusion of wheeled vehicles. One of the battalions assigned to lead in the attack, which had been on the march most of the night, was forced to move at a run for the last few hundred yards, reaching its place just as the barrage started.[1]

The 2d Division headquarters found itself on the 16th with no knowledge of the terrain and no detailed instructions for the attack. Going toward the front over the congested roads, Harbord and his Chief of Staff on the evening of the 16th found the headquarters of the French XX Corps at Retheuil, where they were given the directive for the attack, from which they issued the division orders for distribution the following day.

The country over which the XX Corps advanced consisted of a succession of wooded ravines that lay across the line of advance. Scarcely any roads led toward the front. The German main defenses along the ridges of the Soissons plateau were naturally strong. With the added obstacle of his entrenchments the enemy evidently felt himself reasonably secure. It was harvest time and the ripening grain that covered the rolling landscape gave excellent cover for the enemy's infantry and machine guns and also helped to hide our advance.

Without the usual preliminary artillery preparation, the assaulting battalions, accompanied by light tanks, plunged forward behind the barrage. The enemy was caught by surprise and the 1st and 2d Divisions, supported by the Moroccan Division in the center, quickly overran his forward positions and broke through the zone of his light artillery. Though constantly confronted by fresh enemy troops, this American-Moroccan corps took the lead and its progress was beyond expectations. By noon it had captured half of the great plateau on its front, with many prisoners, and later the forward elements reached the day's objective.

The 2d Division encountered and overcame strong opposition, especially at Vierzy. In a determined assault launched after 6 P.M., the town was captured and a line overlooking the valley of

---

[1] One unnecessary cause of delay reported was that the French officer in charge of the truck trains insisted upon counting the men carried and obtaining receipts for their transportation.

the Crise River was occupied. The 1st Division had also carried everything before it, capturing fortified farmhouses and other points where it met stiff resistance, finally taking Missy-aux-Bois and establishing its front line slightly beyond that town.

The attack of the corps was resumed on the morning of the 19th against the German lines which had been heavily reënforced with machine guns and artillery during the night. The 1st Division, leading the French division on its left, encountered fire from both the front and left flank. Tanks were sent to its as-

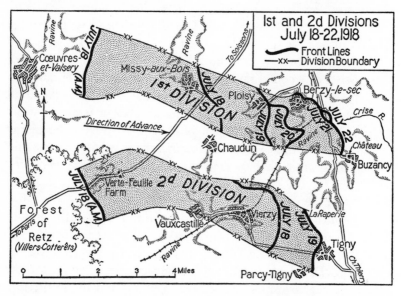

sistance and with close artillery support the division was enabled slowly to gain ground, but at considerable cost.

The 2d Division, with the reserves of the first day in the lead, forged ahead against stout opposition to the main Château-Thierry road, but was compelled to withdraw to the vicinity of La Raperie. After very severe fighting, it finally established a line just west of Tigny, with the road under the control of its guns. The division was relieved by a French division on the night of the 19th, having advanced 6½ miles, captured 3,000 prisoners and 75 guns, and sustained about 5,000 casualties.

On the 20th, the 1st Division doggedly continued its progress in spite of a determined stand by the Germans in front of Berzy-le-Sec, which the French attempted to take without success. In the afternoon Summerall directed that the town be taken by the 1st Division, but the effort failed. However, on the 21st, assisted by the skillful use of artillery and with consummate dash, in the face of intense artillery and machine gun fire, the town was captured by the 2d Brigade (Buck). Meanwhile, the right of the division and the French division which had relieved the Moroccans, had crossed the Soissons—Château-Thierry highway and reached the château of Buzancy. The line now ran parallel to the Crise, with Soissons commanded by our artillery.

The 1st Division, throughout four days of constant fighting, had advanced nearly 7 miles, taken 3,500 prisoners and 68 guns from seven different German divisions employed against it, and had suffered about 7,200 casualties.

The thrust of the XX Corps, in conjunction with the Franco-American attacks farther south, along the western face of the salient, was made with such dash and power that the enemy's position within the salient was rendered untenable. As a result he was forced into the decision of retiring from the salient, and the movement began on the 20th. We had snatched the initiative from the Germans almost in an instant. They made no more formidable attacks, but from that moment until the end of the war they were on the defensive. The magnificent conduct of our 1st and 2d Divisions and the Moroccan Division marked the turning of the tide. Pétain said it could not have been done without our divisions.

General Mangin, who commanded the French Tenth Army, said this about it in his general orders:

"Officers, noncommissioned officers and soldiers of the United States III Corps, shoulder to shoulder with your French comrades you were thrown into the counteroffensive battle which commenced on the 18th of July.

"You rushed into the fight as to a fête.

"Your magnificent courage completely routed a surprised enemy and your indomitable tenacity checked the counterattacks of his fresh divisions.

"You have shown yourselves worthy sons of your great country and you were admired by your brothers-in-arms.

"Ninety-one guns, 7,200 prisoners, immense booty, ten kilometers of country reconquered. This is your portion of the spoil of victory.

"Furthermore, you have really felt your superiority over the barbarous enemy of the whole human race against whom the children of Liberty are striving.

"To attack him is to vanquish him.

"American Comrades: I am grateful to you for the blood so generously spilled on the soil of my country.

"I am proud to have commanded you during such days and to have fought with you for the deliverance of the world.

"MANGIN."

The German Chancellor, Von Hertling, said later:

"We expected grave events in Paris for the end of July. That was on the 15th. On the 18th even the most optimistic among us understood that all was lost. The history of the world was played out in three days."

Field Marshal von Hindenburg, in "Out of My Life," says:

"From the purely military point of view it was of the greatest and most fateful importance that we had lost the initiative to the enemy and were at first not strong enough to recover it ourselves. We had been compelled to draw upon a large part of the reserves which we intended to use for the attack in Flanders. This meant the end of our hopes of dealing our long-planned decisive blow at the English army.

"In these circumstances the steady arrival of American reënforcements must be particularly valuable for the enemy. Even if these reënforcements were not yet quite up to the level of modern requirements in a purely military sense, mere numerical superiority had a far greater effect at this stage when our units had suffered so heavily.

"The effect of our failure on the country and our allies was even greater, judging by our first impressions. How many hopes, cherished during the last few months, had probably collapsed at one blow! How many calculations had been scattered to the winds!"

The following extracts from a special report by Colonel, later Brigadier General, Paul B. Malone, who commanded the 23d Infantry regiment of the 2d Division in this battle, give a vivid picture of the difficulties which the troops of the division encountered in reaching the line of deployment, and their progress thereafter:

"The road to the front was found completely blocked, the troops endeavoring to thread their way through and between vehicles of all kinds. It began raining early in the evening and the night became so dark that it was impossible to see at more than a pace distance. No opportunity of any kind could be given to the company or platoon commanders to reconnoiter the way to the front, through an intricate network of roads and trails in the forest. * * * Proceeding to the Post of Command of the French Regimental Commander I stationed noncommissioned officers to guide the troops as best they could in the proper direction. At 2:30 A.M. the Regimental Adjutant reported that all three battalions had secured ammunition and were moving along their proper routes to the front. The French troops at the front were sending in reports that the American troops to relieve them had not arrived, and throughout the night the most disquieting reports constantly arrived, indicating that our troops were lost in the woods.

"The attack was to start at 4:35 A.M. At about ten minutes to four the Sergeant Major of the First Battalion arrived at my P.C. [Post of Command] with the information that Companies 'A' and 'B' had lost their way and that he thought only a small portion of the First Battalion had reached position for the attack. A moment later I was advised that two battalions of the Marines were then passing the P.C. en route to the front, from which it was apparent that they could not possibly reach the jumping-off trenches in time. I immediately left the P.C. with my entire staff, the French regimental commander, all of his runners and all of mine. The French regimental commander turned over all of his runners to the Marines and Lieutenant Colonel Feland placed them with his troops to guide them as rapidly as possible to the front. I personally moved to the front with Companies 'A' and 'B,' picking up along the way some troops of the 9th Infantry and the 23d Infantry that had been lost in the darkness. It seemed futile to hope that any attack under such circumstances could be a success. Nevertheless, the troops were led as rapidly as possible along the road through the woods and at 4:35 A.M. our artillery barrage came down with a crash. A guide led me for a few minutes in the wrong direction but the proper direction was finally recovered and at 5:00 A.M. myself and this detachment, with my staff officers and runners, emerged from the eastern extremity of the Forêt de Retz at the proper point prescribed in the orders for the attack. The attack was already under way, the Second Battalion leading the attack had gone over the top at H hour (4:35 A.M.), but to reach its position it had been necessary to advance during the last ten minutes at a run, the men reaching the jumping-off trenches breathless and exhausted. * * *

"From the time the troops left the vicinity of Montreuil-aux-Lions (near Château-Thierry) they had received no food and practically no water; they had had no sleep and had fought continuously since the beginning of the operation. * * * No more difficult circumstances could have confronted a command than that which presented itself to this regiment on the night of July 17th-18th.

"Without reconnaissance of any kind it was compelled to move through an absolutely unknown terrain during a night which was intensely dark and rainy, to thread its way through a road blocked to a standstill with traffic of all kinds, find its jumping-off place of which nothing was previously known, form in three echelons for an attack, all three of which must move in harmony under an artillery barrage, the exact timing of which could not be secured because of the unknown incidents of the attack, and attack over a terrain which it had not previously seen, the attack changing in direction twice during its progress. The troops actually ran to their destination and met the enemy in an entrenched position with no other weapon than the rifle; yet they were completely and overwhelmingly successful."

While the 1st and 2d Divisions were waging a bitter contest for the possession of the crucial point near Soissons, our troops around the western rim of the salient also had been steadily driving ahead. The brigades of the 4th Division (Cameron) were at first assigned to French divisions. In the attack of July 18th, one brigade captured Noroy, and on the 19th advanced about two and one-half miles. The other brigade, in the attack of the 18th, assisted in the capture of Hautevesnes and Courchamps, took Chevillon and made further substantial gains. On the 19th and 20th, it made a gain of about two miles.

The I Corps (Liggett), serving with the French Sixth Army and composed of our 26th and the French 167th Divisions, took part in the movement. Attacking from the line near Belleau, the 26th Division (Edwards) captured the villages of Torcy and Belleau on July 18th and elements reached the base of the dominating Hill 193, which was in the sector of the French division.

On the 19th and 20th the French failed to take Hill 193, which commanded the Allied lines, but on the 20th the 26th Division succeeded in taking Gonetrie Farm and secured a foothold on Hill 190. On the 21st, it was found that the Germans had withdrawn during the night and the division moved forward with little or no opposition until it reached the new German line near Épieds, east of the Soissons—Château-Thierry highway. On the 22d Trugny was taken and a foothold secured in Épieds, but a strong German counterattack forced a retirement to Breteuil Wood.

Although the success of the 1st and 2d Divisions near Soissons on the first two days of the attack had started the withdrawal of the German armies, they fought desperately from position to position and their retirement was skillfully conducted throughout in an effort to save men and matériel from capture. They were faced with the problem of saving what they could from the enormous quantities of supplies and equipment which had been brought into the salient. A subsequent statement of the Germans declared that their artillery column alone would occupy a road space of 375 miles. To obtain the necessary time for the removal of stores and matériel their retreat was conducted by stages, and the successive defense lines were prepared accordingly.

In the counteroffensive beginning July 18th, the French and American troops east of Château-Thierry did not advance immediately. On the 20th, however, patrols from the 3d Division (Dickman) discovered that the Germans had withdrawn and on the 21st the division crossed the Marne in pursuit, capturing Mont St. Père and driving machine guns out of Chartèves. Jaulgonne was taken on the 22d and gains made beyond the town, but the ground could not be held. On the 23d, the division wrested Mont l'Evèque Wood from the Germans, who that night retired to the line Vincelles-Coincy, leaving machine guns to delay our advance on Le Charmel.

On the 20th, I visited the commanders of our units engaged and found all roads west of the salient greatly congested. No one who has not been an eye-witness can visualize the confusion in traffic conditions that exists immediately behind the lines during the progress of a great modern battle. It is a most difficult problem to regulate circulation over the roads and keep them from becoming seriously blocked, especially at night, when vehicles must travel without lights and frequent halts are necessary due to accidents of various sorts.

On this trip, my first call was at the headquarters of the 3d Division, where General Dickman gave me details of the fighting on July 15th, when his troops showed such remarkable coolness and heroism in repulsing the Germans who assaulted and partially surrounded some units of his division.

Going from there to the 28th Division (Muir), farther to the east, I found that several companies of its 55th Brigade, through some misinterpretation of instructions, had been assigned to French battalions and were serving in the front lines at the time of the attack on the 15th. The French gave way before the German assault, but our companies, which had not been told that the French were retiring, gallantly held their positions and as a result found themselves surrounded and only fought their way to the rear under the greatest difficulties. This was another striking illustration of the danger of having our small units serve in Allied divisions.

At the headquarters of the I Corps, I reviewed Liggett's situation and found his divisions making satisfactory progress. We went forward to the 26th Division which, with the French division comprising this corps, was attacking the enemy, who was stubbornly fighting to cover his retirement.

While traveling northward through the Forest of Villers-Cotterêts it was almost impossible to make any headway, as the road was filled with columns moving in both directions over the badly cut-up road. In the middle of the forest, at the main cross-roads, I met General Mangin, the Army Commander, trudging along on foot, followed by his automobile, which was working its way through the jam of troops, trucks, artillery, wagons, and ambulances, including some with wounded. Although we talked but a moment, it was long enough for him to speak in high praise of the brilliant dash of the American divisions under his command. Moving on toward the front, we soon found ourselves at the command post of the 1st Division, sheltered in an underground quarry west of Cœuvres-et-Valsery. The Chief of Staff, Colonel Campbell King, gave me a full account of the fighting and explained the division's position. Leaving a message of congratulations for Summerall, who was still somewhere on the battlefield, we proceeded on our journey.

Arriving later at Taillefontaine, we located General Bullard, who, much to his regret and my own, had not been able to organize his III Corps Staff in time to take command of our 1st and 2d Divisions in this attack. However, he was just as elated over their work as if he had commanded them himself. En route from there to the 2d Division, which had just been withdrawn from the line, we passed a Scottish division going toward the front to relieve our 1st. At the headquarters of the 2d, I saw General Harbord, who always wore his tin hat, and his Chief of Staff, Colonel Preston Brown. They were both in fine spirits and could hardly find words to express their enthusiasm over the achievements of the division and I was happy to congratulate them on its splendid conduct. I recall saying to Harbord that even though the 1st and 2d Divisions should never fire another shot they had made themselves and their commanders immortal.

Having received a telephone request from General Pétain to meet him that evening for dinner and a conference, I went on to Provins. On account of being held back by traffic in reaching the 1st and 2d Divisions, darkness overtook us and we were also caught in a heavy rain storm. We were delayed further by crowded roads and by time lost examining sign-boards and maps, but about 1:30 in the morning we finally reached Provins, where I spent the night with our Chief of Mission, Major Paul H. Clark.

(Diary) Paris, Sunday, July 21, 1918. Saw Pétain this morning. He said that all French commanders were enthusiastic over American troops. Held conference with him about employment of other divisions and reached an agreement which we jointly presented to Foch this afternoon. This being Belgian national holiday, I telegraphed the greetings of the A.E.F. to His Majesty, the King, commanding the

Belgian Army. Chemical Warfare Service organization officially approved. War Department cables difficulties of diverting tonnage for shipment horses and suggests expedition of motor transport instead.

With every new demonstration of the efficiency of Americans in battle, the French became louder in their praise, and it looked as though they were ready to welcome the formation of an American army as soon as the various elements could be assembled. In talking it over with Pétain, I proposed anew that we should now take positive steps to plan for a sector for the American Army near Château-Thierry, or at some other active part of the front. I also suggested that we should have a quiet front of our own where we could send exhausted divisions from the battle line for rest and recuperation and where untrained divisions could go for preliminary line experience. Moreover, it was very important that an active sector be chosen at once in order to plan definitely the necessary installations. To all of this he agreed in principle.

I told him that I expected to take command of the American First Army when it was organized, and that, while retaining entire independence regarding plans and the conduct of operations, it seemed best in the beginning to place our army on the same footing as the French armies in order to secure their full coöperation. The practical effect of this would be that the French would handle many intricate questions concerning the civil population behind the lines and would feel under obligations to provide French artillery, aviation, truck transportation and tanks, much of which we still lacked and which could be supplied and managed efficiently only by the most intimate coördination between the French and ourselves.

In the first appearance of an American army beside the Allied armies, it was clearly my place to take personal command, which I was now in position to do, as our problems of supply were soon to be under efficient direction that would largely relieve me from the necessity of constant supervision. Furthermore, it accorded with my own desire from the purely military point of view.

Regarding the rest sector, Pétain and I agreed that it could be on the southern side of the St. Mihiel salient for the present, both of us having in mind our previous plan to make this the active American front later on. With the understanding that we should limit our conversation with General Foch and not go too much into details about the future, we went to see him at Bombon and laid the proposal before him. After some discussion and the approval of Pétain, he agreed to think the matter over and let me know.

(Diary) Paris, Tuesday, July 23, 1918. Saw Dawes yesterday about Spanish decree forbidding exportation of horses. McFadden working on problem. Mott brought letter from Foch approving Toul sector for Americans. Visited our wounded in Paris hospitals; impressed by their fine spirit. Mr. Nitti, Italian Prime Minister, requests more American troops for Italy. Our divisions progressing in Marne sector against strong enemy resistance.

Met Mr. Stettinius, Assistant Secretary of War, to-day and am certain he will be very valuable in handling munitions and financial questions.

Sir Douglas Haig, General Lawrence, Colonels Bacon and Boyd took dinner with me this evening.

The horse supply question now became more serious, due to a Spanish decree, which had been issued on July 22d, forbidding the exportation of horses. It looked as though this would prevent us from obtaining the 25,000 or 35,000 that we had hoped to get. It was said, and was doubtless true, that the embargo had been laid to force our War Trade Board to permit the shipment to Spain of cotton and other raw materials and manufactured articles required by her industries. After consultation with Dawes, the task of handling this matter was delegated to Mr. George McFadden, who had an intimate knowledge of the situation. I went over the question with him and concurred in his opinion that the War Trade Board should be urged to make some trade concessions to Spain. He cabled Washington, recommending that the State, Treasury, and War Departments should agree upon the policy to be followed, and also suggesting in some detail the method of procedure.

Spain was then in the throes of economic and commercial depression, with her cotton mills at Barcelona operating only three days per week and with three-fourths of her railway service discontinued for lack of equipment and fuel. It was believed that concessions on our part would influence Spanish public opinion in favor of the Allies and make it possible for us to obtain at least the 17,000 animals we had already contracted for. Eventually an export permit for upwards of 40,000 animals was granted, but only a few were received prior to the Armistice.

On the evening of the 23d, I had the pleasure of Marshal Haig's company at dinner. It was always interesting to talk with him and as we had not met for some time we discussed recent events, especially the success of the combined French and American counteroffensive. It was recalled that before the enemy's offensive of May 27th the French had thought that he intended to make a further effort against the British, and had declined to take the view that he was likely to attack on the Aisne. The French believed, Sir Douglas said, that the strength in reserves behind the armies of Prince Rupprecht, which confronted the British, led to that conclusion. On the other hand, they seemed to overlook their own front, which was very weak in reserves, a considerable number of which had been sent to aid the British. Sir Douglas referred to the fact that several British divisions sent to the French front for rest had been used against the German attack. He said that reports indicated that all of Prince Rupprecht's army was still in front of the British, with thirty to forty divisions in reserve.

Sir Douglas was as aggressive as ever and was then planning to start another offensive in about three weeks. Under the circumstances I was expecting a definite request for the use of the five American divisions remaining in the British area. I was prepared, however, to decline, well knowing that if they should become involved in this operation it would be impossible for me to obtain them in time to organize an American army as planned. Marshal Haig seemed somewhat apprehensive as to what might be proposed at the conference we were to have with the Allied Commander-in-Chief the next day. I outlined my project for uniting our divisions as an army but did not mention the probable early recall of our units from his front.

CHAPTER XXXVIII

Conference of Commanders-in-Chief—Initiative with the Allies—Plans Approved—Preliminary Operations—St. Mihiel American Task—First Army Organization Under Way—American Troops Ordered to Russia —President's Declaration of Aims and Purposes of the United States— Harbord to Command Services of Supply—Proposal that Washington Control Supply—Letters from and to Secretary of War

(Diary) Chaumont, Wednesday, July 24, 1918. To-day attended conference of Commanders-in-Chief at General Foch's headquarters to discuss plans for offensive operations. Present: Generals Foch, Pétain, Weygand and Buat; Field Marshal Haig and General Lawrence; and Colonel Conner, Chief of Operations, Boyd and Hughes with me. Told General Foch after the conference that Washington directed sending troops to Murmansk if he approved. He offered no objections. Pétain and I confirmed plan to group American divisions under the I Corps. Went to I Corps headquarters, located in tumbledown house at Buire; also went to 26th Division. Returned to Chaumont this evening. Orders for organization of First Army issued to-day, to take effect August 10th.

THERE was a pronounced air of good feeling and confidence as we assembled for this conference. General Foch began by reading from notes giving a résumé of the general situation as it existed at the moment, with which, of course, we were all familiar. He stated that he proposed no definite plan but submitted his remarks to us as the basis of discussion. The main point was that the fifth German offensive of the year had been checked and the Allied counteroffensive beginning July 18th had transformed it into defeat. It was the general opinion that every advantage should be taken of this fact and that the Allies should continue their attacks with as much vigor as possible. Foch stated with satisfaction that we had now reached an equality in the numbers of combatants and an actual superiority in reserves. As the enemy would soon be required to relieve a considerable number of tired divisions from the active front, the Allies would rapidly gain further superiority through the constantly increasing number of Americans. All information went to show that the enemy had two armies, so to speak, he continued, one an exhausted holding army and the other a shock army, already weakened, maneuvering behind this frail front. Unquestionably we had material advantage in aviation and tanks and, to a smaller degree, in artillery, although this would be augmented by the arrival of personnel and armament of American artillery.

As to the reserve strength behind the Allies, it would soon be powerful indeed if the rate of 250,000 per month at which the Americans were pouring in could be maintained. One could sense an approaching crisis, on the enemy's side, probably not so very remote, because of the difficulty which he was having in keeping up the effective strength of his units. Beyond these advantages of material force in our favor, there was also the moral ascendancy we had gained by our recent victories and his failures. Foch also felt, as we all did, that the Allies now held the initiative and that from this time on they should abandon the defensive attitude that had been so long imposed upon them and continue the offensive without cessation. He mentioned a series of operations on the different fronts which should aim at results of immediate importance to subsequent progress. These preliminary actions would be of limited extent and would be executed as rapidly as possible with the number of troops available. He then pointed out the following offensives which it was evident would be indispensable to later operations:

The release of the Paris-Avricourt railroad in the Marne region as the minimum result of present (Franco-American) operations;

The freeing of the Paris-Amiens railroad by a concerted action of the British and French;

The release of the Paris-Avricourt railroad in the region of Commercy by the reduction of the St. Mihiel salient by the American Army. By thus reducing the front, it would bring the Allies within reach of the Briey region and permit action on a larger scale between the Meuse and Moselle.

Further offensives were foreseen having in view the recapture of the mining section to the north by definitely driving the enemy from the region of Dunkirk and Calais.

With the armies working together, operations could be continued at such brief intervals as to prevent the enemy from using his reserves to advantage and without giving him time to build up depleted units. No one could tell then just how far these efforts might take us, but possibly they would, if successful, pave the way for something more important in the late summer or autumn, which in turn would still further increase our advantage. No one suggested that the plans of the moment or those to follow might be carried so far as to terminate the war in 1918. Concerning the part each should play, Foch then asked expressions of opinion of the respective Commanders-in-Chief as to how these or any other operations that we might propose should be conducted.

Marshal Haig gave his views and plans, which agreed with the general outline suggested, as did General Pétain, who wanted further to consider the possibilities. As far as these preliminary operations applied to the Americans, they were simply a restatement of the plans we had been leading up to ever since our entry into the war. I, therefore, advised him that details of organization and supply were receiving every consideration in preparation of the American Army to do its part.

In this connection, I brought up again the question of obtaining artillery, and the understanding that we should have the coöperation of the French in this respect was confirmed. The progress by the United States in the manufacture of guns was discussed and the hope was expressed that it might reach a point which would enable the French to turn their attention to making shells, and this brought out the critical situation regarding steel. I had been urging haste in our home production of artillery and remarked that we had all learned from experience that programs for manufacture of munitions had rarely been fully met.

The pressing need of cross-country transportation was then considered and it was agreed to urge upon our respective Governments the utmost celerity in this regard. General Foch suggested the importance of tanks, but we were without tanks and there was little prospect that the plan of joint production by the British and ourselves, previously undertaken, would provide them in any quantity for use in the immediate future. The proposal that we should develop our own tanks at home had come to naught. Marshal Haig reported that the British had three brigades with 700 or 800 tanks in all, but General Pétain said the French were short. Finally, however, the hope was held out by both of them that they would be able to let us have some tanks by the time we should need them.

While this conference was primarily held for the exchange of views, it decidedly confirmed the principle of coöperation and emphasized the wisdom of having a coördinating head for the Allied forces. The conclusions regarding operations, though more or less tentative, became the basis of action for the future. The general plans definitely contemplated that the American forces would constitute an independent army.

Frequent references have already been made to the difficulties and delays encountered in forming a distinctive American army, which I had contended was essential to Allied success. Not only was it demanded by the existing situation but by all the circumstances of our participation in the war. Not the least important consideration was that until such an army should be actually formed and successfully carry out an operation our position before our people at home would not be enviable.

Although General Pétain and I, in accordance with our first conversation, more than a year before, had definitely planned the transfer of the line north of Toul to American control, the demands for our divisions during April and May had been so great that this could not be done. Later, when it was agreed that the Americans should take over the sector as soon as four divisions could be united there, the German assault on the Chemin des Dames had disrupted the arrangement and our most effective divisions had to be sent to the Château-Thierry front. Thus each successive German offensive had brought a crisis followed by pressure for modifications of plans, and each had operated to delay the time when an American army could be assembled.

It was imperative that we should meet these conditons as they arose, although sending our regiments, brigades or divisions to aid the Allied armies caused a wide dispersion of our units that made it difficult to assemble them now that the time had come to take that step. The worst feature was that the special shipments of infantry and machine gunners made the organization of corps and armies impossible without obtaining from the French or British, at least temporarily, the units corresponding to those we had omitted.

The situation, however, demanded a very definite understanding. The Allies were resuming offensive operations, the enemy seemed to be entirely committed to the defensive and we now had more than 1,200,000 American soldiers on French soil. The important part our divisions had played gave me every reason to press my determination to have our own army. It was a matter of no special importance for the moment where our combat units should be assembled, whether near Château-Thierry or elsewhere, as any front other than that in the northeast would probably not be permanent.

While at General Foch's headquarters I arranged with General Pétain for the expansion of the I Corps, then operating in the Marne sector, by which four American divisions were to be placed in the line with two in reserve. It was tentatively understood between us that the III Corps should be placed beside the I Corps to form an army on that front. At that time it was also planned to form a second army in the St. Mihiel sector as soon as practicable. My formal order creating the First Army was issued on July 24th, to take effect on August 10th, with headquarters at La Ferté-sous-Jouarre.

The Supreme War Council was prone to listen to suggestions for the use of Allied troops at various places other than the Western Front. One of these, on which the British seemed to be especially insistent, was to send troops to help the so-called White Army in Russia in order to keep open the communications through Murmansk. I was opposed to the idea, as it would simply mean scattering our resources, all of which were needed to build up the A.E.F. But the President was prevailed upon to help and I was directed to send a regiment provided General Foch had no objections. As apparently he had already considered the question, he gave his approval. The 339th Infantry, Lieutenant Colonel George E. Stewart commanding, together with one battalion of engineers, one field hospital company and one ambulance company, were designated for this service.

Now that we were to assume the offensive and our divisions were likely to be sent into battle at once upon arrival, it was more important than ever that those yet to come should receive careful training prior to reaching France. A few days before I had again drawn attention to the defects we had found and emphasized as strongly as possible the urgency of greater supervision of training at home. As a guide, I sent to Washington an intensive four months' program based upon our experience and also recommended that officers of all grades be subjected to the most careful general staff inspections during their period of preparation.

A recent conference with Mr. Shearman and Colonel Bruce Palmer revealed facts of the utmost significance and I again urged an increase in shipping. For the time being, sufficient deadweight cargo tonnage had been placed in our service to give us, with a 60-day turn-around, a little more than 600,000 tons of freight per month, but this was not nearly enough to keep our supplies going. According to our information only one-quarter of the 126,000 tons so far built at home for the Shipping Board, not all suitable for transatlantic service, and less than half of the 500,000 tons of Dutch and 200,000 tons of Swedish and other shipping taken over, had been allotted to the Army. Restating it as my judgment that the successful outcome of the war was dependent upon the fulfillment of the 80-division program, which could not be transported and supplied with the tonnage allotted, I urged that no less than 500,000 tons then employed on commercial routes be withdrawn for use in supplying our forces.

Realizing that the hesitancy of the War Department to increase cargo tonnage was partly on account of the fear of swamping both their ports and our own, I again stated emphatically that the increased tonnage could and would be handled at our end of the line with reasonable rapidity. While conditions were improving at the ports, I had already planned certain changes, which will appear later.

> (Diary) Chaumont, Sunday, July 28, 1918. Saw Foulois on Thursday about aviation for the First Army. Representative Isaac Siegel called to urge independent welfare organization for Jewish soldiers.
>
> Conferred with Mr. Stettinius on Friday. Tardieu wants priority on Liberty motors; Stettinius will handle. Cable received giving President's statement to Allies. Discussed First Army organization with Logan and Moseley. Need for trucks, motor cars, ambulances, motorcycles and horses urgently reiterated by cable. Harbord spent the night with us. Appointed him Chief of S.O.S., much to his regret. General Kernan designated from Washington as representative at conference with Germans at Berne on handling prisoners.
>
> General Trenchard, British Air Chief, and Lord Weir, British Air Minister, came yesterday to consider aiding us in aviation.
>
> M. Claveille and Atterbury came this morning to talk over railway matters; discharge of cargo and evacuation improving; French coöperating better. Congratulations received from the Secretary of War on work being done by our army; also from Chief of Staff, Japanese Army.[1] Germans continue giving way in Marne salient. Am leaving to-night on inspection trip S.O.S.

The statement of "Aims and Purposes of the United States" which the President handed the Ambassadors of Great Britain,

---

[1] "July 28, 1918. Accept our hearty and grateful congratulations on the brilliant work done by your Army. The whole country is thrilled with pride in our soldiers. We follow eagerly every move they make. Their courage and success make us all prouder than ever that we are Americans and are represented by such heroic soldiers. They are worthy of their country and the cause.

"BAKER."

"July 28, 1918. Please accept my sincere congratulations on the recent brilliant success won by your gallant army on the French battlefield. I am looking forward with absolute confidence to the continued favorable development of the situation, and I feel fortified in my conviction of the final triumph of our common cause.

"GENERAL BARON Y UYEHARA."

France and Italy at this time, and which was cabled to me, set forth at some length in diplomatic language the position of the United States in the war. It began by saying: "The whole heart of the people of the United States is in the winning of this war. The controlling purpose of the Government of the United States is to do anything that is necessary and effective to win it." The statement then said in substance that the war could be won only by common council and intimate concert of action. It further said that our Government had adopted a plan for fighting on the Western Front using all its resources; that it had put into the plan the entire energy of the Nation and that it was then considering the possibility of increasing its effort; but, that if the larger program were at all feasible, the industrial processes and the shipping facilities of the associated powers would be taxed to the utmost.

The reasons given for not diverting any part of the American military forces from the Western Front to other points or objectives were that the instrumentalities to handle our army in France had been created at great expense and they did not exist elsewhere. Moreover, while the army had been sent a great distance, it was much farther to any other field of action. The President said: "The United States Government therefore very respectfully requests its associates to accept its deliberate judgment that it should not dissipate its forces by attempting important operations elsewhere." In the statement the Italian front was considered a part of the line of the Western Front and sending troops there would be, of course, subject to the decision of the Supreme Command.

As to Russia, it was made clear that intervention was out of the question, as it would serve no useful purpose nor be of advantage in the prosecution of the war. Russia should not be used in an attempt to make an attack on Germany from the east. The only justifiable reason for entering Russia, the President said, would be to aid the Czecho-Slovakians to consolidate their forces and to steady any efforts at self-government or self-defense in which the Russians might accept assistance. It was set forth that the Government of the United States by restricting its own action did not wish to be understood as seeking, even by implication, to influence the action or define the policies of its associates.

The statement referred to the willingness of our Government to coöperate with the Allies and send a small force to Vladivostok, where the necessity seemed immediate, and with the approval of the Supreme Command to send another to Murmansk to guard stores and make it safe for Russian forces to come together in the north. It was also stated that solemn assurance by the governments united for action should be given the people of Russia that no interference with her political sovereignty or intervention in internal affairs or impairment of territorial integrity was intended.

The statement gave no promise that the 80-division project had been adopted; in fact, it implied some misgiving as to whether such an extensive plan could be carried out by our Government. It did, however, as a result of its frankness, no doubt put an end to the importunities of the Allies to send American troops here and there and confirmed the attitude that I had taken that the war must be won on the Western Front.

In view of the decision for the assembly of corps and divisions to form our army, it became urgent that the plans for its organization be hastened with all possible speed. The outlines had been determined and members of the First Army staff were at work on the details, yet several questions pertaining to final selection of troops and their assignments had to be decided and directions given to the staff.

In view of our increased program, consideration had to be given to improvement in the general supply system. Although the recent reorganization had helped, it had been my purpose for some time to make changes in personnel in the S.O.S., particularly in the position of commander, which demanded great administrative ability. After much thought, the choice fell on General Harbord. His knowledge of organization, his personality, his energy and his loyalty made him the outstanding selection.

Reluctance to lose his services in command of troops, where he had shown himself to be a brilliant leader, caused me to delay until his division could be relieved from the active front.

I had recently received a letter from the Secretary of War which confirmed reports reaching my headquarters from other sources, in which he stated that it had been proposed that General George W. Goethals be sent over to take charge of the Services of Supply. The idea was that he would have coördinate authority with me and be in control of supplies from the source at home, thence across the Atlantic and up to the Zone of the Armies, and be directly under orders from Washington. The theory was that this arrangement would enable me to devote my time exclusively to military operations. The Secretary wished to know what I thought of the suggestion.

I much appreciated the Secretary's desire to relieve me of every burden that might interfere with the direction of operations, but there appeared to be an exaggerated view concerning the personal attention required in handling the details of administration. As a principle of military organization, the suggestion did not meet with my approval. The command had been organized carefully with just this situation in view and the supply system was fulfilling its functions as an essential part of the organic military structure so far as the conditions of delayed material and of limited and inexperienced personnel would permit. I was in control through my General Staff, which in turn was handling directly a multitude of questions immediately vital to military success. The system, to be successful, could have no divided authority or responsibility.

The man who directed the armies was the one to control their supply through a military commander responsible to him alone. This military principle, under the peculiar circumstances, could not be violated without inviting failure. It was applied in the British armies and as far as possible in the French. In each of the Allied armies the general in charge of the Services of Supply and the Lines of Communication of their forces was subordinate to the Commander-in-Chief. In our case it only remained to invest the commanding general of the supply system with necessary authority to enable him to take the initiative under my general direction.

One example borrowed from my experience in October will illustrate the soundness of the principle. During the battle of the Meuse-Argonne our situation at the front was such that the S.O.S. had to be literally stripped of every available man and all means of transportation—animals, trucks, and railroad rolling stock—that could possibly be spared. Assistance was given cheerfully, but it was done in compliance with my orders. One can imagine the chances of failure if it had been necessary to request these things from an official responsible not to me but to the War Department at Washington. The officer or group of officers who proposed such a scheme to the Secretary could not have had the success of the High Command in France very deeply at heart or else they lacked understanding of the basic principles of organization.

A reply to the Secretary of War regarding his suggestion concerning Goethals was sent at once by cable, in which I urged him not to permit any violation of the foregoing principles, and asked him to await my letter, which he advised he would do. The real answer, however, was the assignment of Harbord to command the Services of Supply. No further action was taken with reference to the proposed assignment of Goethals. I should have been glad to have him under other conditions.

The following letter from the Secretary containing his reference to the command of the supply system is given in full, especially because of his discussion of other important matters under consideration at the time, and because it shows in detail the personal attention the Secretary himself gave to such questions:

"July 6, 1918.

"My Dear General Pershing:

"I have your letter of June 18,[1] which reached me promptly. I have been studying with more than ordinary care and interest the dispatches of the past week or two with reference to the enlargement of our

[1] Chapter XXXII.

military effort and program. When your cablegram suggesting a 60-division [1] program came I immediately set about the necessary inquiries to discover just how far it fell within the range of industrial possibility. When the 100-division program came it occurred to me that we ought to study the situation with the view of determining the maximum amount we can do. I have the feeling that this war has gone on long enough and if any exertion on our part or any sacrifice can speed its successful termination even by a single day, we should make it. We are therefore now having studies made to show the things necessary to be done for three possible programs, one involving 60, one 80, and the other 100 divisions by the first of July, 1919. As soon as these programs are worked out we will, in consultation with the War Industries Board, determine how far manufacturing facilities already in existence or possible to be created can supply the necessary material, and the assistance we shall have to have in the way of heavy artillery and transportation from the British and French. It will then be possible to take up with those Governments a frank exhibition of the possibilities and to arrange for concerted action among us which will lead to the increase in our effort which you and General Foch recommend. In the meantime, I have asked the British Government to continue the troop ships which they have had in our service during June through July and August, and have told them frankly that we are considering an enlargement of our program which may require for a time at least the uninterrupted service of all the ships which we have been using. If we are able in July and August to match the performance of June, it will mean another half-million men in France, as the June embarkation figures from this country show slightly more than 279,000 men. Our own ships carried during that month something more than 100,000, which is, of course, doing better than our part as we originally calculated it. I think it highly important that neither General Foch nor the British and French Governments should assume our ability to carry out an enlarged program until we ourselves have studied it. There is no disposition on the part of the United States to shrink from any sacrifice or any effort, and yet experience has taught us that great as our capacity is in industry it takes time to build new factories, get the necessary machine tools, and bring together the raw materials for any large increase in industrial output, and I am especially concerned that there should be no disappointment on the part of our Allies. I would very much rather they expect less and receive more, than to expect more and be disappointed in the result. One of the happy effects of the recent accelerated shipment

[1] Evidently this refers to the 66-division program.

of troops has been that we have out-stripped our promises and, if I judge correctly the effect of this in Europe, it has been most agreeable and heartening.

"The Operations Committee of the General Staff is pressing forward the necessary studies. They involve, of course, questions of clothing, small arms, ammunition, transportation, and training. On the latter subject I am beginning to be fairly free from doubts; the troops which we have recently sent you have admittedly been of an uneven quality, chiefly because we have made up deficiencies in divisions about to sail by taking men from other divisions, with consequent disorganization of those divisions from which men were repeatedly taken, and when we got to a place where we could no longer carry out this process, fairly raw men had to be used in order to keep divisions from sailing short. The plan inaugurated by General March of having replacement divisions in this country from which deficiencies could be supplied without robbing other divisions and disorganizing them, seems to me to solve the problem, and the divisions which come to you in August and September will, I am sure, show highly beneficial results from this policy. In the meantime, we have discovered two things about training in this country which apparently nobody knew or thought of before we went into the war; first, that while it may take nine months or a year to train raw recruits into soldiers in peace time, when there is no inspiration from an existing struggle, it takes no such length of time now when the great dramatic battles are being fought and men are eager to qualify themselves to participate in them. We are certainly able to get more training into a man now in three months than would be possible in nine months of peace-time training. And, second, we have learned that to keep men too long in training camps in this country makes them go stale and probably does as much harm by the spirit of impatience and restlessness aroused as it does good by the longer drilling. The men in our training camps are champing at the bit, and this applies not only to the officers, who naturally want their professional opportunity, but to the men as well. Indeed, one of the difficulties in America is to make people content with the lot which keeps them here for any length of time, so impatient are we all, military men and civilians alike, to get to France where the real work is being done. As a consequence of these discoveries, I feel that we will be perfectly safe if we have a million men in training in the United States at all times. That will enable us to feed them out to you at the rate of 250,000 a month and bring that number in by draft at the other end, which will always give us an adequate supply of men who have had as much training as they can profitably secure here in the

United States. The finishing touches in any event will have to be given in France, and I think you will find that men who have had four months' training here are pretty nearly ready for use in association with your veteran and experienced troops, and that no prolonged period of European training, for infantry at least, will be found necessary. This makes the problem very simple from the point of view of the draft and the training camps. A number of the camps originally established by us have now been developed for specialized technical uses, but we still have a large number, and I think an adequate number, of camps which can be enlarged without great expense, and there seems little likelihood of our being obliged to resort to the billeting system, although of course we should not hesitate to do it if the need arose.

"All accounts which we receive in this country of the conduct of our men are most stimulating and encouraging. Apparently the common opinion is that we have rendered valuable, if not indispensable, service already, in a purely military way, in the great battles. I saw a letter a day or two ago from Mr. Cravath to Mr. Leffingwell, in which he gave the opinion of British and French men of affairs on the subject of the American troops, and it was enthusiastic. I was a little afraid that too enthusiastic comment might create a feeling of resentment on the part of our allies. Their men, of course, have stood these attacks for a long time, and it would only be human if they resented the newcomers getting too much attention at the expense of organizations which are battle-scarred and have had their valor tested in great conflicts; and I have a little feared, too, that if our people here at home were fed too many stories of success they might get the notion that this great task is going to be easy for Americans and be ill-prepared for any reverse, no matter how slight, which might come. For that reason I have exercised a good deal of self-restraint in my own discussion with the newspapermen and in such public addresses as I have made, seeking always to couple up the British and the French with our American soldiers and to make the whole war a matter of common effort, rather than of our own national effort. This has been especially easy because the spirit of America is now very high. The country is thoroughly unified and is waiting only to be shown how it can make further effective sacrifices and efforts. It occurs to me in this connection that it might be wise for you in your communiqués, from time to time, to refer to slight repulses suffered by our men; but of course I do not want our men to be repulsed merely to balance the news.

"On the 1st of July I wrote the President that 1,019,000 men had embarked from the United States for France. There had been so much speculation about numbers that it seemed necessary to be frank and tell the facts. The American people are accustomed to demanding the facts and there was some impatience manifested with the Department for its continued policy of silence on this subject. I realized when I made the statement that in all likelihood I should have to discontinue further reference to numbers, at least further specific references. The Germans, French, and British of course make no such announcements, and our allies will not like to have us adopting a different course. There are doubtless good military reasons for not being very generous with information of this kind, which finds its way to the enemy and enables them to make more certain calculations. Still, if the rate of shipments which we have maintained for the last two or three months can be kept up for another six months, I am not very sure that exact news carried to Germany of the arrival of Americans in France might not be helpful to us, rather than harmful. The German Government cannot fail to be impressed by this steady stream of fresh soldiers to the Western front.

"The President and I have had several conferences about your situation in France, both of us desiring in every possible way to relieve you of unnecessary burdens, but of course to leave you with all the authority necessary to secure the best results from your forces and to supply all the support and assistance we possibly can. As the American troops in France become more and more numerous and the battle initiative on some parts of the front passes to you, the purely military part of your task will necessarily take more and more of your time, and both the President and I want to feel that the planning and executing of military undertakings has your personal consideration and that your mind is free for that as far as possible. The American people think of you as their 'fighting General,' and I want them to have that idea more and more brought home to them. For these reasons, it seems to me that if some plan could be devised by which you would be free from any necessity of giving attention to services of supply it would help, and one plan in that direction which suggested itself was to send General Goethals over to take charge of the services of supply, establishing a direct relationship between him and Washington and allowing you to rely upon him just as you would rely upon the supply departments of the War Department if your military operations were being conducted in America, instead of in France. Such a plan would place General Goethals rather in a coördinate than a subordinate relationship to you, but of course it would transfer all of the supply responsibilities from you to him and you could then forget about docks, railroads, storage houses, and all the other vast industrial undertakings to which up to now you have given a good deal of your time and, as you know, we all think with superb success. I would be very glad to know what you think about this suggestion. I realize that France is very far from the United States and that our reliance upon cables makes a very difficult means of communication, so that you may prefer to have the supply system as one of your responsibilities. I would be grateful if you would think the problem over and tell me quite frankly just what you think on the subject. The President and I will consider your reply together, and you may rely upon our being guided only by confidence in your judgment and the deep desire to aid you.

"One other aspect of your burdens the President feels can be somewhat lightened by a larger use of General Bliss as diplomatic intermediary. The President is adopting as a definite rule of action an insistence upon Inter-Allied military questions being referred to the Permanent Military Representatives. Our difficulty here has been that the British representative would present something for consideration without the knowledge of the French, or the French without the knowledge of the British, and when we took the matter up for decision we would sometimes find that the other nation felt aggrieved at not being consulted. As each of the Allied Nations is represented at Versailles, the President is now uniformly saying with regard to all Inter-Allied military questions, that their presentation to him should come through the Permanent Military Representatives who, in a way, are a kind of staff for General Foch and undoubtedly maintain such close relations with him as to make any proposition which they consider one upon which his views are ascertained.[1] As the President deals in matters of military diplomacy with General Bliss, it would seem that he could with propriety relieve you of some part of the conferences and consultations which in the early days you were obliged to have with the British War Office and the French War Office, thus simplifying the presentation of Inter-Allied questions to the President.

"Mr. Stettinius will leave very shortly for Europe; I enclose you copy of a letter which I have given him, outlining the inquiries which I desire to have him make. You will find him a very considerate man in the matter of demands upon your time, as he is accustomed to

[1] The Military Representatives were advisers to the Supreme War Council and their recommendations were presented to the Council in the form of joint (unanimous) notes which took effect only upon approval by the Council. In case the recommendation affected the American Government or Army, the approval of President Wilson was also required. General Bliss was the intermediary between the Council and the President. The Military Representatives had no relation to the Supreme Commander, Marshal Foch.

dealing with busy men and not prolonging conferences beyond their useful limit.

"It seems not unlikely at present that I shall myself come over to Europe in connection with our enlarged military program. If we find that our ability to do the thing depends upon French and British coöperation it will be a good deal simpler to put the whole question up to the British and French Cabinets and get definite agreements of coöperation and concerted action. Cablegrams are of course inconclusive and uncertain, and I constantly find that even letters fail to carry just the spirit in which they are dictated. When I write you, of course I know that our personal relations and knowledge of each other are too cordial and entire to allow any sort of misunderstanding, but I haven't the same acquaintance with the British and French Cabinet officers, and with them the presumptions do not obtain which are always implied in our correspondence. I confess I am somewhat moved to this idea of the necessity for my going by my desire to go; it is a tremendous inspiration to see our forces and to look at the work which you and they have done.

"Cordially yours,

"NEWTON D. BAKER
"Secretary of War."

In reply, the following letter was sent the Secretary by return messenger:

"JULY 28, 1918.

"MY DEAR MR. SECRETARY:

"I have your letter of July 6th and have gone over it very carefully.

"I realize that a very large undertaking has been proposed in the 80 to 100 division program, and that to carry it out is going to require very great sacrifices on our part. But, as you say, the war has gone on long enough and should be brought to a close as early as it is possible for us to do it.

"The main reason for an extreme effort on our part next year is the stimulating effect that our immediate entry into the war in a large way will have upon our allies. If we should not demonstrate our wish thus to bring the war to a speedy end our allies might not hold on over another year, and we shall need every ounce of fight they have left in them to win, not that we have not the men and the resources at home, but that if left to carry on the war alone, even on French soil, we would soon come to the limit of our ability to bring them over and supply them.

"I realize that we shall be put to it to furnish all the equipment, the aviation, the artillery, the ammunition, the tanks, and especially the horses, but if we can win next year it will be worth the supreme effort necessary to provide all these things. I do not, of course, overlook the shipping, nor the very strenuous work necessary at this end to handle the immense quantity of freight that will be required. Our port facilities must be increased, our railroads must be improved, and we must have a large increase in cars and locomotives. These things must come along rapidly from now on. We are preparing estimates for what we shall need and will forward them by cable as soon as finished.

"Just now we are passing through a very critical time. When the shipment of infantry and machine guns was increased during May, June and July, of course we had to reduce, or rather postpone, the corresponding troops for our service of the rear, with the result that we now find ourselves shorthanded and unable to handle as quickly as we should like the increase of supplies incident to the great expansion of our combatant forces.

"To add to the difficulties there has been a shortage of replacements in men, as we have had to throw all available troops into the lines to stop the German advance. So that we have not even had any troops to spare for work to help out the rear, making it appear that we are unnecessarily falling behind in unloading ships. I have cabled a request for service of the rear troops to be sent at once and hope they will not be delayed. We have a lot to do to catch up and get our ports and lines of communication in shape to meet the heavy demands that are to be made upon them.

"On June 23d, when Mr. Clemenceau was at my headquarters for the conference, I had an opportunity to speak about the use of our troops. I told him that they were being wasted and that instead of the Allies being always on the defensive, an American Army should be formed at once to strike an offensive blow and turn the tide of the war.[1] He was very much impressed at such boldness, as he had heard only of our men going into French divisions as platoons or at most as regiments. Soon after that Pétain was called to Paris and I have heard was told my views. Anyway Pétain soon began to take another view. * * *

"Our troops have done well for new troops and the part they have taken has encouraged our allies, especially the French, to go in and help put over a counteroffensive. This offensive, between Soissons and

[1] In conversation with M. Clemenceau it was further suggested that we could put in at least six fresh divisions, and possibly eight, for a counteroffensive south of Soissons or Reims, and stress was laid on the fact that we were still on the defensive and that in my opinion opportunities were being lost by not using our troops for a counteroffensive, which I urged upon him as well as upon Foch and Pétain.

Château-Thierry, was planned some time ago, to be undertaken especially in the event of the Germans attempting to push their line south of the Marne; or to the east between the Marne and Reims. I had conferred with General Pétain and had arranged to put the 1st, 2d, and 26th Divisions in the attack north of the Marne, supported by the 4th, while the 3d and 28th were to be used south of the Marne. As it turned out, all these troops were engaged with results you already know. The participation by our troops made this offensive possible and in fact the brunt of it fell to them. Our divisions in this advance completely outstepped the French and had to slow down their speed occasionally for them to catch up.

"Two American corps are now organized and on the active front. These are to be organized into the Field Army which will take its place in line under my immediate command on August 10th. We shall occupy a sector north of the Marne and probably replace the 6th French Army. At the same time we shall take over a permanent sector north of Toul and Nancy, where I shall organize a second army at an early date. After that we shall soon have troops enough for a third army. So that before long I shall have to relinquish command of the Field Army and command the group.

"I have had to insist very strongly, in the face of determined opposition, to get our troops out of leading strings. You know the French and British have always advanced the idea that we should not form divisions until our men had three or four months with them. We have found, however, that only a short time was necessary to learn all they know, as it is confined to trench warfare almost entirely, and I have insisted on open warfare training. To get this training, it has been necessary to unite our men under our own commanders, which is now being done rapidly.

"The additional fact that training with these worn-out French and British troops, if continued, is detrimental, is another reason for haste in forming our own units and conducting our own training. The morale of the Allies is low and association with them has had a bad effect upon our men. To counteract the talk our men have heard, we have had to say to our troops, through their officers, that we had come over to brace up the Allies and help them win and that they must pay no attention to loose remarks along that line by their Allied comrades.

"The fact is that our officers and men are far and away superior to the tired Europeans. High officers of the Allies have often dropped derogatory remarks about our poorly trained staff and high commanders, which our men have stood as long as they can. Even Mr.

Tardieu said some of these things to me a few days ago. I replied, in rather forcible language, that we had now been patronized as long as we would stand for it, and I wished to hear no more of that sort of nonsense. Orders have now been given by the French that all of our troops in sectors with the French would be placed under our own officers and that American division commanders would be given command of their own sectors. This has come about since my insistence forced the French to agree to the formation of an American Field Army.

"At a conference called by General Foch last Wednesday, the 24th instant, plans for assuming the offensive this year were discussed, as well as tentative plans for 1919. This is the first time the American Army has been recognized as a participant, as such, alongside the Allies. I shall give you from time to time an outline of what our plans are, but hope you will soon be here so that I may discuss them with you.

"I entirely agree with what you say regarding General Bliss as a diplomatic intermediary. However, very little of my time has been taken up with that sort of thing, except as it concerned questions of troop shipments and their use with British and French. As you know, I have the highest regard for General Bliss and our relations have been the most pleasant. I think he is admirably fitted to represent the President in many of these perplexing diplomatic questions that come up. He has excellent judgment, and is very highly regarded by the Allied official world.

"Mr. Stettinius has arrived and we have had several conferences. I am very much delighted to have him here. His presence is going to relieve me entirely of all those difficult questions pertaining to the allocation of materials, and the determination of manufacturing programs and the like. His action will be able to prevent the continuous flow of cablegrams from the Allies to our War Department on all these subjects.

"On the subject of General Goethals, I have about covered it in my cablegram of to-day. I thank you very much for referring this matter to me. Mr. Secretary, our organization here is working well. It is founded upon sound principles. May I not emphasize again the principle of unity of command and responsibility. It has always been my understanding that you believed that full power should be given to the man on the spot and responsible for results. I would say this regardless of the person in command. Our organization here is so bound up with operations, and training, and supply, and transportation of troops, that it would be impossible to make it function if the control of our service of the rear were placed in Washington. Please let us not make the mistake of handicapping our army here by attempting to control these things from Washington, or by introducing any coördinate authority. All matters pertaining to these forces, after their arrival in France, should be under the General Staff here where they are being and can be handled satisfactorily.

"Mr. Secretary, I have been more or less puzzled about this question of sending over General Goethals. I thought he was in charge of transportation over there and that he was considered necessary in that position. So, it is difficult to see just why he should have been proposed for this place. I do not wish to appear unappreciative of any suggestion from you because I know that it is your desire to do the best possible to help, and have satisfied myself by a knowledge of this fact. I do think, however, that General Harbord can handle it as well as, or better than, any one I know; besides, I have every confidence in General Harbord and know that he is going to pull in the team. I should have put Harbord in some time ago but his division was in the line. Now it goes to a quiet sector and his services can be spared.

"May I say a word about our training. Our successes here should not be hastily accepted as the basis for conclusions on the possibilities of building up efficient units by intensive training for short periods. Four months should be the minimum for drafts that are to enter as replacements in among old soldiers in organized units. But, it requires a much longer time than that to build units from the ground up. Eight or nine months, or even a year, would be better, so that if we could get all of next year's army in the ranks by November we should be much better prepared in the Spring for the immense task we are preparing for.

"May I again express my warm appreciation of your confidence, and say also how gratifying it is to me to enjoy the personal relations that exist between us.

"Will you please convey to the President my best compliments and the Army's faith in his leadership.

"With very warm regards and sincere good wishes, I am
"Very faithfully,
"JOHN J. PERSHING."

CHAPTER XXXIX

Inspect Services of Supply with Harbord—At Headquarters, Tours—Confer with Supply Chiefs—Visit Wounded—Bordeaux Works Immense—La Rochelle—Nantes and St. Nazaire Activities—Brest Well Organized—Other Installations—S.O.S. Monument to American Initiative

(Diary) Paris, Monday, August 5, 1918. Returned yesterday from tour of principal installations and activities of Services of Supply with Harbord, McAndrew and other staff officers, including Colonels Wilgus, Andrews and Boyd, Major Bowditch, and Lieutenant Adamson. General Foch called informally after my return.

Held conference to-day on transfer of greater authority to Commanding General, S.O.S. Saw Felton, Atterbury, and Langfitt on needs of port improvements and rail transportation.

THIS trip of inspection was made to note the progress and acquaint myself, the Chief of Staff, and General Harbord, by actual observation, with conditions in the S.O.S., and also with a view to making such changes in personnel and such improvements in methods as would insure the complete fulfillment of the increased obligations imposed upon that service by the enlarged troop and supply program that had been undertaken.

Our first stop was on the 29th, at Tours, which, being the location of the Headquarters of the S.O.S., with a large American military garrison of 2,400 officers and 4,360 men, had become a center of great activity. After the usual greetings from the préfect, the mayor and the local French commander, we went

Note: Total strength of the A.E.F. on July 31st, 54,224 officers, 1,114,838 enlisted men.
Divisional units arriving during July included elements of the following divisions: 36th Division (National Guard, Texas and Oklahoma), Maj. Gen. William R. Smith; 76th Division (National Army, New England and New York), Maj. Gen. Harry F. Hodges; 79th Division (National Army, northeastern Pennsylvania, Maryland and District of Columbia), Maj. Gen. Joseph E. Kuhn; 91st Division (National Army, Nebraska, Montana, Wyoming, Utah, Alaska, Washington, Oregon, California, and Idaho), Brig. Gen. Frederick S. Foltz.

directly to General Kernan's headquarters to meet and confer with the several chiefs of services.

Speaking for the Medical Department, Brigadier General Ireland said that although short of personnel his organization was working satisfactorily, and that he then had 59,000 beds in the various hospitals from seaports to battle front. For the present he felt prepared to meet any ordinary emergency, but as to the future, a greater number of buildings for hospitals would be required. Although we had considerable new construction under way at various points, I had already urged the French Minister of War to let us have more buildings.

Brigadier General Jadwin, the head of the Department of Construction and Forestry, gave an account of good progress, in spite of lack of building material before our own sawmills had reached capacity output. This department had charge of the building of docks, the erection of storehouses at ports and depots, and of general construction.

The Chief Quartermaster, Brigadier General Rogers, stated briefly that the quantities of food and clothing on hand were ample to meet the immediate requirements of the forces. His Department had accumulated at various storage plants and base ports 45,000,000 rations, or about 90,000 tons, equivalent to forty days for the command. There was a shortage of horses, forage and labor. The 80,000 horses promised by the French would be only about one-half the number required for the forces then in France, but a study was under way with a view to reducing the number of horses needed by using motor transportation instead. There were only about 32,000 non-American laborers of all nationalities available, including prisoners of war, and every effort was being made by the Labor Bureau to obtain more from France, Italy, and Spain. We also had about 50,000 American labor and forestry troops, including 3,000 combatant troops, on this work.

The Motor Transport Service, under Brigadier General Meriwether Walker, was increasing in efficiency, but there was difficulty in obtaining trained chauffeurs and mechanics. Only about half the number of automobiles and trucks actually needed in the S.O.S. at that time had reached France.

The Chief of Aviation, Major General Patrick, said that while our planes were arriving in increasing numbers, we were far behind expectations and still dependent upon the French. We had only one-third the number of squadrons in combat service that we expected. Our Liberty motors, in the opinion of the Air Service, had proved to be the last word, and it was thought then that there would be no further delay in supplying our own and Allied needs.

Brigadier General C. B. Wheeler, the Chief of Ordnance, who had succeeded Brigadier General Williams, said that the automatic supplies were coming regularly. Thus far no guns had been received from home and we should probably have to rely upon the Allies for the larger program. The indications were, however, that the French would be unable to produce enough for both their army and ours. The powder and explosive program was up to requirements, but on account of lack of steel the manufacture of ammunition for artillery, which had also been left to the French, was slowing down.

The task of the Services of Supply was very great and its successful accomplishment vital, yet, even from the beginning, the idea prevailed in the minds of its personnel, especially at the ports, that they were not exactly doing the work of soldiers, and hence, their efforts lacked enthusiasm. So, beginning with Tours, I took every opportunity during this trip to speak directly to groups of officers and men, giving them an account of the splendid conduct of our soldiers in battle and impressing upon them that forwarding supplies of food and ammunition to the front was quite as important as the actual fighting.

We visited every activity at Tours, beginning with the Central Records Office, established by Brigadier General Davis as a large branch of the Adjutant General's Office, where the personal record of every man in the A.E.F. was kept. At Camp de Grasse, near the city, we found the railway operators, numbering thousands, comfortably situated in portable barracks. Certain engineer

troops were kept at Tours for railway work, ready to respond
to calls from any direction. The well-managed camp of German
prisoners contained several hundred men used as laborers.

A number of British women, known as the Women's Auxiliary
Army Corps, were lent to us by their Government to assist in
clerical work. The 250 women located at Tours occupied neat
and comfortable temporary barracks and presented a very military appearance on parade. Some fifty of them were ill in
quarters at the time and I gave instructions that they should
be transferred to our hospital. This force with us eventually
numbered about 5,000. Its members rendered valuable and efficient service with our forces, releasing an equal number of men
for duty elsewhere.

The base hospital at Tours was filled with men wounded in
the recent engagements. They were receiving the best of care
under the efficient group of medical officers and nurses. In
speaking to the men in our hospitals during this tour of inspection, I told them how much the country appreciated their services
and assured them that no pains would be spared to hasten their
recovery.

Passing through one of the wards of this hospital, I spoke to a
fine-looking young soldier who was sitting up in bed and asked
him where he was wounded, meaning to inquire as to the nature
of his wound. In reply, he said: "Do you remember, Sir, just
where the road skirts a small grove and turns to the left across
a wheatfield, and then leads up over the brow of the hill? Well!
right there, Sir." He was clearly describing the advance south
of Soissons which pierced the Château-Thierry salient. Of
course, I was not there at the time, but it touched me that he
should feel that I must have been very close to him.

The Aviation Instruction Center for Observers gave us a
favorable impression in every particular. While there I said
a few words to the smart-looking company of mechanicians on
the importance of their work.

At the end of our inspection, Boyd and I went for a walk
and incidentally visited the fine old *pension* in which I had spent

two happy months with my family back in 1908. The beautiful garden, the shade trees, the swing, the children's sand pile, all were the same, but the management had changed and I was a stranger.

On the way to our train, I went to the Y.M.C.A. hut and was greeted by the large crowd of men who had finished their day's work and had gathered there to enjoy the facilities for reading and recreation which our people at home, through the Y.M.C.A., so generously provided our troops abroad.

During the evening, Eltinge, the Deputy Chief of Staff, at Chaumont, reported by telephone to my train that the Supreme War Council had recommended that the United States establish a few training camps in Italy, with the idea that the presence of American soldiers would stimulate the morale of the Italians. I was as much opposed to any dispersion of our forces as ever and at once telegraphed General Foch to that effect. Although he was also against it, I feared he might be persuaded to recommend it, and that the War Department might fail to see that it was not the innocent proposition it appeared to be. My telegram seemed to settle the question, as nothing more was heard of it.

We left Tours that night and arrived the next morning at Bordeaux, where we were met by the base commander and General Hallouin, the French military commander. This base section covered fourteen French political departments, and all American establishments within this territory were under the commanding general of the section. Our main interests there centered around the docks at Bordeaux and Bassens. Other activities included the base depot at St. Sulpice, the large refrigeration plant, the engine terminal and other railroad facilities, the stevedore camp and the rest and embarkation camps at Grange Neuve and Génicart. There were smaller depots at Coutras and Sursol, with ammunition storage facilities at St. Loubès. Farther out were the extensive artillery training camps at Souge and Le Courneau, the remount stations and hospitals of various types located throughout the section, and numerous sawmills established by our Forestry Bureau in different forests.

The inspection began at the receiving camps for incoming troops, where everything was found in excellent condition. The next stop was at the main storage plant for the port, at St. Sulpice. Over half of the construction was then completed and everything appeared to be in fine shape.

Speaking to the colored stevedores for a few minutes I referred to my service with a colored regiment and how proud we were of its conduct in the Spanish-American War. Among other things, I told them that later they might be given the honor of serving as combat troops at the front. At the conclusion of the talk, Colonel Boyd asked one of the corporals if he understood what I had said, and inquired whether he would like to take part in the fighting. After some hesitation, the corporal replied, very seriously, that he understood, but said he hoped the Colonel would please tell the General that he was very well satisfied where he was.

On the opposite bank of the Gironde River and about six miles below Bordeaux lies Bassens, where the French had ten berths which they turned over to us. Near them we constructed an additional ten berths. My inspection showed that the unloading of ships was being carried on in a perfunctory sort of way, with apparently little realization of the necessity for haste. I minced no words in demanding a change to a more energetic attitude by all concerned.

We next visited the combined artillery and balloon training camp at Souge, several miles west of Bordeaux, where the artillery brigade of the 27th Division seemed to be making good progress under Brigadier General G. A. Wingate.

At the base hospital we found about 500 of our wounded, most of whom were soon to be sent home. No matter how severely wounded they were, I never heard a word of complaint from any of our men. There could not have been found in the hospitals of any army a more cheerful lot. Their fine courage was a lesson in fortitude; indeed, an inspiration. Some would never again see the light of day, others would never be able to walk again, but they all seemed proud of their sacrifice, which many of their countrymen are often prone to forget all too soon.

Considering the extreme importance to us of Bordeaux as one of our ports, the general conditions were not satisfactory. There was a lack of appreciation by the officials of the urgency of expediting the turn-around of vessels, and virile direction seemed to be wanting. In view of the necessity of promptly meeting our new obligations, several of the officers at base headquarters were replaced by others of greater activity.

The following day found us at La Rochelle, later the headquarters of Base Section No. 7, embracing the territorial department of Charente-Inférieure. A large part of our coal was received through the ports of this section, which included, among other activities, our main storage depot for oil and gasoline at La Pallice, and a cement plant at Mortagne.

Brigadier General Charles Gerhardt was in command of this section and at an early hour, under his guidance, we started on our inspection, visiting the docks, the well-kept camp and the car shops, where cars from home were being assembled by the 35th Engineers at the rate of sixty per day. This work was well systematized and the energy put into their task by the personnel was very gratifying.

We went by train to Nantes, where we were met by Colonel J. S. Sewell, commanding Base Section No. 1, Colonel E. T. Smith, commanding Nantes, and the préfect and other French officials. Nantes, some thirty miles up the Loire from St. Nazaire, was the second port in importance in this base section, but it was available only for vessels of light draft. The permanent warehouses assigned to us were rapidly being filled, making temporary structures necessary later on. The motor reception park was manned by a smart-looking lot of men doing their work well and promptly sending forward the limited amount of motor transport as it arrived. The two base hospitals there, both with many sick and wounded, presented every sign of good management.

The next day, August 1st, was spent at St. Nazaire, our principal port of entry, and the headquarters of the base section commander. Beginning the inspection at the remount station, we found it well regulated and sufficient in accommodations. The horses and mules recently arrived were in good condition, considering the sea voyage, and were receiving special attention by the veterinary hospital force. There was a camp for 2,400 stevedores, which was clean and neat, though somewhat cramped, and a casual camp with 16,000 men just in from the States.

At the Locomotive Repair and Erection Plant, the 19th Engineers, working at high pressure, were setting up American locomotives, then being received in parts. This labor was avoided when, upon our insistence, locomotives were shipped in vessels with holds large enough to take them without being dismantled. This method of transporting locomotives across the Atlantic had never before been undertaken, but loading was accomplished successfully at home, not without considerable difficulty, and eventually only complete engines were shipped. I spoke to the men of the 19th Regiment during the noon hour, and also to over 5,000 laborers and stevedores assembled in the broad square near the docks.

Montoir, the port depot of St. Nazaire, probably the largest of its kind ever planned or constructed, was the last word in efficient arrangement. It covered about 2,000 acres and, as planned, required over 200 miles of track, with over 4,000,000 square feet of storehouses and 10,000,000 square feet of open storage space. An engine pulling a flat car took us around the plant, and I used the rear end of the car as a speaking platform. At no place was there more enthusiasm for their work than that shown by the 2,000 railway troops at Montoir.

To supplement the port accommodations at St. Nazaire, the construction of a wharf with berths for eight vessels at once was begun on the Loire River at Montoir. Due to lack of material, it was not completed before the Armistice, but three berths were finished in January, 1919.

The base hospital at Savenay, near St. Nazaire, was the main point for the assembly of the sick and severely wounded being sent home. All patients there maintained the same cheerful attitude that was the surprise and admiration of those who so tenderly looked after their welfare.

The base section of St. Nazaire included five geographical departments and embraced several towns in which there were A.E.F. activities. Angers was one where we had a large training base for incoming engineer casuals, and where a base hospital and a replacement depot for railway troops were located. At Coët-quidan and Meucon there were artillery training camps and aerial observation schools. At Saumur was the large artillery school for officers.

Continuing our journey, we arrived at Brest, the headquarters of Base Section No. 5, on the morning of the 2d and found the Commanding General, G. H. Harries, and staff at the station to meet us. Brest was our leading port of debarkation. The section included four French territorial departments. Cherbourg was the other important landing port for troops in this base section. A large locomotive terminal and repair shop was located at Rennes and a coal port at Granville.

It was a reminder of frontier days to see Harries. After the campaign of 1890-1891 against the Sioux Indians, I was sent to Pine Ridge Agency, South Dakota, to command a company of Ogallala Sioux Scouts and Harries was there as a member of a commission sent to investigate the Indians' troubles and settle their differences with the Government. At Harries' headquarters at Brest we met Admiral Henry B. Wilson, who, under Admiral Sims, was commanding the Naval District. It was very gratifying to hear from both of these commanders how perfectly they were pulling together.

After an inspection of the storehouses and the new construction for additional storage on the piers, I asked for the chief stevedore, Major John O'Neil, who came up apparently quite embarrassed. To put him at ease, I took him by the arm and we walked together to where some lighters were being unloaded. As the port had made the record of handling 42,000 arriving troops and their baggage on May 24th, entirely with lighters, I asked him to tell me about it. By this time he had regained his composure, and pointing to two officers, each down in the bottom of a lighter directing the work, he said, "Sir, do you see those two captains down there in their shirt sleeves? Well, that's the secret. I say to them, 'Don't stand off somewhere and puff yourselves up in your uniforms, but take off your Sam Brownes and your coats and get down close to your men.' Of course, those captains have now become experts. I did the same thing when I started, but since they are trained I manage things generally and they carry out my orders. I can wear my uniform now that I have won the right to wear it." "Well," I said, "O'Neil, you're just the man that I have been looking for, and I am going to send you to every port we use to show them your secret."

We next went to the large French infantry barracks at Pontanezen, which were utilized for incoming troops, a part of Major General W. R. Smith's 36th Division being there at the time. The new arrivals were impatient when they could not be promptly moved to the front, which was often the case, and these men were no exception. There was a German officers' prison camp at Fort Penfield, nearby, which we found in satisfactory condition. Incidentally, it was everywhere noticeable that whether in prison or at work the German soldier always retained his military bearing and his excellent discipline.

Of the three remaining base sections, none of which we visited at this time, the most important was that which embraced all the American agencies in the British Isles engaged in forwarding troops and supplies to France, with headquarters in London. Large numbers of air service personnel were trained in this section, and we had several base hospitals there. Rest camps for our troops were located along the route from Liverpool to Southampton.

There was another base section established on the French side of the Channel for receiving troops and supplies arriving from England. With headquarters at Le Havre, it embraced also the ports of Rouen, Boulogne, and Calais. The only other base section in operation at this time was on the Mediterranean, with headquarters at Marseille, which was used mainly for freight.

What was called the Intermediate Section covered all territory lying between Base Sections 1 and 2 and the French Zone of the Armies. It included the two great storage depots of Gièvres and Montierchaume, an ordnance depot and repair shops at Méhun-sur-Yèvre, a large replacement depot at St. Aignan, and the re-classification camp for officers at Blois. The main air service training center at Issoudun, a large air service production center and acceptance park at Romorantin, an aviation instruction center at Clermont-Ferrand, large hospital centers at Mars, Mesves-sur-Loire, and Allerey, and base hospitals at Châteauroux and Orléans were also in this section. The section headquarters was at Nevers, which was also the center for hospital trains and the location of a locomotive repair shop. The motor transport repair shops were at Verneuil and the Central Records Office of our forces was located at Bourges, after its removal from Tours.

The final link in the system of supply was the distribution to troops at the front, which was accomplished through the regulating stations in the Advance Section. We constructed two of these stations, one at Is-sur-Tille and another at Liffol-le-Grand, and used one at St. Dizier turned over to us by the French during the St. Mihiel operation. The details of distribution by the regulating stations have already been given in Chapter XI.

After leaving Brest, we arrived the next day, August 3d, at Blois, where Colonel H. R. Lee, commanding, met us at the station. At the reclassification camp for the A.E.F., officers found unfitted for a particular assignment were examined as to fitness for other duty and those recommended for discharge were assembled there until their cases could be disposed of.

From Blois we went to the replacement depot at St. Aignan, where part of the 41st Division was encamped. Our next stop was at Selles-sur-Cher, one of our many remount stations, commanded by Captain A. Devereux, of international polo fame. We then went to Gièvres, our greatest supply depot, which has been fully described in Chapter XXIII.

Near Gièvres was Romorantin, one of our large air service centers. We saw here several DeHaviland airplanes equipped with Liberty motors, and the well-kept camp sheltering about 1,000 railway troops. These men were all skilled workmen, but with most commendable spirit were doing any kind of work assigned to them.

The next stop was at Montierchaume, near Châteauroux, where another large depot was under construction. It was being built in anticipation of the enlarged program for the A.E.F. Our trip ended with a brief visit to Méhun, our mammoth ordnance station, with its large storehouses and shops designed to repair ordnance of all sorts, including the relining of worn-out artillery up to 155-millimeter guns.

The development that had taken place at the ports and along our lines of communication had surpassed our calculations, even though there had been a constant shortage of labor and material and a much larger flow of troops than had been anticipated. Although we had visited but a small proportion of the numerous activities, the system and local management, except in one or two instances, were encouraging. The principal criticism of S.O.S. administration up to that time was its lack of coördinating direction, initiative, and driving-force.

Our railway authorities had already caused the repair of 13,000 French freight cars and the number eventually reached over 57,000, besides a total of 1,900 damaged engines. They had risen to every emergency in a remarkable way, confronted as they had been during the preceding months by the unusual demands on rolling stock. In handling supplies for the front, the railroads had been so successful that even with our units widely scattered, supply trains had rarely failed to reach their destinations on time, and the number of our troops that went without food a single day through fault of the railway service was negligible.

Notwithstanding the difficulties encountered in perfecting the organization of the S.O.S. and the several changes that had been found necessary, the solutions of the problems generally were being worked out through the coöperation of able men in every line. With the recent adjustment of details, it was evident that the organization of this vast structure was now on a sound basis. With the expected improvement in methods and a more aggressive spirit in some quarters, there could be no question of the capability of the S.O.S. to fulfill the utmost requirements that might be imposed upon it provided the needs in personnel and material from home were reasonably met. My visit of inspection accompanied by the new commanding general of the S.O.S. had the effect of impressing the personnel with the vital significance of increased effort.

In order to relieve G.H.Q. of many details involved in handling questions of supply, which had been retained under its direct supervision during the formative period, it was decided to transfer to the S.O.S. the control of procurement, reception, maintenance, and distribution of supplies. Large questions of policy, the immediate direction of military transportation and supply in the Zone of the Armies, and the determination of quantities and the control of munitions remained under G.H.Q. The promise with which the new arrangement began almost immediately to operate afforded a definite indication of early and permanent improvement.

Some idea of the magnitude of this great supply organization of the A.E.F. may be obtained by giving the numbers of men employed in this problem of supply. On August 1st there were 1,169,062 officers and enlisted men in the A.E.F., of whom 275,-000 pertained to the S.O.S.; and even this was below requirements, as the proportion estimated for the work was somewhat less than one man in three. An adequate conception of the immense business organization behind the lines cannot be given by a mere recital of territory embraced or numbers of men employed. There was scarcely a town in France south of the latitude of Paris that had rail connections with our main railroad arteries to the front that did not boast some important American activity connected with the S.O.S.

Speaking of the situation in a cable to the Secretary of War, dated August 7th, I said, among other things:

"I have just returned from a thorough inspection of the Services of Supply, having spent a day at each of the western ports of France and visited all of the principal depots, remount stations and hospitals.* * * The results are especially gratifying in view of the handicap of the shortage of labor and material that has existed since April on account of tonnage being devoted to transportation of combatant troops to the exclusion of S.O.S. troops. I am satisfied now that we have builded properly and that there is no question whatever that the ports and our Services of Supply will be able to provide for the needs of our extended program.

" * * * Right now there is a capacity approximating 25,000 tons per day at all our ports including Marseille and this will continue to increase *pari passu* with our needs. Port efficiency will increase with experience and additional men and equipment.

" * * * With the increased personnel and material called for, the rail facilities will be adequate. There need be no worry as to our ability to handle supplies as fast as our expanding tonnage will require. Even with scant labor supply, we have repaired about 13,000 French cars and a proportionate number of engines.

" * * * Notwithstanding the scattered units of the command, supply trains have never failed to reach our troops, who have never been short of food for a day.[1] * * *

"The work of engineers in construction is now only a matter of men and material, both of which are in sight. * * * The great warehouses at Gièvres, Châteauroux, Méhun, and Is-sur-Tille are well advanced and will prove adequate for all requirements.

" * * * A change of the system to one of coördinate control is not indicated. Although there has been some lack of push in the S.O.S. yet I am as confident of the perfect working of the organization under the selected head, General Harbord, as I am of ultimate military victory. He has taken hold in splendid fashion. I shall transfer to him the entire subject of routine supply and related subjects, including transaction of cable business with the War Department on such subjects. There is no sort of doubt in my mind that the Services of Supply with him at its head, under direction of the General Staff, will continue to function satisfactorily regardless of the size of this command, leaving me free to devote my attention to the military problems.

" * * * There is no line of cleavage between the supply of troops and their tactical operations. All must be under one head to insure success. It is a sound military principle the wisdom of which the experience gained in all wars has clearly shown."

[1] This was true when the cable was sent, but during operations there were instances when it would not apply.

Regarding our rail situation in its relation to railway procurement at home, it was fortunate that Mr. Samuel M. Felton, who was in charge, should have been in France at this time. With the limited amount of sea transportation available, he had done everything possible to help equip and man our railways, but the immediate cry was still for more locomotives, more cars, and more port equipment. Despite the ever-increasing demands, we had received only about 7,600 cars, with about 21,000 on order that we had urgently asked for. Looking into the next year, to meet our program of 3,000,000 men, and allowing for all the cars that could be built or repaired in France or obtained elsewhere, we would need to receive from home over 60,000 more by the following July.

As to locomotives, it was the same story. We had obtained only 555 from the States and our actual needs by July, 1919, would be about 3,000 more, or 250 per month from then on.

Many other essential articles vitally needed to equip our docks for the prompt discharge of vessels had not yet arrived. Cablegrams that would fill volumes had been sent on all these matters, but there seems never to have been a clear conception at home of their relative importance. It is likely, however, that troop shipments during recent months had absorbed the attention of the home authorities to such an extent that many other important demands were postponed. Whatever may have been the reason for not meeting our requirements, the effect was to retard materially the necessary expansion of our supply system and thus to delay seriously the upbuilding in France of a well-balanced force. As indicated in my cable to the Secretary of War, it was simply a question of obtaining from home the necessary men, material and equipment.

CHAPTER XL ✦

Reduction of Château-Thierry Salient Completed—President Poincaré's Visit to Chaumont—Mr. Hoover Discusses Allied Food Supply—I Take Command of First Army—33d Division Attacks with British—King George Visits 33d Division—Bestows Decorations—Withdraw Divisions from British—Vicissitudes of Forming Independent Army —Foch Suggests Control of Allied Supply Under One Head—War Department Appears Swamped

(Diary) La Ferté-sous-Jouarre, Saturday, August 10, 1918. The enemy has been pushed beyond the Vesle River.

M. Poincaré came to Chaumont Tuesday to present me with decoration of Grand Cross of the Legion of Honor. Mr. Hoover and M. Boret, French Minister of Agriculture, came for conference. Colonel the Marquis Saigo, Japanese Army, whom I knew in Manchuria, took dinner with us. In reply to inquiry from Washington, cabled that A.E.F. does not pay for trenches used or occupied.[1] Commanding General, French XXXVIII Corps, highly commends the 28th and 32d Divisions.[2]

Talked Wednesday with Mr. Shearman, of the Shipping Board, who is returning to Washington in the interest of our shipping. Also

[1] My cablegram, dated August 7th, was as follows: "Reference your cablegram 1766, the following statement of facts and explanation is made by Director of Renting, Requisition and Claims Service. 'Paragraph 1. The American E. F. have not paid rent for trenches occupied or used for offensive or defensive purposes, nor, so far as I know, has any request or suggestion that payment for such use been made. Paragraph 2. In divisional areas back of the line used for training purposes, the lands are leased. Where trenches are constructed on such land for training purposes the damages to the land caused by such construction are paid for under exactly the same principles as if such damage to land occurred in the United States.' "

[2] The following order was issued by General de Mondésir:

"The time having now come for him to hand over the command of the zone of battle to General Bullard, commanding the III Corps, A.E.F., General de Mondésir, commanding the French XXXVIII Corps, addresses all his thanks to the splendid troops of the 28th and 32d American Divisions, who have proved during the pursuit which is still being continued not only their courage but also their staying qualities.

"The casualties, the toils and hardships due to the difficulties of bringing up rations during the marching and fighting of this period were unable to break their high morale, their élan, and their war-like spirit.

"General de Mondésir is proud to have commanded them. He hopes that the day will come when he will have them next to him as comrades in our common fight."

saw Brigadier General W. D. Connor, leaving to command Bordeaux District. Sent Foch congratulations on his appointment as Marshal of France.

On Thursday considered First Army plans with Chief of Staff and Chief of Operations. Discussed tractor and railway artillery with Chief of Artillery. Martin Egan came for brief talk. Combined French and British attack begun between Montdidier and Albert going well. Left for Paris.

Called at Sarcus yesterday concerning transfer of First Army to St. Mihiel sector, receiving Foch's approval. Later, de Chambrun went with me to see Pétain, with whom an understanding was reached on details.

Advised Major General Degoutte, who came to call to-day, of agreement with Pétain to leave two divisions on Vesle front temporarily. Orders from Washington establish the Army of the United States, placing Regulars, National Guard and National Army on same footing. First American air squadron completely equipped by American production crossed the German lines on the 7th.

WE have seen how the powerful attack by our 1st and 2d Divisions south of Soissons beginning on July 18th seized the initiative from the enemy, hastened his withdrawal from the south bank of the Marne, and forced upon him the decision to retire from the salient. In the vigorous Franco-American offensive against the enemy, our attacks were directed northward through the center of his position, driving him back relentlessly from one position to another, and finally breaking through his determined stand on the Ourcq River and compelling his withdrawal beyond the Vesle.

It will be recalled that the 26th Division had crossed the Château-Thierry—Soissons road and was attacking Epieds on July 23d. That night, the division was reënforced by a brigade of the 28th Division, which on July 24th took up the pursuit of the enemy, who had withdrawn to La Croix Rouge Farm. Up to this time, the 26th Division had progressed nearly 11 miles, captured 250 prisoners, and suffered about 5,000 casualties. The division front was taken over on July 25th by the 42d Division, which later also replaced two adjoining French divisions and occupied the entire front of the I Corps, about two miles in extent.

The 3d Division, it will be remembered, was north of the Marne, engaged before Le Charmel, on July 23d. On the following day, the division advanced to a line just south of the town, which was captured on July 25th. Operations carried out the next day in coöperation with a French division and the 42d Division on its left were only partially successful. The 42d captured the strongly held La Croix Rouge Farm, but the French division could not advance. The leading battalions of the 3d

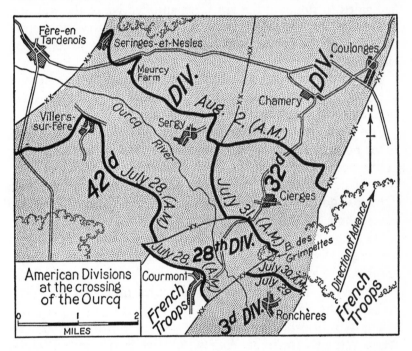

American Divisions at the crossing of the Ourcq

Division entered Le Charmel, but were withdrawn after dark. During the night, the hard-pressed Germans retired to the Ourcq River.

On July 27th, the 28th Division relieved a French division near Courmont, and the 3d Division occupied a line southeast of that town. During the morning of the 28th, the 3d Division captured Ronchères, and the 28th Division crossed the Ourcq, but was unable to hold its gains north of the river. Neither the 3d Division nor the 28th Division on its left was able to make progress against the Bois des Grimpettes on July 29th, but on the following day these woods were captured by the 28th Division in a hard-fought attack made jointly with the 32d Division, which had relieved the 3d Division that morning. That night the 28th Division also was relieved by the 32d.

The 3d Division had been in the line continuously for about two months and had taken part in three major operations. It had aided in stopping the last German offensive of the war and had advanced ten miles through difficult country stubbornly defended by the enemy. Its casualties were about 6,000 officers and men.

The 42d Division, on July 28th, had established its line beyond the Ourcq, and on the 29th, assisted by elements of the 4th Division, captured Sergy and Seringes-et-Nesles.

The enemy made an obstinate defense along the strong ridges to the north of the Ourcq River and some of the bitterest fighting of the war occurred on this line. However, his efforts to hold were of no avail against the gallant and persistent attacks of our divisions and on the night of August 1st he withdrew to the Vesle River, about ten miles farther back.[1]

On August 3d, the 42d Division in the I Corps was relieved by the 4th Division. The III Corps (Bullard) relieved the French corps on the right of our I Corps, so when the lines stabilized on the Vesle River we had for the first time two American corps side by side.

The 6th Brigade (3d Division) entered the line in the III Corps east of Fismes on August 6th, while the 28th Division relieved the 32d Division at Fismes on the 7th. The 77th Division took over the front of the 4th Division in the I Corps near

---

[1] The American communiqué of August 3d read as follows: "The full fruits of victory in the counteroffensive begun so gloriously by Franco-American troops on July 18th were reaped to-day when the enemy, who met his second defeat on the Marne, was driven in confusion beyond the line of the Vesle.

"The enemy, in spite of suffering the severest losses, has proved incapable of stemming the onslaught of our troops fighting for liberty side by side with the French, British, and Italian veterans. In the course of the operations 8,400 prisoners and 133 guns have been captured by our men alone."

Bazoches on August 12th. Elements of all these units succeeded in crossing the Vesle River, encountering tenacious defense. The bridgeheads established at Fismette and in the vicinity of Château du Diable became localities of intense hand-to-hand fighting.

Thus the Second Battle of the Marne came to an end. Our strenuous efforts to place sufficient American troops in battle in time to deprive the enemy of victory in the summer of 1918 bore fruit in the Allied counteroffensive against the German salient about Château-Thierry. While our forces had played important rôles in halting earlier German offensives, there were available here for the first time sufficient American divisions to join with those of the Allies in striking a decisive blow. The power of American arms brought to bear in the Marne salient made it possible to crush the last enemy offensive and commit him entirely to the defensive. He suffered a costly and disastrous defeat by the determined attacks of our 1st, 2d, 3d, 4th, 26th, 28th, 32d, 42d, and 77th Divisions, which constituted a force equal to eighteen Allied divisions. To these should be added considerable numbers of American air units and corps artillery, medical and transportation troops. The preponderance of Americans at the critical periods of this offensive, coupled with their successes in the vital areas of the battle, brought about this victory. Nearly 300,000 American soldiers were engaged in these operations, sustaining more than 50,000 casualties.

While the battle was in progress, arrangements for the formation of the American First Army, to be composed of the I and III Corps comprising the American divisions then on the battlefield, had been completed, and transfer of command from the French to the Americans was planned for August 10th. However, the favorable turn of the situation, resulting in a slowing down of activity along the Vesle River by August 6th and the discontinuance for the time being of further extensive offensive operations in that direction, made it inexpedient for the First Army to assume command on that front.

The situation to the north also affected this decision. On August 8th, the French and British armies had combined, under

Marshal Haig, in a drive against the German lines between Mont-didier and Albert. The attack came as a surprise to the Germans and was the beginning of a splendid success. By the end of the first day, an advance of more than six miles had been attained. The time appeared propitious for activity farther east.

The First American Army had been recognized as an accomplished fact, with headquarters at La Ferté-sous-Jouarre. Now it seemed advisable to begin preparations immediately to carry out the plan of campaign adopted on July 24th, providing for a distinctly American operation against the St. Mihiel salient.

I motored to Sarcus on August 9th, and, after discussing with Marshal Foch the changed conditions in the Marne sector and the practical stabilization of the front on the Vesle, I suggested shifting the First Army Headquarters to the St. Mihiel region, where it could begin immediate preparations for the proposed offensive. We roughly considered the outline of my plans and, as expected, he at once acquiesced in the transfer. Returning to Paris the same afternoon, I then went to Provins to talk the matter over further with General Pétain. We took stock of available units for the St. Mihiel operation and he said that I could count on him definitely to do everything within his power to furnish whatever we might require. Having thus reached a general understanding regarding the preliminary details of the move, and after spending the night at the quarters of Major Clark, I drove the following morning to La Ferté-sous-Jouarre to take formal command of the First Army and to give instructions to my staff regarding the movement of headquarters to Neuf-château.

The French Government had expressed a desire to bestow their decorations on American officers and men and advised that they wished to confer upon me the Grand Cross of the Legion of Honor. As Congress had recently granted permission for members of our forces to receive foreign decorations, the French Government was informed accordingly, and it was for this purpose that M. Poincaré paid his first brief visit to Chaumont on August 6th. I met him at the station with a military escort

General Ferdinand Foch, field commander of the French forces, confers with General Pershing in his quarterss at Val des Écoliers, Chaumont, France, on June 17, 1918. (National Archives photograph)

General Pershing and King George V of England review a contingent of U.S. Marines near Chaumont, France, in the fall of 1918. (National Archives photograph)

General Pershing and the King and Queen of Belgium enter the Hotel de Ville in Chaumont, France, to attend a reception on March 20, 1919. The mayor of Chaumont is on the left. (National Archives photograph)

General Pershing leads his staff down the Champs-Élysées in Paris during a victory parade on July 14, 1919. (National Archives photograph)

Baseball star Babe Ruth enlists in the U.S. Army in 1924 and is welcomed on board by General Pershing. (The photograph is a reproduction from the collections of the Library of Congress.)

General Pershing places a wreath on the Tomb of the Unknown Soldier of World War I on Memorial Day, November 11, 1938. (National Archives photograph)

and conducted him to my headquarters, where the senior officers of the staff were presented. After that formality, we repaired to the small area of barracks, where the headquarters troop and band were drawn up in line for the ceremony.

Meanwhile, the entire headquarters personnel, consisting of several hundred men and women, had turned out to witness the proceedings. Both national airs were played and the troops were presented to the President, after which he addressed me briefly in perfect English and pinned on the decoration. He said:

> "I am very glad to present to you to-day, before your gallant staff and your brave soldiers, the insignia of the high distinction bestowed upon you by the French Government.
>
> "It is an especial pleasure to take this opportunity of congratulating you and your splendid army for the great successes already attained and for the precious services you render to right and freedom."

I replied thanking him for the honor and saying:

> "I value this decoration as a mark of recognition by France of the services of the American Army and of friendship for the American people."

Then, according to the French custom, he kissed me on both cheeks, but not without some difficulty, as he was not so tall as I and it was necessary for him to rise on tiptoe and for me to lean somewhat forward.

I was not insensible to the high personal honor, but regarded it mainly as an appreciation on the part of the French Government of the assistance America had already given to the cause. Without implying the slightest criticism of the form of salutation used in the ceremony, I cannot refrain from confessing my embarrassment, especially as I could hear the restrained laughter of the irreverent Americans in the area who witnessed my situation, no doubt with sympathy. I thought that M. Poincaré himself was probably quite as much embarrassed as I was. Moreover, he must have heard the suppressed mirth as plainly as I did.

At this time there was some apprehension as to food supply for the civilian population of the Allies, especially for certain districts in France. Mr. Herbert Hoover, who came to Chaumont in company with the French Minister of Agriculture, was conversant with the food situation in general. He thought that England could be of immediate assistance, but I was not so hopeful, feeling that her stores must be low due to the employment of so much of her shipping to carry American troops, but I was willing to accept his views and assured him that in any event we would stand ready to assist.

My days, from the time of my arrival in France, had always been too short, but it now seemed that several days of arduous work had to be crowded into one. The sphere of our activities had become extended and many important matters required my personal attention, necessitating a great deal of travel. After the hurried trip to the Services of Supply, it was necessary to spend a day or so here or there—at Paris, Chaumont, on the Marne, or in the St. Mihiel region—holding frequent conferences with Foch, Pétain, Haig and others. I was much relieved to have the S.O.S. in good hands.

(Diary) Chaumont, Tuesday, August 13, 1918. Came through Paris Sunday and directed the Chief of Staff by telephone to announce to the press the formation of American First Army. Went to 33d Division, which was still engaged in British offensive.

King George visited the Division Headquarters Monday and decorated General Bliss, me, and several men of the 33d. Went to see Field Marshal Haig to arrange release of three of our divisions. Returned to Paris and saw Winston Churchill, Lord Weir, and Stettinius about artillery and aviation. British can provide us with additional artillery.

Told Clemenceau this morning of my talk with Sir Douglas and asked Mott to advise Marshal Foch. Have asked for Hugh S. Gibson, now in Paris, to supervise propaganda in enemy countries.[1] Returned to Chaumont in afternoon.

The 33d Division (Bell) was still in training when the combined attack of the British and French in the Montdidier-Albert

[1] This request was disapproved, as the Department did not think it wise that Mr. Gibson, who was in the Diplomatic Service, should be associated with that work, the responsibility for propaganda having been placed upon the Committee on Public Information.

sector began on August 8th. The division was attached to the British III Corps for the operation, the 131st Regiment of Infantry being assigned to the British 58th Division. This regiment joined in the attack on August 9th and captured in splendid fashion the Morlancourt—Chipilly ridge north of the Somme. During the next few days, it extended its gains and finally reached a line just west of Bray-sur-Somme. The other three regiments of the division were not engaged. The 131st Infantry was relieved on August 20th, having advanced over three miles and suffered heavy casualties.

I motored to the British front on Sunday to be present at 33d Division Headquarters, near Molliens-aux-Bois, on the occasion of the visit of His Majesty, King George, who was then spending some days with his armies. General Bliss had preceded me and we both spent the night there. That evening General Bell, in relating the details of the participation of his troops with the British, said that their services had been urgently requested and that they had acquitted themselves well.

The King and his suite arrived on the morning of the 12th, having come for the purpose of presenting decorations, especially to selected men of the 33d Division who had participated in the recent attacks of the British army. Soon after his arrival, the King invited General Bliss and me to his room, where he bestowed upon me the Grand Cross of the Order of the Bath, and upon General Bliss the order of St. Michael and St. George. The presentations were informal, as he simply handed the decorations to us in turn, at the same time expressing his appreciation of American assistance.

His Majesty, speaking of the employment of the American troops, said he was anxious to have as many as possible serve with the British Army, that their presence had an excellent effect in stimulating the morale of his men, and that although the British troops had never lost spirit they had been very sorely tried. He remarked that he was not a politician and did not see things from their point of view, but he thought it would be advantageous to have some Americans serving with his armies.

He suggested that our troops might be brought in through the port of Dunkirk, which could be placed at our disposal. He spoke of the friendly sentiments he held for America and of how much it would mean after the war to be able to say that the two English-speaking peoples had fought side by side in this great struggle.

I expressed entire agreement that friendly relations ought to be stronger after the war, but explained that we were now forming an army of our own and would require practically all our troops as soon as they could be brought together. He said he appreciated that fact but hoped that some divisions might continue with the British, but of course I could make no promises. At the conclusion of our brief conversation, we accompanied the King to the place where the men were assembled for the ceremony. He was gracious in his compliments as he pinned the decorations on our men, and needless to say the recipients were extremely proud of the honor conferred upon them.

As soon as the King departed, I left with Boyd for Sir Douglas Haig's advance headquarters to ask for the relief of some of the American divisions then with the British armies. When last at Marshal Foch's headquarters I had suggested that he should make the request of Marshal Haig for these divisions. But he had hesitated, for some reason, which I presumed to be either the coolness that was said to have arisen between him and Marshal Haig regarding the active use he had made of some British divisions sent to the French front near the Marne salient to recuperate, or his knowledge of how badly our troops were needed on the British front. In any event, he asked me to discuss the matter myself with Marshal Haig.

We found the Marshal on his train near Wiry-au-Mont and took luncheon with him and his staff, during which we chatted about everything except the object of my visit. Repairing to his office car after lunch, I brought up the subject and spoke to the Field Marshal of the letter he had written me a few days before saying that he would like to use some of our American divisions in an attack he was about to undertake. I referred to our plans then in progress to form an American army for the reduction of the St. Mihiel salient and said that I should be compelled to withdraw from his front at least three of the five American divisions still there in training. Referring to the conference with Marshal Foch in July, I pointed out that under the circumstances it would not be possible to leave our troops here and there among the Allies any longer, as their services would be required with our own armies.

In reply, he said that he had understood that the American divisions had been sent there to be trained and to serve on the British front and that now, just as they had become useful, it was proposed to take them away. He had hoped, he said, that these divisions would remain and was disappointed to have them removed. I reminded him of our agreement that these troops were at all times to be under my orders and that while they had been placed behind his armies for training they were to be used there in battle only to meet an emergency. I emphasized the fact that we were all fighting a common enemy and that in my opinion the best way to help toward victory was for the Americans to fight under their own flag and their own officers.

I could well understand the Field Marshal's feelings. His armies had suffered very heavy casualties, were worn with continuous fighting, and defeat had stared them in the face. Now that the tide had apparently turned and the offensive was to be resumed, it could not have been otherwise than disheartening to have our large divisions of vigorous, keen young Americans transferred to another field of action. I gave him my assurance that his desire was fully appreciated and that I regretted the necessity which impelled me to make this decision just at this moment, but in accordance with our agreement I must insist on having them. He acknowledged the understanding and said that although he needed our troops he realized my position and my reasons for their withdrawal. He then concluded, in his frank, straightforward way: "Pershing, of course you shall have them, there can never be any difference between us." On leaving British headquarters with the matter satisfactorily arranged, I felt that Marshal

218 MY EXPERIENCES IN THE WORLD WAR

Foch would be much relieved that his intervention would not be required.

On the following morning I called on M. Clemenceau and told him of my visit to British Army Headquarters and we spoke of the progress toward the formation of an American army. A record of what he said, as set down in my notes, is as follows:

"M. Clemenceau told me that when I first began insisting on using American divisions in an American army under an American command, he frankly did not agree with me, but that he wished to say to me now that I was right and that every one who was against me on this proposition was wrong; that he fully agreed with me now and thought that the Americans should operate separately as an American army."

We then discussed a telegram he had received from Lloyd George endeavoring to arrange for a number of American divisions to be retained with the British. This message was handed to me by M. Clemenceau. In part Mr. Lloyd George said:

"I did not ask for the transfer of American divisions to the British front. The brilliant part taken by them in the second great Marne victory has more than justified the use General Foch made of them. What I asked was that a few American divisions at most from among those recently arrived in France and which could not be put in the line without some training should be sent to complete their training behind British lines. My purpose was to form a reserve capable of being used in the critical situation of a break in our front by the enemy, permitting the holding with our local reserves until the arrival of divisions from the general reserve of the Allied Armies on the Western Front. I did not consider my demand excessive for it must not be forgotten that the greater part of the American troops were brought to France by British shipping and that because of the sacrifices made to furnish this shipping our people have the right to expect that more than five divisions of the twenty-eight now in France should be put in training behind our lines. We are informed that a serious attack on the British front is still probable now. I do not wish to hamper you now, but in the interest of that unity of command for which I made so great an effort, I urgently ask you to support the very modest request made by me from our Commander-in-Chief."

Not only were the British anxious to get our units, but the whole question of the employment of American troops continued to be considered among the Allies. One program which the British clung to contemplated the use of Dunkirk as the supply port for an American army which they hoped would be sent to their front for service under their control. M. Clemenceau told me that the Italian Ambassador and Mr. Lloyd George had been in conference in London regarding the disposition of our troops, the former urging that every influence be brought to bear upon Marshal Foch and myself to obtain divisions for Italy. This was not the first time that the British had shown an interest in having our units go to Italy, having previously suggested that they be grouped with the British forces there.

Another proposal which was again submitted to Marshal Foch about this time was that of placing American infantry and other services in the reduced divisions of all the principal Allies—British, French, and Italian—but the French had changed their attitude and were opposed to any of these schemes, none of which thereafter came up for formal consideration. I could not believe that Mr. Lloyd George was lending himself to any of these plans in view of his positive declaration at the Abbeville Conference in favor of the formation and use of an American army as such. The impression left on our minds was, first, that the British desired to discourage the concentration of our forces into one army, and, second, that perhaps there was a desire to check the growth of too friendly relations between Americans and French.

(Diary) Chaumont, Thursday, August 15, 1918. Senator J. Hamilton Lewis had luncheon with us yesterday. Several Congressmen and naval officers visited us to-day.[1] Foch suggests single control of supply systems, which I do not favor. Wrote Sir Douglas Haig approving request that 27th and 30th Divisions remain with British temporarily to function under our II Corps. Doctor Jacob Gould Schurman, of Cornell University, called.

Marshal Foch sent copy of proposed cable to President Wilson

[1] The party included: Representatives L. P. Padgett, J. J. Riordan, F. C. Hicks, S. E. Mudd, W. B. Oliver, W. J. Browning, and Paymaster J. S. Higgins, U. S. N., who took luncheon with us, the others being Representatives J. A. Peters, W. W. Venable, J. C. Wilson, J. R. Farr, J. R. Connelly, W. L. Hensley, T. S. Butler and T. D. Schall and Captain R. H. Jackson and Lieutenant M. H. Anderson of the Navy.

urging the 100-division plan. I sent back word to Foch that it would probably irritate the President and advised against sending it.

Our members of Congress from home were always welcome and particular care was taken to give them opportunity to become acquainted as far as practicable with our plans and the state of our preparations. The members of this group of Representatives were intensely interested, each one especially so in what the units from his own section of the country were doing. They were shown through our organization at General Headquarters and the projects we were about to undertake were explained to them. As representatives elected by the people, their personal and official interest in our effort and their expressed belief in our success were encouraging.

In its practical application through the Military Board of Allied Supply, our theory of pooling certain supplies was proving effective in solving a number of questions of greater or less importance. There was, however, a tendency to carry it beyond the limits under which it operated and the suggestion was presented that it be made general, with the entire control under one supreme head. In order to get my views, Marshal Foch sent one of his officers to discuss it with my staff, but I thought we had gone as far as it was safe to go in this direction. The matter of handling our supplies was bound up with our system of ports, depots, and means of transportation to such an extent that the control could not be delegated to any other authority.

While strategical use of the armies had been placed in the hands of the Allied Commander-in-Chief, the responsibility for their tactical direction necessarily remained in the hands of their respective commanders. If there had been a general mingling of units regardless of national integrity, then a general supply system applicable to the entire front under a single head might have been logical. But it was only by establishing the principle of unanimity that even the Inter-Allied Board was made acceptable, as no Commander-in-Chief would forego control of his supplies any more than he would yield the military command over his army. The system was already giving excellent service and in my opinion it was more satisfactory than any plan of arbitrary control could be. Among other things, such problems as procurement of labor, storage facilities, and forage supply were in process of solution. A reserve of light railway[1] material and of motor transport, though small, was being formed and systematic methods of handling traffic were being studied.

I took early occasion to explain my views to Marshal Foch and convinced him that the suggestion of a supreme head for supplies was not practicable, at the same time urging an extension of the scope of authority of the Inter-Allied Board as far as possible without interfering with the machinery of supply behind each army.

(Diary) Neufchâteau, Sunday, August 18, 1918. Saw press correspondents on Friday and gave confidential talk on plans. General Ireland came to report difficulties in obtaining buildings for hospitals, and although the French have been generous, I have asked M. Clemenceau for further concessions. Delay at Washington in answering cables indicates they must be swamped.

General George W. Read (II Corps) came for conference yesterday. Went to Neufchâteau to-day and worked with First Army staff. Tonnage falling off, many idle berths at ports. Cable reports that recommendations for promotion have finally been approved.

As it was the policy to let the press have just as much information as could safely be given out, the correspondents came in occasionally to receive news of our progress and plans. Although most of what was told them at these meetings was confidential, it gave them a background for intelligent action and their patriotic interest was sufficient safeguard that the information would not be divulged. It was understood that the publication of news

[1] The 60-centimeter railway, about 20 inches between rails, was used immediately behind the lines to transport ammunition and other supplies and was often used to carry troops and remove the wounded. The track came in sections and was easily and quickly laid, though oftentimes on soft ground a foundation of stone or the use of wooden ties was necessary. The engines and cars were relatively small, but the cars were supposed to carry about ten tons and often carried more than that. The operation of these lines was conducted by the engineers under the organization known as the Light Railway Department.

had to be limited and I think the members of the press fully appreciated the necessity of the restrictions imposed.

The decrease in the number of transport arrivals at this time caused some apprehension. The accumulation of the immense quantity of supplies needed could only be assured by a constant flow from home ports. Improvement in the rapidity of discharging cargo was almost instantaneous with the change made in the administrative personnel of the Services of Supply. This, combined with the fewer vessels arriving, had left many idle berths. A loss in tonnage deliveries could not readily be made up by sending very large groups of transports later on, as that would produce a certain amount of congestion and consequent delay of vessels. We were constantly increasing the capacity of our ports and were now able to discharge 25,000 tons a day, but only about 16,000 tons per day were arriving.

With the great number of our troops then in France and the continued arrival of others, there was danger of running still further behind in many things of which we were already short. Our imperative needs in motor transport, rolling stock for railways, and construction material were not being met, and yet they were indispensable. At that moment, when we were asking the French to lend us trucks, they made the same request of us. We actually needed 1,300 automobiles, thousands of trucks, and all other kinds of motor vehicles. The ambulance situation was critical, several sanitary units were completely immobile, and twenty base hospitals had arrived without equipment. The Ordnance Department was little better off, with shortages of machine guns, carts, and trench mortar ammunition. The Quartermaster Corps needed rolling kitchens, combat wagons, water carts, and many other things, without which troops were practically confined to training areas. The Signal Corps reported lack of many essentials of unit equipment for battle. It was not believed that the Secretary of War himself was being kept informed of these matters and often in reporting conditions it was requested that his especial attention be called to the cablegrams.

The following shows my thought at the time, as expressed to the Secretary of War:

"France, August 17, 1918.

"DEAR MR. SECRETARY:

"Inasmuch as you asked me to speak to you frankly I know you will permit me to refer to the subject of coöperation between here and the General Staff at Washington. I do so only to give you my point of view and possibly aid you in getting over some difficult places which I am sure you must encounter and which are beginning to affect us here. There is an impression here that our cablegrams are not being carefully studied and thoroughly coördinated. There seems to be energy enough behind things, but, perhaps, it is not as well directed by the Staff as it might be. It may possibly be due to faulty General Staff organization, which, as nearly as I can learn, has not yet reached that point of perfection which would enable all these matters to be handled systematically. In any event, there is not the satisfactory teamwork with us over here that should exist. It is not easy for me, at this distance, to understand all the reasons, but it may be due to a disinclination to accept our views.

"I fully realize that it may be difficult to get the perfection that you should have and that there may be some of the personnel that is not entirely satisfactory. In order to have full coöperation, there must, of course, be entire sympathy and unity of purpose. The system should be one thoroughly tested out, such as is in operation here, and upon which every successful army organization must depend. I have at times doubted whether you will get it going smoothly without taking some one who has actually gone through this organization here from beginning to end, as you know this is the only general staff organization that our army has ever had. All this comes to my mind following the idea of an occasional change, of which you spoke when here as being your intention.

*   *   *   *   *   *   *

"With very high personal and official regard, I am,

"Faithfully yours,

"JOHN J. PERSHING."

The tonnage allotted to our use was less in July than in June, notwithstanding our greater need. Consequently, it was again urged that more tonnage be pressed into service. Only a limited amount of the new tonnage from our own yards was then in military use and continuance of British assistance had become doubtful.

The following cable from Mr. Lloyd George to M. Clemenceau, handed to me by the latter some days before, showed some doubt about the continuance of aid, despite the confident assurances which Mr. Lloyd George and Lord Milner had given when the increased program was discussed:

"Recent dispatches from Washington give reason to believe that the United States Government has abandoned its program for putting 100 divisions on the Western front by July, 1919, and that the greatest possible number would only comprise 80 divisions.[1] We have also been advised that this program reduced can only be realized if Great Britain should continue to furnish its help for naval transportation. Because of the serious character of this information, I immediately made a preliminary study of the questions with Minister of Naval Transportation, Sir Joseph Maclay. I regret to declare that we shall not be able to continue our help as far as cargoes of merchandise are concerned and that we shall probably have to cut down tonnage assigned for troop transportation. In the last few months we have lost several troop transports of large tonnage. * * *

"In Lancashire 40,000 cotton workers, at least, are idle because of lack of raw material and to increase the cotton supply we have been forced to cut short our program for cereal supply. Another very serious difficulty results from the lack of coal by reason of our need of manpower to keep the armies going in the recent military crisis. The coal situation is giving me the greatest anxiety because the situation in France and Italy as well as our own munition production depend upon a suitable coal supply. By reason of the lack of coal a large number of ships have been subjected to delay in our ports and our whole program of naval transportation has been shaken up by this fact. This increases our difficulty to help the Americans in executing their program with regard to merchant shipping. While continuing to do our best for the Allies in the future as we have in the past, I think it best to let you know without delay what difficulties we may meet in attempting to realize the American program in its entirety."

[1] This would equal 160 French or British divisions, which was a larger force than the combined armies of the French and British then on the Western Front.

CHAPTER XLI

Preparations for St. Mihiel Offensive Begun—Composition of First Army —Concentration Half Million Men—French Services Required—First Army Staff Working Well—Colored Troops—Conferences with Foch and Pétain—Two Divisions Left with British—Heavy Artillery Delayed—St. Mihiel Postponed—Urge Maximum Effort at Home— Recommend Withdrawal Allied Instructors in Training—Advance Headquarters, Ligny-en-Barrois—Ruse Near Belfort Successful— Cabled President Wilson Suggesting Possibility of Victory, 1918

(Diary) Chaumont, Thursday, August 22, 1918. Left Neufchâteau Monday to inspect new divisions. Stopped to see General de Castelnau, Commander of French Group of Armies, and express appreciation for his coöperation. Spent the night at Belfort.

On Tuesday saw 29th Division (Morton) in line near there. Visited Bandholtz's and M. A. Reckord's brigades in trenches.

Spent yesterday with 92d Division (Ballou). Colored officers deficient in training.

To-day at First Army Headquarters considered engineer, tank and artillery questions with Brigadier Generals J. J. Morrow, Rockenbach, and E. F. McGlachlin, respectively. Major Generals Dickman and Cameron appointed corps commanders. Had letter from Tardieu on control of commodity prices in our areas. Sent letter to Marshal Foch requesting fifteen to seventeen observation squadrons and three night bombardment groups for St. Mihiel attack.

THE final decision that the First Army would undertake the reduction of the St. Mihiel salient as its first operation was transmitted to army headquarters on August 10th, and the army staff immediately began the development of plans for the concentration of the troops necessary for its execution.

It was certain that the psychological effect on the enemy of success in this first operation by the American Army, as well as on the Allies, our own troops, and our people at home, would be of signal importance. The attack must, therefore, not only carry through, but a serious hostile reaction must be made impossible.

The headquarters of the First Army were transferred to Neufchâteau between August 11th and 16th. The special army troops assembled north of Château-Thierry were moved eastward during the same period. Neufchâteau was centrally located with reference to all parts of the front from St. Mihiel to the Swiss frontier, and as considerable American activity had been carried on there for many months, we thought that its selection would probably keep the enemy in ignorance as to the exact sector we were to occupy.

The corps and divisions placed at the disposal of the First Army for the St. Mihiel operation and their condition may be summarized as follows:

> The 1st and 2d Divisions were excellent as to training, equipment and morale. They had attacked July 18th in the Soissons drive.
>
> The 3d, 4th, 26th and 42d Divisions were of fine morale and considerable experience, as they had fought in the defense about Château-Thierry and in the advance toward the Vesle River.
>
> The 89th and 90th Divisions were going through their sector training on the front between Toul and the Moselle River, and the 5th and 35th Divisions were taking their sector training in the Vosges.
>
> The 33d, 78th, 80th and 82d Divisions had been training in rear of the British front, one brigade of the 33d having had front-line service with the British. The 91st Division had never been in the front line and had received less than four weeks' training in France.
>
> As to Corps Headquarters, the I Corps was well organized and had operated in the Aisne-Marne defensive and offensive. IV and V Corps Headquarters had taken no part in operations and had very few corps troops.
>
> Except for one brigade of corps artillery and three or four air service squadrons, all of the American corps and army troops to be employed were at this time in their preliminary training period in France.

The final instruction of the divisions for the coming operation was directed by the Training Section of General Headquarters. The equipment of these units, their supply, and the handling of replacements devolved upon the First Army, as did the reception, equipment and supply of thousands of corps and army troops arriving from the Services of Supply or directly from transports.

Preparations were being hastened in the hope that the St. Mihiel attack might be made by the 7th of September. Our divisions were scattered and it seemed doubtful whether sufficient rail or truck transportation could be found to bring them in the area, together with the corps and army troops and auxiliaries, before the rainy season, which usually starts about the middle of September and which, it was said, might seriously hinder operations in that sector. It was necessary to assemble in all 550,000 troops for this operation, and this gigantic task, imposed mainly upon the First Army General Staff, which itself was yet in the formative state, might well have caused dismay, even under the most favorable circumstances.

The almost total inactivity on the St. Mihiel front since 1916 made many installations necessary in preparation for an operation of such magnitude. The telephone and telegraph lines, to insure effective communication throughout the area, needed many miles of wire. Artillery ammunition, calculated on the basis of at least five days of battle, was necessary in the amount of about 3,300,000 rounds. Engineering material for building roads across no-man's-land behind the advancing army ran into thousands of tons. Railway spurs, advance depots, and hospital accommodations for sick and wounded had to be provided and aviation fields prepared. Many other things were required, such as the construction of light railways for distribution beyond the railheads, personnel and equipment pertaining to searchlights, the development of water supply, installations for sound and flash ranging for artillery, arrangements for traffic control and the camouflage of positions, roads and material. Each item was the subject of consideration by qualified specialists and all had to be coördinated by the newly formed staff.

The actual movement for the concentration of the more than one-half million men, whether by rail, truck, or on foot, generally took place at night. The troops bivouacked during the day in forests or other sheltered places hidden from the observation of enemy airplanes, resuming the movement at nightfall.

The rail and most of the truck transport belonged to the French and was handled by them. Changes were constantly necessary in schedules on account of the nonarrival of trucks as planned, usually due to their being used elsewhere by the French.

All ranks of the staff and line were filled with enthusiasm at the prospect of the coming operation. Officers of the rapidly expanding First Army Staff worked with the greatest energy under their new responsibilities. The French officers assigned to my headquarters gave material assistance in expediting the arrival of French troops and in handling the civilian population within the Zone of the Armies. These officers were deeply interested and the spirit of coöperation between French and Americans in the untiring efforts given to preparation foretold the favorable outcome of our first offensive.

During my visit to the 92d Division (colored) it was learned that the situation as to training, especially of colored officers, was not entirely satisfactory. This National Army division had been in the service since October, 1917, and was composed of units from different parts of the United States. None of the junior officers had received more than superficial training and most of them were unaccustomed to the management of men. The general officers of the division, who had all served with colored regiments of the Regular Army, were not sanguine regarding the possibility of reaching a high standard of instruction among their troops.

It was well known that the time and attention that must be devoted to training colored troops in order to raise their level of efficiency to the average were considerably greater than for white regiments. More responsibility rested upon officers of colored regiments owing to the lower capacity and lack of education of the personnel. In the new army, with hastily trained colored officers relatively below white officers in general ability and in previous preparation, the problem of attaining battle efficiency for colored troops was vastly more difficult. It would have been much wiser to have followed the long experience of our Regular Army and provided these colored units with selected white officers.

On account of the rapidly increasing numbers of American troops in France, M. Tardieu, Commissioner General for Franco-American Affairs, writing on behalf of the Minister of Agriculture and Supplies, called attention to the necessity of controlling prices on sales of articles of food and drink. The French Government desired to prevent excessive charges, not only to benefit us, but to avoid the increased cost of living for the French people themselves. The efforts of the French Minister and M. Tardieu to regulate prices to our soldiers proved to be only partially successful, but the attempt was nevertheless much appreciated.

(Diary) Chaumont, Sunday, August 25, 1918. Harbord came up on Friday; reported increasing activity in S.O.S. Have cabled for 39,000 extra engineer and service troops for port expansion. Conferred with Colonel Andrews. Major Perkins, Red Cross, has requested service in the army.

Went yesterday for conference with Foch on operations. Franklin Roosevelt, Assistant Secretary of Navy, called. Had dinner with Pétain at Chantilly.

General Bliss came to-day to propose coöperation in urging the 100-division program. General Bridges, British Army, called to discuss machine gun organization, training, and repartition of lines. Told him that we were not in favor of training with the Allies. Lunched with Dawes; discussed Allied Board activities. Saw Foch at Bombon again to-day and reached Chaumont at 10:30 P.M.

My visit to Marshal Foch on the 24th was to discuss preparation for the coming operation in the St. Mihiel sector and especially to urge haste in the assignment of the required French auxiliary units. In our conversation, Marshal Foch referred to the letter he had written the previous day requesting that our 27th and 30th Divisions, which were still with the British, should remain there. He considered it important, he said, to have them ready to assist if necessary in the British operations then in progress. I replied that not only were these troops needed with our own army but they were eager to serve under their own flag. Moreover, it had been clearly understood that they should join the American Army when it was formed. I think Foch fully appreciated the situation and the sentiment involved, but he said the battle was going well on the British front from Arras to the Oise and he hoped that it would extend farther and produce still greater results. Therefore, he wanted to count on the assistance of our two divisions.

While he did not give any other reason, I thought it probable that he also wished thus to satisfy the demand of the British for their share of American troops. Moreover, it was certain that he would also ask for American divisions to aid the French and his action in this case would make the latter request appear more consistent. I felt that if our divisions should once become engaged in battle as part of another army it would be unlikely that they could be withdrawn, yet, under the circumstances, I accepted military emergency as the real reason for the request and assented, with the understanding that these divisions should not remain with the British indefinitely.

I was opposed to the suggestion made by Mr. Lloyd George in his telegram to M. Clemenceau that we should leave a few of our divisions behind the British lines, and felt that compliance with Foch's request for two divisions temporarily was as far as I could go. Our experience with the British had shown that, due to differences in national characteristics and military systems, the instruction and training of our troops by them retarded our progress.

As it was likely that further demands would be made on us, I told Foch that it should be definitely understood that we would thereafter instruct our troops according to our own methods and use them in our own army. He took the view that Mr. Lloyd George should not complain as to where our troops were used so long as they were winning victories, a view which, if given general application, might cause the continued dispersion of our units. I wished to be of assistance so far as consistent with the formation of an active, independent American army and when he asked that two other divisions be held for use wherever they might be needed I agreed only after much the same discussion as before and under the condition that such assignment, when it came, would be only temporary.

We then took up the question of tanks, to find, not at all to my surprise, that the British now said they could not spare any, although at the conference on July 24th it was understood that they would be able to furnish us some heavy tanks when we needed them. Foch said the French would let us have five battalions of light tanks, three with French personnel and two to be manned by Americans. I later sent my tank commander, Brigadier General Rockenbach, to confer with the British in an endeavor to obtain an equitable allotment of the heavy type, but without success.

The shortage in tanks made it necessary to plan for greater artillery or other preparation to overcome obstacles such as barbed wire entanglements and concrete machine gun shelters, or pill boxes, as they were called. Steps had already been taken to procure an extra supply of wire cutters, and the interest was such that various other means were improvised by engineers and by the troops themselves to enable them to cross the sea of entanglements on the St. Mihiel front.

I went from Bombon to Pétain's headquarters at Chantilly to talk over various details with him. We fixed the boundary between the American sector and that of the French Second Army, which was to attack on our left with six divisions. When we took up the questions of truck transport and additional artillery, he told me that he had issued orders directing all services to give us every assistance. He also said that all the aviation that we had asked for would be brought into the sector, and more besides. It could not yet be definitely determined how much artillery the French could furnish, as a considerable number of the necessary heavy guns were to come from Mangin's Tenth Army, which was then preparing for an operation. I was anxious to begin the attack by the 7th of September, if possible, or by the 10th at the latest, but it looked as though the delay in getting these guns would make it necessary to postpone the date until perhaps the 12th. General Pétain and I felt that it would be necessary to have this heavy artillery to insure our success. But there was danger of being held up by the mud in the plain of the Woëvre if the operation should be deferred too long. Moreover, it was desirable that the attack should be made before the season closed, as the Woëvre would be very difficult in the spring.

Returning to Bombon the following afternoon for further conference with Marshal Foch, I asked him particularly to expedite the arrival of the artillery, advising him that in order to save time the necessary reconnaissance had already been made and the positions for the guns chosen. I pointed out that we should hasten the St. Mihiel operation in order to have more time to prepare for subsequent offensives. We had to wait for the heavy artillery from Mangin's army, however, and were held up until the 12th and there was no way to avoid it.

Marshal Foch and I also spoke of the large program proposed for America in 1919. I mentioned the coming visit of the Secretary of War and suggested that we should get together upon his arrival and go thoroughly into all questions involved. In order that Foch might visualize our problem and be prepared to discuss it with the Secretary, I explained that our War Department feared we should not be able to provide supplies for the contemplated large increase in our forces, but that I thought there should be no hesitation, at least as to subsistence, as we were not making war in a barren country and there would be no danger of serious shortage of food.

Speaking of shipping, I said that we might obtain more for military purposes if only our Government could be induced to commandeer additional tonnage from commercial channels. As to the British, there seemed to be considerable doubt whether they would make much more of an effort, in view of the cable Mr. Lloyd George had sent M. Clemenceau and also of his statement that the amount of tonnage the United Kingdom might furnish could not be determined until after the American Government had declared how much it could provide.

The Marshal really needed no coaching, as he was thoroughly committed to the larger program. He said that in his opinion the Allies should make every effort to win the war in 1919, that the British were tired, that the French were worn out, and that we must hasten the arrival of American divisions. He said that he was doing and would continue to do all in his power to obtain the necessary sea transportation and that his requests had included the British, American and Italian shipping. I suggested that he should go into these details in his conversation with our Secretary of War.

Feeling that possibly Allied effort might be weakened by peace propaganda, then being circulated, I said positively, "We must not let the people listen to rumors that the Germans are ready to make peace; there should be no peace until Germany is completely crushed. We should emphasize this point. We have pacifists who are lukewarm * * * and too much inclined to accept any proposition to have the war stopped."

In support of the 100-division program, General Bliss came to see me and suggested closer coöperation between us in advocating its adoption. As no definite advice had been received from the War Department regarding the greater plans, I continued to urge that the 80-division program be completed by April, 1919, and the 100-division by July, basing my action in recommending the higher number mainly on the probability that the War Department would thus be spurred on to greater effort.

It was my thought also, and I so advised the War Department by cable on the 17th, that if we ourselves should decide to send over 100 divisions the Allies would be the more willing to concede additional tonnage and supplies. Moreover, it was certain that if our people at home could be brought to realize the possible eventual demands, they would be prepared for the necessary sacrifice the effort would entail and we should be all the more likely to attain at least the 80-division program. I conferred with Mr. Hoover on the question of food supply, with Mr. Stettinius on production of munitions, and with Marshal Foch on the military requirements, and all agreed that the maximum should be the goal. Hence, with the thought that insistence would at least insure the 80-division plan being carried out, it was again recommended that there be no hesitation or delay in entering upon the larger plan. I sent the following letter to the Secretary on the subject:

"France, August 17, 1918.

"DEAR MR. SECRETARY:

"I hope you will pardon me for referring so persistently to the large program for next year already recommended by Marshal Foch and myself, but I consider it such a vital matter and so important to our success within a reasonable time that I cannot refrain from again impressing it upon you, knowing that you will fully understand my motives.

"It seems to me that there has never been a full realization of our urgent requirements by those who control the Government's shipping, and this control, as understood over here, rests largely with Mr. Hurley's Board. But whoever may control, they must prepare to meet the program that the Government decides upon, regardless of temporary commercial or other sacrifices that it might entail upon our people. There will be little use for shipping, or little advantage in keeping up commerce if we lose this war. I firmly believe, Mr. Secretary, that if these interests could realize the vital need for more tonnage, they would stand ready to meet it as far as possible, even to the abandonment of certain fruit and other trade with South America.

"The food question, in general and in particular, must, of course, be given every consideration, but after all the fact remains that we are not making war in a country destitute of food supplies and that France has fairly good crops this year. French food supplies, with what England can furnish, would always tide us over any temporary emergency that might arise. Of course, I realize that all in all it is going to require considerable sacrifice to make the necessary saving in Allied food, but with 220,000,000 people in the Allied European countries the supply of 2,000,000 or 3,000,000 men, even though our contribution might be limited, is not likely so to deplete stocks as ever to bring us anywhere near the danger point of starvation. Therefore the question of food should not frighten us off.

"I sincerely hope that the President may decide on the 100-division program as a minimum and establish that as the aim toward which every energy shall be directed. Such a decision would stimulate our Allies to further effort, which, in itself, would be also of almost vital significance. Our own various supply departments and shipping interests, as well as those of our Allies, will then be brought to realize that much greater concessions will have to be made in order to carry out this high purpose of our Government. I am afraid that now they are inclined to hold back and discuss the matter and wonder whether it can be done or not. My strong opinion is that a leap must be made into this big program, and that those who fail to follow must take the consequences. Even though we may fall short, we shall have shown our full appreciation of its importance and our desire to carry it out.

"I am enclosing a copy of my cable of to-day on this subject.

"With expression of my high personal and official esteem, believe me, as always,

"Faithfully yours,

"JOHN J. PERSHING."

In a cablegram dated September 25th the War Department informed me that the 80-division program had been approved by the President and Secretary of War on July 26th. The message expressed the view that it would be impracticable to carry out any larger plan, citing the lack of camp space for having more than eighteen divisions in training at home at the same time. The cable made it clear that the War Department expected to have eighty divisions, or approximately 3,200,000 men, actually in France by July, 1919.

(Diary) Ligny-en-Barrois, Thursday, August 29, 1918. At G.H.Q. all day Monday. Conferred with Andrews, Moseley, Bethel and Eltinge. Saw Walter Damrosch, who has assisted in improving our bands.

Sent cable Tuesday supporting Liberty Loan.[1] Cabled objections

---

[1] "The men of the American Expeditionary Forces expect that the Fourth Liberty Loan will be subscribed.

"In the camps and villages of France we have been training and preparing these many months for the supreme test. In the ports and along the roads that reach from the sea to the battle front, we have been organizing, constructing, and achieving.

"We have toiled cheerfully against the day of battle, and the spirit that has urged us on through the discomfort and drudgery of the winter, in muddy field and sodden trench, in storm-swept port, in rain and sunshine, has been the determination to be worthy of those whom we left behind when we crossed the seas. By the side of the Allied veterans of the four years' conflict we have made a beginning as proof of what we hope to accomplish.

"The news of America awake, of the national spirit more strong, more unified, more determined day by day thrills us all. We have a thousand proofs that our people are behind us. The past successful loans, the fleets that are being launched, the voluntary to plan of starting school at home for higher commanders with French and British instructors. Issued General Order [1] commending I and III Corps.

Went to Neufchâteau Tuesday afternoon to confer with First Army Staff and returned yesterday. Sent de Marenches to French G.H.Q. to see about tanks, airplanes, and gas shells. Washington complains not receiving prompt report of casualties. Received Sir Connop Guthrie, British Shipping Board, and stressed Allied obligation to pool shipping. Saw Moseley regarding St. Dizier regulating station.

Arrived at Ligny-en-Barrois this morning. Visited headquarters I Corps (Liggett) and IV Corps (Dickman). Preparations for attack going well. Sent confidential message to the President.

I was very desirous of improving the music of the bands throughout the A.E.F., particularly on account of its beneficial effect upon the morale of the troops. For this purpose a number of musicians were selected from the various regimental bands and assembled in Chaumont for instruction. My idea also was to organize our bands so that it would be possible to separate each one into three parts when necessary to furnish music to the battalions, especially on the march. Out of the assembly of musicians grew the Headquarters Band. To Mr. Damrosch is largely due the credit for the development of this very remarkable organiza-

economies willingly undergone for the cause of world freedom, make us proud that we represent you.

"The American spirit of liberty and freedom urges us to continue until the end. It is the knowledge of that spirit which makes us certain that our people at home will stand behind us as they have from the beginning so that we may return soon to you, the victory won."

[1] France, August 28, 1918.

General Orders ⎱
   No. 143. ⎰

It fills me with pride to record in General Orders a tribute to the service and achievements of the First and Third Corps, comprising the 1st, 2d, 3d, 4th, 26th, 28th, 32d and 42d Divisions of the American Expeditionary Forces.

You came to the battlefield at the crucial hour of the Allied cause. For almost four years the most formidable army the world had as yet seen had pressed its invasion of France, and stood threatening its capital. At no time had that army been more powerful or menacing than when, on July 15th, it struck again to destroy in one great battle the brave men opposed to it and to enforce its brutal will upon the world and civilization.

Three days later, in conjunction with our Allies, you counterattacked. The Allied Armies gained a brilliant victory that marks the turning point of the war. You did more than give our brave Allies the support to which as a nation our faith was pledged.

tion, in which many of the bandsmen from different units of the army had an opportunity to serve. Most of these men were returned to their own bands, thus exerting an excellent influence on the music of the A.E.F.

The question of training came up again, this time through the receipt of a cable saying that an advanced course of military instruction for higher commanders would be conducted at home by selected French and British officers. Our experience in France and our observation of the results of training at home under foreign officers did not point to the success of this higher course. As we had already abandoned the use of such instructors in the A.E.F., I cabled my objections to the plan, and suggested that competent American officers be employed. My cable stated that too much tutelage by Allied officers tended to rob our officers of a sense of responsibility and initiative. It was well known that many of these officers sent to the States were not professional soldiers, but were men whose knowledge was limited to personal experience in subordinate grades in trench warfare. Moreover, the French doctrine, as well as the British, was based upon the cautious advance of infantry with prescribed objectives, where obstacles had been destroyed and resistance largely broken by artillery. The French infantryman, as has been already stated, did not rely upon his rifle and made little use of its great power. The infantry of both the French and British were poor skirmishers as a result of extended service in the trenches. Our mission required an aggressive offensive based on self-reliant infantry.

The organization of our army was radically different from that of any of the Allied armies and we could not become imitators

You proved that our altruism, our pacific spirit, our sense of justice have not blunted our virility or our courage. You have shown that American initiative and energy are as fit for the test of war as for the pursuits of peace. You have justly won the unstinted praise of our Allies and the eternal gratitude of our countrymen.

We have paid for our success in the lives of many of our brave comrades. We shall cherish their memory always, and claim for our history and our literature their bravery, achievement and sacrifice.

This order will be read to all organizations at the first assembly formation after its receipt.

JOHN J. PERSHING,
General, Commander-in-Chief.

of methods which applied especially to armies in which initiative was more or less repressed by infinite attention to detail in directives prepared for their guidance. It was my belief, as cabled the War Department, that efficiency could be attained only by adherence to our own doctrines based upon thorough appreciation of the American temperament, qualifications and deficiencies. I recommended the withdrawal of all instruction in the United States from the hands of Allied instructors. This recommendation was promptly approved by the Chief of Staff, who entirely agreed with my views.

In preparation for the coming offensives, the Advance Headquarters of the First Army was moved from Neufchâteau on August 29th to Ligny-en-Barrois, a small town some twenty-five miles southwest of St. Mihiel. It was from Ligny that activities were directed during the St. Mihiel operation.

When we arrived, the French General who was being relieved and his Chief of Staff, all dressed up in their red trousers and blue coats, came formally to turn over the command. The Chief of Staff carried two large volumes, each consisting of about 150 pages, the first being the Offensive Plan and the second the Defensive Plan for the St. Mihiel salient. These they presented to me with considerable ceremony. My orders had been already prepared, the one for the attack comprising six pages and the one for the defense eight pages. This incident is cited merely to show the difference between planning for trench warfare, to which the French were inclined, and open warfare, which we expected to conduct.

At Ligny-en-Barrois we were in close touch with the front. The I Corps Headquarters was established at Saizerais, northeast of Toul, and the IV at Toul, as both corps were to be engaged on the south side of the salient. During my visit on the 29th, I went over their plans and examined the progress they were making in the assembly of troops. Each corps headquarters was charged with the location and general control of divisions and other elements arriving within the sector of the corps for assignment to its organization.

The I Corps staff had gained much experience in the Marne battle and although the staff of the IV Corps was without such experience both were well handled during the St. Mihiel battle and later.

The considerable circulation of troops in the St. Mihiel area naturally started our officers and men and the people talking about the possibility of an attack against the salient. It was feared that the enemy would hear rumors to this effect and conclude that the danger was immediate and either reënforce his position or withdraw to a line farther back. Up to this time our movements had not been definite enough to indicate the exact sector in which the attack was to be made. However, it was thought advisable to attract the enemy's attention elsewhere. Hoping that it would reach his ear, the news was quietly given out at headquarters that our first offensive might be in the direction of Mulhouse, in the Rhine valley beyond the Vosges Mountains, northeast of Belfort.[1]

It was also decided to make a diversion in that direction and as a preliminary step an officer was sent to lease necessary buildings in Belfort for the use of headquarters. At the same time, confidential instructions were given to Major General Bundy, commanding the VI Corps, to proceed to Belfort with a limited staff and prepare detailed plans for an offensive in the direction of Mulhouse and the heights to the southeast, with the object of eventually establishing our line along the Rhine. In the letter of instructions seven divisions were mentioned as having been designated for the attack and three officers from each of these units were detailed to report to General Bundy to assist in reconnaissance work. He was directed to expedite preparations and was informed that the movement would probably begin about September 8th, under my personal command.

The presence of a major general and an active staff in Belfort must have caused some apprehension among the Germans. In any event, two days later reports began to come in that a hospital

[1] To further this rumor, division radios were secretly directed to become active north of Lunéville.

and considerable numbers of the population were moving to the other side of the Rhine. Meanwhile, plans were being prepared in all seriousness, when one day Colonel A. L. Conger, who was in the secret and was acting as my representative, carelessly (?) left in his room at the hotel, as directed, a copy of instructions to the commander of the VI Corps, only to find upon his return that it had disappeared, no doubt at the hands of some spy. This apparently served to confirm the worst of German fears, for within a few days one of his reserve divisions was reported moving up to that front while another was sent to Mulhouse and two more to the Vosges farther north. The French staff gave valuable assistance by circulating false rumors about our plans. So the ruse apparently had been successful and the result quieted our anxiety over the situation for the time being.

The progress of the Allies since July 18th had been greater than expected and as a consequence the Allied program had been extended. At the same time, the weakness among Germany's allies was becoming more evident. With the prospect of three months of seasonable weather for active operations on a large scale, with every assurance of victory in our first independent offensive, and confidence in the plans in preparation for further offensives to follow, it seemed to me not unreasonable to hope for the successful conclusion of the war in 1918. In order that President Wilson might be apprised of my views, I sent word to him that there was such a possibility, and suggested that the utmost pressure, both diplomatic and commercial, be brought to bear upon neutrals as well as upon Germany's allies to the end that Germany might be forced to regard a continuance of the war as futile.

CHAPTER XLII

Thirty-second Division at Juvigny—St. Mihiel Transferred to American
Command—Foch Makes Impossible Proposition—Would Break up
American Army—Decline Approval—Conference with Pétain—Further Discussion with Foch—Agreement Reached—Americans Assigned
to Meuse-Argonne Front—Lord Reading Advocates American Army
near British—Diaz Requests Twenty-five American Divisions

(Diary) Paris, Monday, September 2, 1918. Our 32d Division has
done splendid work in attack as part of French Tenth Army.

On Friday, the 30th, assumed command over definite American
sector extending from Port-sur-Seille to Watronville. That same evening Marshal Foch called at Ligny-en-Barrois and proposed a new
American front and the assignment of several divisions of the French
armies, which I flatly disapproved.

On Saturday at Nettancourt saw Pétain, who disagrees with Foch's
idea and favors an American sector from the Moselle to the Argonne.
Had dinner with Pétain on his train. Generals McAndrew and
Conner conferred with Weygand, Foch's Chief of Staff.

Visited the I and IV Corps Headquarters yesterday. Pétain and I
met Marshal Foch this afternoon and after prolonged discussion
reached an understanding with him regarding American operations.

THE attack of the French Tenth Army which began on the
morning of August 29th was undertaken to force the
retirement of the enemy from the Vesle and Aisne Rivers.
On its relief from the Vesle on August 7th, the 32d Division
(Haan) was assigned to the Tenth Army and entered the line

NOTE: Total strength of the A.E.F. on August 31st, 61,061 officers, 1,354,067 enlisted
men.

Among divisional units arriving in August were elements of the following divisions:
7th Division (Regular Army), Brig. Gen. Charles H. Barth; 39th Division (National
Guard, Arkansas, Mississippi and Louisiana), Maj. Gen. Henry C. Hodges, Jr.; 40th
Division (National Guard, California, Colorado, Utah, Arizona and New Mexico), Maj.
Gen. Frederick S. Strong; 81st Division (National Army, North Carolina, South Caro-
lina, Florida, and Porto Rico), Maj. Gen. Charles J. Bailey; 85th Division (National
Army, Michigan and Wisconsin), Maj. Gen. Chase W. Kennedy; 88th Division (Na-
tional Army, North Dakota, Minnesota, Iowa and Illinois), Brig. Gen. William D.
Beach.

on August 28th, immediately undertaking a series of local operations, in which gains were made in the face of very heavy fire. The ravines and the numerous caves in the region provided ideal cover for the defending troops. The general attack of the army on the following day met with but slight success, the enemy resisting desperately along his entire front, but on the 30th, by a flank attack from the south, the 32d Division captured Juvigny, pushing a small salient into the German lines. Hard fighting

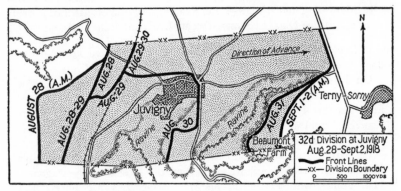

continued on the 31st, but by the end of the day the division had reached the important Soissons-St. Quentin road, where it was relieved on September 3d. The 32d Division had advanced nearly three miles and its success contributed greatly to the forced withdrawal of the German line to the Aisne River.

As pre-arranged between General Pétain and myself, the sector from Port-sur-Seille (east of the Moselle River) to Watronville (north of Les Eparges), forty-two miles in extent, then occupied by the entire French Eighth Army and a part of the French Second Army, was transferred to my command on August 30th. The front included the St. Mihiel salient, and embraced the permanent fortresses around Toul. We had three divisions in line on the southern face of the salient, but the mass of our battle troops were not to take over the trenches until the night before the attack.

As we have seen, there had been a great deal of discussion leading up to the agreement regarding the St. Mihiel offensive.

On August 16th, preliminary instructions had been issued by me and these had been supplemented from time to time by verbal directions, and now everything was moving smoothly toward readiness for the attack, with Marieulles—Mars-la-Tour—Etain as the objective. In my conversation with Foch as late as August 25th, he had even suggested the extension of our front on the west of the salient. Two French corps in the sector had been assigned to my command and arrangements for the transfer to the area of auxiliary troops and services had been agreed upon with no hint that he was not in full accord with our plans.

On August 30th, the day when I assumed command of the sector, Marshal Foch, accompanied by Weygand, his Chief of Staff, came to my residence at Ligny-en-Barrois and after the usual exchange of greetings he presented an entirely new plan for the employment of the American Army. He began by saying that the German armies were in more or less disorder from recent attacks by the Allies and that we must not allow them to reorganize, that the British would continue their attack in the direction of Cambrai and St. Quentin and the French toward Mesnil. Then, much to my surprise, he proposed that the objectives in the St. Mihiel operation should be restricted and the attack be made on the southern face only, and that upon its completion two other operations be undertaken by combined Americans and French, a number of our divisions going *under French command*. His plans, defining the operations after St. Mihiel, were as follows:

"(a) An attack between the Meuse and the Argonne executed by the French Second Army reënforced by a few American divisions (4 or 6), to be prepared at once and launched as soon as possible after that in Woëvre.

"(b) A French-American attack extending from the Argonne to the Souain road, to be prepared also without any delay so that it may be launched a few days after the preceding one. This attack will be executed by: On the right, an American army acting on each side of the Aisne—on the left the French Fourth Army extending its action to the Souain road."

244 MY EXPERIENCES IN THE WORLD WAR

He said, "I realize that I am presenting a number of new ideas and that you will probably need time to think them over, but I should like your first impressions," which I did not hesitate a moment to give.

I said, "Well, Marshal, this is a very sudden change. We are going forward as already recommended to you and approved by you, and I cannot understand why you want these changes. Moreover, I think that to make an attack in the salient with limited objectives would cost little less than to carry out the original idea, which would put us in much better position."

He then said, "That is true, but the fate of the 1918 campaign will be decided in the Aisne region and I wish to limit the Woëvre (St. Mihiel) attack so that the Americans can participate in the Meuse offensive, which will produce still greater results."

"But," I said, "Marshal Foch, here on the very day that you turn over a sector to the American Army, and almost on the eve of an offensive, you ask me to reduce the operation so that you can take away several of my divisions and assign some to the French Second Army [1] and use others to form an American army to operate on the Aisne in conjunction with the French Fourth Army, leaving me with little to do except hold what will become a quiet sector after the St. Mihiel offensive. This virtually destroys the American army that we have been trying so long to form."

He suggested that if I could give a satisfactory solution which would permit the execution of the operations in view he would be glad, but he did not think it possible. He said that he had studied the question carefully and had sincerely looked for some way to avoid dividing the American Army, but he did not believe it could be found.

I suggested that, "One way might be to withdraw the Americans from other sectors and put them in with their right on the Meuse and let them extend as far to the west as possible."

He then said, "That might be considered, although it would

[1] With the American First Army then in the St. Mihiel sector, the French Second Army was the next on our left and the French Fourth Army on the left of the Second.

be difficult to execute the St. Mihiel operation and have time to shift the command to another front for an operation there, but there would be no objection to relieving American divisions from the Woëvre (St. Mihiel) by tired French divisions later so that they could be sent to one or both of the proposed American groups."

He then requested me to send reserve divisions toward the Aisne while the St. Mihiel battle was going on and said that later, having made studies and general preparation for the attack, I could go and take command when the army was formed.

Referring again to the St. Mihiel operation, I argued that there would be less risk if we should attack on both sides of the salient. He seemed to think there was danger of our becoming too deeply involved in that sector, although in the conference in July he had stated that clearing the salient would bring us within reach of the Briey Basin and permit action on a larger scale between the Meuse and the Moselle.

However, he now clung to the idea that the objective should be the line Regniéville—Thiaucourt—Vigneulles and that the attack should be made only on the southern face. But I did not think it wise, at this eleventh hour, to make changes in our solution of the problem. I was willing to accept the limited objectives, but held out in favor of the secondary attack from the west.

Supporting his plans further, Marshal Foch suggested that for the operation in the Aisne he could put General Degoutte, who was thoroughly familiar with that region, and General Malcor, who was also acquainted with the country, having been Chief of Artillery of the Fourth Army, at my disposal to aid an American staff, while I was engaged in the Woëvre. This was only a round-about way of attempting to assign General Degoutte to command our forces. Many officers who had served under him on the Vesle felt that because of his orders American troops had been unnecessarily sacrificed, so for both reasons I disapproved the suggestion. The Marshal then restated his proposal and added that if the two American contingents, one being the group assigned to the French Second Army and the other the proposed

246 MY EXPERIENCES IN THE WORLD WAR

American army on the opposite side of the Argonne, should eventually join hands, he could only see advantage in this.

The further we proceeded in the discussion the more apparent it became to me that the result of any of these proposals would be to prevent, or at least seriously delay, the formation of a distinct American army. In this event, it was certain that despite the contribution of our splendid units whatever success might be attained would be counted as the achievement of the French armies and our participation regarded entirely secondary.

I asked why these Americans which he proposed should go to the Aisne should not replace French divisions in the French Second Army, then between the Meuse River and the Argonne Forest. In other words, why should not the Americans take over the whole sector then occupied by the French Second Army west of the Meuse, thus making the French troops relieved available to reënforce the French Fourth Army. I repeated what I had often said that the American Government and people expected the army to act as a unit and not be dispersed in this way. I pointed out that each time we were about to complete the organization of our army some proposition like this was presented to prevent it.

Marshal Foch then said, "Do you wish to take part in the battle?" I replied, "Most assuredly, but as an American Army and in no other way." He argued that there would not be time, whereupon I said, "If you will assign me a sector I will take it at once." He asked, "Where would it be?" I replied, "Wherever you say." He then referred to our lack of artillery and other auxiliary troops. I reminded him that the French had insisted on our shipping to France only infantry and machine gun units and had said that they would supply us temporarily with auxiliary troops when needed. I pointed out that he himself had made repeated and urgent requests for such shipments and had promised that we should be furnished whatever units were necessary to complete our organization until our artillery and other troops should arrive. I then demanded that he fulfill these promises.

He said, "It is now August 30th, and the attack must begin on September 15th; it is a question of time," adding that he was quite ready to listen to any proposition, but we must start on the 15th. My reply was that I was willing to send divisions west of the Argonne Forest as part of an American army, but that I did not approve of putting any divisions in the French Second Army. He then asserted that this would not leave the Second Army enough troops with which to attack.

Among my other suggestions, one was that we should operate east of the Meuse River, and another that we should have two armies, one west and the other east of the Argonne Forest. Both proposals were rejected. When I offered definitely to extend the front of our army to include the sector between the Meuse and the Argonne, he said this had been his original idea.

However, he pleaded lack of time, and continued to reiterate his requests for the adoption of his plan until I was provoked to say: "Marshal Foch, you have no authority as Allied Commander-in-Chief to call upon me to yield up my command of the American Army and have it scattered among the Allied forces where it will not be an American army at all."

He was apparently surprised at my remark, and said, "I must insist upon the arrangement," to which I replied, as we both rose from the table where we sat, "Marshal Foch, you may insist all you please, but I decline absolutely to agree to your plan. While our army will fight wherever you may decide, it will not fight except as an independent American army." I then pointed out to him that I had depended upon him to assist in completing the organization of our army, and that we had all been criticized for parcelling out our troops here and there. I drew his attention to the message President Wilson had sent to the embassies in Washington stating that the American Army should fight as such on the Western Front.

He said he was disposed to do what he could toward forming an American army. He then picked up his maps and papers and left, very pale and apparently exhausted, saying at the door, as he handed me the memorandum of his proposal, that he thought that after careful study I would arrive at the same conclusion he had.

The impression this meeting left on my mind was that Marshal Foch was inclined to approve the formation of an American army, but had allowed himself to be persuaded that after the reduction of the St. Mihiel salient it should be split up as proposed. With the added support of American divisions, making the Second Army largely American, Foch's advisers no doubt thought that the French themselves would then be able to push forward and cut Germany's vital lines of communication.

I was ready to use our forces wherever it seemed best, but not under French commanders, except as a temporary measure. The plan suggested for the American participation in these operations, with a considerable number of our divisions under their command, was not in any sense acceptable to me. It was directly contrary to my belief that an American army under its own flag could best serve the Allied cause.

An enormous amount of preparation had been made in our area in the construction of roads, railroads, regulating stations, hospitals, and other installations looking to the use and supply of our armies on a particular front. Our divisions had already begun to move up to their battle positions. Moreover, the inherent disinclination of our troops to serve under Allied commanders had grown to open disapproval and if continued under the changes proposed would have been entirely destructive of American morale.

Because of its importance, the principal points of my formal reply to Foch of August 31st are given below:

"I have carefully examined your note of August 30th, in which you point out the fact that the successes already obtained are far beyond those foreseen by your decision of July 24th. I agree with you that it is now essential to exploit to the utmost the present situation.

" * * * I can no longer agree to any plan which involves a dispersion of our units. This is a matter whose importance is such as to demand very frank discussion. Briefly, American officers and soldiers alike are, after one experience, no longer willing to be incorporated in other armies, even though such incorporation be by larger units. The older American divisions have encountered so much difficulty in their service with the French and British that it is inadvisable to consider the return of such divisions to French or British control. The same is true of our corps staffs.

"It has been said that the American Army is a fiction and that it cannot now be actually formed because it lacks artillery and services. Unfortunately, this lack is evident. But our shortages in this respect are due to the fact that America brought over infantry and machine gunners to the virtual exclusion of the services and auxiliaries. Permit me also to recall that when this decision was made, there was coupled with it a promise that the Allies would undertake to provide the necessary services and auxiliaries, and that you yourself have repeatedly guaranteed the formation of a real American army. It seems to me that it is far more appropriate at the present moment for the Allies temporarily to furnish the American Army with the services and auxiliaries it needs than for the Allies to expect further delay in the formation of an American army. I am writing faithfully my own ideas, which are those not only of every American officer and soldier, but also of my Government.

" * * * Since our arrival in France our plans, not only with the consent but at the initiative of the French authorities, have been based on the organization of the American Army on the front St. Mihiel-Belfort. All our depots, hospitals, training areas and other installations are located with reference to this front, and a change of these plans cannot be easily made. For instance, the care of our wounded must be foreseen. We have already had very grave difficulty and no little dissatisfaction in those of our divisions serving under conditions which made us dependent on the French for the handling and care of our sick and wounded.

"With reference to the objective to be considered in the St. Mihiel operation, I agree, of course, with you that an advance to the line Thiaucourt-Vigneulles would accomplish the primary result sought by the operation. I think, however, that it is advisable, even in limiting the result sought, to make the attack north of Les Éparges, at least as a secondary operation. Unfortunately, both the French and the Americans have talked and it now seems certain that the enemy is aware of the approaching attack. Nevertheless, I believe that the attack should be made and that decision as to the extent to which any success should be exploited should be reserved. To do this it seems essential that I should hold available all the divisions I am now concentrating for the St. Mihiel operation.

"The number of American divisions which will be available immediately after the attack cannot, of course, be foretold with any certainty. However, it would appear entirely impracticable to carry out the St. Mihiel operation and to assemble the 12 to 16 American divisions for an attack in the direction of Mézières between the 15th and 20th of September. In fact, it would be necessary to begin at once the movements preliminary to the assembly of the 12 or 16 divisions contemplated by your note. It is improbable that any of the divisions actually engaged in the St. Mihiel operation could be withdrawn and placed in position for the Mézières operation by September 20th. Then, too, the second-line divisions which will not become involved even in the limited attack can hardly exceed six, and these could not be the most experienced divisions.

"Assuming, however, that six of the divisions from the St. Mihiel operation would be available, we should still have to find six to ten divisions in order to make up the 12 to 16 divisions which your note contemplates for employment in the Mézières operation, and we must seek these divisions elsewhere. * * *

"It seems apparent to me that it is impracticable to carry out even the limited St. Mihiel operation and yet assemble 12 to 16 American divisions, suitable for undertaking an offensive, by September 15th or 20th. It therefore follows that the St. Mihiel operation must be abandoned or that the Mézières operation must be postponed if 12 to 16 American divisions are to participate in the latter operation. Moreover, if the St. Mihiel operation is carried out, it is only after its completion that it would be practicable to fix a date upon which it would be possible to have available 12 to 16 American divisions fit for a powerful offensive.

" * * * In your capacity as Allied Commander-in-Chief, it is your province to decide as to the strategy of operations, and I abide by your decisions.

"Finally, however, there is one thing that must not be done and that is to disperse the American forces among the Allied armies; the danger of destroying by such dispersion the fine morale of the American soldier is too great, to say nothing of the results to be obtained by using the American Army as a whole. If you decide to utilize American forces in attacking in the direction of Mézières, I accept that decision, even though it complicates my supply system and the care of sick and wounded, but I do insist that the American Army must be employed as a whole, either east of the Argonne or west of the Argonne, and not four or five divisions here and six or seven there."

In my letter I also brought out the possibility that the American Army could carry out the St. Mihiel offensive and immediately thereafter attack in the vicinity of Belfort or Lunéville; the entire sector from St. Mihiel to the Swiss Border being eventually turned over to us. It was my plan that after the above operations we should advance either to the northeast or to the east.

On the afternoon of the 31st, General Pétain and I held a conference on his train at Nettancourt to consider the change in arrangements that would be required by the limited St. Mihiel operation. The point first to be decided was whether or not the attack planned against the western face of the salient should be abandoned. Originally three or four American divisions, with five or six French divisions on their left, were to make this assault, while the principal blow was being struck by a wholly American force against the southern face. The newly proposed operations would make unnecessary the participation of the six French divisions and at least two of the American divisions.

Being decidedly of the opinion that an attack on the western face would be necessary to give us the maximum benefit from the effort to be made north of Toul, I proposed that there should be at least one or preferably two divisions in the attack from the west, to support the seven divisions in the first line on the southern face. Opening a map on which he had sketched a project for this offensive, Pétain showed exactly the same dispositions and number of divisions which I had planned in an independent study. It was our opinion that once Marshal Foch had determined the strategical use of an army by prescribing the direction and extent of its employment, the details were solely the province of the Commander-in-Chief of the army concerned and that Foch had nothing further to do with it.

We then considered the question of putting the American Army astride the Aisne as proposed by the Marshal. A glance at the map showed the difficulty of working along the valley of the Aisne, as the heights of the left bank dominated those on the right, while deep ravines and projecting ridges offered serious obstacles. The main objection, however, was that, in addition to putting units under the French, our army would be separated into two parts, with a French army between them. Pétain was strongly of my opinion that this should not be done, but that the American Army in the Woëvre should continue to hold that sector and expand from there.

We agreed that, beginning with the Moselle, its then eastern flank, the American front could gradually be extended to the west as the forces increased. By retaining its position in the Woëvre, it would, in fact, be possible to widen its front in either or both directions. We concluded that eventually the American First Army might extend to Douaumont, the Second to the Suippe River and the Third to Reims, relieving the French Second Army and then the Fourth. Pétain thought the Americans would later deliver the final blow.

Referring to Metz, I expressed the view that it would have a tremendous moral and material effect on Germany if we should make an advance in that direction. Pétain considered that it could not well be undertaken until after the line had been straightened out along the Meuse. It was evident that the Marshal thought all could be settled on the left of that line. I referred to the dependence of Germany on the mines north of Metz and pointed out how jealously guarded that region was by the Germans. Eventually, Pétain thought, developments should lead to offensives in two directions, one toward Belgium and the other toward Metz, but he did not think the latter would be feasible until the Germans were back of the Ardennes. He was, however, anxious to see it carried out.

Marshal Foch did not favor an extended operation east of the Meuse on account of lack of communications, he said, although, as we have seen, he had previously suggested it. In my opinion, an advance in that direction would encounter less elaborate defenses than west of the Meuse and it was the shortest route to the German line of communications and supply.

After some further discussion, Pétain definitely proposed that he should transfer to the Americans the whole of the front from the Moselle River to the Argonne Forest, which was what I had suggested to Foch the day before, as he opposed an advance to the northeast. In the event that we should attack between the Meuse and the Argonne, Pétain thought all that could be done before winter would be to take Montfaucon, and that we could not contemplate this attack to the west of the Meuse until the St. Mihiel salient had been reduced.

My Chief of Staff, McAndrew, and Chief of Operations, Fox Conner, were sent to confer with Weygand on the 1st of September and returned to Ligny-en-Barrois with word that Marshal Foch desired to see General Pétain and me the following day. Motoring to Pétain's headquarters with Boyd and de Marenches, we found McAndrew and Conner had preceded us, and after lunch we went to Bombon. The others present at the conference were Marshal Foch and his immediate staff and General Pétain with his Chief of Staff, General Buat, and Colonels Dufieux and Payot.

As a result of the several conversations that had taken place since the 30th, it seemed probable that we would reach an understanding. When we met, there was little of the atmosphere of the meeting of August 30th. In opening the conference, Foch referred to the note he had handed me at that time and to my reply and asked for my observations. Stating my opinion that we should unite in carrying out vigorous offensives to the fullest possible extent, I explained that if it should be deemed necessary to abandon the St. Mihiel project in order to begin the larger offensive, which he had decided should be west of the Meuse, I would abide by his decision.

I would have regretted, however, to leave the salient unmolested. One reason was that it had been in possession of the Germans since September, 1914, and covered a very sensitive section behind the enemy's position on the Western Front, which included the Mézières—Sedan—Metz railway system and the Briey iron basin. Moreover, its reduction would relieve the threat against the French region opposite, including the railway from Paris to the east, and would afford the victors a new line of departure for further operations toward the northeast. If left undisturbed, it would render precarious the circulation in the rear of an army operating west of the Meuse or on the Nancy front. Finally, and this was a very important consideration, Pétain and I believed that its capture by the Americans would immensely stimulate Allied morale.

Taking up my reply, Marshal Foch said that, if he understood me correctly, I wished to postpone the St. Mihiel operation and concentrate entirely upon operations west of the Meuse. I explained that this was not exactly correct, but that to begin an operation west of the Meuse between the 15th and 20th of September, as he had suggested, would be impossible if we were to conduct the St. Mihiel offensive on the 10th, unless we could have plenty of transportation.

In the ensuing discussion, while there was considerable sparring, including a review of the number and state of preparation of our divisions and the length of front we should take over, it was agreed that the American Army should operate as a unit under its own commander on the Meuse-Argonne front. In my opinion, with which some of the French fully agreed, none of the Allied troops had the morale or the aggressive spirit to overcome the difficulties to be met in that sector.

Marshal Foch concluded that the date for the operation should be postponed so that we could first carry out the limited attack at St. Mihiel. We finally reached the definite understanding that after St. Mihiel our First Army should prepare to begin this second offensive not later than September 25th. The French Fourth Army was to advance at the same time west of the Argonne. The line from the Moselle to the Argonne, ninety miles long, was to be under my command and was to include certain French divisions to be left in the sector, the details of boundaries between the French and American sectors to be settled by General Pétain and myself.

Our commitments now represented a gigantic task, a task involving the execution of the major operation against the St. Mihiel salient and the transfer of certain troops employed in that battle, together with many others, to a new front, and the initiation of the second battle, all in the brief space of two weeks. Plans for this second concentration involved the movement of some

600,000 men and 2,700 guns, more than half of which would have to be transferred from the battlefield of St. Mihiel by only three roads, almost entirely during the hours of darkness. In other words, we had undertaken to launch with practically the same army, within the next twenty-four days, two great attacks on battlefields sixty miles apart.

Each of the Allied armies already occupied its own front, and the necessary installations, more complicated than the public utility services of a great city, were established. We were confronted with the problem of taking over an inactive portion of the line and had to put in many facilities required in an active sector. The time was very short. A million tons of supplies and munitions had to be transported to the Meuse-Argonne front before the day of the attack. As most of our truck transportation was involved at this time in connection with the St. Mihiel operation, only a limited amount was at once available for use in preparing for the second attack. When viewed as a whole, it is believed that history gives no parallel of such an undertaking with so large an army.

At that moment, it could not be said that my staff in the First Army was perfect, but it had done exceedingly well so far and was being rapidly whipped into shape under the able direction of Colonel H. A. Drum, the First Army Chief of Staff, and his principal assistants. The staffs of two of the four army corps had gained profitable experience, but the other two had just recently been organized. It was only my absolute faith in the energy and resourcefulness of our officers of both staff and line and the resolute and aggressive courage of our soldiers that permitted me to accept such a prodigious undertaking.

It was a relief to have a decision. While certain changes were necessary in plans under way, nevertheless the limits placed on the St. Mihiel operation made the preliminary work somewhat lighter. In spite of this fact, the additional burden on my First Army staff imposed by the second offensive was so great that I at once assigned several officers from G.H.Q. to assist. Immediate instructions were issued to carry out the amended program.

(Diary) Ligny-en-Barrois, Friday, September 6, 1918. On Tuesday Lord Reading called on me in Paris to discuss shipping. He also pointed out the advantages of having the American Army near the British. General Diaz came to request American divisions. Arrived at Ligny-en-Barrois 11 P.M.

Spent Wednesday at First Army Headquarters, reaching Chaumont for dinner. General Ireland reported 100,000 hospital beds available.

Held conference yesterday on instruction of divisions. Returned to Ligny, stopping at aviation center, Colombey-les-Belles.

Harbord came up to-day, giving encouraging account of race between ports in handling cargo. Sent cable urging that army artillery, engineers, signal troops and field hospitals be hurried over. Reports indicate President urging economic and political pressure against Germany by Scandinavian countries.

In my discussion of shipping with Lord Reading, the increase of British tonnage for our use seemed to hinge on the allotment of a greater proportion of our troops for service with their armies. He advocated having the American Army near theirs, especially maintaining that our supply and equipment would really be facilitated, all of which was a repetition of arguments other British officials had advanced. But the question as to the employment of our troops was settled. Lord Reading's engaging personality made it interesting to talk with him, even though we were on different sides of the question, he as an advocate without particular conviction and I entrenched behind the sound principle involved.

Later in the day, General Diaz, the Italian Commander-in-Chief, with whom I was on very friendly terms, called to see me, and in the course of our conversation it developed that the real purpose of his visit was to ask that American troops be sent for service with the Italian armies. In framing his request, he at first mentioned twenty divisions, and as I showed no evidence of surprise, having become quite accustomed to that sort of thing, he possibly thought that was a favorable sign, so while the interpreter was translating what he had said he interrupted and raised the number to twenty-five divisions. With all the auxiliary services that would have been required to constitute an army of that many divisions, it would have reached the modest total of 1,000,000 men.

This request, coming from one in his position, was so astonishing that it was difficult to regard it seriously. In reply, it seemed unnecessary to go into details, so I merely let him know very politely that we were in need of troops ourselves and could not send any more to Italy. But taking up the question of operations, I suggested to General Diaz that it would be of immense help to the Allies if the Italian armies could assume the offensive also and take advantage of the situation in which the Germans found themselves with all their forces in France engaged on the defensive. He said his staff was studying the matter, but that if his troops should attack now he would have no reserves left for operations the following spring, a course of reasoning which was not easy to follow.

Other conferences filled a busy day, to which was added a motor trip to Ligny-en-Barrois, with a brief stop at Vitry-le-François for dinner. This journey took me through portions of the scene of the First Battle of the Marne, where the successive phases of the battle could be traced by the crosses over the graves of those who had fallen. Whenever I passed through this district I could not help thinking of the dreadful toll in human life that modern war demanded. As we were now about to enter into an active campaign, the thought came to me, perhaps as never before, that many an American boy would likewise be buried on the battlefield before the contest in which we were engaged should come to an end.

Since the war the remains of those of our men who were left in France have been gathered into a few cemeteries, where they lie in precise rows under the shadow of our own flag within the sacred limits of their small bit of America. Most of these spots mark the field of valor where they fell and each has become a shrine where devoted comrades and countrymen may come in remembrance of American youth who consecrated their lives to a sublime cause. It has been a great privilege for me to be at the head of the commission to erect suitable monuments in our cemeteries and on our battlefields, through which a grateful people may commemorate the heroism of their sons. But no matter what else we may do to beautify the hallowed ground where our dead lie buried, nothing can ever take the place of the white marble crosses and stars that mark their graves. These stand as memorials of sacrifice and as symbols of our faith in immortality.

CHAPTER XLIII

Preparations for St. Mihiel Completed—Description of Terrain—Plan of
Battle—Order of Battle—Attack Begins—Objectives Taken First Day
—Salient Wiped Out—Visit Town with Pétain—Our Victory Inspiring—Congratulatory Messages—Clemenceau on our Front—President
and Madame Poincaré Visit Ruins of Home

(Diary) Ligny-en-Barrois, Tuesday, September 10, 1918. On Saturday visited 90th, 2d and 89th Divisions and found much enthusiasm
regarding the coming offensive. Presented decorations to men of the
1st, 3d and 42d.

Chief of French Aviation, General Duval, came Sunday to place
French air units under our control.

General Pétain called Monday and seemed surprised at completeness
of our plans of attack.

Secretary Baker arrived at Brest on the 8th and came from Paris
this morning. He at once visited various corps and division headquarters. Final conference was held this afternoon with corps commanders and their chiefs of staff. Germans seem to suspect an attack
by Americans.[1] Mr. Baker speaks highly of officers and men of the
Mount Vernon.[2]

---

[1] Extract from German paper, *Taeglische Rundschau*, of Sept. 1st: "General von
Siebert foresees an early blow from American forces. Even though the German official
communiqué says 'all is well and our front holds good,' and though French and British
attacks have failed and their fronts have not been enlarged lately, there is another
danger against which we must guard; a danger coming from the south, on the Aisne-
Vesle. We must reckon with America's strength and numbers we have learned to
know and understand. We shall see soon in what form they intend to participate. * * *
As Americans pay strict attention to clock-like working of their machine, we must
expect them to take their time while making minute studies and preparations for their
attack."

[2] Mr. Baker sent the Secretary of the Navy on Sept. 8th, through our headquarters,
the following message: "I have just visited and viewed the *Mount Vernon*. The high
spirited morale of its men and the masterful seamanship of its Captain and officers
makes such a stirring story of heroism that I wish all the nation might know the
splendid way in which that huge transport met and foiled the attempt to destroy it at
sea. The traditions of your service are enriched by the conduct in this emergency."
It will be recalled that this vessel was torpedoed 250 miles out of Brest and though
seriously damaged was successfully brought back into port.

THE actual concentration of troops and matériel to form our First Army was begun in the St. Mihiel region in early August.[1] The greater part of the American troops had previously been serving at other points along the Western Front. As railway and motor transport became available, units were brought from the British front, from the French armies about Château-Thierry, and from the Vosges. They were assembled in billeting areas some distance behind the battle lines, where they received necessary replacements and equipment and continued their training.

The transfer of certain auxiliary units and the French artillery could not be carried out until after September 2d, as much of the motor transportation which came from the French was in use farther west. On account of the scarcity of roads and the necessity for the crossing of columns, complete march tables had to be prepared by First Army Headquarters for this concentration, which was conducted with efficiency and celerity. The organization of the First Army was completed in the back areas. Beginning at the end of August, the battle concentration was started, when all combatant units were quietly moved to their battle positions.

The aviation force, consisting of nearly 1,400 planes, under Colonel Mitchell, was the strongest that had been assembled up to that time. It included the British Independent Bombing Squadrons, under General Trenchard, which Marshal Haig had

---

[1] We had 3,010 artillery guns of all calibers, none of which were of American manufacture. Of the total, 1,681 were manned by Americans and 1,329 by French. Before the attack, 40,000 tons of ammunition were placed in dumps. Signal communication consisted of telegraph and telephone lines, radio and pigeons. The central switchboard was at Ligny-en-Barrois with 38 circuits with separate nets for command, supply, artillery, air service and utilities. There were 19 railheads for daily supplies such as food, clothing and equipment. In addition to our own limited motor transportation, we borrowed from the French trucks capable of moving at one time 2,000 tons of material and 20,000 men. The Medical Department provided 15,000 beds for the southern and 5,900 for the western attack and 65 evacuation trains for patients. Engineers provided material, including rolling stock and shops, for the reconstruction and operation of over 45 miles of standard gauge and 250 miles of light railways. A bridge of 200 feet at Griscourt was built, and 15 miles of road reconstructed. Road rock used was over 100,000 tons. 120 water points were established, furnishing 1,200,000 gallons per day, replenished by night trips of railroad or truck water trains.

generously sent and which were particularly useful for attacking important rail centers in rear of the enemy's line. General Pétain placed at our disposal a French air division of 600 planes. Thus we started with a superiority over the enemy in the air which was maintained throughout the offensive.

Unfortunately, we could obtain no heavy tanks and only 267

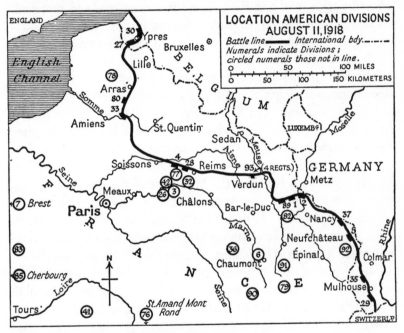

light tanks, which were all of French manufacture, and of these 154 were manned by American troops.

In addition to the American divisions, four French divisions, three of which were then serving under the French II Colonial Corps around the tip of the salient, were assigned to our army for the operation. The total strength of the First Army when ready for battle was about 550,000 American and 110,000 French troops.

The engineers were on hand with personnel and material to begin the reconstruction of roads and light railways. The signal troops were there to extend communications. Arrangements to give medical aid were ready, many installations having been taken over from the French, who assisted us materially in this work. The size and shape of the salient made it necessary to organize two systems of supply, one to serve troops operating against the southern face and the other those attacking from the west.

The preliminary arrangements were completed expeditiously and efficiently, and the First Army was now ready to undertake its first independent operation. Except for delay in the arrival of part of the French heavy artillery, the attack could have been made as early as the 10th.

The St. Mihiel salient lay between the Meuse and the Moselle Rivers and was roughly outlined by the triangle Pont-à-Mousson, St. Mihiel, Verdun. On the western side of this area the wooded heights of the Meuse extend along the east bank of the river. Beyond these heights lies the broad plain of the Woëvre with its large forest areas and numerous lakes and swamps. High wooded bluffs follow both banks of the Moselle, and the deep ravines and heavy forests on the western bank offer difficult terrain for offensive operations. Between the Moselle and Meuse Rivers, the only stream of any importance is the Rupt de Mad, which flows northeast through Thiaucourt and empties into the Moselle.

The principal forests in the plain of the Woëvre are the Bois le Prêtre, the Bois de Mort Mare and the Bois de Vigneulles. From the heights of Loupmont and Montsec, and from the steep eastern bluff of the heights of the Meuse, practically every portion of the plain can be seen.

Our possession of the eastern edge of the heights of the Meuse northwest of Les Éparges was a distinct advantage. But farther south the enemy held sections of these heights, which gave him important observation stations and enabled him to conceal masses of artillery that could fire either against our lines to the south on the plain of the Woëvre or to the west into the valley of the Meuse. It was, therefore, especially advisable, in order to prevent the concentration of his artillery fire in one direction, for us to attack the enemy from the west face of the salient in conjunction with our attack against the southern face.

The main rail lines and roads run along the river valleys, with subsidiaries passing through the heart of the salient and along the eastern slope of the heights of the Meuse.

The Woëvre is seriously affected by the wet season which begins about the middle of September. In dry weather, the water supply is difficult, while during the rainy period the country becomes flooded, making many of the roads impassable.

During the period of four years' occupation, the Germans had strengthened the natural defensive features by elaborate fortifications and by a dense network of barbed wire that covered the entire front. There were four or five defensive positions, the first of which included the outpost system, the fourth being the Hindenburg Line, back of which were a series of detached works, and in rear the permanent fortifications of Metz and Thionville. The strength of the defenses had been fully demonstrated earlier in the war when powerful efforts by the French against various points of the line had been defeated with heavy losses.

The salient was practically a great field fortress. It had, however, the characteristic weakness of all salients in that it could be attacked from both flanks in converging operations. Our heaviest blow was to be from the south where there were no great natural features to be overcome, while the secondary attack was to come from the west and join the main drive in the heart of the salient. The accompanying sketch illustrates the essentials of the First Army's plan for this offensive.

In our original plans it had been my purpose after crushing the salient to continue the offensive through the Hindenburg Line and as much farther as possible, depending upon the success attained and the opposition that developed.

As we have seen, however, the agreement reached in conference on September 2d limited the operations to the reduction of the salient itself. The basic features of the plan were not altered, but its objectives were defined and the number of troops to be employed was reduced.

A tactical surprise was essential to success, as the strength of the position would permit small forces of the enemy to inflict heavy losses on attacking troops. The sector had been quiet for some time and was usually occupied by seven enemy divisions in the front line, with two in reserve. It was estimated that the enemy could reënforce it by two divisions in two days, two more in three days, and as many divisions as were available in four days.

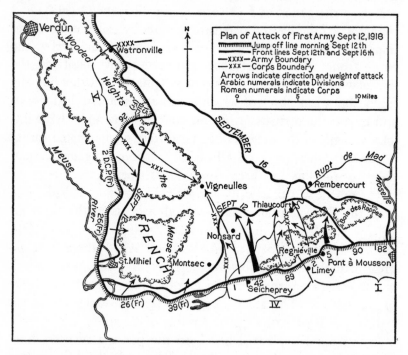

From captured documents and other sources of information, it seemed reasonable to conclude that the enemy had prepared a plan for withdrawal from the salient to the Hindenburg Line in case of heavy Allied pressure. There was no doubt he was aware that an American attack was impending. Therefore, it was possible that he might increase his strength on our front. In that case, our task would be more difficult and as anything short of complete success would undoubtedly be seized upon to our disadvantage by those of the Allies who opposed the policy of forming an American army, no chances of a repulse in our first battle could be taken. These considerations prompted the decision to use some of our most experienced divisions along with the others.

As the plans for the battle neared completion, the duration of the preliminary artillery bombardment came up for consideration as affecting the element of surprise. Practically all previous attacks by the Allies had been preceded by severe bombardments, in some instances lasting for days. In the event that we should pursue the same method the enemy would of course be fully warned of our intentions. I decided, therefore, that there should be only enough preliminary artillery fire to disconcert the enemy and still not leave him time to withdraw or bring up reserves in any number before we could strike. A reasonable amount of firing would give encouragement to our own troops and would be especially advantageous in case rain should make the ground difficult for the tanks. The length of time for the preliminary bombardment was therefore fixed at four hours, which proved to be wise.

In the order of battle for the main attack, the I Corps (Liggett) was on the right, with the 82d Division (Burnham) astride the Moselle, and the 90th (Allen), the 5th (McMahon), and the 2d (Lejeune) in order from east to west. Then came the IV Corps (Dickman) with the 89th Division (Wright), the 42d Division (Menoher), and the 1st Division (Summerall). The V Corps (Cameron), with the 26th Division (Edwards), and part of the 4th Division (Hines), assisted by the French 15th Colonial Division, was to conduct the secondary attack against the western face. In this corps the 26th Division alone was to make a deep advance, directed southeast toward Vigneulles.

At the point of the salient was the French II Colonial Corps composed of the French 39th and 26th Infantry Divisions and the 2d Dismounted Cavalry Division. This corps was to make a supporting advance on the left of the principal drive from the south, and also on the right of the western attack. Troops at the apex were to hold the enemy in their front.

Of the three American corps and nine divisions in the front

line, the IV and V Corps and the 5th, 82d, 89th and 90th Divisions had never before been engaged in offensive combat. Our divisions in reserve were, for the I corps, the 78th (McRae); for the IV Corps, the 3d (Buck); and for the V Corps, the 4th Division (Hines). The army reserve consisted of the 35th (Traub), 91st (Johnston), and 80th (Cronkhite) Divisions.

On the date of the attack the enemy had in the salient proper the equivalent of nine divisions in line, and one in reserve. These troops consisted of one division and two brigades of the Metz group, four divisions of the Bavarian I Corps, and three of the Combres group, V Corps, with one division in reserve. The sector was under the command of General von Fuchs.

The plan presented an especial difficulty in that the troops on the south were required to make a change in direction of sixty degrees during the advance. The long-range guns of Metz covered the Moselle valley as far as Pagny-sur-Moselle, and the enemy's positions on the heights to the east and west of the Moselle gave each other mutual support. These factors made it advisable not to attempt initially to carry the heights on the west bank of the river.

The infantry deployment along the line of departure was delayed generally until the night of September 11th-12th to avoid the possibility of the enemy gaining information of the additional strength on his front by the capture of prisoners. The artillery went into position from two to three nights before the attack.

(Diary) Ligny-en-Barrois, Friday, September 13, 1918. The First Army attacked yesterday and the reduction of St. Mihiel salient is complete. Our troops behaved splendidly. The Secretary of War visited two corps headquarters; returned to Ligny much delighted at our success.

Pétain and I went to the town of St. Mihiel to-day and were warmly greeted by the people. This is my birthday and a very happy one.

The attack on the southern face of the salient started at 5:00 o'clock on the morning of the 12th, and before that hour I went with several staff officers to old Fort Gironville, situated on a commanding height overlooking the battlefield from the south. The secondary attack on the west was launched at 8:00 A.M. as an element of surprise and in order to give more time for artillery preparation there.

A drizzling rain and mist prevented us from getting a clear view, but the progress of our troops could be followed by the barrage which preceded them. Notwithstanding a heavy rainfall on the night of the 11th-12th, the weather gave us an advantage, as the mist partially screened our movements from the enemy. There was a chill breeze blowing and its direction was such that no sound of firing could be heard from the artillery in our immediate front, although the more distant artillery bombardment on the western face was heard distinctly.

The sky over the battlefield, both before and after dawn, aflame with exploding shells, star signals, burning supply dumps and villages, presented a scene at once picturesque and terrible. The exultation in our minds that here, at last, after seventeen months of effort, an American army was fighting under its own flag was tempered by the realization of the sacrifice of life on both sides, and yet fate had willed it thus and we must carry through. Confidence in our troops dispelled every doubt of ultimate victory.

As we returned from Gironville, groups of prisoners were already being marched to stockades in the rear. About 9 o'clock reports began to come in to army headquarters at Ligny from all portions of the twenty-five mile front that everything was going well, with losses light.

Mr. Baker returned from his observation point near the battlefield much elated over the success of the troops. He had been a witness to the first effort of an American army and it was a proud day for him to feel that as Secretary of War his directing hand had led to such results. He took much pleasure in going about to all parts of the army, and scorned being treated as a guest.

Thanks to the thorough preparation beforehand, the wire entanglements were more easily overcome than we had expected.

Trained teams of pioneers and engineers, with bangalore tor-
pedoes,[1] wire cutters and axes, assisted in opening gaps in the
masses of barbed wire protecting the German positions.   The
leading troops themselves carried along rolls of chicken wire
which was thrown across entanglements here and there, forming
a kind of bridge for the infantry.   In all their offensives the Allies
had spent days in destroying these obstructions with artillery fire,
or had used a large number of heavy tanks, but we had only
a few light tanks, which were ineffective for such work.   The
fact that we had smothered the enemy artillery was an advantage, as it enabled the leading waves deliberately to do their
work without serious loss.

The quick passage through these entanglements by our troops
excited no little surprise among the French, who sent a large
number of officers and noncommissioned officers to St. Mihiel
several days later to see how it had been done.[2]   One of these
officers, after his reconnaissance, remarked in all seriousness that
the Americans had the advantage over Frenchmen because of
their long legs and large feet.

In making our dispositions for battle our older divisions, the
1st, 2d, and 42d, had been given positions on the southern face
opposite the open spaces to enable them to flank the wooded
areas quickly, thus aiding the advance of less experienced units
assigned to these areas.   The whole line, pivoting as planned
on the 82d Division on the right, advanced resolutely to the
attack.   The entire operation was carried through with dash
and precision.

[1] A bangalore torpedo is a long tin or sheet-iron tube containing T.N.T.

[2] The following extract is from General Pétain's order: "It is desirable for a certain
number of French officers, noncommissioned officers and soldiers to visit the terrain
so that they can fully understand the manner in which the American infantry has
been able, during the last attacks carried out by the American First Army, to overcome
the obstacles encountered during the advance and not destroyed by artillery or by
tanks.

"The American units have cut themselves a passage with wire-cutters through the
thick bands of wire or they have walked over these wire entanglements with much
skill, rapidity and decision.   It is interesting that our infantry soldiers should see for
themselves the nature of the difficulties thus overcome and that they should persuade
themselves that they also are capable of doing as much on occasion."

By afternoon the troops had pushed beyond their scheduled objectives and by evening had reached the second day's objective on most of the southern front. The divisions of the IV Corps and those on the left of the I Corps overwhelmed the hostile garrisons and quickly overran their positions, carrying the fighting into the open. The German resistance on this part of the front was disorganized by the rapidity of our advance and was soon overcome.

When the 1st Division, on the marching flank of the southern attack, had broken through the hostile forward positions, the squadron of cavalry attached to the IV Corps was passed through the breach. At 1:45 P.M. it pushed forward to reconnoiter the roads toward Vigneulles, but encountering machine guns in position, was forced to retire.

On the western face of the salient progress was not so satisfactory. The 26th Division, in its attempt to make a deep advance toward Vigneulles, met with considerable resistance and except for a battalion sent from the division reserve had not reached the day's objective.

The French at the tip of the salient had attempted to follow up the flanks of our successful penetrations, but made only small advances. Upon the request of General Blondlat, commanding the French II Colonial Corps, a regiment of the 80th Division, in reserve, was sent to his assistance.

On the afternoon of the 12th, learning that the roads leading out of the salient between the two attacks were filled with retreating enemy troops, with their trains and artillery, I gave orders to the commanders of the IV and V Corps to push forward without delay. Using the telephone myself, I directed the commander of the V Corps to send at least one regiment of the 26th Division toward Vigneulles with all possible speed. That evening, a strong force from the 51st Brigade pushed boldly forward and reached Vigneulles at 2:15 A.M. on the 13th. It immediately made dispositions that effectively closed the roads leading out of the salient west of that point. In the IV Corps the 2d Brigade of the 1st Division advanced in force about dawn of the 13th, its leading elements reaching Vigneulles by 6:00 A.M. The salient was closed and our troops were masters of the field.

The troops continued to advance on the 13th, when the line was established approximately along the final objectives set for this offensive. In view of the favorable situation that had been developed just west of the Moselle River by our successes farther to the left, a limited attack, in accordance with our previous plans, was made on that part of the front by elements of the 82d and 90th Divisions, with good results. During the night, our troops were engaged in organizing their new positions for defense, preparatory to the withdrawal of divisions and corps troops for participation in the Meuse-Argonne battle. On September 14th, 15th, and 16th, local operations continued, consisting of strong reconnaissances and the occupation of better ground for defensive purposes. Beginning on the 13th, several counterattacks were repulsed. The line as finally established was: Haudiomont—Fresnes-en-Woëvre—Doncourt—Jaulny—Vandières.

Reports received during the 13th and 14th indicated that the enemy was retreating in considerable disorder. Without doubt, an immediate continuation of the advance would have carried us well beyond the Hindenburg Line and possibly into Metz, and the temptation to press on was very great, but we would probably have become involved and delayed the greater Meuse-Argonne operation, to which we were wholly committed.

During the fighting from September 12th to 16th, the German 125th, 8th Landwehr, 88th and 28th Divisions reënforced the enemy's line and several other divisions arrived in reserve positions. On September 16th in front of the First Army there were ten German divisions and two brigades in line and seven divisions in reserve.

Nearly 16,000 prisoners were taken and some 450 enemy guns had fallen into our hands. Our casualties numbered about 7,000. As the enemy retreated he set fire to many large supply dumps and several villages. The few remaining French inhabitants who found themselves within our lines were overjoyed to be released from the domination of the enemy, but many were left destitute by the burning of their homes at the very moment of deliverance.

On the 13th, General Pétain came by my headquarters and we went together to St. Mihiel, where the people, including the children carrying French flags, gave us a welcome which may well be imagined when one realizes that they had been held as prisoners, entirely out of touch with their own countrymen, for four years, though always within sight of the French lines. They had heard only such vague reports of the war as their captors cared to furnish them, which were mainly accounts of German successes, and they were quite ignorant of the momentous events that had taken place during the previous two months.

The people were assembled at the Hôtel de Ville, where we talked with the assistant mayor. He told us that in their retreat the Germans had taken away all the Frenchmen between the ages of sixteen and forty-five years. Fortunately, the flight was so rapid that these prisoners were abandoned after a ten-mile march and returned to St. Mihiel the following day. The assistant mayor said the Germans had treated the inhabitants well.

General Pétain explained to the people that although the French troops had driven the enemy through St. Mihiel, they were serving as a part of the American Army and were able to reoccupy the town because the American attacks had crushed in the salient on the south and west. He arranged to reëstablish the city government and give aid to the people and we departed. Just as we were leaving the town we met Secretary Baker entering and I regretted that he could not have gone in with General Pétain and me.

On my visit to several corps and division headquarters the following day, I found all jubilant over the victory and overflowing with incidents of the fighting, reciting many feats of heroism among the troops. In one or two cases, the keen rivalry between adjoining divisions had resulted in friendly controversies between them as to which should have the credit for the capture of certain localities. Important villages along their boundaries were sometimes entered by elements of each without the knowledge of the other, and these instances formed the basis of claims for honors which were upheld with insistence by the units concerned. However, distinction in achievement among the attacking troops on the southern face could not be made with any assurance, as all had done more than was expected of them.

It is never difficult to discover the attitude of a commander, as it is almost certain to be reflected in his unit. If the commander lacks energy or is disloyal, his officers and men are likely to be affected accordingly. If he is aggressive and loyal, his command will show it. I recall one incident which illustrates the point. In the course of a conversation with one division commander he was asked the condition of his unit, to which he replied that the men were very tired. Whereupon, I remarked that there could be no reason for that, as they had been in the line only a short time, and I added with some emphasis that it was probably the division commander who was tired. Not long afterward his division lost its cohesion in battle and became much disorganized. He was relieved and another commander appointed, who was tireless and efficient, and under him the division served with exceptional distinction.

The reduction of the St. Mihiel salient completed the first task of the American Army. Its elimination freed the Paris—Nancy rail communications and the roads that paralleled the Meuse north from St. Mihiel. These at once became available for our use in the greater offensive to be undertaken immediately. We had restored to France 200 square miles of territory and had placed our army in a favorable situation for further operations. The new American position in the Woëvre, almost within reach of Metz, now stood as a threat against the great fortress on the Moselle that defended Germany on that part of the front. I was somewhat familiar with the strength of the fortifications, having visited Metz and the surrounding country, including the battlefields of 1870, some years before, little dreaming, however, that one day an American army would be so near and be so eager to measure swords with the defenders.

This striking victory completely demonstrated the wisdom of

building up a distinct American army.   No form of propaganda could overcome the depressing effect on the enemy's morale of the fact that a new adversary had been able to put a formidable army in the field against him which, in its first offensive, could win such an important engagement.   This result, after nearly a year and a half of working and waiting, must have tremendously heartened our people at home, as it gave them a tangible reason to believe that our contribution to the war would be the deciding factor.   It inspired our troops with unlimited confidence which was to stand them in good stead against the weary days and nights of battle they were to experience later on.   The St. Mihiel victory probably did more than any single operation of the war to encourage the tired Allies.   After the years of doubt and despair, of suffering and loss, it brought them assurance of the final defeat of an enemy whose armies had seemed well-nigh invincible.   The French people of all classes were loud in their praise of Americans.

Many were the messages of congratulation that poured into the First Army Headquarters from all sources, some of which are quoted, as follows:

"Pershing,
    "Amexforce, Paris.
    "Accept my warmest congratulations on the brilliant achievements of the Army under your command.   The boys have done what we expected of them and done it in a way we most admire.   We are deeply proud of them and of their Chief.   Please convey to all concerned my grateful and affectionate thanks.   "Woodrow Wilson."

"My dear General:
    "The American First Army, under your command, on this first day has won a magnificent victory by a maneuver as skillfully prepared as it was valiantly executed.   I extend to you as well as to the officers and to the troops under your command my warmest congratulations.
                                            "Marshal Foch."

"General Pershing,
    "Headquarters,
        "American Expeditionary Forces.
    "All ranks of the British Armies in France welcome with unbounded admiration and pleasure the victory which has attended the initial

offensive of the great American Army under your personal command. I beg you to accept and to convey to all ranks my best congratulations and those of all ranks of the British under my command.

"HAIG."

(Diary) Ligny-en-Barrois, Sunday, September 15, 1918. Met M. Clemenceau at station and sent Colonel Quekemeyer and Captain de Marenches with him into recaptured territory. President and Madame Poincaré came to-day to Sampigny, their home town; took luncheon with them on his train. Sent Colonel Boyd with the President, who went to Thiaucourt. Troops made minor advances yesterday and to-day to straighten line and secure advantageous ground. Stettinius, in coöperation with Chief of Ordnance, directed by the Secretary to negotiate with Allies for ordnance material.

On Sunday, M. Clemenceau, who usually spent that day on some portion of the front, came to visit our army and was most enthusiastic in his congratulations. He wished to go over the field and particularly to visit Thiaucourt, but it seemed to me still too dangerous and I said, "Mr. President, we cannot take the chance of losing a Prime Minister." Moreover, the roads were filled with traffic moving in both directions, so, much to his disappointment, I gave instructions that he should not be allowed to go.

During luncheon with President and Madame Poincaré they expressed themselves as being much pleased at our success, especially so because Sampigny was no longer under the enemy's guns. After lunch we visited the site of their residence only to find that it had been completely demolished by German artillery. It had been a beautiful though modest house and its location especially well chosen to give one a fine view of the Meuse valley. It was a sad occasion for them as they looked over the ruins, but they accepted it in the usual courageous French way by saying simply, *"C'est la guerre,"* as did thousands of others in northern France, many of whose homes had been destroyed leaving scarcely a trace.

As we strolled about, two American artillerymen whose brigade happened to be billeted in the village came forward. When I told them who the visitors were, they seemed to regard my remarks as an introduction. Both walked up and warmly shook hands with the President and Madame Poincaré, and then quietly went about with us. It was just another illustration of our democracy and the President and his wife were very gracious, though much amused by the cordial and rather unconventional manner of their guests. I returned to army headquarters leaving the President and Madame Poincaré to be escorted by Colonel Boyd, who was compelled by the President's insistence to take them to Thiaucourt. M. Clemenceau, who dined with me that evening, was much annoyed when he learned about it, since I had denied him the opportunity to go that far to the front.

CHAPTER XLIV

Red Cross Coöperation—Cable for Auxiliary Services—No Improvement in
Rifle Training in United States—Visit St. Mihiel with Marshal Foch—
We Turn to the Meuse-Argonne—Simultaneous Allied Attacks Planned
—Meuse-Argonne Vital Front—Description of Sector—German Defen-
sive Lines—Concentration Hurried—Complicated Movements—Use of
Partially Trained Divisions—Visit to Verdun

(Diary) Ligny-en-Barrois, Wednesday, September 18, 1918. Spent
Monday visiting front line divisions. Tuesday had discussion with
McAndrew on new offensive. Conferred with Personnel Section on
promotions. Martin Egan, also Mr. Julius Rosenwald, who has been
visiting the front, came to luncheon.

Mr. Davison, General Ireland, Colonel Wadhams, and Mr. Perkins
came to-day to discuss Red Cross matters. Called at headquarters
French corps and division commanders serving in the First Army. All
appear to be very efficient. Visited Hattonchâtel, from which German
lines can be plainly seen.

THE experience in the St. Mihiel battle brought out the
necessity of closer coöperation between the Red Cross and
the Medical Corps hospital services. Mr. Davison, the head
of the Red Cross, and General Ireland, Chief Surgeon, had
worked out a plan by which certain elements of the Red Cross
personnel would be taken into the Medical Corps. I think that
Mr. Davison had some doubt as to how the proposal would be
received, for, when I approved it without a moment's hesitation,
he seemed somewhat surprised. The American Red Cross represented in rather a personal way all those who had contributed
to its support, and I felt that it should be given a definite status
with respect to the care of our sick and wounded, although the
scheme was never entirely put into effect.

In recognition of the devoted service of the Red Cross, the
following order was published to the A.E.F. on October 3d:

"The American Red Cross is the recognized national organization for relief work with the Army and Navy in time of war. It is through this organization that the men and women of America contribute their funds and their labor for the relief and comfort of the men in service.

"To the millions of women whose hearts and hands are consecrated to the service, to the millions of men, rich and poor alike, throughout the country who have contributed and sacrificed, and even to the millions of children of our schools who are doing their part, it should be made clear that the relief and comfort contributed by them through the American Red Cross to the men in service is essential.

"The Commander-in-Chief desires to express for the entire American Expeditionary Forces the deep sense of appreciation of the services being rendered by the American Red Cross."

Having completed one major operation successfully and being now engaged in preparing for a second, our lack of personnel for certain services and our deficiencies in material became still more disturbing. In our cables to Washington every possible emphasis was laid on the urgency of supplying the items we needed most. In addition, our requirements for 1919 must be foreseen and provided for. In explaining the situation to the War Department, one of my cables stated that "as a consequence, before deciding upon any plan of operations, I must have assurance of not only sufficient fighting troops for the execution of the plan, but also sufficient labor and S.O.S. troops to permit of necessary construction that must be completed in advance." As to the training and shipment of later divisions, it was pointed out that they should be called into service in ample time to provide efficient units, it being important "that divisions should be organized far enough ahead so that the flow of fully trained divisions may keep every available troop transport busy from now on until the program is completed."

During the formative period most of our special services had only temporary personnel, that is, they were manned by officers and men from other branches. This was objectionable and was conducive neither to the esprit de corps nor the efficiency which permanent interest and status would inspire. In anticipation of another year of activity, cables had been sent the latter part of

May requesting authority to place the Chemical Warfare Service, Motor Transport Service, Transportation Corps, and Army Service Corps on a permanent footing. It was essential that their officers should be appointed with their proper grades, instead of being detailed temporarily and separated from their regular assignments. Although these services were established by War Department orders within a reasonable time, full details of organization had not yet been received, and we were forced to limp along with detailed personnel until the necessary action was taken.

Among our troops recently arrived there was a serious lack of training in the use of the rifle. It seemed inexcusable to send over men who were deficient in this very elementary step in preparation, even though there may not have been time to train them otherwise. The idea apparently prevailed at home that three months' instruction was sufficient, but it was never conceded by me that this was anything like adequate. Even though the shipment of troops was much more rapid than was ever expected, making it often necessary to send units whether their personnel was trained or untrained, some instruction in the use of the rifle should have been given. As already pointed out, this deficiency might have been avoided by beginning earlier in the spring to increase the monthly drafts. The following cable on this subject was sent on September 15th:

"Am mailing you report on serious lack of training in replacements recently arrived from Camp Lee, Virginia. These men have received little instruction gas defense, bayonet exercise and combat, interior guard, march discipline, school of soldier, care and use of rifle. Some had never handled a rifle. Nevertheless these men had been in service about two months. Essential replacements should receive instruction in fundamentals before departure United States provided flow of replacements not thereby impeded. Current shortage in replacements requires men to be sent to first line divisions within five or six days after arrival in France. Unfair individual and ruinous efficiency his organization send recruits into battle without adequate training. Thorough instruction in United States must be given in school of soldier, use individual field equipment, personal hygiene, first aid, military courtesy. Particularly important infantry be given rifle practice to include 600 yards in United States. Do not understand why this condition should prevail with anything like proper supervision over training in camps at home. Suggest fullest investigation of methods and policies as to instruction."

(Diary) Ligny-en-Barrois, Saturday, September 21, 1918. Visited St. Mihiel yesterday with Marshal Foch, drove to Hattonchâtel, over-looking St. Mihiel battlefield, thence back to Ligny for lunch. Am very busy these days in preparation for the coming offensive. The staff is carrying a tremendous burden efficiently.

To-day held conference with Pétain at Nettancourt; discussed co-operation with Fourth Army. Saw Hirschauer, who says the discipline and concealment of our infantry best he has ever seen, but road discipline not so good. Took luncheon with Liggett (I Corps) at Rarécourt; called on Cameron (V Corps) at Ville-sur-Cousances; then on Bullard (III Corps) at Rampont; found them all busy and everything moving up to schedule. Saw Claudel, French XVII Corps, and went over the situation on his front. He thinks the Germans do not anticipate our attack. Visited citadel at Verdun. First Army Headquarters moved to Souilly. Complete requirements for December cabled Washington.

Marshal Foch and I, accompanied by General Weygand and my aide, Colonel Boyd, went to St. Mihiel, where we found the people generally going about their business as though nothing had happened. The destruction of buildings was not so great as might have been expected and the work of reconstruction had already begun. Marshal Foch was very devout and wanted especially to visit the cathedral. When we entered, he reverently knelt, and following his example all of us did likewise, remaining some minutes at our devotions. Weygand told me that it was Foch's custom to visit church whenever he had an opportunity. We went from there to Hattonchâtel, where we had a fine view overlooking the St. Mihiel battlefield, and as we stood on this prominent point Foch spoke with enthusiasm regarding the battle. We returned to my quarters at Ligny-en-Barrois for luncheon, having spent a very interesting half-day.

In accordance with the understanding of September 2d, we were now moving rapidly toward our second great offensive. Questions concerning the concentration and supply of the elements of the First Army in the battle areas were being worked out by the staff of that army, which was given every possible assistance by the staff at G.H.Q. In my dual capacity as Commander-in-Chief and Commander of the First Army, I was able promptly to place every facility of the A.E.F. at the disposition of the First Army. With the Headquarters General Staff and the Services of Supply both in excellent working order, the business of the A.E.F., once general directions were given, was well conducted and I was free to devote my time to operations.

The general plan of action of the Allied armies, as agreed upon at the conference of Commanders-in-Chief on July 24th, was, to state it simply and briefly, that the offensive should continue, each army driving forward as rapidly as possible. The Allied and American operations during the summer had resulted in the reduction of the Château-Thierry, Amiens and St. Mihiel salients, and our greater offensive would soon combine with those of the Allies. Immediately west of the Meuse River the battle lines had remained practically unchanged since 1917. It was on this front that the American Army was to play its part. In accordance with Marshal Foch's idea, offensives were to be launched by the Allies as follows:

"(a) A British-French attack on the general line St. Quentin-Cambrai, advancing between the Oise and the Scarpe Rivers.

"(b) A French-American attack on the general line Reims-Verdun, advancing between the Suippe and the Meuse Rivers.

"(c) A combined Allied attack east of Ypres.

"(d) Between the attacks mentioned above, liaison was to be maintained by intervening armies."

The operations were to be as nearly simultaneous as possible all along the Western Front. If successful they would force the enemy either to disperse his reserves and weaken his defense generally, or else concentrate his reserve power at what appeared to be the vital points, to the jeopardy of the remainder of his line. The disposition of the Belgian, British, French, and American armies between the North Sea and Verdun was such that they would naturally converge as they advanced. So long as the enemy could hold his ground on the east of this battle line, frontal attacks farther west might drive him back on his successive positions, yet a decision would be long delayed.

His main line of communication and supply ran through Carignan, Sedan and Mézières. If that should be interrupted before he could withdraw his armies from France and Belgium, the communications in the narrow avenue between the Ardennes Forest and the Dutch frontier were so limited that he would be unable adequately to supply his forces or to evacuate them before his ruin would be accomplished. As our objective was the Sedan—Carignan railroad, it was evident that the sector assigned to the American Army was opposite the most sensitive part of the German front then being attacked.

The danger confronting the enemy made it imperative that he should hold on in front of the American Army to the limit of his resources. From his point of view this was the vital portion of his defensive line, because here it was closer to his main artery of supply (Carignan—Sedan—Mézières) than at any other point. He could afford to retire his armies gradually from all fronts west of the Meuse except ours, where he must hold until the last. The strategical value of success against this part of the enemy's line had been apparent from the beginning, and his preparations for its defense had been thoroughly carried out.

The operation against this important sector was to consist of an attack by the American First Army between the Meuse River and the Argonne Forest, supported by the French Fourth Army to the west of the Argonne. Our thrust east of the forest, by threatening the left flank of the enemy's position in front of the French Fourth Army, on the Aisne River, would force his withdrawal, and the combined or successive advances of both armies would throw him back on the line Stenay—Le Chesne—Attigny, and eventually on Mézières.

Once the Argonne should be captured, these two armies would continue their joint attacks in the general direction of Mézières and Sedan, with the object of severing the enemy's line of rail communications between Carignan and Sedan. The bulk of his armies farther west would be cut off as the Ardennes, a rugged, heavily wooded area, would limit them to the line of communication and supply through Liège.

At this moment, the American First Army, holding the sector from the Moselle River to Watronville, southeast of Verdun, and flushed with success, stood as a menace against the German lines that protected Metz and the Briey iron region. The second offensive about to take place required the extension of our lines to the north of Verdun, and from there to the western edge of the Argonne Forest, giving us a total front of ninety-four miles, or one-third of the total active portion of the lines from the North Sea to the Moselle.

The area between the Meuse River and the Argonne Forest was ideal for defensive fighting. On the east, the heights of the Meuse commanded that river valley and on the west the rugged, high hills of the Argonne Forest dominated the valley of the Aire River. In the center, the watershed between the Aire and the Meuse Rivers commanded both valleys, with the heights of Montfaucon, Cunel, Romagne and of the Bois de Barricourt standing out as natural strong points. From these heights, observation points completely covered the entire area in front of the German lines.

The terrain over which the attack was to be made formed a defile blocked by three successive barriers, the heights of Montfaucon, then those of Cunel and Romagne, and farther back the ridges of the Bois de Barricourt and of the Bois de Bourgogne. The Meuse River was unfordable and the Aire River fordable only in places. In addition to the heavy forest of the Argonne, there were numerous woods with heavy undergrowth which were serious obstacles.

These natural defenses were strengthened by every artificial means imaginable, such as fortified strongpoints, dugouts, successive lines of trenches, and an unlimited number of concrete machine gun emplacements. A dense network of wire entanglements covered every position. With the advantage of commanding ground, the enemy was peculiarly well located to pour oblique and flanking artillery fire on any assailant attempting to advance within range between the Meuse and the Argonne. It was small wonder that the enemy had rested for four years on this front without being seriously molested. He felt secure in the knowledge that even with few divisions to hold these defenses his east and west lines of rail communication in rear would be well protected against the probability of interference.

The system of defensive positions prepared by the Germans

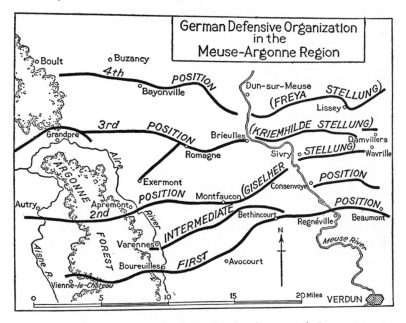

along the Western Front and farther back toward Germany consisted of four distinct lines extending from Metz to the northwest. These lines were widely separated near their greatest dip toward Paris, but converged as they approached that portion of the front protecting the communications which were the objective of the American Army. The location of these successive lines opposite the First Army is shown on the accompanying sketch.

Rapid concentration of the large force required for the battle was most urgent, and even before the beginning of the St. Mihiel offensive troops of some of the services were en route. At the end of the first day's fighting at St. Mihiel the success of the attack was assured, and, as prearranged, I immediately directed the transfer of certain combat troops from that battlefield to the Meuse-Argonne region. Army reserves, corps reserves and all spare artillery were moving by trucks and otherwise over circuitous routes to the new battle front, and other combat troops from the St. Mihiel area were now able to use the route near the tip of the former salient made available by our recent success.

In the area behind our Meuse-Argonne battle front, restricted as it was by the curve in the German line from Verdun to the south, there were but three standard gauge railroads available for the movement of troops and their supplies. One ran east and west between Ste. Menehould and Verdun, another north from Bar-le-Duc to Clermont-en-Argonne, and the third, northeast from Bar-le-Duc via Commercy and St. Mihiel to Souilly and Verdun.

There were only three roads leading into no-man's-land, one through Esnes, another through Avocourt and a third through Varennes; one for each corps. None of them, even though in good repair, was more than adequate for the normal supply of the attacking divisions dependent upon it. We realized that any excess of traffic would likely cause serious congestion, so that the greatest preparations were made to rebuild these roads by calling to that front all available engineer personnel and accumulating beforehand as much road material as possible.

On September 3d the French Second Army held the front from Watronville to the Argonne Forest with three army corps. In vacating the sector the French had to move two corps headquarters with corps troops, eleven divisions, and several army units, leaving the French XVII Corps behind to become a part of our army.

Our concentration required the entrance into the area of three corps headquarters with corps troops, fifteen divisions, and several thousand army troops. All movements were made under cover of darkness, by rail, autobus and marching. Approximately

220,000 men were moved out of the sector and 600,000 into it, making a grand total of 820,000 men handled.

As in the concentration prior to St. Mihiel, the route and length of each day's march for each unit had to be prescribed in order to prevent road congestion and insure the necessary daily delivery of supplies. It was a stupendous task and a delicate one to move such numbers of troops in addition to the large quantities of supplies, ammunition and hospital equipment required.[1] That it was carried out in the brief period available without arousing the suspicions of the enemy indicates the precision and smoothness with which it was calculated and accomplished. The battle at St. Mihiel followed the plan so closely, however, that it was possible to withdraw troops exactly as intended. It seldom happens in war that plans can be so precisely carried out as was possible in this instance. The details of the movements of troops connected with this concentration were worked out and their execution conducted under the able direction of Colonel George C. Marshall, Jr., of the Operations Section of the General Staff, First Army.

A well-known British war correspondent, an ex-officer of the British Army, in writing for the London *Post* said of this concentration:

"Few people in England know that this operation (the Argonne-Meuse Offensive), was preceded by one of the most interesting and difficult Staff operations of the war, namely, the transfer within four-

[1] Some idea can be formed of the amount of material involved by the following: Of artillery used in the Meuse-Argonne battle there were 3,980 guns of all calibers, most of which were in position for the opening of the battle; American gunners manned 2,516 and French 1,464. Artillery ammunition amounting to 40,000 tons was placed by September 25th, replenished by 12 to 14 trainloads, or 3,000 tons, daily; the amount fired by the divisional and corps artillery reached 350,000 rounds daily. There were 19 railheads for the automatic supply of the army. Depots established were: 12 for ordnance, 24 ammunition, 9 gas and oil, 9 quartermaster supplies, 12 engineer supplies, 8 engineer water supply, 6 chemical warfare, besides depots for medical, signal, motor, and tank supplies. There were 34 evacuation hospitals. The total number of animals was 93,032. Of motor transportation there were 3,500 truck tons capable of carrying 20,000 men in one load; 428,000 men were transported to the area by truck, average haul 48 miles. Light railway lines constructed and rebuilt 164 miles, and 215 miles were operated. As to standard gauge, we built 12 miles, Aubréville to Apremont, and reconstructed 65 miles.

teen days of the bulk of the 1st American Army from the Metz front to that of the Meuse-Argonne, and its replacement by the 2nd American Army. No less than 10 divisions began the Meuse-Argonne attack on September 26, * * * * while there stood in reserve, all eventually to be thrown into the fight, the 1st, 2nd, 3rd, 5th, 29th, 32nd, 82nd and 92nd Divisions. A comparison of these divisional units with those which fought at St. Mihiel shows that 10 divisions were withdrawn from the Metz front and aligned for the new operation. It was a fine piece of Staff work and no other Staff could have done it better."

On the new front, the army ammunition dumps were piling up and equipment for road building and for light railways was going forward. Hospital arrangements were being perfected, signal communications going in, remount stations constructed, battalion replacement camps located, and work had begun on a new railroad line from Aubréville to Varennes that had been projected to give us necessary additional rail transportation. Regulating stations, especially at St. Dizier, had to be greatly expanded and completely organized under American personnel in order to distribute efficiently the vastly multiplied volume of freight that must be provided before and during the battle. Aviation fields were being occupied by the constant arrival of the personnel and matériel of our squadrons. The services of water supply, camouflage and sound and flash ranging were being rapidly installed.

Specific instructions were sent to all troops calling attention to defects noticed during the St. Mihiel battle, such as ineffective liaison between units, passage through woods, regulation of barrages and the use of accompanying guns. The training staff was kept on the go to assist those divisions which would have no further opportunity to hold practice maneuvers with their artillery and the air service. Further instruction of the military police, who had lacked experience in the previous offensive, was carried out as far as possible, especially in the duty of controlling the immense amount of traffic even then crowding the area.

As we have seen, some of our most experienced divisions, the 1st, 2d, 26th and 42d, were used at St. Mihiel. This prevented their transfer to the Meuse-Argonne in time to open the fight, and compelled the employment of some divisions which had not entirely completed their period of training. Four of the nine divisions that were to lead the assault were without their own artillery and had brigades of that arm assigned to them with which they had never previously been in contact. It was realized that difficulties were likely to develop in handling these organizations in battle for the first time. Therefore instructions for the opening phases were made to cover as far as possible the details of maneuver ordinarily taught beforehand through combat exercises.

As Verdun was soon to become a part of my command, I went on the 21st to see the town and make a casual inspection of the citadel. The commanding officer showed me the various chambers, including those occupied by the local civil authorities during the period of the German drive to wrest the stronghold from the French, and finally we reached the Officers' Club. As we entered, my eye fell upon Pétain's famous declaration, *"On ne passe pas,"* in bold letters on the wall opposite me. It would be difficult to describe my feelings, and as I stopped in my tracks the party, realizing the reason, with one accord remained silent for some minutes.

Several years later, at the dedication of the Ossuary near Douaumont, it was my privilege to speak, and I addressed myself as follows to the distinguished commander who uttered the above inspiring phrase:

"The poignant horror of the tragedy enacted here has been brought home to me anew, and my triumphant sense of victory has been entirely overwhelmed by my sympathy for the men who fell, the victims of the sacrifice. Their patience and courage, their unalterable will to follow to the end the long and dolorous road of martyrdom which they were treading, have been celebrated in words more appropriate than any I could utter. But the grief of the man who commanded them has been too often forgotten by all who have commented on these battles. I have often felt, when you and I were together, that I could read your thoughts and follow your mind as it reviewed the days and weeks of your struggles on this soil, when your country's fate hung in the balance. Only those who know the kindness of your heart can appreciate the weight of sorrow which it carried. The fall of each one of your soldiers was a stab in the heart of his general, and the impassive expression under which you hide your feelings masked constant and unremitting grief.

"As an old friend and comrade in arms, I feel my thoughts dwelling on those who did not return, and like you, I think of them with infinite sympathy."

CHAPTER XLV

First Army Takes Command of Meuse-Argonne Sector—Order of Battle
—Plan of Battle—Battle Begins—Strong Defense Encountered—
Montfaucon Taken—Counterattacks—New Divisions Yield—Success
of First Four Days—Difficult Problems—Visit by M. Clemenceau—
27th and 30th Divisions Attack with British

(Diary) Souilly, Wednesday, September 25, 1918. Assumed command of Meuse-Argonne sector the 22d. General Gouraud, commanding the French Fourth Army, called to discuss joint operation.

General Deletoille, Director of the Zones des Étapes, reported on Monday and was given charge of relations with civil authorities in our area. Have spent the past three days working with staff on final details of preparation.

To-day visited headquarters of all front line divisions. Satisfied that they appreciate and understand their missions.

THE I, V, and III Corps Headquarters, located at Rarécourt, Ville-sur-Cousances and Rampont, respectively, worked in coöperation with the corresponding units of the French Second Army, which, under General Hirschauer's able and friendly direction, did everything possible to expedite preparations. He was of the greatest assistance in helping to place installations and in assigning units that were moved into the sector during the two weeks preceding the battle. The command passed to the First Army on September 22d and at that time, except for the XVII Corps, the last of the French troops and two Italian divisions serving with them were withdrawn, leaving a few detachments in the first line trenches which were maintained until the night of the 25th.

On the front of the American Army, the tactical missions varied for the different sectors. It was not intended to attempt a further advance on the Moselle-Watronville front, but to hold that portion of our line for the time being and utilize all available divisions for the extension of the front west of the Meuse. On that part of our line from Watronville northwest to the Meuse it was planned to keep the enemy busy by demonstrations while the attack between the Meuse and the Argonne was developing.

Of the eighteen enemy divisions on our front from the Moselle west, with twelve in reserve, five were in line between the Meuse and the Argonne. Judging from the number in the vicinity of Metz, it seemed probable that the German commander expected a renewal of the offensive in the St. Mihiel sector. It was estimated that the enemy could reënforce the front of attack between the Meuse and the Argonne with four divisions the first day, two the second, and nine the third day.

At the beginning of this battle most of the light and heavy guns, including corps and army artillery matériel and supply trains, as at St. Mihiel, were provided by the French, some by the British, and practically none from home. We had 189 light tanks, all of French manufacture, 25 per cent of which were handled by French personnel, but no heavy tanks could be obtained. In aviation, we had 821 airplanes, over 600 of which were flown by American aviators.

The order of battle of the First Army from the Moselle River to the Meuse River for September 25th, from east to west, was as follows: The IV Corps (Dickman) with the French 69th Division and our 90th (Allen), 78th (McRae), 89th (Wright) and 42d (Menoher) Divisions in line and the 5th (McMahon) in reserve; French II Colonial Corps with the French 39th and 2d Divisions and our 26th Division (Edwards) in line; French XVII Corps with the French 15th, 10th and 18th Divisions in line and the French 26th Division in reserve.

In the order of battle on the Meuse-Argonne front, from east to west, the III Corps (Bullard) was on the right, with the 33d Division (Bell) nearest the Meuse to cover the river and protect the flank of the army, the 80th Division (Cronkhite) in the center, and the 4th Division (Hines) on the left, with the 3d Division (Buck) in reserve. The V Corps (Cameron) consisted of the 79th Division (Kuhn) facing Montfaucon, the 37th (Farnsworth), and the 91st (Johnston), in that order, while the 32d Division (Haan) was in reserve. The I Corps (Liggett) was on the left of the army with the 35th Division (Traub) on its right, the 28th Division (Muir) next, west of the Aire River, and the 77th Division (Alexander) facing the Argonne, with the French 5th Cavalry Division and the American 92d Division (colored) (Ballou) in reserve, except one regiment which was attached to the French Fourth Army. The 1st Division (Summerall), the 29th (Morton), and the 82d (Burnham) formed the army reserve.

In accordance with the principal mission, which remained the

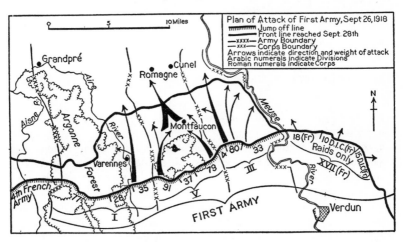

same throughout this offensive, the main attack by the First Army was to be launched west of the Meuse River, its right to be covered by the river and by the operations of the French XVII Corps on the east of the river, that corps being a part of our army. Our left was to be supported by a simultaneous advance by the French Fourth Army. Our attack, to include the Argonne Forest, was to be driven with all possible strength in the general direction of Mézières. The operations of the American First Army and the French Fourth Army were to be coördinated under agreement between General Pétain and myself.

The first operation of our army was to have for its objective the Hindenburg position on the front Brieulles-sur-Meuse—Romagne-sous-Montfaucon—Grandpré, with a following development in the direction of Buzancy—Mézières in order to force the enemy beyond the Meuse and outflank his positions on the Vouziers—Rethel line from the east.

In conjunction with our advance, which would outflank the enemy's position south of the Aisne, the French Fourth Army, by attacking successively the positions between the Aisne and the Suippe Rivers, would be able to occupy the line Vouziers—Rethel. After that it would operate in the directions of the plateau east of the Rethel—Signy-l'Abbaye road.

A liaison detachment under the French Fourth Army was designated to operate along the western edge of the Argonne Forest as a connecting link between the French and American armies.

In detail, it was actually planned by the First Army to make:

> (a) An advance of ten miles to force the enemy to evacuate the Argonne Forest and insure our junction with the French Fourth Army at Grandpré.
>
> (b) Then, a further advance of about ten miles to the line Stenay—Le Chesne to outflank the enemy's position along the Aisne River in front of the French Fourth Army and clear the way for our advance on Mézières or Sedan.
>
> (c) An operation to clear the heights east of the Meuse River, either by an attack in an easterly direction or by an attack northwards along the east bank of the Meuse River between Beaumont and Sivry-sur-Meuse, to clear the crest south of Bois de la Grand Montagne, or by a combination of these two attacks.

The plan for the initial attack was based on penetrating the enemy's third position by capturing the commanding heights of Romagne.

The V Corps, after outflanking the Bois de Montfaucon and the Bois de Cheppy, and passing the hostile second position near Montfaucon, was to drive on, without waiting for adjacent corps, and penetrate the hostile third position about Romagne. The III Corps' main mission was to support the advance of the V Corps by turning Montfaucon from the east and protecting the right flank along the Meuse River. At the same time the I Corps, on the left, was to assist the advance by flanking the Argonne Forest from the east and protecting the left of the V Corps. The artillery of the two flank corps was specially charged with suppressing the enemy guns located on the dominating heights of the Meuse, to the east, and those in the Argonne Forest, to the west.

Thus, in the initial advance two salients were to be driven into the German defenses, one to the east and one to the west of Montfaucon. These two advances would carry the enemy's second position and outflank Montfaucon. The troops driving in the two salients just mentioned, having been joined by the troops attacking in the interval, would advance until the penetration of the third hostile position about Romagne and Cunel had been accomplished.

Our purpose was to effect a tactical surprise if possible and overcome the enemy's first and second positions in the area of Montfaucon and capture the commanding heights (Côte Dame Marie) of his third position before he could bring up strong reënforcements. This plan would require a rapid advance of ten miles through a densely fortified zone. From an estimate of the enemy's reserves and their location, it was realized that we must capture Montfaucon and seize Côte Dame Marie by the end of the second day.

It was thought reasonable to count on the vigor and the aggressive spirit of our troops to make up in a measure for their inexperience, but at the same time the fact was not overlooked that lack of technical skill might considerably reduce the chances of complete success against well organized resistance of experienced defenders. General Pétain had already given it as his opinion that we should not be able to get farther than Montfaucon before winter. Foreseeing clearly the difficulty under the existing conditions of reaching in one stride an objective ten miles away, alternative plans were made to continue with more deliberation but with every determination to win in the contest which, if not successful in the first rush, was certain to become extremely severe.

On the afternoon of the day before the attack I visited the headquarters of corps and divisions to give a word of encouragement here and there to the leaders upon whom our success on the following days would depend. They were all alert and confident and I returned feeling that all would go as planned.

(Diary) Souilly, Monday, September 30, 1918. Our attack started well Thursday morning and good advances were made along the whole front. Montfaucon was captured on Friday. The Secretary of War left for Paris. Assistant Secretary of War John D. Ryan took lunch with us.

Visited all American corps headquarters on Saturday. Approved Muir's request for temporary assignment of Brigadier General Nolan and Colonel Conger to 28th Division to replace inefficient officers. Gave orders yesterday for the relief from front line of 35th, 37th and 79th Divisions and their replacement by 1st, 32d and 3d Divisions.

German resistance stubborn. Yesterday counterattacks forced us to give ground in places. Our II Corps, with the British, attacked and broke through the Hindenburg Line. General Pétain called, much pleased at our progress. M. Clemenceau, who also came, very enthusiastic and started to Montfaucon, but road congestion prevented his reaching there. Some counterattacks to-day repulsed.

First Phase—Meuse-Argonne Operations

The Meuse-Argonne offensive opened on the morning of September 26th. To call it a battle may be a misnomer, yet it was a battle, the greatest, the most prolonged in American history. Through forty-seven days we were engaged in a persistent struggle with the enemy to smash through his defenses. The attack started on a front of twenty-four miles, which gradually extended until the enemy was being actively assailed from the Argonne Forest to the Moselle River, a distance of about ninety miles.

In all, more than 1,200,000 men were employed and the attack was driven thirty-two miles to the north and fourteen miles to the northeast before the Armistice terminated hostilities. The numbers engaged, the diverse character of the fighting and the terrain, the numerous crises, and the brilliant feats of individuals and units make a detailed description of the battle extremely complicated and necessarily confusing to the reader. The outstanding fact that I desire to emphasize is that once started the battle was maintained continuously, aggressively, and relentlessly to the end. All difficulties were overridden in one tremendous sustained effort to terminate the war then and there in a victorious manner.

After three hours' violent artillery preparation, the attack began at 5:30 A.M. At the same time, to divert the enemy's attention elsewhere, local raids and demonstrations were made on the Meuse-Moselle front. The French Fourth Army (Gouraud) to our left, on the west of the Argonne Forest, began its advance half an hour later. The battle opened favorably. Our attack at that particular place and at that time evidently came as a surprise to the enemy and our troops were enabled quickly to overrun his forward positions. The vast network of undestroyed barbed wire, the deep ravines, the dense woods, and the heavy fog made it difficult to coördinate the movements of the assaulting infantry, especially of some divisions in battle for the first time, yet the advance throughout was extremely vigorous.

The III Corps (Bullard), nearest the Meuse, carried the enemy's second position before dark. The 33d Division (Bell), wheeling to the right as it advanced, occupied the west bank of the Meuse to protect the flank of the army. The Bois de Forges, with its difficult terrain and strong machine gun defenses, was carried in splendid fashion.

The right of the 80th Division (Cronkhite) had by noon cleared the Bois Juré in the face of machine gun fire and established its line north of Dannevoux. On its left, after an all-day fight, the division forced its way through the strong positions on Hill 262 and reached the northern slopes of that hill.

The 4th Division (Hines), on the left of the 80th, took Septsarges and firmly established itself in the woods to the north. It was abreast of Nantillois and its left was more than a mile beyond Montfaucon, but through some misinterpretation of the orders by the III Corps the opportunity to capture Montfaucon that day was lost. Three counterattacks against the division during the afternoon were broken up.

In the center, the V Corps (Cameron), with the exception of the 91st Division (Johnston), on its left, fell short of its objectives. The 79th Division (Kuhn), on the right of the corps, took Malancourt but in the open ground beyond encountered considerable opposition and the advanced elements were not in position before Montfaucon until late afternoon. The attack of the division launched against this strongpoint early in the evening was met by the fire of artillery and machine guns from the southern slopes of the hill which held up further progress.

The 37th Division (Farnsworth), in the center of the V Corps, after overcoming strong machine gun fire, pushed through the Bois de Montfaucon, and its attacks in the afternoon carried the line up to west of Montfaucon. The left of its line, facing stiff opposition, cleaned up the woods in its front and established itself just south of Ivoiry.

The 91st Division (Johnston) overcame strong initial resistance and advanced rapidly to Épinonville, which it entered but did not hold. Crossing into the sector of the 35th Division during the day, it occupied Véry.

On the left of the Army, the I Corps (Liggett) made excellent progress. The 35th Division (Traub) cleverly captured the strong position of Vauquois and took Cheppy against stubborn opposition. Elements of the division reached the corps objective east of Charpentry but were withdrawn to a line west of Véry. On the left, the division captured that part of Varennes east of the Aire River, but was held up between Varennes and Cheppy. At this time, a fresh regiment took the lead, giving a new impetus to the attack, and pushed the line forward to the high ground south of Charpentry.

In the 28th Division (Muir) the right brigade captured the western half of Varennes and continued about a mile farther. The left brigade, facing the eastern spurs of the Argonne, which constituted the enemy's chief defense of that forest, was unable to overcome the intense machine gun fire from the vicinity of Champ Mahaut. The 77th Division (Alexander) in the difficult terrain of the Argonne made some progress.

The advance on the first day was generally rapid, as the forward elements of the German defensive zone were usually not strongly held and they had not yet been reënforced in any numbers. By the second day, however, his nearby reserves had arrived, and the enemy took full advantage of the stand at Montfaucon on the first day to strengthen his defenses.

The Germans made every use of the favorable terrain to oppose our advance by cross and enfilading artillery fire, especially from the bluffs on the eastern edge of the Argonne Forest and the heights east of the Meuse. His light guns and the extensive use of machine guns along his lines of defense, in the hands of well trained troops, were serious obstacles, and the advance after the second day was more difficult.

By the evening of the 27th, the V Corps was almost abreast of the I and III on its flanks. The 79th Division captured Montfaucon on the morning of the 27th, and on the 28th Nantillois and the Bois de Beuge were passed despite determined resistance. Twice on the 28th elements of the division penetrated the Bois des Ogons but could not hold on. Again on the 29th it attacked the wood, severe casualties once more compelling retirement to the ridge north of Nantillois. Other troops of the division advanced more than a mile beyond the Bois de Beuge but were forced to fall back.

I went to III Corps headquarters on the 28th to confer with Bullard, who spoke well of the divisions under his command. The 80th had taken the Bois de la Côte Lemont after hard fighting, but assault after assault made with dogged determination across the open space toward Brieulles-sur-Meuse was rolled back by the galling fire of the enemy from the town and its vicinity and by the artillery firing from the east of the Meuse.

The 33d Division maintained its position on the 27th and 28th and on the 29th relieved the 80th Division by extending its left along the northeastern edge of Bois de la Côte Lemont, where it occupied difficult ground under the dominating heights east of the Meuse.

The 4th Division captured Nantillois on the 27th but was forced by enemy counterattacks to retire. The town was retaken and held on the following day by troops of the 4th and 79th Divisions. After three days of almost continuous fighting, the 4th had taken the Bois de Brieulles and entered the Bois des Ogons, but could not hold the latter against counterattacks and the deadly machine gun and artillery fire of the enemy. The fortitude and courage of the 4th Division in these operations were inspiring.

The 37th Division on the 27th attempted to advance beyond the Ivoiry—Montfaucon road but each time it reached there was driven back by heavy shelling. On the 28th, however, it pushed forward to a position north of the Cierges—Nantillois road. Cierges was entered but not held. On the following day it again attacked Cierges but the advance was abruptly halted by concentrated artillery fire.

The 91st Division on the 27th encountered strong opposition at Épinonville, which was reached but could not be retained. Eclisfontaine was taken but was evacuated as an artillery barrage was to be laid on the road through the town during the night. Épinonville was finally captured on the 28th and the Bois de Cierges was occupied after hard fighting. Two attacks of the division from the Bois de Cierges on the 29th crumbled under fierce artillery and enfilading machine gun fire, but on the third attack, despite severe losses, Gesnes was taken. The full advantage of this important gain was lost, however, through the inability of the 37th Division to advance its left. This placed the right flank of the 91st in a dangerous position and it had to be withdrawn. During the afternoon the 35th Division was subjected to a heavy counterattack which also involved the left of the 91st, but made no progress against it.

Three new German divisions had appeared by September 30th on the front of the I Corps and the battle continued with increased intensity. The 35th Division was stopped by heavy fire soon after its attack opened on September 27th, but later in the day it captured Charpentry and advanced to the ridge northeast, though suffering severe casualties. When I called to see General Traub at his P.C. at Cheppy, on the 28th, his communications with his front had been seriously damaged and it was difficult to tell what was happening. The division, however, took Montrebeau Wood on that day. Early on the morning of the 29th a detachment reached Exermont valley, but being nearly surrounded withdrew to the starting-point. Encountering very heavy artillery fire and an advance of the German 52d and 5th Guard Divisions, the 35th withdrew from Montrebeau Wood, which it had taken the day before. The 35th suffered greater casualties than any other division during these four days of continuous fighting.

On my visit to the headquarters of the 28th Division, then at Varennes, General Muir complained of a lack of trained officers. Two general staff officers, General Nolan and Colonel Conger, were there at the time, and I assigned them both temporarily to the division. Though subjected to strong artillery and machine gun fire from the bluffs of the Argonne, the 28th Division captured Montblainville on September 27th. It could make only slight headway, however, against firm opposition from positions in the vicinity of Champ Mahaut, but carried them on the 28th and also captured Apremont. On the 29th, after repulsing a German counterattack, a slight advance was made against the defenses of Le Chêne Tondu.[1]

The 77th Division encountered stiff resistance in the Argonne on the 27th and was held to a small gain, but moved forward about a mile on the 28th. On the 29th its right was advanced with but little opposition.

During the first four days of fighting, the First Army, west of the Meuse, had made a maximum advance of about eight miles,

---

[1] Brig. Gen. Edward Sigerfoos, while en route to assume command of the 56th Brigade, 28th Division, was struck by shell fragments on Sept. 29th, near Apremont, and died of wounds on Oct. 7th.

reaching the line Bois de la Côte Lemont—Nantillois—Apremont. The enemy had been struck a blow so powerful that the extreme gravity of his situation in France was obvious to him. From the North Sea to the Meuse his tired divisions had been battered, and nowhere with more dogged resolution than in front of the American First Army, his most sensitive point. The initial moves of the German Government to stop the fighting occurred at this time and without doubt because of the results of these four days of battle.

The enemy must have realized that the complete loss of his positions on the west bank of the Meuse was only a question of a short time. Meanwhile, he had to hold his third line of defense on our front as long as possible to protect his vital artery of communications and the flank of his troops opposing the French Fourth Army. He was, therefore, compelled to weaken his power of resistance on other fronts to provide reënforcements for his struggle with our First Army. It should be recorded that in this dire extremity the Germans defended every foot of ground with desperate tenacity and with the rare skill of experienced soldiers.

The enemy quickly brought up reënforcements, one division arriving on the afternoon of the 26th. By the 30th he had added six fresh divisions to his lines with five more ready in close reserve. The 76th Reserve Division entered in the Argonne, the 5th Guard Division on the Aire, the 52d near Exermont, the 115th Division near Cierges, the 37th Division west of Nantillois, and the 5th Bavarian Division near Nantillois. Our initial gains had been made against eleven enemy divisions.

The difficulties encountered by our inexperienced divisions during this phase of the fighting were not easily overcome. Liaison between the various echelons was hard to maintain owing to the broken nature of the terrain and the numerous wooded areas. Supported in most instances by artillery units with which they had never before maneuvered, perfect teamwork between the artillery and the infantry was not at once attained. The tanks gave valuable assistance at the start, but they became especial targets for the enemy's artillery and their numbers were rapidly diminished.

The question of supply during the Meuse-Argonne operation, especially in the beginning, gave us much concern. The three roads crossing no-man's-land over which artillery and supply trains had to move were impassable in many places. After four years of neglect and frequent bombardment, scarcely more than traces were left. In addition to having been blown up in spots where repair was difficult, they were further damaged by the explosion of contact mines planted by the retreating enemy. The French earlier in the war had also blown enormous craters in these roads to hinder the German advance. Trucks and artillery were delayed and could often be gotten forward only by the troops hauling them by ropes. The whole terrain in front of the enemy's first line was one continuous area of deep shell holes. After the sunshine of the first day, the heavy rainfall on the second and third days added immeasurably to the task of road repair. Considerable portions of the roads over no-man's-land had to be entirely rebuilt.

Notwithstanding the limited time available and the scarcity of labor, the task of moving combat troops, supplies and ammunition under the circumstances was accomplished in a most commendable manner, due mainly to the energetic work of pioneer, road, railroad, and truck train troops. Most of the divisional artillery and a considerable portion of the corps artillery got forward on the first day, and all but a few batteries of heavy artillery on the second day.

During the first four days, especially, although we had a superiority in the number of guns, the enemy's artillery had the advantage of hidden flank positions on the heights of the Meuse and in the Argonne. It had almost full play on the more exposed elements of the advance, and its cross-fire caused us many casualties. The tremendous numbers of machine guns, located in inaccessible places, gave us much trouble.

The tenacity with which the eastern heights of the Argonne Forest were held by the Germans is indicated in the orders of their divisions and the corps holding the Argonne and Aire valley sectors. The corps advised the Argonne sector on September 26th to reënforce the eastern edge of the forest; on the 27th positive orders were issued that the troops in the Aire valley were to be supported with every piece of artillery in the Argonne. The artillery so concentrated along the edge of the forest poured its deadly flanking fire into the 28th, 35th and 91st Divisions, particularly the 35th. A German account written on the 28th gives the number of tanks shot to pieces in the vicinity of Chaudron Farm and Montblainville as thirty. By the morning of the 28th, according to German report, there were thirteen batteries enfilading the American attack from the eastern rim of the Argonne.

Telephone communications were difficult to maintain, mainly due to destruction wrought by the enemy's artillery, although somewhat due to the inexperience of our personnel. In the V Corps the signal battalion joined on the eve of battle and had to learn its duties under fire. Without some means of sending messages between the elements of a command, there can, of course, be no direction and no concerted action, and consequently little chance of success.

The severity of the fighting, the heavy casualties, and the intermingling of troops in some of our divisions were such that it seemed advisable to place in the line more experienced divisions which had now become available. It was also thought best to limit activities to local attacks for two or three days. The 32d (Haan) and the 3d (Buck) Divisions were brought in to relieve the 37th (Farnsworth) and 79th (Kuhn), and the 1st Division (Summerall) took the place of the 35th (Traub). The 91st (Johnston) was withdrawn to corps reserve and the 92d (Ballou) was placed at the disposal of the French XXXVIII Corps, which was on the left of the I Corps.

These changes, involving the movement of more than 125,000 men over the limited routes available, already severely taxed with the transportation of ammunition, food, and the evacuation of wounded, were successfully made and the army was ready for the renewal of its attacks.

It was a matter of keen regret that the veteran 2d Division was not on hand at this time, but at Marshal Foch's earnest request it had been sent to General Gouraud to assist the French Fourth Army, which was held up at Somme Py. At no time did I refuse to comply with Foch's requests to send divisions to the assistance of the Allies, no matter how inconvenient it may have been. I always insisted, however, that these divisions should operate as American units and should return to my command when they had accomplished their emergency mission.

It was one thing to fight a battle with well trained, well organized and experienced troops, but quite another matter to take relatively green troops and organize, train and fight them at the same time. Some of our divisions that lacked training could not have been considered available for this operation had it not been for our belief that the morale of the enemy in general was rather low and that this was the opportunity to throw our full strength into the battle with the intention of winning the war in 1918.

During this phase and throughout the battle, I frequently visited corps and divisions to give personal encouragement to commanders and staffs, to point out deficiencies, to adjust difficulties, to keep myself directly informed as to progress, and to indicate the most advantageous methods of handling the troops in these attacks. In order to keep in closer touch with the activities of our forces, my personal staff and other officers especially qualified for this duty were sent to the front to observe the progress of the different units.

On Sunday, the 29th, M. Clemenceau came to visit the First Army. He was pleased with our progress and was especially delighted at the capture of Montfaucon. He insisted on going there notwithstanding my warning that it was dangerous to do so and that the roads were filled with traffic. I felt real solicitude for his safety as Montfaucon was a prominent target for the enemy's artillery. The road he took was crowded with trucks that morning, due especially to the trains of the 1st Division, which was going to the front to relieve the 35th. He failed to reach Montfaucon and left rather disappointed, thinking, no doubt, that our transportation was hopelessly swamped, as we soon began to hear of criticisms to that effect not only by the French but even by some Americans.

The truth is that while the roads were at times congested in places, no such general condition existed. This is shown by the relief of three divisions by three others, making a large increase in the number of men handled over the roads at this time, in addition to the heavy regular traffic. Under the circumstances, the movement of the truck trains required for this purpose was especially well managed. The number of troops moved in this change was greater than the entire Northern Army in the battle of the Wilderness. There was no major offensive during the World War in which a certain amount of congestion on roads leading to the front did not occur until those across no-man's-land could be opened up and put in good shape. I have already referred to the confused conditions behind Mangin's army during his attack on the Château-Thierry salient in July, and this was another case in point.

Good reports came in regarding the operations on the 29th of our II Corps (Read), which was with General Rawlinson's British Fourth Army. With both the 30th (Lewis) and the 27th (O'Ryan) Divisions in line, this corps formed the main wedge in the attack against that portion of the German lines which included the Bellicourt tunnel of the Cambrai—St. Quentin Canal. This tunnel, which is about 6,500 yards in length, served as an excellent shelter for the protection of German troops in that sector.

The II Corps, attacking on September 29th against stiff resistance, gallantly captured the ridge of the tunnel, which was a part of the Hindenburg Line. The 30th Division did especially well. It broke through the Hindenburg Line on its entire front and took Bellicourt and part of Nauroy by noon of the 29th. The Australian 5th Division, coming up at this time, continued the attack with elements of the 30th Division and the line advanced a considerable distance.

The 27th Division, due to no fault of its own, had been unable to take full advantage of the accompanying barrage, which was laid down over 1,000 yards ahead of the line from which the troops started the attack. Despite the handicap, it took the

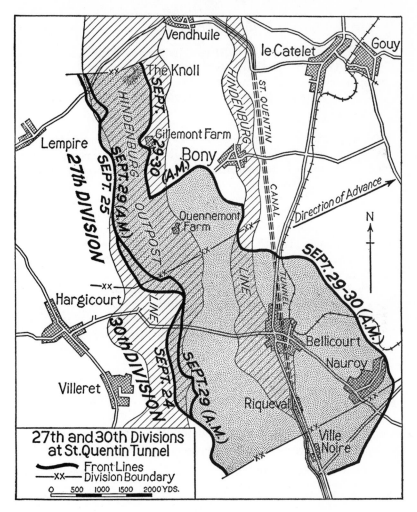

enemy trenches of the Hindenburg Line south of Bony, captured The Knoll, and established its line south from that position to a point just west of Gillemont Farm.

CHAPTER XLVI

New Proposal by Foch—Would Divide First Army—Flatly Disapprove—
Motor Transport Woefully Short—Rail Transportation Inadequate—
Shipments Haphazard—Mr. Baker Obtains Additional Tonnage from
British—Personnel Falling Behind—Secretary's Departure—Letters
Exchanged

(Diary) Souilly, Thursday, October 3, 1918. Was surprised Tuesday by proposal of Marshal Foch, brought by General Weygand, to
interject the French Second Army between us and French Fourth
Army, which I disapproved.

Claudel [1] came yesterday to discuss an attack by his corps which
he had been directed to prepare. Sent letter to the Secretary of War.

Minor engagements have occurred since the 29th. Captured positions being consolidated.

This afternoon saw corps commanders about the attack to-morrow.
Roads rapidly improving and conditions better.

Serious situation as to motor transport again cabled to Washington.
Shortage in tonnage reducing supplies to danger point. The French
have agreed to import locomotives and turn over cars made for them
in the United States. Atterbury has cabled Felton complete rail requirements.

AS noted in the diary, the proposal from Marshal Foch,
brought by Weygand, contemplated placing the French
Second Army between the American First and the French
Fourth Armies. It was suggested by Weygand that the Second
Army should take over those divisions from the left of our First

[1] General Claudel commanded the French XVII Corps at Verdun, which formed a
part of the American First Army.

NOTE: Total strength of the A.E.F. on September 30th, 71,172 officers, 1,634,220 enlisted
men.

Divisional units arriving in September included elements of the following divisions:
34th Division (National Guard, Nebraska, Iowa, South Dakota, North Dakota and
Minnesota), Brig. Gen. John A. Johnston; 84th Division (National Army, Kentucky,
Indiana and southern Illinois), Maj. Gen. Harry C. Hale; 86th Division (National
Army, Wisconsin and Illinois), Maj. Gen. Charles H. Martin; 87th Division (National
Army, Arkansas, Louisiana, Mississippi and Alabama), Maj. Gen. Samuel D. Sturgis.

Army that were in and near the Argonne Forest, leaving the rest of the army under my command. The idea seemed to be that this would accelerate the advance. The plan was similar to the one of August 30th, which had been so firmly opposed that I thought the matter settled once for all.

Just what prompted the proposal was not clear. However, I suspected at the time that it was made in deference to some suggestion or direction from Clemenceau, who often jumped at conclusions. Although he might not have expert knowledge of military situations or of operations, this would not have deterred him from judging as though he were quite competent to do so.

As Chairman of the Supreme War Council, Clemenceau had been granted no authority to issue directions to the Allied Commander-in-Chief. But in his capacity as Prime Minister he had authority over Marshal Foch as an officer of the French Army. The Marshal fully realized this, and although he had been chosen by the Allied Governments and was responsible to them jointly, his tenure of office naturally depended upon their pleasure, and especially upon that of his own Prime Minister. This would readily account for any action he might take at the suggestion of the latter.

The proposition Weygand submitted was not sound because the different features of that front were interdependent and the advantages they afforded the enemy's defense could best be overcome by a strong attacking force under one control. Another objection was that there was only one road leading to the part of our front which was proposed for the French Second Army and its use by two different armies would have resulted in many complications. Moreover, the fact was again overlooked that our men seriously objected to service in the French Army. I pointed out these objections to Weygand and told him that the change, in my opinion, instead of increasing Allied progress would retard it. He left with the view that I was right, and my reply by letter disapproving the plan seemed to settle the matter. So we continued our attacks as planned.

We were woefully deficient in motor transportation now that we had undertaken large operations, although the shipment of motor vehicles had been repeatedly urged upon the War Department. Once more we were almost wholly dependent upon the French for land transport to move our troops and to handle about half of our ammunition supply. To carry on operations, we had to strip the S.O.S. of trucks, and this seriously interfered with work at the base ports, with construction projects at other points, and with supply of troops in general. The shortage of ambulances to move the sick and wounded was critical and we had been compelled to borrow fifteen American ambulance sections from Italy. But we had reached the point where we were no longer able to borrow. This condition was not easy to reconcile with the suggestion from Washington made a short time before that motor transportation be largely substituted for horses.

All these facts were pointed out plainly to the War Department, but we received little encouragement. According to the Department's detailed program of shipments, just received, the best we could expect in the near future was only about one-fifth of our requirements. After another urgent cable, we were promised 10,000 motor vehicles in October but the promise was only partially fulfilled. The question was to some extent dependent upon tonnage, although the shipping authorities continuously failed to take advantage of deck space available on most of our transports.

The following quotation from my cable to the Chief of Staff on the subject, sent September 13th, will indicate our situation:

"At the present time our ability to supply and maneuver our forces depends largely on motor transportation. The shortage in motor transportation is particularly embarrassing now due to shortage of horses for our horse-drawn transport. We are able to carry out present plans due to fact that we have been able to borrow temporarily large numbers of trucks and ambulances from French. We have also borrowed fifteen American ambulance sections from Italy. The shortage of ambulances to move our wounded is critical. * * * The most important plans and operations depend upon certainty that the home government will deliver at French ports material and equipment called for. It is urged that foregoing be given most serious consideration.

* * * The need of motor transportation is urgent. It is not understood why greater advantage has not been taken of deck space to ship motor trucks. Trucks do not overburden dock accommodations or require railroad transportation * * * . Can you not impress this upon shipping authorities?"

The absence of motor vehicles would not have been quite so serious if we had not been in such a crippled state as to horses. Due to lack of animals our divisional transport and artillery were rapidly becoming immobilized. We still hoped to obtain a number from the French, and from Spain and Portugal, but after cutting down the requirements as far as possible we needed 30,000 per month additional from home from October to June, 1919, even with our full quota of motor vehicles. It became evident in July that to meet our pressing needs the shipment of horses would have to be resumed and a request was cabled July 16th for 25,000 per month. It was not to be expected that shipments could begin at once, but it was disappointing that in the three months preceding our entry into battle we should receive less than 2,000 horses.

In the matter of locomotives and cars the situation continued much the same and came to such a pass that the French said they could do no more. They offered to import for us as many locomotives as could be produced in excess of our monthly program, the non-fulfillment of which had left us short, and to turn over sufficient cars manufactured on their orders to bring monthly shipments up to 7,500. As to rails, they suggested that if there was not enough steel for shell production and for rails we should abandon railroad repair and tear up existing track at home, as both they and the British had done. Marshal Foch urged increased rail facilities as necessary to win the war and himself submitted the above suggestions.

In considering questions of supply, we were always forced back to the subject of shipping. Our tonnage allotments were not keeping up to our increasing demands. In July, for instance, we were allotted 475,000 tons against my request for 750,000, and we received 438,000 tons. It was the same in August, when we were allotted 700,000 tons and received 511,000, and on the basis of receipts for the first two weeks of September it seemed probable we would run some 200,000 tons short in that month.[1]   The situation was so grave that in my cable of October 3d setting forth the deficiencies I said, "Unless supplies are furnished when and as called for, our armies will cease to operate."

To aggravate matters, shipments seemed to be haphazard. For instance, there were sent in August 50,000 tons of quartermaster supplies of which we already had a surplus, and in that month the shipments showed a deficiency of 50,000 tons pertaining to the transportation department and motor transport. In cabling these facts to Washington, I stated, "You must prepare to ship supplies we request instead of shipping excess amounts of supplies of which we have a due proportion."

To get an idea of the situation, it may be noted that for June, July, and August, shipments of Ordnance material were 33 per cent short of estimated allotments, in Signal Corps material 52 per cent, in Chemical Warfare requirements 51 per cent, in Medical Corps supplies 23 per cent, in railway transportation, principally rolling stock, 20 per cent, while in motor transport we were desperate as the deficiency was 81 per cent.

It was next to impossible to consider with complacency a situation which left us not only short of supplies but almost without modern means to move our armies. When a nation is forced into war without preparation, neither men nor equipment are at once forthcoming and time is required to develop the flow of all that is needed, which is difficult because of the pressure for haste from all quarters. Yet after nearly eighteen months of war it would be reasonable to expect that the organization at home would have been more nearly able to provide adequate equipment and supplies, and to handle shipments more systematically. It was fortunate indeed that we were not operating alone, for, in that case, the failure to meet our demands would have caused us serious trouble, if not irreparable disaster.

[1] The difference in the amount of supplies asked for by the A.E.F. and the amount received in September was 330,000 tons and in October 398,000 tons.

There was hope, however, of some improvement in the tonnage situation. The Emergency Fleet Corporation of the Shipping Board at home, under the energetic and able direction of Mr. Charles M. Schwab, was turning out new ships at a greatly increased rate. Undoubtedly, had the war lasted a few months longer, our deficiency in this respect would have been entirely overcome.

As for the immediate future, when Mr. Baker came back from England to be with us at the beginning of the Meuse-Argonne battle, he brought the welcome news that he had succeeded in getting an allotment of 200,000 tons of shipping from the British, on the condition that we should help them out later in the shipment of cereals, if it should become necessary. He cabled the President asking approval of an agreement he wished to make with Lord Reading that there would be no diversion of tonnage from the amount needed for the maintenance of our forces in Europe if we would agree to coöperate with the Allies by using our tonnage for their supply programs as their needs should become paramount.

The arrivals of personnel were not keeping up with the 80-division program, even as construed in Washington. Our contention was that these eighty divisions should be combat troops, and that in addition we should have a corresponding number for the various units connected with the S.O.S., but Washington took another view. At any rate, for the forces then in France there was needed to balance the command, 129,000 army troops, 93,000 corps troops, 83,000 S.O.S. troops and 65,000 replacements. In order to make definite plans for the future, it was necessary for us to have the troops for the various purposes in due proportion. However, it was evident from the correspondence that in the opinion of the War Department 3,000,000 men would be the highest number that could be trained, transported, and supplied.

The Secretary was now about to leave for home and as it was not possible for me to see him again I wrote him touching on these and other matters that had been the subject of conversation:

"France, October 2, 1918.

"MY DEAR MR. SECRETARY:

"I very much regret that it will be impossible for me to meet you in Paris before you leave for the States. It seems that I have not had more than a glimpse of you, and our conversations have been so few and so short that I feel as though I had not brought out clearly many things of mutual interest and importance. Our whole problem here is of such magnitude that details sometimes are apt to get little attention, and yet only by carefully watching these details shall we be able to keep the machinery going. If one part of the mechanism gets weak, then, under great stress, the whole might fail. It all requires the most watchful care. There is no one quite so sensitive to this as the engineer who is getting the machinery into perfect working order, putting it under way, and trying to keep it moving until it has attained its full momentum, and then holding it there in a true course.

"The one general principle, which you so clearly understand, much to my gratification, and the enforcement of which will insure perfect coöperation, is that the General Staff and every supply department at Washington should strive to provide us promptly with the necessary personnel and material in the order called for, the whole scheme, of course, to be coördinated by your General Staff. As you know, our personnel and some kinds of material and supplies, including transportation, are in a very unbalanced condition. I hope that your own high position and your personal force will serve to regulate many of these matters with which no one but yourself over there can be familiar.

"In sending General McAndrew up to Paris to see you, I have asked him to take certain cables which illustrate our situation and show the insistence with which we have placed our needs before the Department, and the apparent routine attitude with which they are too often viewed at the other end. Of course, it may be difficult for them to see the problem as we see it, but that is all the more reason for their accepting our view instead of adhering to their own.

"The operations here have gone very well, but, due to the rains and the condition of the roads, have not gone forward as rapidly nor as far as I had hoped. But this terrain over which we now operate is the most difficult on the Western Front. Our losses so far have been moderate. I have taken out three of the newest divisions and replaced them by older ones. We shall be prepared to advance again in a day or two more.

"I did not mean to write at such length, but our success here depends so much upon the coöperative support that the General Staff and the supply departments, including shipping, at Washington give us that I have ventured again to appear garrulous. No doubt it will be much improved upon your return. If I have seemed too positive, it is because I am prompted by my wish and by your own strong desire to have things go as we have planned.

"May I ask you to convey to the President my most cordial greetings and very best wishes.

"Believe me, with warmest personal and official regard,

"Yours sincerely,   "JOHN J. PERSHING."

Written on the same date, his letter advised me of shipping and other matters of great interest:

"France, October 2, 1918.

"MY DEAR GENERAL PERSHING:

"I am returning to Paris to-day, having completed, so far as it can be done, the shipping matters in London. On Friday night I shall go to Brest and thence home. I am taking back to the United States with me, Mr. Ryan, General Hines, Mr. Hostetler, Mr. Day and Mr. Gifford, who came over with Mr. Stettinius. Before we leave, General Hines is going to see General McAndrew for a final talk about shipping matters. I think we will all go home to the United States with fresh enthusiasm for our end of the work and I hope you will soon feel in Europe the effect of our work in the States.

"The four main problems are, of course, the shipping of motor transport, animal transport, general supplies and of men. In addition to these I will assuredly be mindful of the discussion of the promotion question and the schools question.

"As you know, the British have already placed at our disposal for October sailings, substantially 200,000 tons cargo carrying capacity of ships. In London we found every disposition to assist us to the full extent of the needs of the eighty-division program, and after very careful studies of the question the whole matter was brought up at the Inter-Allied Maritime Council in session attended by Lord Reading and me. Apparently the only obstacle grew out of a fear on the part of the European Allies that the diversion of tonnage from their cereal import program at this time would leave them short of food later in the year. They were aware of the fact that our shipbuilding progress would, on present appearance, give us a surplus of ships beyond our Army needs beginning in March, 1919, but they wanted some sort of assurance that we would use this surplus to replenish their food stocks. As it is obvious that we cannot allow this period of the civil populations of the European Allies to be broken by insufficient food, I felt quite ready to give the necessary assurance and we have now this understanding embodied in the resolutions of the Inter-Allied Maritime Council, namely that the eighty-division American Military Program is approved and thought necessary. Shipping to effect it is to be placed at our disposal with the understanding that should a food, or other need of any of the European Allies become so pressing as to become critical, the United States will confer through the Inter-Allied Maritime Council with the representatives of other nations and participate with them in meeting the crisis out of any surplus shipping it may have or any such other way as the character of the crisis dictates. In effect this amounts to a present approval of our program with the reservation that in view of the constantly changing situation we are all free to meet any new crisis should it arise, by fresh consultations and determinations.

"Among the ships already diverted to our use are three horse-ships and I impressed upon the executives of the Maritime Council the importance of further diversion of ships of the same kind. One result of this arrangement will be that the Inter-Allied Maritime Council will be constantly studying America's need for shipping and this of course will mean principally the Army need. I stated to the Council quite frankly that America could never under any circumstances regard any other need as paramount to the necessary supplies of so much of our Army as is in Europe at any given time. This position was recognized as just and Messrs. Stevens and Rublee, who represent the United States on the Maritime Council, have assured me that they will keep themselves constantly advised as to the Army needs and represent them for us in the deliberations of the Maritime Council so that no diversion of shipping will be made by that body which will prejudice the necessary supplies of the Army.

"I hope to see General Harbord and to explain to him the importance of keeping Messrs. Stevens and Rublee fully acquainted with the Army needs from time to time and have arranged to have Mr. Morrow come to France and confer with General Harbord frequently so that he can be the means of inter-communication between our S.O.S. Headquarters and Mr. Stevens and Mr. Rublee. I am told that you have already met Mr. Morrow and I need not therefore enlarge upon his splendid abilities and fine spirit. It may be that he may ask to see you should any peculiarly difficult question arise and I am therefore explaining in detail the service which he has undertaken to perform and its importance in assuring the continuance of the necessary shipping for our use.

"I had rather expected that the Italian delegates to the Maritime Council might raise some question about American troops serving in Italy. They did not bring up the subject, nor was anything said at the meeting of the Council by the British on that subject, but an interesting incident took place about which I feel that you ought to have for your information a rather detailed account.

" * * * The conversation was very general until dinner time, but as soon as we had finished dinner, the Prime Minister brought up the shipping question. Sir Joseph Maclay, who was present, was called on to state the situation, which he did in a few words, and I made a brief comment which was accepted by everybody as showing that we were all in hearty accord and would be able to work out the problem. Then Mr. Lloyd George squared himself around and said that he had something which he felt it very important to say to me and to say with great frankness. We all kept quiet and he talked, I should say, for half an hour without interruption. I cannot of course reproduce verbally what he said, but in effect it was this:

"That the British had brought over from the United States an enormous number of troops in the firm expectation that they would be trained with the British and would assist the British in their Flanders fighting. That they had gone to great lengths to supply and equip our troops and finally had some ten divisions of them about ready to engage in conflict and included in Sir Douglas Haig's plans of attack, when suddenly the five best trained divisions were taken away just at the time when they would have been of most service with Sir Douglas Haig's troops. That later, of the five divisions then with the British, three were taken away and that he was informed that the other two came near being taken away so that the effect of the whole business was that for all their pains and sacrifices for training our troops there and equipping them they had gotten no good out of them whatever, and that the American troops had not been of any service to the British. That at one time when some American troops were about to go into action with the British, peremptory orders had been issued that they should not go into action as they were not adequately trained.

"From this he went on to say that he was earnestly desirous for opportunity of the American and British soldiers to fraternize. He felt that large issues to the future peace of the world depended upon the American and British peoples understanding one another and that much the best hope of such an understanding grew out of intermingling our soldiers so that they could learn to know one another, but that it seemed to him that there was some influence at work to monopolize American soldiers for the assistance of the French and to keep them from the association of the British.

"When he had about finished, I replied to him that I was profoundly surprised at the feeling he expressed, since Lord Reading and I had quite definitely understood in Washington, and our understanding had been set up in a memorandum of which copy had been sent him, that the American troops brought over by the British were expedited because of the lack of reserves by the British and French, which would be made up by August 1st. That I had stated to Lord Reading and put into the memorandum that these American troops assigned for training with the British were to be subject to your call at any time at your discretion and that their training and use was constantly to be such as you directed. I had, therefore, no thought that there could be any ground for misunderstanding your right to take the American troops at any time you wanted them. I pointed out to him that the President and I had repeatedly, both verbally and in writing, insisted that the American Army as such was the thing we were trying to create. That we had no intention of feeding our soldiers into the French or British Army and intended to have an American army in exactly the same sense that Great Britain had a British army and France a French army. That we all recognized the right of Marshal Foch to send divisions of Americans or French or British from one part of the line to another for particular operations or to create a composite reserve which would have troops of all three nations for use as reserves, but with that exception American troops in France were as completely under your control as British troops in France were under the control of Sir Douglas Haig. I then took up the question as to whether American troops had been of any service to the British and told him quite frankly that I did not see how it was possible to hold the view he had expressed for three reasons at least. First— the work of our troops at Château-Thierry and elsewhere had been so valuable a contribution to the whole cause, and I had been repeatedly told, in France by Frenchmen and in England by Englishmen, that they had saved the whole situation. Second—that our occupation of a substantial portion of the line in Lorraine and our operations there had undoubtedly both cost the enemy heavily and required the German high command to remove divisions from the British fronts, thus rendering Sir Douglas Haig's operations easier by diminishing the forces opposed to him; and third, I pointed out that our soldiers actually with the British at this time were bearing their full share of the heavy fighting and I said this must have been going on for some time, since I have visited several hospitals in England which are filled with wounded American soldiers, many of whom have been from three to five weeks in the hospitals recovering from wounds received by them in August, when according to the original understanding they would not have been with the British at all but would have been back with your Army.

"Long as this account of the conversation is, it is nevertheless but a summary of it. It left on my mind a very strong feeling that Lloyd George frankly wants Americans to remain with the British both as a stimulus and for the fraternization which he describes and that he is very suspicious that the French are desiring to monopolize the Americans and so come out of the war as our principal friends without there having been any real opportunity for coöperation and understanding between the British and Americans.

"I, of course, gave him no assurances whatever, and when he asked me what expectations I thought he ought to have about the use of American troops I replied shortly that I thought he ought to expect the American Army as such to exist in the same sense as the British Army and to be used there as a whole or by the detachment of divisions here and there wherever the largest good could be accomplished for the cause in the judgment of the Commander-in-Chief as he considered the problem from time to time.

"In the course of his statement that the American troops had been of no service to the British he pointed out that we had relieved the French of some forty or forty-five miles of front line and I remarked that when we took over forty miles of the entire front that was a help because it enabled the French and British to hold the remainder of the line more strongly with the same aggregate force. He then asked me whether I thought the French ought to take over some portion of the line held by the British in view of the fact that the Americans had relieved the French of so much of their portion of the line. I told him I knew nothing about the way that such matters were decided but that it would seem equable to have the relief afforded by the American assumption of a portion of the line insure to the benefit of both the French and the British in some such way.

"I am particular to describe this part of the conversation to you because I thought I could see an intention on his part to press Marshal Foch to take over for the French Army some part of the present British lines and he may quote me on the subject to the Marshal. I should be sorry to have the Marshal imagine that I undertook to express any opinion on such a subject beyond the mere generality that the American relief ought to be, as far as just and practicable, a benefit to both of our Allies in the line.

"The dinner party broke up pleasantly enough by our turning the conversation to other subjects.   Later Lord Reading and Lord Milner communicated to me privately to the effect that they were very glad that the Prime Minister had brought up the subject and that we had discussed it so frankly.   They were both perfectly proper in their attitude but as far as they could, gave me to understand that they were glad he had it off his chest and were equally glad that I had stood my ground and argued it out.   So far as I can learn neither Lord Reading nor Lord Milner has had any special sympathy with the Prime Minister's view in this matter, although, of course, he is the head of the Government and they are loyal to his expressed views.

"I spoke with General Read, whose corps is participating very heavily in the present fighting, and I venture to suggest that it be not withdrawn from the British section for the immediate present.   It will doubtless need to be rested up after this fighting is over and I would imagine it might be given its rest with the British so as to prolong its stay in their area and not immediately raise the question again, but I make this suggestion entirely subject to your own determinations which were originally made final and from which I have allowed nothing to be subtracted.

"I delivered your message of invitation to Lord Milner and he seemed heartily pleased at your having thought to convey a special invitation to visit your front through me.   Last night, just before I left London, Lord Milner took me aside and said as a parting word, about this: 'I want to say to you, Mr. Secretary, that all my relations with your officers and your Army have been and are most cordial and sympathetic.   I have had no disagreements or misunderstandings with them.   From General Pershing down, I regard them highly and there is not likely to be any misunderstanding between us.'   He told me that he had planned to visit you, but found out that the battle was on and knew that a visit would be more acceptable a little later so doubtless he will go over to see you pretty soon.

"I ought not to add a word to this long letter, but cannot leave France without thanking you heartily for all these fresh kindnesses you have shown me on this visit.   Colonel Collins has been so graciously helpful and is personally so charming a companion that every minute of my stay here has been made delightful, and, of course, the opportunity to see your great Army in action was the crowning event of a very interesting visit which I hope sincerely will prove useful to you in your work.

"With cordial regards, believe me
"Sincerely yours,
"NEWTON D. BAKER."

The Secretary's letter impressed me, as did almost every communication received from him, with his earnest purpose to do everything possible for our success.   His desire to aid in the solution of the multitude of problems which confronted me, his clear comprehension of their magnitude, his sympathy, his infinite tact and understanding, were qualities that served to lighten my burden and inspire loyalty to his direction of America's military effort.   No American general in the field ever received the perfect support accorded me by Mr. Baker.   His attitude throughout the war, in so far as it concerned me personally and the Army in France, is a model for the guidance of future secretaries in such an emergency.

CHAPTER XLVII

Vigorous Attacks Continued—Terrific Hand-to-Hand Fighting—I Corps Makes Important Gains—1st Division, I Corps, Drives Through— Other Corps Advance—French Fourth Army Stopped—Helped by Brilliant Work of 2d Division—Heavy Casualties, Much Sickness— Relief of "Lost Battalion"—Attack Extended East of the Meuse—Second Corps Does Well with British

(Diary) Souilly, Sunday, October 6, 1918. General attack in the Meuse-Argonne resumed the 4th, meeting stubborn resistance. Communications improving.

General Pétain took lunch with us yesterday; fully appreciates difficulty of our task. Summerall's 1st and Hines' 4th Divisions did well yesterday. Everything quiet on Dickman's IV Corps front in St. Mihiel sector. Conferred with Provost Marshal General Bandholtz; road circulation going better.

Our advance continued to-day. Mr. Baker cabled Washington directing appointment of general officers recommended by me.

Second Phase—Meuse-Argonne Operations

THE period of the battle from October 1st to the 11th involved the heaviest strain on the army and on me. There was little time to make readjustments among the troops heavily engaged, without giving the enemy a respite in which to strengthen his defenses and bring up reserves. The battle could not be delayed while roads were being built or repaired and supplies brought up. The weather was cold and rainy and not the kind to inspire energetic action on the part of troops unaccustomed to the damp, raw climate. A few commanders lacking in those stern qualities essential to battle leadership or in physical stamina so necessary under these conditions were inclined to pessimism or inertia. An exhibition of either of these tendencies was quickly reflected in the troops. The real leaders, those indomitable characters whose spirits rose to master every difficulty, stood forth, a tower of strength to me during this period of the fighting. For the thing to do was to drive forward with all possible force.

Our army in the Meuse-Argonne was confronted by the enemy strongly fortified on his main position of defense—the Hinden-

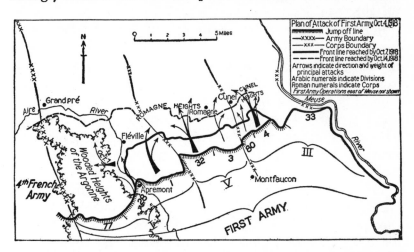

burg Line.[1] Romagne heights was a part of this defensive area and its dominating feature was Côte Dame Marie, which lay west of the town of Romagne and southeast of Landres-et-St. Georges. The approaches to the area could be plainly seen from the enemy's observation points and were covered thoroughly by his flanking artillery. The Cunel heights were flanked by fire

[1] The German estimate of the importance of holding this front is shown by the following order to his army issued by General von der Marwitz:

"October 1, 1918.

"According to information in our hands, the enemy intends to attack the 5th Army east of the Meuse in order to reach Longuyon. The objective of this attack is the cutting of the railroad line Longuyon-Sedan, which is the main line of communication (Lebensader) of the Western Army. Furthermore, the enemy hopes to compel us to discontinue the exploitation of the iron mines of Briey, the possession of which is a great factor in our steel production. The 5th Army once again may have to bear the brunt of the fighting of the coming weeks on which the security of the Fatherland may depend. The fate of a large portion of the Western Front, perhaps of our nation, depends on the firm holding of the Verdun front. The Fatherland believes that every commander and every soldier realizes the greatness of his task, and that every one will fulfill his duties to the utmost. If this is done, the enemy's attack will be shattered."

on the east from the heights of the Meuse and on the west from the heights of Romagne. The latter positions were supported by fire from Cunel heights and the heights of the Argonne Forest about Châtel-Chéhéry and Cornay. In other words the German positions then occupied in that sector afforded each other mutual support.

In the entire area on our front, as well as on the dominating heights mentioned, the large groups of woods were staggered in such a way that local flanking maneuvers caused excessive losses. Concealed in each group of woods were machine guns without number, covering the flanks and front of adjacent woods, and the timber lessened the effectiveness of our artillery fire. These machine gun positions were usually carried by direct infantry assault, with accompanying artillery. Such operations had to be carefully planned and executed to insure success.

The purpose of our attack on October 4th was to carry the above important positions or make gains that would lead to their capture. I visited our three corps headquarters on the day preceding this attack to discuss the plans with corps commanders. They all realized that we had hard fighting ahead of us, but they were acting with great vigor and determination and were confident of the outcome. The III Corps (Bullard) and the V (Cameron), acting in concert, were to take the heights of Cunel and Romagne. Their main effort was to be made against the western flank of Cunel heights, to avoid the enemy's fire from east of the Meuse. They were also to move against the eastern flank of Romagne heights. Heavy counterbattery fire with high explosives and gas was to be maintained and the observation stations beyond the Meuse were to be blinded by similar fire and smoke screens. The I Corps (Liggett) was to neutralize the flanking fire from the Argonne and was also to assist the V Corps by capturing the western portion of Romagne heights. Its plans involved a drive against the enemy east of Fléville to gain space for an attack northwest through Cornay and Châtel-Chéhéry, which would outflank the Argonne Forest.

To correct certain defects disclosed by our initial advance, special instructions were sent out regarding flanking maneuvers, mixing of units, and close coöperation between commanders.

Our order of battle to the west of the Meuse from right to left was as follows: III Corps (Bullard), with the 33d Division (Bell), the 4th (Hines), and the 80th (Cronkhite) in the front line; the V Corps (Cameron), with the 3d Division (Buck) and the 32d (Haan), both fresh, in line, with the 42d (Menoher) and the 91st (Johnston) in reserve; the I Corps (Liggett), with the 1st Division (Summerall), the 28th (Muir), and the 77th (Alexander) in line, and the 82d (Duncan) and the French 5th Cavalry Division in reserve. The army reserves were the 29th Division (Morton), the 35th (Traub), and the 92d (Ballou).

Between the Meuse and the Moselle the order of battle remained unchanged except that the 42d Division had been transferred to the reserve of the V Corps.

The general attack was resumed at 5:00 A.M. on October 4th, meeting desperate resistance by the enemy. In this attack, the 4th Division of the III Corps, in three days' bitter fighting, captured and held the Bois de Fays, making a gain of over a mile. Advances into the Bois de Peut de Faux were forced back by vicious counterattacks. In similar hard fighting, the 80th Division gained a foothold in the Bois des Ogons against very heavy machine gun fire.

In the attack of the V Corps, the 3d Division pushed forward in the face of strong resistance. During the next two days this division extended its gains, but could make no headway against the Bois de Cunel. The 32d Division, which had taken Cierges on October 1st, advanced to just south of Gesnes on the 4th, despite very severe hostile fire, and on the next day captured that town.

On the left of the army, the I Corps was very successful. The 1st Division, in a fine display of power on October 4th, drove a deep wedge into the enemy's line which was of great value in affording space for the attack toward the Argonne which was to be launched later. The fighting here was characterized by the stubborn nature of the German resistance and the offensive spirit of the division. In spite of heavy casualties, its determination was in no way weakened and by the evening of the 5th it had taken Arietal Farm and with great courage captured Hill 240. Its gains at this time totalled three miles.

The right of the 28th Division fought its way down the Aire River in liaison with the 1st and captured Chéhéry. The left of the division encountered much opposition and made but slight gain notwithstanding its repeated attacks. The division was now facing west for nearly three miles along the Aire River. The 77th Division between September 29th and October 4th continued its attacks in the Argonne, advancing about a mile over difficult terrain. In the assault of October 2d, a mixed battalion of the division moved forward more rapidly than the troops on its right and left and was completely surrounded by the enemy. It became popularly known as the "Lost Battalion." For several days every effort by the 77th Division to relieve this beleaguered force was unsuccessful and attempts by the Germans to compel its surrender were without avail.

Throughout this period the fighting was severe, with innumerable hand-to-hand combats between the opposing infantry. On the whole our new divisions were showing greater technical skill and their interior communications were much improved. By October 6th the attack had reached the general line: Bois de la Côte Lemont—Fléville—Le Chêne Tondu.

The enemy's lines were being reënforced by his best divisions, the total number then confronting the First Army having been increased to twenty-seven in line and seventeen in reserve. The Germans supported the defense by the use of innumerable machine guns and intense artillery fire from dominating crests and forests. That the danger which they foresaw from our violent attacks caused them grave apprehension was shown by their continued withdrawal of troops from other parts of the front for use against us. Although we were attacking, our estimate was that the enemy losses at least equalled our own.

In the meantime the French Fourth Army, on our left, had been held up at Blanc Mont. As a consequence, Marshal Foch appealed to me for assistance. Although I was loath to spare any troops from our front, so serious was our own replacement situation, I sent, in accordance with my promise, the 2d Division (Lejeune), which was followed later by the 36th (W. R. Smith). On October 3d, the 2d Division, accompanied by French tanks, in

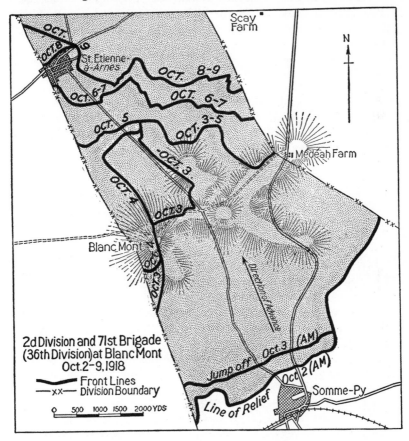

2d Division and 71st Brigade (36th Division) at Blanc Mont Oct. 2-9, 1918
Front Lines
—xx— Division Boundary
0 500 1000 1500 2000 YDS

a brilliant maneuver against heavy machine gun resistance, stormed and captured the dominating German positions on the Médéah Farm—Blanc Mont Ridge, and continued on toward St. Étienne, which was taken on October 8th with the assistance of a brigade of the 36th Division. This success carried forward the French divisions on its right and left, and, as reported by

General Gouraud, enabled the whole Fourth Army to advance.

The importance of this aid to the French Fourth Army is indicated by the following extracts from the French résumé of operations:

"The two brigades were side by side, the 4th Brigade of Marines on the left, and the 3d Brigade of Infantry on the right. Each of these two brigades had at its disposition a battalion of light tanks. * * *

"After a short but extremely violent artillery preparation the attack started at 5:50 A.M. on the 3d of October. Despite a considerable number of machine guns and heavy artillery fire, the two brigades with admirable dash attained the assigned objective, Blanc Mont— Médéah. In the course of its advance, the 5th Regiment of Marines sent a detachment to the XI Corps to help it clean out the German trenches. During this time, the division was subjected to violent artillery fire, as well as machine gun fire upon its left flank.

"At 4:00 P.M. the attack started anew. In the woods, filled with machine guns, the advance continued, and at 6:30 P.M., the forward movements of the American 2d Division reached the line marked by the Scay Farm and the crossroads at a point one kilometer south of St. Etienne-à-Arnes.

"The advance realized by the American 2d Division during the course of the day was remarkable, and reached a depth of about six kilometers. Numerous prisoners, cannon, machine guns, and material of all kinds, fell into its hands.

"The rapid advance of the XXI Corps, and, in particular that of the American 2d Division, on October 3d, brought about the most favorable results.

"The enemy, placed by this rapid advance of the center of the Fourth Army in a very difficult position upon the Monts, as well as in the valley of the Suippe, decided to evacuate the Monts and to retreat upon the Arnes and the Suippe. * * *

"On the 8th of October, a new attack took place on the whole Army front; the XXI Corps, strengthened by tanks, was directed to advance in the direction of Machault. The attack started at 5:15 A.M. The American 2d Division occupied St. Etienne-à-Arnes."

The 2d Division was relieved by the 36th on the night of October 9th-10th. During the night of the 10th the enemy withdrew, and the 36th went forward in pursuit, reaching the Aisne River on the 13th and establishing its line on the south bank.

The division maintained its position there until the night of the 28th-29th, when it was relieved by the French.

Although all classes of transportation were badly needed, it was imperative at this time to increase the rail facilities in the zone of our army. Truck trains were now being handled regularly and efficiently, yet the enormous supply of artillery ammunition that had to be brought up was beginning to bear heavily on them. The French were demanding the return of their trucks for use behind their own lines farther to the west, where transportation was also being overtaxed.

Our supply system was on a well regulated basis under the able coördination of Brigadier General Moseley and his assistants at G.H.Q., although we sorely felt the deficiencies in motor vehicles. These operations were hard on horse flesh, but our losses were being partially replaced from the limited numbers in the French armies, mainly through Marshal Foch's direct orders, and some were obtained from the British. Colonel John L. DeWitt, as the coördinator of supplies for the First Army, displayed rare ability in meeting the tremendous demands and overcoming the difficulties of transportation.

Influenza in the Army had assumed very serious proportions, over 16,000 cases additional having been reported during the week ending October 5th. Large numbers of cases were brought in by our troop ships. The total number of cases of influenza treated in hospitals was nearly 70,000, of whom many developed a grave form of pneumonia. The death rate from influenza rose to 32 per cent of cases for the A.E.F. and was as high as 80 per cent in some groups.

Although short of equipment and personnel, especially nurses,[1] the medical units of the First Army gave splendid service, regardless of the arduous character of their duties. In many instances they were under constant exposure on or near the battlefields for long periods. Their supply truck trains and ambulance trains went back and forth at all times, and were often hit by artillery

---

[1] In a cable dated October 3d it was requested that 1,500 nurses be sent to France at the earliest practicable date.

fire or shot up from airplanes. Evacuation hospitals were frequently bombed, and several nurses were wounded. Altogether, the Medical Department deserves the greatest praise for its services in this operation.

It was recognized that our divisions were required on other parts of the front to sustain and encourage the Allies and often to aid at points where the other armies were unable to advance without our help. At the same time, the absence with the French and British of four divisions, among which were some of our best, made it necessary to keep units in line on our front without the normal withdrawal for rest and refitting. Five of our divisions were kept in line on the active front for an average of twenty-four days of continuous service.

Once our army was committed to continuous attacks, the replacement of men became a problem of vital importance. The losses were mounting daily and the number of effectives was decreasing at a rapid rate. Casualties since September 26th had grown to nearly 75,000, and our need for replacements had increased to 80,000. It was necessary at this stage to reduce the size of our infantry companies from 250 to 175 men, and to keep up their strength even to this reduced figure some of our combat divisions had to be broken up and the men used as replacements. The offensive had to be continued without cessation, regardless of the expedients required to fill the depletion in our ranks.

On October 3d the following cable was sent supporting previous cables on the same subject:

"Over 50,000 of the replacements requested for the months of July, August, and September have not arrived. Due to extreme seriousness of the replacement situation it is necessary to utilize the personnel of the 84th and 86th Divisions for replacement purposes. Combat divisions are short over 80,000 men. Vitally important that all replacements due, including 55,000 requested for October, be sent early in October. If necessary, some divisions in the United States should be stripped of trained men and such men shipped as replacements at once."

(Diary) Souilly, Saturday, October 12, 1918. Series of attacks on different portions of front began the 7th, Germans fighting desperately to hold us. Confidential reports from the Inspector General (Brewster) and his assistants indicate improved conditions. Dawes reports petty criticisms in Paris of our supply management.

Visited French XVII Corps (Claudel) Monday to give final directions concerning attack next day.

Lewis' 30th Division, with the British, attacked on the 8th.

Colonel Logan, Tardieu and Ganne came Wednesday to discuss horse and forage questions.

Orders for organization of Second Army issued Thursday. Liggett will command First and Bullard the Second.

Discussed operations with Chief of Staff and Chief of Operations yesterday. Attack progressing well.

Liggett dined with us to-day on my train. Saw a number of officers, including Harbord, Patrick, Dickman and Hines, discussing with each some detail of his task. Important gains made during last few days.

The operations carried out between October 7th and 11th consisted of four specific attacks, as follows:

(1) October 7th. The I Corps, employing the 82d Division between the 1st and 28th Divisions, attacked the eastern edge of the Argonne Forest.

(2) October 8th. The French XVII Corps, reënforced by the American 33d and 29th Divisions, attacked east of the Meuse on the front Beaumont—Brabant-sur-Meuse, with the object of seizing the heights there.

(3) October 9th. The V Corps, reënforced by including within its front the 1st Division, to which was attached a brigade from the 91st Division, attacked the heights of the Bois de Romagne.

(4) October 10th-11th. A general attack on the 20-mile front from Beaumont west to the Aire River.

The French Fourth Army had not been able to keep abreast of the American First Army and it was evident that clearing the Argonne Forest would materially aid its advance. The opportunity presented itself just at this time. Although on October 6th the enemy continued to hold the heights of Cunel and Romagne, nevertheless sufficient space had been secured along the Aire River to warrant an attack to the west with the object of striking the rear of the enemy's positions in the Argonne Forest. There was another important factor that entered into the decision to force the withdrawal of the enemy from the Argonne at this time. This was the predicament of the "Lost Battalion," already mentioned, which, under Major C. W. Whittlesey, had been holding out near Binarville since October 2d. As efforts to relieve it had so far failed, the men had consumed their rations and expended most of their ammunition. Our aviators had attempted to drop small amounts of food to them, but, as learned later, they had not been successful. The battalion was resisting heroically against great odds.

Pursuant to the plan, an attack was made by the 28th and 82d Divisions against the left and rear of the enemy's positions in the region of Châtel-Chéhéry and Cornay. After a night march of eight miles, the 82d Division (Duncan) entered the line between the 28th (Muir) and the 1st (Summerall). In a series of daring movements to the west by the 28th and 82d Divisions, Châtel-Chéhéry and the dominating hills northwest of Apremont were captured.

The 82d Division captured Hill 180 with dash on the 7th, but the attack against Cornay was broken up by heavy fire. After occupying the hill north of Châtel-Chéhéry, which had been taken over from the 28th Division, the 82d suffered severe casualties in repulsing an enemy counterattack. On the 8th, while executing a change of direction from west to north, elements of the division entered Cornay, but heavy shelling, claimed to be from our own artillery, forced their retirement. The town was again occupied on the following day, but was recaptured by a counterattack of the fresh German 41st Division. On this same day the 82d Division took over the front of the 28th and made a substantial advance.

The 28th Division on October 7th captured Châtel-Chéhéry in splendid fashion. Troops of the division crossed into the sector of the 82d Division and occupied a portion of the hill north of the town which had menaced its flank. The 28th advanced again on the 8th against heavy machine gun fire and on the following day was relieved by the 82d Division. For twelve days it had faced the almost impregnable defenses of the Aire with fine courage and endurance and had well earned a rest.

Although the continued operation of these two divisions was attended by severe fighting, the results were immediate. The enemy was forced to withdraw from that region, the Argonne Forest was cleared, and the 77th Division was enabled to advance to the relief of its "Lost Battalion." It then pushed on to the north in pursuit of the retreating enemy.

On my visit to the French XVII Corps, east of the Meuse, I reviewed with General Claudel the plans for his attack the fol-

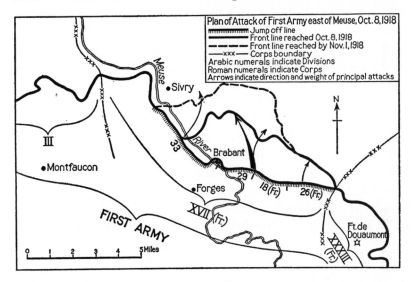

lowing day, October 8th. The object of the operation was to seize the heights northwest of Beaumont. At that time, the corps consisted of two French divisions and the two American divisions, 33d and 29th, making it two-thirds American in numerical strength. Though opposed by strong German resistance, the assault was successfully conducted and our lines were further advanced during the next few days to the commanding ground between Beaumont and Richêne Hill.

In a well directed operation, the 33d Division (Bell) crossed the Meuse early on the morning of the 8th by means of bridges constructed during the night, captured Consenvoye and progressed up the neighboring slopes. On the following day a further advance was made, but heavy fire from the Borne de Cornouiller and the failure of the troops on the right to keep up forced a retirement to the morning line. This ground was re- taken despite strong resistance and by the night of the 10th the division had established itself on the west slopes of Richêne Hill.

The 58th Brigade of the 29th Division (Morton), under com- mand of the French 18th Division, against considerable opposi- tion pushed forward into the woods south of Richêne Hill on the 8th and during the next two days completed the capture of those woods. Its 57th Brigade, also under the French 18th Division, on the 12th made important gains in the Bois d'Ormont.

This advance of the French XVII Corps deprived the enemy of many important observation points and battery positions. The main purpose of the attack, however, was to increase the fighting front of the army and thus engage and consume the maximum number of German divisions. In this latter respect, the attack was particularly successful, aimed as it was directly at the pivot of the German line on the Western Front. From this time on until the Armistice, the threat in this region forced the enemy to maintain east of the Meuse at least two additional divisions.

The narrowness of the ridge east of and parallel to the Meuse River and the difficulty of the terrain limited the number of troops that could be employed there. This restriction, coupled with the heavy hostile artillery fire directed from the vicinity of Romagne-sous-les-Côtes and from north of Damvillers, prevented a deeper advance or the clearing of the heights of the Meuse until we were able to attack from south of Dun-sur-Meuse, as originally planned.

In conjunction with the operations by the French XVII Corps, the V Corps (Cameron) attacked in force on October 9th and continued its efforts during the next two days. The 3d Division (Buck) progressed on the 9th and after fierce fighting seized Madeleine Farm, which had previously proved a stumbling-block, and partially cleared the Bois de Cunel. On the following day it completed the possession of that wood and on the 11th ex- tended its gains to the northwest.

The 32d Division (Haan) reached Romagne on October 9th, and penetrated the enemy trenches on Côte Dame Marie on the 10th, but was driven from the latter and established its lines on the southern slopes of the hill.

The 91st Division (Johnston), on the left of the 32d Division, fought all day on the 9th for possession of Hill 255, suffering heavy casualties, and on the following day occupied the position. The advance then continued until stopped at Hill 288 and the Côte Dame Marie. The division was relieved on the night of October 11th.

The 1st Division (Summerall) in a resolute attack captured the difficult enemy positions on and near Hill 272 on October 9th and established its line on the north slope of the Côte de Maldah on the 10th. It also was relieved on the 11th. During the operations of the 9th and 10th, the 181st Brigade (John B. McDonald) of the 91st Division was attached to the 1st Division, and was transferred to the 32d Division on the night of the 10th.

The advance of the III Corps (Bullard) was bitterly contested by the enemy, but on October 10th the 4th Division (Hines) fought its way forward beyond the Cunel—Brieulles road. Two determined assaults against the Bois de Peut de Faux were broken up, but on the third attempt the northern edge of that wood was attained. The division gained the far side of the Bois de Forêt on the 11th against severe opposition.

The 80th Division (Cronkhite) on the 9th pushed forward in the face of very heavy fire to a short distance north of the Bois des Ogons. The division's attacks continued and when relieved two days later it had reached a line slightly south and east of Cunel.

On the front of the I Corps (Liggett) the opposition encountered on the 10th was less determined and the 82d Division (Duncan) by midnight had established its line beyond Marcq; while the line of the 77th Division (Alexander) ran westward from there. On the 11th, however, the fighting was severe, yet the 82d, regardless of heavy casualties, advanced to a position north of Sommerance. This town, though in the sector of the 1st Division, was occupied by the 82d to protect its own flank.

On the night of October 11th our line ran from east to west roughly as follows: Molleville Farm—Bois de la Côte Lemont—part of Bois de Forêt—South of Côte Dame Marie—Sommerance —Grandpré.

While these operations on our First Army front were in progress, the 30th Division (Lewis) of the II Corps (Read) attacked on October 8th as a part of the British Fourth Army, aiding materially in the general advance of that army. The attack, although meeting considerable opposition, was successful and the progress continued for three days. When relieved on the night of the 11th, the 30th Division had driven the enemy back seven miles and had reached the Selle River.

CHAPTER XLVIII

Second Army Organized—Liggett takes First, Bullard Second—General Attack Resumed—Côte Dame Marie Captured—Hindenburg Line Broken—Germans Treating for Peace—Diplomatic Correspondence— Foch Fears President Wilson may Commit Allies too Deeply—British Views on Armistice

(Diary) Souilly, Wednesday, October 16, 1918. On Sunday, visited Pétain at Provins to discuss organization of group of armies. Called on Marshal Foch at Bombon and pointed out strength of Germans on our front. Told him of organization of group of armies. Spent the night in Paris and returned here Monday. Visited several corps and divisions yesterday.

Remained to-day at Souilly. Saw Chief of Staff regarding promotions. Brigadier General Wm. Chamberlaine came to confer on use of naval railroad artillery. Received cable from Griscom giving British views of armistice. Marshal Foch requests two divisions be sent to Belgian front to reënforce French Sixth Army near Ypres, which is making slow progress. Have selected 37th and 91st. Colonel Walter D. McCaw appointed Chief Surgeon, A.E.F., and Brigadier General John H. Rice, Chief Ordnance Officer.[1] Discussed with Mitchell better employment of aviation. War Department expects increase of shipping and promises motor transport, railway material and horses for November.

THE broadening of the front of attack to the east of the Meuse, and the probability that we should soon become engaged along our whole line made it advisable to establish another army. Accordingly the Second Army was formed of troops then on the front extending from the Moselle to Fresnes-en-Woëvre and placed under the command of Major General Bullard on the 12th. The remainder of our front, from

[1] The appointment of Col. McCaw followed the relief of Maj. Gen. Ireland, who was returned to Washington to become Surgeon General of the Army; and that of Brig. Gen. Rice to relieve Brig. Gen. Charles B. Wheeler in order that he might be available for service on the Inter-Allied Board of Ordnance.

Fresnes-en-Woëvre to the Argonne Forest, inclusive, remained under the First Army, to which Major General Liggett was assigned. Both commanders were recommended by me for promotion to the grade of lieutenant general.

My status now became that of Commander of a Group of Armies. Major General Summerall was placed in command of the V Corps to relieve Major General Cameron, who was given command of the 4th Division. Major General Hines was promoted to the command of the III Corps in place of General Bullard. Major General Dickman, commanding the IV Corps, was given the I Corps, and Major General Muir the IV. These changes generally took effect on the 12th, but I retained the immediate command of the First Army until the 16th.

The higher commanders and their staffs of the First Army, as well as the troops of all arms, were gaining in efficiency with every day of actual experience in battle. Nevertheless, I insisted that commanders should make closer examinations of the details of plans and give greater personal attention to their execution. Against the strong and thoroughly organized defense of the enemy, only the most determined and well directed efforts could insure success. Granting that the local plans were sound and arrangements perfected for support by the artillery, aviation, machine guns, and tanks, if any, it was the skill of the officers and men of the smaller units in the front lines that determined the final result of the battle.

On the particular visit to corps and divisions made on the 15th, I saw Generals Summerall and Hines, commanding the V and III Corps, respectively, and went to the command posts of the 5th, 3d, 89th, 32d and 42d Divisions, or saw their commanders. They were all very aggressive, but some of our troops had been forced out of captured positions by enemy counterattacks. It was, therefore, impressed upon every one that ground once taken should be quickly organized for defense and then held at all hazards.

In the series of attacks which began on the 7th and continued up to the 12th, the enemy contested every inch of ground and the severe fighting that occurred before positions could be captured was scarcely realized outside of our own army. Our troops were engaged in some of the most bitter fighting of the war, forcing their way through dense woods, over hills and across deep ravines, against German defense conducted with a skill only equalled by that of the French in front of Verdun in 1916. Yet all our corps advanced their lines, the V capturing elements of the Hindenburg Line, which our troops were now facing.

Early in the Meuse-Argonne offensive, most of the French air division was withdrawn from the First Army front. This considerably reduced our strength in aviation, and the German fliers began to do more serious damage to our troops. Therefore, it was necessary to concentrate our attention on the enemy's aviation and to make every effort to obtain superiority over it. The tendency of our air force at first was to attach too much significance to flights beyond the enemy's lines in an endeavor to interrupt his communications. However, this was of secondary importance during the battle, as aviators were then expected to protect and assist our ground troops. In other words, they were to drive off hostile airplanes and procure for the infantry and artillery information concerning the enemy's movements.

The best results were not obtained until we sent additional aviators to serve awhile with the infantry and study the problem from its point of view. Selected infantry and artillery officers were also sent to fly with air pilots. Once in command of the air, the enemy's artillery and ground troops became the object of their attacks. Individually, our aviators were unsurpassed in boldness, in fortitude, and in skill. These daring fliers who fought their opponents in the air vied with their fearless comrades of the infantry who grappled with the enemy on foot. Men of both arms left a record of heroic deeds that will remain a brilliant page in the annals of warfare.

Third Phase—Meuse-Argonne Operations

The increasing intensity of the resistance in our front indicated the enemy's fear of losing his hold on this vital sector before he could retire his armies facing the Allies farther to the west. His retirement in front of the Allies was being accelerated by our persistent gains in the east. He was clearly trying to save himself from complete disaster, which it was urgent that we should strive all the more vigorously to hasten.

The attacks during the preceding phase, although reaching the Hindenburg Line and even capturing portions of that position near Romagne and Cunel, left in the enemy's hands the strong defenses in the Bois de Romagne and the Bois de Bantheville,

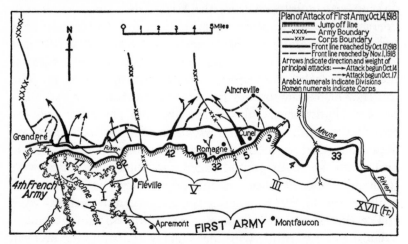

both of which had to be reduced before further considerable progress could be made. To the west of Romagne heights, we faced the strongly fortified position which included Côte de Châtillon, Landres-et-St. Georges, St. Juvin, Bois des Loges, and Grandpré.

Plans for a general attack were prepared, based on the following:

(a) The French XVII Corps, under our army, was to continue its offensive east of the Meuse River.

(b) The III and V Corps, with fresh divisions (the 5th and 42d), were to drive salients through the hostile positions on both flanks of the Bois de Romagne and of the Bois de Bantheville.

(c) The I Corps was to hold the enemy on its left flank while advancing its right in conjunction with the left of the V Corps.

(d) The French Fourth Army, which had now come up on our left and held the south bank of the Aire and the west bank of the Aisne as far as Vouziers, was ordered by General Pétain to attack on the same day, so as to outflank the enemy opposing our left.

We had set October 15th as the date for this offensive, but upon the request of the French Fourth Army, which intended to attack on the 14th, our arrangements were hastily changed to conform with theirs.

The order of battle in the Meuse-Argonne was now, from right to left: the French XVII Corps east of the Meuse, with the French 10th Colonial, 26th, and 18th Divisions and the American 29th (Morton) and 33d (Bell) Divisions; west of the Meuse the III Corps (Hines), with the 4th Division (Cameron), 3d (Buck), and 5th (McMahon); then the V Corps (Summerall), with the 32d Division (Haan) and 42d (Menoher); and on the left the I Corps (Dickman), with the 82d Division (Duncan) and the 77th (Alexander). On the front of our offensive the enemy had the equivalent of twenty-four divisions actually in the front line.

Our attacks on the 14th, 15th and 16th in conjunction with Gouraud's French Fourth Army met violent opposition, especially at the beginning, and although ground was often taken and retaken several times, our lines were steadily pushed forward.

On the east of the Meuse, in the French XVII Corps, the 33d Division had made some progress, and the 29th Division, despite the difficult terrain and severe casualties, had entered the woods north of Molleville Farm.

The III Corps was held up by very heavy machine gun and artillery fire from the Bois de Bantheville and the Bois des Rappes, in spite of precautions to neutralize these localities. The 4th Division remained inactive during this period. The 3d Division made a small gain west of the Bois de Forêt and cleaned up the eastern edge of the wood north of Cunel in conjunction with the 5th Division, but could make little headway northward. The 5th Division, in the face of intense fire on its front and flanks, on the 14th reached the top of the slopes northeast of Romagne and cleared the wood north of Cunel. Elements of the division pushed through to the northern edge of the Bois des Rappes, but were withdrawn.

By dint of the superior determination of our troops, the enemy's lines were broken at a vital point by the V Corps. Unstinted praise must be given the 32d Division. Notwithstanding heavy losses, its 64th Brigade (Edwin B. Winans) on October 14th brilliantly captured Côte Dame Marie, perhaps the most important strong point of the Hindenburg Line on the Western Front. The town of Romagne and the eastern half of Bois de Romagne were also taken by this division on that day; while on the following day its line was advanced about a mile to the southern edge of the Bois de Bantheville.

The 42d Division fought aggressively against the most obstinate defense, forcing its way through the western half of Bois de Romagne, its 84th Brigade (Douglas MacArthur) scaling the precipitous heights of the Côte de Châtillon and carrying its line on beyond that position. The desperate resistance on the left of the division, south of St. Georges and Landres-et-St. Georges, however, could not be overcome.

The advance of the I Corps was to a large extent dependent upon that of the V Corps, the left of which had been held up. The 82d Division, on the right of the I Corps, attacked October 14th and pushed forward to north of the St. Juvin—St. Georges road, but during the next two days had only slight success. The 77th Division forced a crossing of the Aire River on the 14th and took St. Juvin. On the following day it moved against Grandpré and after an all-day attempt occupied the island south of the town. On the 16th, the southern part of Grandpré was reached, but all attempts to take the northern part of the town were repulsed. The division was then relieved by the 78th Division.

The importance of these operations can hardly be overestimated. The capture of the Romagne heights, especially their dominating feature, Côte Dame Marie, was a decisive blow. We now occupied the enemy's strongest fortified position on that front and flanked his line on the Aisne and on the Heights of the Meuse. Unless he could recapture the positions we held, our successes would compel him to retire from his lines to the north, as we were within heavy artillery range of his railroad communications.

The main objective of our initial attack of September 26th had now been reached. Failing to capture it in our first attempt, the army had deliberately, systematically, and doggedly stuck to the task in the face of many difficulties and discouragements. The persistent and vigorous effort with which divisions forced their way forward to the goal is the outstanding glory of our service in France.

Our ranks had become further depleted by this severe fighting and we now had to use as replacements the personnel of two more recently arrived divisions, although even these were not enough. In all, we skeletonized four combat divisions and three depot divisions to obtain men for units at the front. Much greater numbers of replacements would have been available if they had been sent in groups as such. It was a source of much regret to me that these organized units should have to be stripped of men, but there was no alternative.

We were also in need of balloons and their personnel, none having arrived from home since July. Although fifty-two companies had been requested for August and September, there seemed to be no hope of receiving them within a reasonable time. A shortage in balloons always existed in our forces and as usual we sponged on the French. But at this time they did not have much more than half the numbers they needed themselves and our demands were creating a serious situation in their army. The loss of observation balloons was very heavy during the continuous fighting of this great battle. Balloons were especially good targets for airplanes. Many of our aviators became expert at destroying those of the enemy. They would wait until about dusk, then, approaching from a great height, swoop down and often surprise several in one flight.

The pressure of the American Army in this great offensive profoundly impressed the enemy.   On October 3d Marshal von Hindenburg sent the following letter to the German Chancellor:

"The High Command insists on its demand of Sunday, September 29th, for the immediate forwarding of an offer of peace to our enemies. * * * There is now no longer any possible hope of forcing peace on the enemy. * * * The situation grows more desperate every day and may force the High Command to grave decisions. * * *"

The Chancellor yielded to this pressure and on October 6th telegraphed, through the Swiss Government, to President Wilson:

"The German Government requests the President of the United States to take in hand the restoration of peace, acquaint all belligerent states with this request, and invite them to send plenipotentiaries for the purpose of opening negotiations.   It accepts the program set forth by the President of the United States in his message to Congress on January 8 and in his later addresses, especially the speech of September 27, as a basis for peace negotiations.   With a view to avoiding further bloodshed, the German Government requests the immediate conclusion of an armistice on land and water and in the air.
"MAX, PRINCE VON BADEN,
"Imperial Chancellor."

Although we knew through our Intelligence Section that the enemy had sued for an armistice, we had no first-hand knowledge of the negotiations that followed.   The development of the situation was so interesting and was so skillfully handled by President Wilson that the various notes that passed between the two Governments are given, some in condensed form.

On October 8th, in reply to the Chancellor's note, the following statement of the President's views was communicated to the German Government by Secretary of State Lansing:

"Before making reply to the request of the Imperial German Government, and in order that that reply shall be as candid and as straightforward as the momentous interests involved require, the President of the United States deems it necessary to assure himself of the exact meaning of the note of the Imperial Chancellor.   Does the Imperial Chancellor mean that the Imperial German Government accepts the terms laid down by the President in his address to the Congress of the United States on January 8 last and in subsequent addresses, and that its object in entering into discussions would be only to agree upon the practical details of their application?

"The President feels bound to say with regard to the suggestion of an armistice that he would not feel at liberty to propose a cessation of arms to the Governments with which the Government of the United States is associated against the Central Powers so long as the Armies of those powers are upon their soil. The good faith of any discussion would manifestly depend upon the consent of the Central Powers immediately to withdraw their forces everywhere from the invaded territory.

"The President also feels that he is justified in asking whether the Imperial Chancellor is speaking merely for the constituted authorities of the empire who have so far conducted the war. He deems the answer to these questions vital from every point of view."

The German reply to this message, sent on October 12th, was as follows:

"In reply to the questions of the President of the United States of America the German Government hereby declares:

"The German Government has accepted the terms laid down by President Wilson in his address of January 8 and in his subsequent addresses on the foundation of a permanent peace of justice. Consequently its object in entering into discussions would be only to agree upon practical details of the application of these terms.

"The German Government assumes that the Governments of the powers associated with the Government of the United States also take the position taken by President Wilson in his address.

"The German Government in accordance with the Austro-Hungarian Government, for the purpose of bringing about an armistice, declares itself ready to comply with the propositions of the President in regard to evacuation.

"The German Government suggests that the President may occasion the meeting of a mixed commission for making the necessary arrangements concerning the evacuation. The present German Government, which has undertaken the responsibility for this step toward peace, has been formed by conferences and in agreement with the great majority of the Reichstag. The Chancellor, supported in all his actions by the will of this majority, speaks in the name of the German Government and of the German People."

The next note was from our Government:

"Washington, October 14, 1918.

"The unqualified acceptance by the present German Government and by a large majority of the German Reichstag of the terms laid down by the President of the United States of America in his address to the Congress of the United States on the 8th of January, 1918, and in his subsequent addresses, justifies the President in making a frank and direct statement of his decision with regard to the communications of the German Government of the eighth and twelfth of October, 1918.

"It must be clearly understood that the process of evacuation and the conditions of an armistice are matters which must be left to the judgment and advice of the military advisers of the Government of the United States and the Allied Governments, and the President feels it his duty to say that no arrangement can be accepted by the Government of the United States which does not provide absolutely satisfactory safeguards and guarantees of the maintenance of the present military supremacy of the armies of the United States and of the Allies in the field. He feels confident that he can safely assume that this will also be the judgment and decision of the Allied Governments."

The message went on to say that the President felt it his duty to add that an armistice could not be granted so long as the armed forces of Germany continued illegal and inhuman practices. The persistence by Germany of the sinking of passenger ships and small boats was cited, and reference was made to the destruction of villages as the armies retired. Continuing, it read in part:

"It is necessary also, in order that there may be no possibility of misunderstanding, that the President should very solemnly call the attention of the Government of Germany to the language and plain intent of one of the terms of peace which the German Government has now accepted. It is contained in the address of the President, delivered at Mount Vernon, on the Fourth of July last. It is as follows:

" 'The destruction of every arbitrary power anywhere that can separately, secretly, and of its single choice disturb the peace of the world; or, if it cannot be presently destroyed, at least its reduction to virtual impotency.'

*   *   *   *   *   *   *

"It is indispensable that the Governments associated against Germany should know beyond peradventure with whom they are dealing. The President will make a separate reply to the Royal and Imperial Government of Austria-Hungary."

In reply, the German Government sent the following:

"Berlin, October 20, 1918.

"In accepting the proposal for an evacuation of the occupied territories, the German Government has started from the assumption that the procedure of this evacuation and of the conditions of an armistice should be left to the judgment of the military advisers, and that the actual standard of power on both sides in the field has to form the basis for arrangements safeguarding and guaranteeing this standard. The German Government suggests to the President that an opportunity should be brought about for fixing the details. It trusts that the President of the United States will approve of no demand which would be irreconcilable with the honor of the German people and with opening a way to a peace of justice."

The German Government protested against the reproach of illegal actions by its land and sea forces and disclaimed any purpose to do such things. It then claimed that a new government had been formed, guaranteed by constitutional safeguards, with which the President could deal.

The State Department then sent the following:

"October 23, 1918.

"Having received the solemn and explicit assurance of the German Government that it unreservedly accepts the terms of peace laid down in his address to the Congress of the United States on the eighth of January, 1918, and the principles of settlement enunciated in his subsequent addresses, particularly the address of the twenty-seventh of September, and that it desires to discuss the details of their application, and that this wish and purpose emanate, not from those who have hitherto dictated German policy and conducted the present war on Germany's behalf, but from Ministers who speak for the majority of the Reichstag and for an overwhelming majority of the German people, and having received also the explicit promise of the present German Government that the humane rules of civilized warfare will be observed both on land and sea by the German armed forces, the President of the United States feels that he cannot decline to take up with the Governments with which the Government of the United States is associated the question of an armistice.

"He deems it his duty to say again, however, that the only armistice he would feel justified in submitting for consideration would be one which should leave the United States and the powers associated with her in a position to enforce any arrangements that may be entered into and to make a renewal of hostilities on the part of Germany impossible.

"The President has, therefore, transmitted his correspondence with the present German authorities to the Governments with which the Government of the United States is associated as a belligerent. * * * Should such terms of armistice be suggested, their acceptance by Germany will afford the best concrete evidence of her unequivocal acceptance of the terms and principles of peace from which the whole action proceeds. * * *

"Feeling that the whole peace of the world depends now on plain speaking and straightforward action, the President deems it his duty to say, without any attempt to soften what may seem harsh words, that the nations of the world do not and cannot trust the word of those who have hitherto been the masters of German policy, and to point out once more that in concluding peace and attempting to undo the infinite injuries and injustices of this war the Government of the United States cannot deal with any but veritable representatives of the German people, who have been assured of a genuine constitutional standing as the real rulers of Germany.

"If it must deal with the military masters and the monarchial autocrats of Germany now, or if it is likely to have to deal with them later in regard to the international obligations of the German Empire, it must demand, not peace negotiations, but surrender. Nothing can be gained by leaving this essential thing unsaid."

To this, Germany replied:

"Berlin, October 27, 1918.

"The German Government has taken cognizance of the answer of the President of the United States. The President is aware of the far-reaching changes which have been carried out and are being carried out in the German constitutional structure, and that peace negotiations are being conducted by a people's Government in whose hands rests, both actually and constitutionally, the power to make the deciding conclusions. The military powers are also subject to it. The German Government now awaits proposals for an armistice, which shall be the first step toward a just peace as the President has described it in his proclamation."

The President's messages were transmitted to the Allied Governments and upon receipt of their replies, the following note was sent:

"November 5, 1918.

"In my note of October 23, 1918, I advised you that the President had transmitted his correspondence with the German authorities to the Governments with which the Government of the United States is associated as a belligerent. * * * The President is now in receipt of a memorandum of observations by the Allied Governments on this correspondence, which is as follows:

"The Allied Governments have given careful consideration to the correspondence which has passed between the President of the United States and the German Government. Subject to the qualifications which follow, they declare their willingness to make peace with the Government of Germany on the terms of peace laid down in the President's address to Congress of January, 1918, and the principles of settlement enunciated in his subsequent addresses. They must point out, however, that Clause 2, relating to what is usually described as the freedom of the seas is open to various interpretations, some of which they could not accept. They must, therefore, reserve to themselves complete freedom on this subject when they enter the peace conference. Further, in the conditions of peace laid down in his address to Congress of January 8, 1918, the President declared that invaded territories must be restored as well as evacuated and freed. The Allied Governments feel that no doubt ought to be allowed to exist as to what this provision implies. By it they understand that compensation will be made by Germany for all damage done to the civilian population of the Allies and their property by the aggression of Germany by land, by sea and from the air.

"I am instructed by the President to say that he is in agreement with the interpretation set forth in the last paragraph of the memorandum above quoted. I am further instructed by the President to request you to notify the German Government that Marshal Foch has been authorized by the Government of the United States and the Allied Governments to receive properly accredited representatives of the German Government and to communicate to them terms of an armistice."

While these diplomatic negotiations were in progress, our own and Allied offensives continued to produce favorable results, and it became more and more evident that the time must soon come when we should have to consider terms and conditions under which hostilities might cease. The discussion of armistice terms in a general way by the Allies had in fact begun. In my conversation with Marshal Foch on the 13th he spoke of the notes that had been exchanged between the Germans and President Wilson and expressed some apprehension about how far the President might commit the Allies. He said he hoped the President would not become involved in a long correspondence and allow himself to be duped by the Germans, and added that so far Mr. Wilson had not consulted the Allies. I replied that he need not have any fear on that score, as of course Mr. Wilson would not act alone. In this discussion I gained the impression that Foch favored demanding the surrender of the German armies.

At my request, Lieutenant Colonel Griscom ascertained and cabled me the views of Lord Milner and General Sir Henry Wilson. Briefly, Lord Milner said that he occupied a middle position between those demanding unconditional surrender and those who wanted peace immediately on the best terms possible. He thought an armistice should be granted only on condition that Germany lay down her heavy guns and give some naval guarantee such as the possession of Heligoland.

General Wilson was in doubt whether it would be possible to inflict a crushing victory before winter, as the British Army was very tired and the French more so, and the Americans not yet prepared to use their great force, but he thought that armistice conditions should make it impossible for Germany to resume operations. He regretted President Wilson's suggestion of German evacuation of Allied territory because he would prefer to fight the Germans where they were than on their own frontiers with a much shortened line. He said the Germans should be required to abandon their heavy guns and retire to the east bank of the Rhine, and in addition to the surrender of Heligoland should also give up some warships and submarines.

General Wilson voiced the extreme British army viewpoint, but the more conservative element in government circles advised against pushing Germany too far for fear of having no government there strong enough to make peace. They feared that widespread revolutions in Germany might unsettle Allied countries and imperil constitutional monarchies. These hints gave the general attitude of the British as it was expressed later on when the time came to dictate the terms.

CHAPTER XLIX

Situation of First Army in Mid-October—Operations Preliminary to Resumption of General Offensive—II Corps with British—General Attack Set for October 28th—Senlis Conference at which Commanders-in-Chief Discuss Armistice Terms—My Views Cabled Washington—President's Comments—My Recommendation for Demanding Unconditional Surrender

(Diary) Souilly, Sunday, October 20, 1918. Admiral Plunkett came Thursday to discuss use of Navy 14-inch railway guns. Spent Friday and Saturday at Chaumont. Sir Arthur Paget came to visit our front; lunched with us on Friday. Representatives Glass, Whaley and Byrnes had dinner with us at Chaumont on Saturday. Brought Fox Conner to Souilly; discussed offensive operations with Liggett Sunday. Some straggling reported; directed energetic measures against it. Received reports of interesting gossip floating around Paris. French desire American director of railways; I have recommended Daniel Willard, of the Baltimore and Ohio.

Fourth Phase—Meuse-Argonne Operations

THE First Army was a tried and seasoned force equal to the best on the Western Front at the time I placed it under the immediate command of Major General Liggett. In order that the Army might understand the value of its recent achievements and realize the urgency of continued vigorous effort, I sent the following message to the new First Army Commander on October 17th:

"Please have the following transmitted as a telegram to Corps and Division Commanders:
"Now that Germany and the Central Powers are losing, they are begging for an armistice. Their request is an acknowledgment of weakness and clearly means that the Allies are winning the war. That is the best of reasons for our pushing the war more vigorously at this moment. Germany's desire is only to gain time to restore order among her forces, but she must be given no opportunity to recuperate and we

350

must strike harder than ever. Our strong blows are telling, and continuous pressure by us has compelled the enemy to meet us, enabling our Allies to gain on other parts of the line. There can be no conclusion to this war until Germany is brought to her knees.

"PERSHING."

The enemy's most important defensive position[1] on the Romagne heights was in our firm possession, and his final defeat was merely a question of time. He had fought desperately to hold his ground, but had been compelled to give way steadily before our effective blows. We could have gone forward without special preparation and succeeded, within a reasonable time, in driving the enemy from the field, but the situation led to the conclusion that his complete defeat could best be accomplished in one powerful stroke by a well organized offensive.

The difficult and continuous attacks since September 26th had been very trying on our troops and had resulted in a certain loss of cohesion. It was, therefore, deemed advisable to take a few days for the replacement of tired units, the renewal of supplies, and the improvement of communications.

The 28th of October was tentatively designated as the date for the beginning of the next general advance, but the French Fourth Army, which was to support our attack on the left, notified us as late as the 27th that it could not get ready in time, so the attack of both armies was fixed for November 1st.

In accordance with instructions issued by me on the 16th, two important preliminary operations were carried out during this period: (1) operations against the Bois des Loges and Bois de Bourgogne to clear the woods east of the Aisne and north of the Aire and thus flank that part of the hostile line on the Aisne, and (2) local operations to secure a suitable line of departure for the general attack.

The I Corps (Dickman), in conjunction with the French Fourth Army, was directed to clear the Bois des Loges and the southern part of the Bois de Bourgogne. An advance in this

---

[1] "The pressure which the fresh American masses were putting upon our most sensitive point in the region of the Meuse was too strong." Marshal von Hindenburg in "Out of my Life."

352 MY EXPERIENCES IN THE WORLD WAR

vicinity would flank the enemy on the Aisne in front of the French and also turn his defenses east of the Bois des Loges which were holding up the I Corps. A study of the characteristics of the terrain will show the difficulties of the task. The enemy, realizing the importance of this position, employed his best troops to defend it.

The fighting on the 78th Division (McRae) front, for a period of ten days, was very severe, especially near the Bois des Loges and Grandpré. Frequent counterattacks, coupled with flanking machine gun and artillery fire, forced our troops back in several instances. However, on October 25th, the I Corps succeeded in gaining a footing on the high ground west of Grandpré and, by October 27th, had driven the enemy from that town. The Bois des Loges remained in the enemy's hands. The above maneuver carried the right of the French Fourth Army forward and a line was thus secured on the left of our Army especially advantageous for the general attack. These engagements had a material effect on the final phase, as they drew some of the enemy's strength to the I Corps front and away from the center, where our main drive was to be made.

Farther to the right, where we had pierced the Hindenburg Line on the Cunel and Romagne heights, it was desirable to force the enemy from the Bois des Rappes, Bois Clairs Chênes and the high ground to the east, and to secure the northern edge of the Bois de Bantheville. These preliminary operations were successfully carried out by the III and V Corps. Some very intense local battles took place during this period.

The 3d Division (Brown)[1] of the III Corps captured Bois Clairs Chênes early on October 20th, then lost the wood in a counterattack, and later in the day recaptured it. On the 22d, the division cleared the Bois de Forêt. The 5th Division (Ely) was unsuccessful in its attacks of October 18th, 19th and 20th against the Bois des Rappes, but on October 21st took the wood, and held it against counterattacks.

[1] On October 18th, Brig. Gen. Preston Brown and Maj. Gen. Hanson E. Ely took command of the 3d and 5th Divisions, respectively.

Although the terrain was difficult and the resistance most determined, the 32d Division (Haan) of the V Corps by night of October 18th had reached the middle of the Bois de Bantheville. Here it was relieved by the 89th Division (Wright), which, on October 20th and 21st, cleared the remainder of the wood.

By the 23d of October, the line of the III and V Corps ran north of Bois Clairs Chênes, Bois des Rappes, and along the northern and western flanks of the Bois de Bantheville and Côte de Chatillon, and then south of Landres-et-St. Georges. This gave us an excellent position in the center and on the right from which to start the next general attack.

To the east of the Meuse, the French XVII Corps, reënforced by the 29th Division (Morton) and the 26th Division (Edwards), continued to progress locally, forcing the enemy to employ fresh troops on that front. The 29th Division captured the ridge north of Molleville Farm on October 23d; while the 26th Division made some gains, and on October 27th, under Brigadier General Frank E. Bamford,[1] penetrated the wood east of the farm.

In the remaining days of this phase local successes continued, especially in the III Corps, Aincreville being captured by the 5th Division on October 30th.

During the Meuse-Argonne battle my personal quarters were on my train, which lay partially hidden in the woods on a spur near Souilly. While there I spent a portion of each day at official headquarters giving directions regarding operations and deciding other important questions. I usually occupied the rest of the day at the front in close touch with corps and divisions. Although I had now relinquished the immediate command of the First Army, its activities and those of the Second Army, carried out under my direction, required close supervision.

Farther west, our II Corps (Read), with the British Fourth Army, was engaged on October 17th south of Le Cateau in the Battle of the Selle. This Corps, with the 30th (Lewis) and 27th (O'Ryan) Divisions in line from right to left, crossed the Selle

[1] Brig. Gen. Bamford took command of the 26th Division on Oct. 25th.

River and advanced four miles in the face of strong resistance, capturing 1,600 prisoners and 12 guns.

The 30th Division captured Molain and St.-Martin-Rivière on the 17th, but heavy fire from Ribeauville prevented further advance until late the following day, when the operations of the British on the right forced the enemy to evacuate the town. Continuing on October 19th, the division captured Mazinghien and was then relieved.

The 27th Division had several hard fights along the railroad southeast of St. Souplet, at Bandival Farm and at the hamlet of Arbre Guernon, all of which were taken on October 17th. By October 19th, the division occupied a position east of the Mazinghien—Basuel road, where it was relieved on October 21st.

Marshal Haig sent the following message to General Read regarding the operations of the II Corps:

> "I wish to express to you personally and to all the officers and men serving under you my warm appreciation of the very valuable and gallant services rendered by you throughout the recent operations with the Fourth British Army. Called upon to attack positions of great strength, held by a determined enemy, all ranks of the 27th and 30th American Divisions under your command displayed an energy, courage and determination in attack which proved irresistible. It does not need me to tell you that in the heavy fighting of the past three weeks you have earned the lasting esteem and admiration of your British Comrades-in-Arms, whose success you so nobly shared."

During the previous weeks of furious fighting against obstinate resistance, the First Army had captured the strongest defenses on the Western Front, and was now engaged in local operations which were preparatory to effective delivery of the final blow. In the face of these splendid achievements, rumors reached me that the French Prime Minister, claiming we were not making satisfactory headway, was contemplating another move to interfere with our control of our own troops and force their distribution more generally among the Allied armies. Certainly, M. Clemenceau was aware of our steady progress and of the fact that we had attained a dominating position. The end was clearly approaching. It was obvious, therefore, that any attempt on his part to discredit our accomplishments would be purely a political gesture designed to minimize America's prestige at the peace conference.

(Diary) Souilly, Thursday, October 24, 1918. Admiral Mayo and party came to visit the army on Monday and had luncheon on my train.

Had conference with M. Clemenceau in Paris on Tuesday and found him in excellent spirits. Talked with Ambassador Sharp and General Bliss about possibility of armistice.

Visited Marshal Foch at Senlis on Wednesday and lunched with Marshal Haig at Bertincourt. Latter takes milder view as to armistice terms than Foch. Captain de Marenches takes up with French the question of civilian services in rear of our armies, which they now want us to handle.

Returned to Souilly this morning. Liggett and Drum came for final consultation on our next operation. Influenza increasing.

In the original plans for the Meuse-Argonne offensive, it was my purpose, after the capture of the Hindenburg Line, to drive through the center of the enemy's position, seize the Bois de Barricourt ridge, and immediately thereafter, by an advance westward to Boult-aux-Bois, outflank the Bois de Bourgogne and the enemy's forces facing the French Fourth Army on the Aisne. The First Army had already issued detailed battle plans for such an attack, to start October 28th, when General Maistre,[1] the representative of Marshal Foch, who had recently been sent to coordinate the activities of the French Fourth Army and our First Army, presented the Marshal's views (set forth in a letter dated October 21st) to the effect that our main blow should be directed along the eastern flank of the Bois de Bourgogne. But, in my opinion, with which General Liggett agreed, the execution of the original plan would be productive of greater results. This plan had been adopted prior to the Meuse-Argonne attack after full discussion with the Chief of Staff, First Army, Gen-

[1] General Maistre commanded a Group of Armies which included the French Fourth Army.

eral Drum, and mainly at his suggestion. Of course, it was quite beyond the Marshal's province to give instructions regarding the tactical conduct of operations. I therefore disregarded his directions and issued the following formal instructions to the Commanding General, First Army:

"October 21, 1918.

* * * * * * *

"2. The First Army will prepare to launch a general attack on October 28th with the object of securing control of Buzancy and the heights immediately to the east of that place. The minimum objective to be reached the first day is marked by the general line: heights south of Aincreville—Bois de Barricourt—hills north of Sivry-les-Buzancy—Bois des Loges. Immediately after reaching the general line above indicated you will proceed to free the Bois de Bourgogne from the enemy and to gain possession of the heights surrounding Briquenay. The operations of your left flank will be conducted in closest liaison with the right of the French Fourth Army. All plans will be made for following up any opportunities to gain possession of the high ground north and northeast of Buzancy.

"3. While preparing for the general attack as above ordered, you will constantly bear in mind that the present situation demands that there be no relaxation in the pressure now exerted on the enemy. You will therefore so time the local operations which are necessary preliminaries to the general attack as to continue the present pressure and will take immediate advantage of any favorable opportunity to advance your lines.

"4. East of the Meuse you will for the present confine your offensive operations to the local attacks necessary to improve your present position."

The changes of divisions and other adjustments necessary in preparation for this attack were being rapidly carried out. Except for those units in the Argonne, which utilized German dugouts, all of our troops had been without shelter of any sort, as none existed north of the Clermont—Verdun road, so that relief for rest and recuperation during this period entailed movements of considerable distance.

The demands of incessant battle had compelled our divisions to fight to the limit of their capacity. Troops were held in line and pushed to the attack until deemed incapable of further effort because of casualties or exhaustion; artillery once engaged was seldom withdrawn.   Our men as a whole showed unrivaled fortitude in this continuous fighting during inclement weather and under the many disadvantages of position.   Through such experience, the Army had developed into a powerful machine, and, with the short respite for readjustment, we had supreme confidence in its ability to carry on successfully.[1]

While the high pressure of our dogged attacks was severe on our troops, it was calamitous to the enemy.   He had been so hard pressed that once a division was engaged in the fight it became practically impossible to effect its relief.   The enemy was forced to meet recurring crises by breaking up tactical organizations and hurriedly sending detachments to different portions of the line.

Every member of the American Expeditionary Forces, from the front line to the base ports, was straining every nerve.   Extraordinary efforts were exerted by the entire Services of Supply to meet the enormous demands made upon it.   Obstacles which seemed insurmountable were overcome daily in hastening the movements of replacements, ammunition, and supplies to the front, and of sick and wounded to the rear.   It was this spirit of determination animating every member of the A.E.F. that made it impossible for the enemy to maintain the struggle until 1919.

On October 26th, Marshal Foch published certain suggestions concerning tactical operations which were most pleasing to me, as they embodied those principles of open warfare for which I had been contending ever since our arrival in France.   The following extract will illustrate his ideas at this time:

"Troops thrown into the attack have only to know the direction of attack.   In this direction they go as far as they can without any thought of alignment, attacking and maneuvering the enemy who resists, the most advanced units working to help those who are momentarily stopped.   In this manner they operate, not toward lines indicated ahead of time according to the terrain, but against the enemy, with whom they never lose contact once they have gained it."

[1] On October 23d, the combat strength of the A.E.F. was 1,256,478, of which 592,300 were in the First Army. The First Army also included approximately 100,000 French combat troops.

No doubt these excellent suggestions were intended for the French armies, as Marshal Foch surely was acquainted with our instructions issued October 25th, directing independent action by army corps in pursuing the enemy to the line of the Meuse River south of Sedan, and also the following instructions which I had issued to the whole American Army on September 5, 1918:

"Combat Instructions (extract)

"From a tactical point of view, the method of combat in trench warfare presents a marked contrast to that employed in open warfare, and the attempt by assaulting infantry to use trench warfare methods in an open warfare combat will be successful only at great cost. Trench warfare is marked by uniform formations, the regulation of space and time by higher commands down to the smallest details * * * fixed distances and intervals between units and individuals * * * little initiative * * *. Open warfare is marked by * * * irregularity of formations, comparatively little regulation of space and time by higher commanders, the greatest possible use of the infantry's own fire power to enable it to get forward, variable distances and intervals between units and individuals * * * brief orders and the greatest possible use of individual initiative by all troops engaged in the action. * * * The infantry commander must oppose machine guns by fire from his rifles, his automatics and his rifle grenades and must close with their crews under cover of this fire and of ground beyond their flanks. * * * The success of every unit from the platoon to the division must be exploited to the fullest extent. Where strong resistance is encountered, reënforcements must not be thrown in to make a frontal attack at this point, but must be pushed through gaps created by successful units, to attack these strong points in the flank or rear."

Now that the end was in prospect, everybody was in much better mood. M. Clemenceau was in fine humor when I saw him at his office on the 22d, and was profuse in his compliments on the success of our army. The object of my visit was to urge his assistance in obtaining more horses for our artillery, which was almost immobile. The French had furnished us 130,000 horses, but they were of inferior quality and were rapidly used up. He hesitated, however, to make a further requisition now that we appeared to be nearing the end of the war.

(Diary) Paris, Monday, October 28, 1918. Met Marshal Foch and Allied Commanders at Senlis Friday to consider terms of armistice. Pétain's views were stiffer than Marshal Haig's and mine more stringent than either. Yesterday sent Mr. House copy of cable reporting conference. Have been laid up with grippe since Saturday.

Although Marshal Foch had told me some days before that if his opinion should be asked regarding the terms of an armistice he expected to call the Commanders-in-Chief together and get their views, I had not made a detailed study of the terms that should be imposed, especially as I had expected some word from Washington on the subject. Having discussed the question in a general way with the Chief of Staff, McAndrew, the Chief of Operations, Fox Conner, and the Judge Advocate, Bethel, they were directed to meet me at Senlis, and we went over the details briefly before the conference.

This meeting of the Commanders-in-Chief was quite in contrast to the one held in July to consider joint action by the armies on the Western Front. What momentous events had taken place in three months! During that short period the Germans had lost the initiative and had been driven steadily backward from their extreme southern and western positions until now they faced certain defeat.

At the opening of the conference, Marshal Foch said in substance: "You are doubtless aware that the Germans are negotiating for an armistice through the intermediary of the American Government, and declare themselves ready to accept the Fourteen Points of President Wilson as a basis." He went on to say that he had called us together to obtain our views and that he thought "the terms should be such as to render Germany powerless to recommence operations in case hostilities are resumed." One of his officers then read aloud from a newspaper the Fourteen Points.

I expressed the opinion that commanders-in-chief should act only on the authority of their respective Governments, and inquired whether the Governments had referred this question to us with directions to draw up the conditions to be imposed in case they should deem it possible to grant an armistice. Marshal Foch

360 MY EXPERIENCES IN THE WORLD WAR

replied that the French Government, with the approval of the Allied and Associated Powers, had directed him to take up the question with the Commanders-in-Chief, and he considered that we were justified in drafting the conditions of an eventual armistice. Although I was in favor of demanding the surrender of the German armies, I accepted this as a conference to decide upon the terms in case an armistice should be granted.

Foch then asked my opinion as to conditions that should be imposed. I replied that as it was a matter of greater concern to both Great Britain and France than to the United States and as their armies had been engaged longer and had suffered more than ours, I thought it appropriate for Sir Douglas Haig and General Pétain to express their views first.

Marshal Haig, being called on, said in substance that the German Army was far from being disintegrated and was still capable of withdrawing to a shorter front and making a stand against equal or greater forces. On the other hand, the Allies were pretty well exhausted. The total shortage of men for the British and French armies, he said, was about 250,000 each, with none available to fill the gaps. As to the American Army, he said something of its lack of training and experience, but later modified his statement, saying in effect that our army was not yet complete and that some time must elapse before it would be large enough to relieve the diminishing Allied armies. He thought the terms should be such that the Germans would not hesitate to accept them. He then proposed the following:

1st. Immediate and complete evacuation of invaded Belgian and French territory.

2d. Occupation by the Allies of Alsace, Lorraine, and the fortresses of Metz and Strasbourg.

3d. Restitution of all rolling stock seized by the Germans in France and Belgium, or its equivalent.

4th. Repatriation of inhabitants of invaded territory.

These conditions, Sir Douglas pointed out, would place us on the German frontier in case of a renewal of hostilities, and we could carry on the war in German territory. The armistice would give the Americans time to build up their army. He continued, "If hostilities should be resumed, I would prefer to find the Germans entrenched behind their old frontier of 1870 than to find them on the right bank of the Rhine."

Marshal Foch then remarked:

"It cannot be said that the German Army is not defeated. Although we are not able to tell its exact condition, still we are dealing with an army that has been pounded every day for three months, an army that is now losing on a front of 400 kilometers, that, since July 15th, has lost more than 250,000 prisoners and 4,000 guns; an army that is, physically and morally, thoroughly beaten. Certainly, the Allied armies are not new, but victorious armies are never fresh. In this matter the question is relative; the German armies are far more exhausted than ours. Certainly the British and French armies are tired; certainly the American Army is a young army, but it is full of idealism and strength and ardor. It has already won victories and is now on the eve of another victory; and nothing gives wings to an army like victory. When one hunts a wild beast and finally comes upon him at bay, one then faces greater danger, but it is not the time to stop, it is time to redouble one's blows without paying any attention to those he, himself, receives."

General Pétain spoke next and spread out a map of the Western Front showing territory between the existing positions and the Rhine, with lines drawn in red indicating proposed stages of retirement of the German armies. He said that in his opinion the best way to render them incapable of further fighting was to deprive them of their matériel, and he recommended that they be required to withdraw promptly according to the schedule he had prepared. If this movement should begin at once, he thought it would be impossible for the Germans to remove their matériel, especially the heavy guns and ammunition. He also suggested that they be required to return to the Allies 5,000 locomotives and 100,000 freight cars. His opinion was that the German armies should retire to the east of the Rhine and that the Allies should establish bridgeheads at Mayence, Coblenz and Cologne.

Marshal Foch then asked my views, which were stated in substance, and the exact terms submitted later in detail:

"The general view that an armistice should provide guarantees against a resumption of hostilities, give the Allies a decided advantage, and be unfavorable to Germany in case hostilities should be resumed, meets with my approval. I think that the damage done by the war to the interests of the powers with which the United States is associated against Germany has been so great that there should be no tendency toward leniency.

"The present military situation is very favorable to the Allies. The German forces since the beginning of the counteroffensive on July 18th have been constantly in retreat and have not been able to recover since that time. The condition of the French and British armies can best be judged by the fact that they have been continuously on the offensive since then and that they are now attacking with as much vigor as ever. As to the American Army, the part it has taken in the operations since July 18th has not been inconsiderable. It is constantly increasing in strength and training; its staffs, its services and its higher commanders have improved by experience, so there is every reason to suppose that the American Army will be able to take the part expected of it in the event of resumption of hostilities.

"I therefore propose:

"1st. The evacuation of France and Belgium within thirty days and of all other foreign territory occupied by Germany without delay.

"2d. The withdrawal of the German armies from Alsace-Lorraine and occupation of those territories by the Allied armies.

"3d. Withdrawal of German armies to the east of the Rhine and the possession of such bridgeheads on the eastern side of the Rhine by the Allies as may be necessary to insure their control of that river.

"4th. The unrestricted transportation of the American Army and its material across the seas.

"5th. The immediate repatriation of all nationals of foreign territory now or heretofore occupied during the war by Germany.

"6th. Surrender of all U-boats and U-boat bases to the control of a neutral power until their disposition is otherwise determined.

"7th. Return to France and Belgium of all railroad rolling stock that has been seized by Germany from those countries."

When I mentioned the surrender of submarines, Marshal Haig interrupted, saying:

"That is none of our affair. It is a matter for the Admiralty to decide."

I replied inviting attention to the fact that the American Army was operating 3,000 miles from home, that the German submarines constituted a formidable menace to our sea communications and that their surrender was a matter of vital importance to us. I said that while the number to be delivered could be decided by the naval authorities, this condition should be exacted so that if hostilities were resumed we should have our communications free from danger.

Marshal Foch said:

"The suggestion of General Pershing regarding submarines seems to me a reasonable one and his demand well founded."

The Marshal expressed his thanks for what I had said and repeated that while it was true the American Army was still young, its spirit was splendid and it was tremendously increasing every day in efficiency and in numbers. He then asked Marshal Haig whether, in view of what General Pétain and I had said, he cared to modify his views on the terms of an armistice, to which Haig replied in the negative. The conference ended here with Marshal Foch's request that each of us submit in writing what we had proposed.

Upon my return to Paris, I cabled a report of the proceedings of the conference to Washington, including my proposals. It may be noted that the views of Marshal Haig were included generally in paragraphs number one, two, five and seven of my proposal, and those of General Pétain were covered practically by paragraphs one, two, three and seven.

Marshal Foch did not definitely express his views at the conference, but on the following day submitted his report to M. Clemenceau. His recommendations embraced the main points proposed by the Commanders-in-Chief and were accepted by the Supreme War Council with practically no change.

(Diary) Paris, Wednesday, October 30, 1918. Cable giving the President's views received yesterday, to which I replied favoring demand for unconditional surrender.

The doctor let me out this morning. Went to Foreign Office, where Bliss and I met Generals Sir Henry Wilson, Sackville-West (British), Di Robilant (Italian), and Belin (French), to consider terms of armistice to be granted Austria, which, as submitted to the Supreme

War Council, included general evacuation of foreign territory and demobilization of armies. Left at 11 P.M. by train for Souilly.

On Sunday Lieutenant Colonel Griscom called to get my views on the terms of the armistice for Mr. House, who did not come himself, fearing that he might catch the grippe. I sent him a copy of my cable of the 25th and also offered to go to see him, but he preferred to wait until Tuesday morning before the meeting of the Supreme War Council. The meeting was later postponed until Wednesday afternoon. Meanwhile, Mr. House sent Frazier with a message to the effect that the military considerations of an armistice had not yet been discussed and that he wanted me to get in touch with Marshals Foch and Haig to see if their views could be reconciled. Although Foch had not expressed his views at the conference, it was evident that, if he favored an armistice, his terms would be greatly at variance with those proposed by Haig. Consequently, it did not seem advisable for me to follow the suggestion.

Inasmuch as no intimation had been sent to me regarding the President's attitude toward granting an armistice to the German armies, and feeling that I could not sit by without expressing my opinion, I prepared a letter to send to the Supreme War Council, giving my views for consideration in case a decision had not been finally reached. In my estimation, the German armies were so badly beaten that they would have no other recourse than to surrender if called upon to do so.

The President's comments on my cable of the 25th were received on the 29th:

"Replying to your cablegram from London,[1] October 26th, the President directs me to say that he is relying upon your counsel and advice in this matter, and in making the following comments he will be glad to have you feel entirely free to bring to his attention any consideration he may have overlooked which in your judgment ought to be weighed before settling finally. * * *

"In general, the President approves of your first, in subparagraph,

[1] My cable was not sent from London, but it frequently happened that the place of origin was not included in cables forwarded through London to Washington.

but suggests wisdom of retention of at least part of German heavy guns, in pledge, and specific enumeration of territory to be evacuated other than France and Belgium. This has to do especially with territory to the East and Southeast, but should not Luxembourg be also included?

"With regard to your second, in subparagraph, the President raises the question as to whether it is necessary for Allied or American (forces) actually to occupy Alsace and Lorraine when evacuated under armistice.

"With regard to your third, in subparagraph, the President doubts advisability of requiring Allied or American occupation on eastern side of the Rhine, as that is practically an invasion of German soil under armistice.

"The President concurs in your fourth, in subparagraph, to the extent of continuing transportation for supplies of troops then in France but would not insist on right to increase American forces during armistice.

"With regard to your fifth, in subparagraph, if this means repatriation of troops now in German Army which have been recruited from non-German soil occupied by Germans, or repatriation of civil population deported from occupied territory, the President approves.

"With regard to your sixth, the President believes it would be enough to require internment of U-boats in neutral waters, as a further pledge and also to further unrestricted transportation of American material referred to in your fourth, but does not think terms of armistice should suggest ultimate disposition of such U-boats, nor that U-boat bases should be occupied under armistice, as that would mean Allied or American occupation of German soil not now in their possession.

"Your seventh, in subparagraph, the President approves.

"In general, the President feels the terms of the armistice should be rigid enough to secure us against renewal of hostilities by Germany but not humiliating beyond that necessity, as such terms would throw the advantage to the military party in Germany.

"The President would be glad to have you confer with Colonel House, who is now in France, showing him copies of your dispatch and this answer, and generally discuss with him all phases of this subject."

Upon receipt of this cable I handed to Mr. House on the 30th, for presentation to the Supreme War Council, the letter I had prepared, and in view of the first paragraph of the message I also cabled the substance of the letter to Washington:

"Paris, October 30, 1918.

"To the Allied Supreme War Council,
  "Paris.

"GENTLEMEN:

"In considering the question of whether or not Germany's request for an armistice should be granted, the following expresses my opinion from the military point of view:

"1. Judging by their excellent conduct during the past three months, the British, French, Belgian and American Armies appear capable of continuing the offensive indefinitely. Their morale is high and the prospects of certain victory should keep it so.

"2. The American Army is constantly increasing in strength and experience, and should be able to take an increasingly important part in the Allied offensive. Its growth both in personnel and matériel, with such reserves as the Allies may furnish, not counting the Italian Army, should be more than equal to the combined losses of the Allied armies.

"3. German manpower is constantly diminishing and her armies have lost over 300,000 prisoners and over one-third of their artillery during the past three months in their effort to extricate themselves from a difficult situation and avoid disaster.

"4. The estimated strength of the Allies on the Western Front, not counting Italy, and of Germany, in rifles is:

Allies	1,563,000
Germany	1,134,000

An advantage in favor of the Allies of 37 per cent.

"In guns:

Allies	22,413
Germany	16,495

An advantage of 35 per cent in favor of the Allies.

"If Italy's forces should be added to the Western Front we should have a still greater advantage.

"5. Germany's morale is undoubtedly low, her Allies have deserted her one by one and she can no longer hope to win. Therefore we should take full advantage of the situation and continue the offensive until we compel her unconditional surrender.

"6. An armistice would revivify the low spirits of the German Army and enable it to reorganize and resist later on, and would deprive the Allies of the full measure of victory by failing to press their present advantage to its complete military end.

"7. As the apparent humility of German leaders in talking of peace may be feigned, the Allies should distrust their sincerity and their motives. The appeal for an armistice is undoubtedly to enable the withdrawal from a critical situation to one more advantageous.

"8. On the other hand, the internal political conditions of Germany, if correctly reported, are such that she is practically forced to ask for an armistice to save the overthrow of her present Government, a consummation which should be sought by the Allies as precedent to permanent peace.

"9. A cessation of hostilities short of capitulation postpones, if it does not render impossible, the imposition of satisfactory peace terms, because it would allow Germany to withdraw her army with its present strength, ready to resume hostilities if terms were not satisfactory to her.

"10. An armistice would lead the Allied armies to believe this the end of fighting and it would be difficult, if not impossible, to resume hostilities with our present advantage in morale in the event of failure to secure at a peace conference what we have fought for.

"11. By agreeing to an armistice under the present favorable military situation of the Allies and accepting the principle of a negotiated peace rather than a dictated peace the Allies would jeopardize the moral position they now hold and possibly lose the chance actually to secure world peace on terms that would insure its permanence.

"12. It is the experience of history that victorious armies are prone to overestimate the enemy's strength and too eagerly seek an opportunity for peace. This mistake is likely to be made now on account of the reputation Germany has gained through her victories of the last four years.

"13. Finally, I believe the complete victory can only be obtained by continuing the war until we force unconditional surrender from Germany, but if the Allied Governments decide to grant an armistice, the terms should be so rigid that under no circumstances could Germany again take up arms.

"Respectfully submitted:

"JOHN J. PERSHING,
"Commander-in-Chief, A.E.F."

That evening I received a note from Mr. House asking me about the views of the other Commanders-in-Chief. In conversation with my aide, Colonel Boyd, Mr. House said that the question as to whether an armistice should be granted was purely political and that all the Prime Ministers were in favor of it. He had shown my letter, he said, to Clemenceau and to Lloyd George. I then wrote him a note to the effect that my opinion was based upon military considerations. I also advised Marshal Foch, through Colonel Mott, that I thought we should demand unconditional surrender. The following day a message came to me at Souilly from Colonel Mott saying that the Marshal was much pleased, as he held similar views.

The correspondence which led up to the Armistice began, as we have seen, as far back as October 6th, by the application of the German Government to President Wilson for an armistice on the basis of the Fourteen Points set forth in his speech to Congress on January 8, 1918. The exchange of notes continued during the month, until finally the Germans accepted the very frank statement by the President, conveyed in the State Department message of October 23d, that "the nations of the world do not and cannot trust the word of those who have hitherto been the masters of German policy," and that "the Government of the United States cannot deal with any but veritable representatives of the German people, who have been assured of a genuine constitutional standing as the real rulers of Germany. If it must deal with the military masters and the monarchial autocrats of Germany now, or if it is likely to have to deal with them later in regard to the international obligations of the German Empire, it must demand, not peace negotiations, but surrender." German compliance with the President's demands was expressed in a note of October 27th, and on November 5th the Germans were advised to apply to Marshal Foch for terms of an armistice.

In the light of later events, we know Germany was more nearly beaten than the Allied leaders realized at that time and was, in fact, in no position to resume the fighting even though her Government had remained intact. Her last division was in

line, her supply system was demoralized, and the congestion behind her lines made it practically impossible for her to move her
armies in the face of the aggressive Allies. Instead of requiring
the German forces to retire at once, leaving material, arms and
equipment behind, the Armistice terms permitted them to march
back to their homeland with colors flying and bands playing,
posing as the victims of political conditions.

If unconditional surrender had been demanded,[1] the Germans
would, without doubt, have been compelled to yield, and their
troops would have returned to Germany without arms, virtually
as paroled prisoners of war. The surrender of the German
armies would have been an advantage to the Allies in the enforcement of peace terms and would have been a greater deterrent
against possible future German aggression.

---

[1] In conversation with M. Poincaré some time after the war, he told me that, as
President of the Republic, he was in favor of demanding the surrender of the German armies, but that M. Clemenceau, his Prime Minister, insisted upon granting them
an armistice.

CHAPTER L

Preparations for General Attack—Plan of Maneuver—Attack Begins November 1st—Enemy Overwhelmed—First Army Forces Crossings of Meuse—Drive Relentless—We Reach Sedan on the 7th—German Delegates meet Foch to Discuss Terms of Armistice—Advance Continues in Meuse-Argonne—Second Army Assumes Offensive—37th and 91st Divisions in Flanders—Foch Appeals to Commanders-in-Chief for Decisive Results

(Diary) Souilly, Sunday, November 3, 1918. Returned here Thursday morning. Visited all corps commanders in afternoon.

General attack resumed Friday morning and our troops everywhere successful.

Arrived in Paris yesterday at Mr. House's request to attend meeting of Supreme War Council, Commanding Generals, and Chiefs of Staff, at Ministry of War, to consider Austrian situation. Austrians given until midnight November 3d-4th to accept terms of Armistice. Met with military men in afternoon to determine procedure in case of refusal of terms. Afterward attended meeting of Supreme War Council at Versailles, where general situation was discussed. Drove back with Mr. House; had satisfactory talk. Awarded first Distinguished Service Medal by the President; cabled appreciation.

Returned to Souilly this morning. The rapid progress of First Army continues. Discussed with General Maistre our proposed advance on Sedan.

Last Phase—Meuse-Argonne Operations

THE American Army had been able for the first time in the war to prepare for an offensive with some deliberation, under reasonably normal conditions, and more nearly on an equal footing with the other armies. It was already on the front of attack, the weather had taken a favorable turn,

NOTE: Strength of the A.E.F. on October 31st, 76,800 officers, 1,790,823 enlisted men. Divisional units arriving in October included elements of the following divisions: 8th Division (Regular Army), Maj. Gen. Eli A. Helmick; 31st Division (National Guard, Georgia, Alabama and Florida), Brig. Gen. Walter A. Harris; 38th Division (National Guard, Indiana, Kentucky and West Virginia), Maj. Gen. Robert L. Howze.

and the morale of the troops was lifted even higher than before.

Our staffs and troops had become veterans. French special units of artillery, pioneers, engineers, rail and service troops had been largely replaced by Americans. The army was operating in a sector which had been under its control for a month and more. Hitherto, as on September 12th and 26th, we had held the front but a brief period instead of being several months on the ground as was usually the case with the Allies.

Preparatory to this general attack, the front line had been reorganized, inefficient commanders had been replaced by active, energetic men, and large quantities of ammunition, supplies and equipment had been brought up. Our line occupied favorable positions from which to start this offensive. From east of Landres-et-St. Georges to the Meuse we were beyond the Hindenburg Line defenses and at the Côte de Châtillon we flanked the enemy's positions in and near Landres-et-St. Georges. Having gained the northern edge of the Bois de Bantheville, we were within striking distance of the heights of Barricourt.

The terrain presented a configuration somewhat similar to that encountered in our initial attack. On the east, overlooking the Meuse River at Dun-sur-Meuse, is a main ridge (called Barricourt ridge), which runs northwest via Buzancy to Stonne. On the west is the high wooded country of Bois de Loges and Bois de Bourgogne. Between these two commanding areas of high ground is lower, rolling country.

We had learned from reports and from photographs taken by our aviators that the enemy had greatly strengthened the most prominent points back of his lines, while captured documents indicated his intention of organizing a position along the west slopes of the Barricourt ridge. The eastern spurs of this ridge commanded all the crossings of the Meuse and formed a connecting link with the high ground east of the river about Côte Saint-Germain.

Our plans, as already indicated, contemplated first a deep penetration in the center of the front west of the Meuse with the object of capturing Barricourt ridge, and, next, a drive to the left to effect a junction with the French Fourth Army near Boult-aux-Bois. The capture of the ridge would give us a flank position which would compel the enemy to withdraw to the east of the river. As previously stated, the operation was to be carried

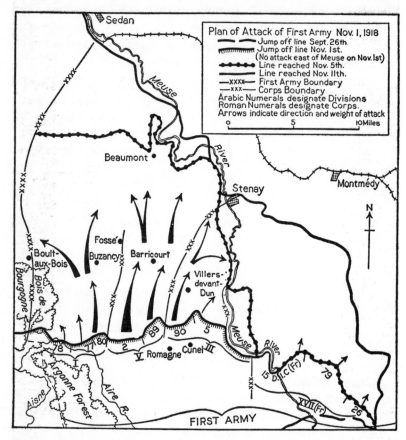

Plan of Attack of First Army Nov. 1, 1918
Jump off line Sept. 26th.
Jump off line Nov. 1st.
(No attack east of Meuse on Nov. 1st)
Line reached Nov. 5th.
Line reached Nov. 11th.
First Army Boundary
Corps Boundary
Arabic Numerals designate Divisions
Roman Numerals designate Corps.
Arrows indicate direction and weight of attack

out in coöperation with the French Fourth Army and both armies were in readiness on November 1st.

The order of battle and general plan of the First Army are well illustrated by the accompanying sketch. On the right, the III Corps (Hines), composed, from right to left, of the 5th Division (Ely) and 90th (Allen), was to support the right of the V Corps, turning the east flank of the Bois de Barricourt and carrying the

Barricourt ridge at Villers-devant-Dun. The V. Corps (Summerall), in the center, with the 89th Division (Wright) and 2d (Lejeune), as the wedge, was to drive to the north, carrying the ridge west of Barricourt and Fossé. The I Corps (Dickman), on the left, consisting of the 80th Division (Cronkhite), 77th (Alexander) and 78th (McRae), was to protect the left of the V. Corps and later to strike toward Boult-aux-Bois. The 1st Division (Parker) and the 42d (Menoher) were placed in close reserve in rear of the V Corps to be passed through the 2d and 80th Divisions when needed to add impetus to the attack.

The personnel of our artillery had quickly absorbed the traditions and the efficiency of this branch of the Regular Army. The value of close coöperation with the infantry was soon recognized, especially where these units of the division were trained together. The advance shipments of infantry and machine gun units prevented combined practice in many divisions, which had to enter the lines supported by strange artillery. A shortage had often compelled us to keep some artillery units in the line to support successive divisions. Notwithstanding such handicaps, the battle efficiency developed in our artillery was unsurpassed in any army. This was shown especially by the striking success in this offensive of the well-planned system of artillery fire which materially aided the infantry's initial penetration of the enemy's lines.

Special arrangements were made for the artillery to employ persistent (mustard) gas against the eastern edge of the Bois de Bourgogne and other selected points. The strongest enemy positions were to be engaged from the front by specified units while all others were to push forward rapidly between these points. In the two-hour violent artillery preparation which preceded the commencement of the attack, all sensitive places such as known batteries, ammunition dumps, strongholds and crossroads were systematically and effectively bombarded.

Three batteries of naval 14-inch guns on railway mounts and manned by naval personnel had been brought into the battle on

October 23d. These guns, with their long range, were used to good advantage against the enemy's main lines of railway communication.

As an aid to our infantry, machine guns were of great value. Capable of direct and overhead fire, and readily concealed in flank positions, the machine gun, alone or in mass, was the primary weapon of the defense. On the offensive our machine guns, often carried long distances, were kept well forward, and played an important rôle in our attacks. In the same way, despite the difficulties, single light artillery guns were advanced with the troops for use against enemy machine gun nests.

The effectiveness of the machine gun was well demonstrated by the exploit of one of our men near Cunel.[1] Repairing and mounting in an abandoned tank a captured machine gun, and holding his position under a hostile barrage and against direct artillery fire, he broke up two counterattacks against our lines.

One serious deficiency, which imposed a harder task on our splendid infantrymen and subjected them to the certainty of additional losses, but which, however, could not be remedied, was the lack of tanks, only eighteen being available instead of several hundred which were sorely needed. It seems strange that, with American genius for manufacturing from iron and steel, we should find ourselves after a year and a half of war almost completely without those mechanical contrivances which had exercised such a great influence on the Western Front in reducing infantry losses. As usual, the American soldier discounted the odds placed against him and carried the day by his dash and courage.

The infantry advanced to the assault at 5:30 on the morning of the 1st, following an accurate barrage of artillery and machine gun fire, which beat down German resistance over a zone 1,200 yards in depth. Squadrons of swift-flying combat planes drove the enemy planes from the air and fired on the hostile infantry, while the bombing squadrons harassed important

---

[1] Private John L. Barkley, Co. K, 4th Infantry, 3d Division. For this feat Private Barkley was awarded the Medal of Honor.

points behind the enemy's lines. The attack went forward with precision, gaining momentum with every mile. For the first time, the enemy's lines were completely broken through. Although he had been badly beaten on all parts of the front, he had hitherto been able to avoid this disaster. By the magnificent dash of our First Army, however, the enemy now found himself in the same situation that had confronted the Allies earlier in the war.

The V Corps, in the center, drove a wedge into the German defenses, swept through the zone of their artillery, and by night had reached the heights of Barricourt, five miles from the front of departure. The enemy's lines here had been decisively crushed, thanks to the splendid performances of the 89th and 2d Divisions.

The III Corps had strongly supported the V Corps, the 90th Division carrying all its objectives without a reverse and the 5th Division, on its right, reaching the Meuse, north of Brieulles, and capturing Cléry-le-Grand.

On the left of the Army, in the I Corps, the 80th Division co-operated with the 2d Division in the capture of Imécourt and reached the corps objective north of Sivry. The remainder of the corps was unable, in spite of great efforts, to make much headway against the strong defense of the Bois des Loges, although the 78th Division did gain a foothold in that wood.

In the meantime, the French Fourth Army, after having been driven back from the Grandpré—Olizy road, was unable to advance beyond the line of the Aisne River, and did not penetrate the Bois de Bourgogne until the American First Army relieved the pressure on its front by capturing Briquenay on November 2d.

By the evening of November 1st, the situation of the enemy was so serious that he had either to deliver a strong counterattack or to withdraw from all territory south of the line, Buzancy—Boult-aux-Bois. The blow struck by the First Army had, however, given him such a shock that he was unable to take strong offensive action, although he still offered serious resistance.

The attack continued with vigor on November 2d and 3d, the III Corps hurling the enemy beyond the Meuse near Dun-sur-Meuse and Stenay. The 5th Division on the 2d captured Doulcon and the 90th took Villers-devant-Dun. On the following day, the 90th pushed through the woods on its front and established its line along the heights overlooking the river in the neighborhood of Villefranche.

In the V Corps, the 89th Division on the 2d captured Tailly in the face of heavy machine gun fire, and on the following day seized Barricourt and drove the enemy backward to Beauclair. The 3d Brigade (Colonel James C. Rhea) of the 2d Division daringly marched through the Bois de la Folie during the night of November 2d, and captured the high ground east and north of Fossé early in the morning of the 3d. That night, this brigade, by another perilous march through the extensive Forêt de Dieulet, passed completely beyond the enemy's lines and captured German troops in their billets. By midnight the head of the column was in firm possession of La Tuilerie Farm, just south of Beaumont. This exploit reversed a scene of the Franco-Prussian War where a French division was surprised in its bivouac around Beaumont, in the opening phase of the Battle of Sedan, by a German night advance through the same forest.

The success of the attack in the center on November 1st compelled the retirement of the enemy on November 2d along the entire front of the I Corps and in front of the right of the French Fourth Army. The 80th Division on the 2d reached the new German defensive position, broke through it, and took Buzancy. On the following day, against heavy fire, the 80th established its line along the road running southeast from St. Pierremont.

The 77th Division now succeeded in passing Champigneulles and by the night of the 2d had reached Harricourt. On the following morning, it drove the enemy to the hill north of St. Pierremont, where it was held up by heavy machine gun fire.

The 78th Division captured the Bois des Loges on the 2d and established its line along the eastern edge of the Bois de

Bourgogne north to Briquenay, and continuing on the 3d captured Germont and Verrières.

(Diary) Souilly, Thursday, November 7, 1918. Had long talk with Stettinius about ordnance on Monday. Visited Second Army Headquarters and found indications of withdrawal on that front.

Issued orders the 5th for operations by First and Second Armies in the direction of Briey-Longwy. Spent the day at front. Went through Grandpré, overtaking Dickman's I Corps Headquarters at Harricourt; he was pushing troops toward Sedan. Returned through St. Juvin and found traffic in difficulties, many trucks having run off the road in the darkness. Gave directions to use lights on all motor transport.

Received letter from Marshal Foch to-day asking for six American divisions for new offensive south of Metz. Our advance has been continuous. Troops reached the heights of Sedan last night. German delegates are meeting Foch to consider terms of armistice. Recommended Harbord and McAndrew for promotion to grade of Lieutenant General.[1]

By November 4th, the enemy, greatly disorganized, was retiring before the vigorous pursuit of our troops on the entire front of the First Army. His withdrawal was strongly protected by cleverly placed machine guns and well organized delaying operations.

The following telegram came to me on the afternoon of the 5th:

"The operations begun on November 1st by the First American Army, due to the valor of the command, (and) to the energy and bravery of the troops, have already assured results of great importance. I am happy to send you my congratulations. * * *

"Foch."

Our success had been so striking since the beginning of the November 1st attack that I felt full advantage should be taken of the possibility of destroying the armies on our front and seizing the region upon which Germany largely depended for her supply

[1] This recommendation met with Secretary Baker's favor, but unfortunately the Tables of Organization made no provision for appointments to that grade except in the line of the army.

of iron and coal. In accordance with these views, the following order was issued on November 5th to the First and Second Armies:

"1. The energetic action of the 1st Army should completely expel the enemy from the region between the MEUSE and the BAR within the next few days. The results obtained by this Army have been felt on the entire front from the MOSELLE to HOLLAND. * * *

"It is desired that, in carrying out the directions that are outlined herein, Corps and Division Commanders push troops forward wherever resistance is broken, without regard for fixed objectives and without fear for their flanks. Special attention will be given to impress upon all officers and soldiers that energy, boldness and open warfare methods are demanded by the present situation.

"2. The 1st and 2nd Armies will at once prepare to undertake operations with the ultimate purpose of destroying the enemy's organization and driving him beyond the existing frontier in the region of BRIEY and LONGWY.

"3. As preliminaries of this offensive, the 1st Army will:

"(a) Complete the occupation of the region between the MEUSE and the BAR.

"(b) Complete the present operation of driving the enemy from the heights of the MEUSE north of VERDUN and south of the FORÊT DE WOËVRE.

"(c) Conduct an offensive with the object of driving the enemy beyond the THINTE and the CHIERS. * * *

"4. The 2nd Army will:

"(a) Conduct raids and local operations in accordance with verbal instructions already given.

"(b) Advance its line between the MOSELLE and the ETANG LACHAUSSÉE toward GORZE and CHAMBLEY.

"(c) Prepare plans for an attack in the direction of BRIEY along the axis FRESNES—CONFLANS—BRIEY. * * * "

Between the Meuse and Chiers Rivers, north and northeast of Stenay, there was a very strong position which commanded the crossings in that vicinity. I believed that if we should cross the river south of Stenay and move in the direction of Montmédy we could turn this position and would have an excellent opportunity to capture large numbers of German troops driven back on the line Sedan—Montmédy. By this maneuver we would also be in an advantageous position to advance on the important supply areas of Longwy and Briey.

In the First Army, an attack by the III Corps to the east across the Meuse, south of Dun-sur-Meuse, in conjunction with the northward movement by the French XVII Corps, was prepared as a preliminary to a new line of advance to the east.

On November 3d, 4th and 5th, the 5th Division of the III Corps, in a brilliant maneuver on a wide front, effected crossings of the Meuse and established bridgeheads south of Dun-sur-Meuse. The heights of the Meuse were gradually cleared by the III Corps and the French II Colonial Corps, which had relieved the French XVII Corps. Now, for the first time since 1914, the French positions around Verdun were completely free from the menace of these heights.

In these operations, the 5th Division, assisted by a regiment of the 32d, on November 5th had captured Milly and established its line from there south to the Bois de Châtillon. By night of the 9th, it had advanced to Remoiville and north of Mouzay.

Our front of attack was also extended to the south and by November 10th an excellent line of departure was secured for an offensive in the direction of Montmédy. The 79th Division (Kuhn), in the French II Colonial Corps, met decided opposition in its attacks of the 4th, 5th, and 6th against the Borne de Cornouiller and this strong point was finally taken on the 7th. On the following day the 79th, with units of the 26th Division (Bamford) attached, advanced on its entire front, and on the 9th took Wavrille.

Between November 3d and 7th the 26th Division, on the right of the 79th, made no attack. On the 8th it took up the pursuit of the retiring enemy and by night of the 9th occupied a line which included Ville-devant-Chaumont.

The 81st Division (Bailey) entered the line as the right division of the French II Colonial Corps on November 7th, relieving the

35th Division (Traub). Attacking on the 9th against stiff defense, it captured Manheulles and Moranville.

In these last days of the fighting some of our troops, including the 81st, operated with a serious shortage of animals, which made it impossible to employ all their artillery in close support of the infantry, and often required the men to drag their guns by hand. The 6th Division (Gordon), which unfortunately did not get into battle, pulled a large part of its transportation many miles by hand in attempting to reach the rapidly moving battle front south of Sedan, where it was planned to use this division in case of necessity.

Taking up again the account of our great drive northward, the 89th Division, V Corps, overcoming stubborn opposition, captured Beaufort on the 4th and reached the Meuse. The Forêt de Jaulnay was cleaned up on the following day and Cesse was occupied. The 2d Division in its attack of the 4th suffered heavy losses and made slight headway, but during the next two days it continued rapidly and by night of the 6th reached the Meuse south of Villemontry.

In the I Corps, the 80th Division on the 4th, in spite of the enemy's stand, captured Vaux-en-Dieulet and Sommauthe. The enemy retired during the night and the division took up the pursuit, overcoming vigorous rearguard resistance until reaching a line north and west of Beaumont. During the night of the 5th, its progress continued, the division being relieved the next morning.

The 77th Division was effectively opposed on the 4th north and east of Oches, but on the 5th its line was pushed forward to the north of Stonne and La Besace. By night of the 6th, the 77th had reached the Meuse; Remilly and Villers being entered by its patrols.

The 78th Division on the 4th captured Les Petites Armoises, and on the following morning advanced more than a mile to the north. The 42d Division relieved the 78th on this line, and by the 6th established itself north of Bulson.

On the morning of November 6th, the 1st Division, V Corps,

took over the front of the 80th Division, I Corps, and at once made a rapid advance to Yoncq, reaching the general line of the Meuse in the vicinity of Villemontry.

It was the ambition of the First Army and mine that our troops should capture Sedan, which the French had lost in a decisive battle in 1870. I suggested to General Maistre that the prescribed boundary line between our First and the French Fourth Army might be ignored in case we should outrun the French, to which he offered no objection, but on the contrary warmly approved.

To reach the objective the left boundary of the First Army would have to be disregarded, as Sedan lay to the northwest beyond that limit. On the afternoon of November 5th, the I Corps was directed to bend its energies to capture Sedan *"assisted on its right by the V Corps."* A misconception in the V Corps of the exact intent of the orders resulted in the 1st Division erroneously going beyond the left boundary of the V Corps and marching directly across the sector of the I Corps during the late afternoon of the 6th and throughout the night. The troops of the 1st Division carried out this unnecessary forced march in fine spirit despite their tired condition.

Considerable confusion resulted in the 42d and 77th Divisions, and their advance was delayed, as roads became blocked by the columns of the 1st Division. The 42d and the 1st then began a race for the honor of capturing Sedan. Part of these divisions had entered the zone of the French Fourth Army and were waging a fight with the enemy for the possession of the heights south and west of Sedan. The morning of the 7th found men of the 42d and the 1st Divisions on the heights overlooking the city.

Under normal conditions the action of the officer or officers responsible for this movement of the 1st Division directly across the zones of action of two other divisions could not have been overlooked, but the splendid record of that unit and the approach of the end of hostilities suggested leniency.

The enemy's main line of communications was now within range of the machine guns of the First Army, which had driven him twenty-four miles since the 1st of November. His position on the Western Front was no longer tenable and he urged immediate consideration of an armistice.

Between November 1st and 7th the western boundary of the First Army was changed several times by Marshal Foch, and the notification in more than one instance reached Army Headquarters too late to be transmitted to the troops in time to become effective. On the 7th of November the left of our army was limited by Mouzon, the original boundary not having been definitely fixed as far north as Sedan. However, this change was not effected until after the Armistice, as the French Fourth Army was not prepared before that time to take over that sector.

> (Diary) Paris, Saturday, November 9, 1918. Had telephone message from Foch yesterday that when hostilities cease troops should hold their lines.
>
> Arrived here to-day by motor to discuss with Foch further operations but found him absent. Word received from Mr. House that the Italians want three or four American regiments sent to Austria with their troops. Went to Neuilly hospital to see our patients. Had talk with Bishop Brent. Japanese Prince Torihito, representing the Emperor, presented me with the highest grade of Order of the Rising Sun.

Late on November 9th Marshal Foch, then in conference with German representatives regarding the terms of the Armistice, sent telegraphic instructions to all Commanders-in-Chief from which it might be inferred that he was uncertain regarding the outcome of negotiations and wished to let the enemy know that there could be no further delay. The following was the message received:

> "The enemy, disorganized by our repeated attack, retreats along the entire front.
>
> "It is important to coördinate and expedite our movements.
>
> "I appeal to the energy and the initiative of the Commanders-in-Chief and of their armies to make decisive the results obtained."

Orders in response to this appeal were immediately issued and their execution by the First Army was under way on November

10th and 11th. Yet here again no sort of urging was necessary. Our troops were determined not to give the enemy any respite. Already the crossing of the Meuse had been planned for the whole army and the V Corps got over during the night of the 10th-11th. Part of the 89th Division crossed on rafts just west of Pouilly, and others in the rear of the 90th Division.

The 2d Division was unable to force a crossing at Mouzon, as planned, but about a mile south of Villemontry the engineers of the division, with exceptional rapidity and skill, threw two bridges across, over which one regiment passed. The 77th Division, now on the left of the V Corps, sent over patrols only on the 10th and 11th, the low ground north of the river opposite its front being flooded due to heavy rains and to damming operations by the Germans.

The I Corps from November 6th to 10th was withdrawing its divisions to points on the Meuse between Dun-sur-Meuse and Verdun, preparatory to a general attack which would have as its object the turning of the enemy's strong position in front of the V Corps.

East of the Meuse, the First Army advanced in conjunction with the Second Army, which had been earnestly preparing for this moment ever since its organization. The Second Army, from left to right, was composed of the French XVII Corps, with the 33d Division (Bell) in line, and the 35th (Traub) in reserve; the IV Corps (Muir), with the 28th Division (Hay) and the 7th (Wittenmyer) in line, and the 4th (Hersey) in reserve; and the VI Corps (Menoher), with the 92d (colored) Division (Ballou) in line; and the 88th Division (Weigel) in the Army reserve. This order of battle is shown on the accompanying sketch.

Under the instructions issued by me on November 5th for the advance of the First and Second Armies, which received approval of Marshal Foch in a personal note of November 8th, the Second Army made progress along its entire front in the direction of the Briey iron basin during the last three days of hostilities. In view of the stubborn resistance encountered, and the extended fronts held by its divisions, the gains realized reflected credit on that command.

Attacking on the 10th, the 33d Division reached the Bois d'Harville and captured Marchéville, but was forced to retire. The 28th Division occupied a part of the Bois des Haudronvilles Bas, as well as Marimbois Farm. The 7th Division took and held against counterattack Hill 323. The 92d Division captured the Bois Fréhaut.

On the front of the First Army, the 90th Division (Allen), on

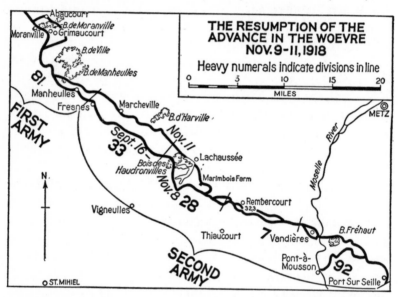

the left of the III Corps (Hines), had crossed the Meuse on the 9th and attacked on the 10th, meeting decided opposition throughout the day. Elements of the division entered Stenay but were unable to clean up the town; while others, after hard fighting in the nearby wood, reached but could not take Baâlon. The 5th Division (Ely) captured Jametz and cleared the Forêt de Woëvre. The 32d Division (Haan) reëntered the line on the 9th as the right division of the III Corps and made substantial progress. On the 10th the division moved forward until stopped by heavy fire from east of the Thinte River.

In the French II Colonial Corps, the 79th Division (Kuhn) engaged the enemy on the 10th and captured Chaumont-devant-Damvillers, while the 26th Division (Bamford) took Ville-devant-Chaumont. The 81st Division (Bailey) continued its attack on the 9th, cleaning up the remainder of the Bois de Moranville and taking Abaucourt. After hard fighting, Grimaucourt was captured, but was later evacuated, the line being established west of the town.

Meanwhile other of our divisions were engaged on distant fronts. In Flanders, our 37th and 91st Divisions, which had been sent to the French Sixth Army at Marshal Foch's request, entered the battle on October 31st. The Cruyshautem ridge was taken by the 37th Division (Farnsworth) on the first day, while the 91st (Johnston), advancing against intense fire, seized the strongly defended wooded area in its front. Both divisions moved forward rapidly to the Escaut River on the following day in pursuit of the enemy. Despite resistance, crossings of the river were effected by the 37th on November 2d and 3d, the division being relieved on the following day. Audenarde was occupied by the 91st Division on the 2d, and the division was relieved on the 3d by the French.

Both divisions reëntered the line for the general attack of the French Sixth Army on November 10th. The 37th Division was directed to relieve two French divisions east of the Escaut on the morning of the 10th, but these divisions had been unable to cross and were relieved on the west bank. In spite of severe losses, the 37th succeeded in again crossing the river and moved forward on the following day, advancing two and a half miles eastward. The 91st Division met slight opposition on the 10th and none on the morning of the 11th, reaching a line east of Boucle-Saint-Blaise.

In the First Army, the V Corps advanced rapidly the morning of the 11th. Elements of the 89th Division occupied Stenay and established a line on the hill to the north. Pouilly-sur-Meuse was mopped up early in the morning and Autreville was occupied. The 2d Division advanced to the ridge west of Moulins; while the 77th Division held its line of the 10th.

In the III Corps, on the morning of the 11th, the 90th Division entered Baâlon, and the 5th and 32d Divisions were preparing to attack. The 79th Division of the French II Colonial Corps attacked against the Côte de Romagne and advanced a short distance; the 26th Division made slight gains; and the 81st Division again took Grimaucourt.

On the front of the Second Army, the attack of the 33d Division on the 11th was held up. The 28th Division carried its line

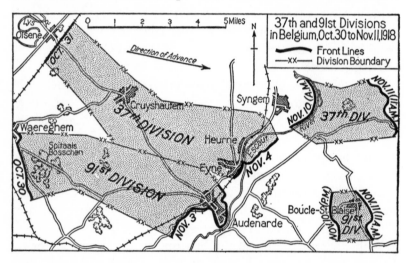

forward north of Marimbois Farm; the 7th Division made no attack; and the 92d Division attacked but did not hold all its gains.

The line of the First Army on November 11th extended from Fresnes-en-Woëvre to Pont-Maugis. The Second Army line ran from Port-sur-Seille to Fresnes-en-Woëvre. Thus both American armies were now in position to carry out the offensive as directed by my orders of November 5th, which was what I had planned and advocated when Marshal Foch insisted that there should be a converging movement of all the armies west of the Meuse, with Mézières—Sedan as the objective of the American First Army.

As noted in the diary of November 7th, Marshal Foch had requested that six American divisions be held in readiness to join in a Franco-American offensive in the direction of Château-Salins, to start from the sector east of the Moselle River. The plan was agreed to, but with the understanding that our troops should be employed as a group under our own command. This combined attack was to begin on November 14th, with twenty French divisions under General Mangin, and a force of six American divisions under General Bullard. It was my intention to have this force known thereafter as the Second Army. I then expected to give General Dickman the command of the old Second Army, which would become the Third, to hold the St. Mihiel front. Of the divisions designated for the operation toward Château-Salins, the 3d, 4th, 29th, and 36th, then in reserve, were scheduled to move eastward on November 11th, while the 28th and 35th were being withdrawn from line on the Second Army front.

CHAPTER LI

Armistice—Résumé—Decoration Foch, Joffre, Pétain and Haig—Call on Clemenceau

(Diary) Chaumont, Monday, November 11, 1918. Arrived here yesterday morning from Paris. Miss Margaret Wilson dined with us last night.

This morning at 6 o'clock message came from Marshal Foch, through Colonel Mott, that hostilities would cease at 11 A.M. Had information on tentative plans for following up Germans. Sent congratulations to the King of Belgium by Comte d'Oultremont on glorious outcome of the war. Assistant Secretary of War F. P. Keppel came to dine. Left on my train for Paris at 11 P.M., taking General McAndrew, Colonels Boyd and Quekemeyer, Lieutenant Colonel Griscom, and Captain Hughes.

AS the conference between Marshal Foch and the German delegates proceeded, and in anticipation of advices regarding the Armistice, telephone lines were kept constantly open between my headquarters and those of the First and Second Armies. When word came to me at 6 A.M. that hostilities would cease at 11:00 A.M., directions to that effect were immediately sent to our armies. Our troops had been advancing rapidly during the preceding two days and although every effort was made to reach them promptly a few could not be overtaken before the prescribed hour.

Between September 26th and November 11th, twenty-two American and six French divisions, with an approximate fighting strength of 500,000 men, on a front extending from southeast of Verdun to the Argonne Forest, had engaged and decisively beaten forty-three different German divisions, with an estimated fighting strength of 470,000. Of the twenty-two American divisions, four had at different times during this period been in action on fronts other than our own.

The enemy suffered an estimated loss of over 100,000 casualties in this battle and the First Army about 117,000. The total strength of the First Army, including 135,000 French troops, reached 1,031,000 men. It captured 26,000 prisoners, 874 cannon, 3,000 machine guns and large quantities of material.

The transportation and supply of divisions to and from our front during this battle was a gigantic task. There were twenty-six American and seven French divisions, besides hundreds of thousands of corps and army troops, moved in and out of the American zone. A total of 173,000 men were evacuated to the rear and more than 100,000 replacements were received.

It need hardly be restated that our entry into the war gave the Allies the preponderance of force vitally necessary to outweigh the tremendous increase in the strength of the Germans on the Western Front, due to the collapse of Russia and the consequent release of German divisions employed against her. From the military point of view, we began to aid the Allies early in 1918, when our divisions with insufficient training to take an active part in battle were sent to the inactive front to relieve French divisions, in order that they might be used where needed in the fighting line.

The assistance we gave the Allies in combat began in May with the successful attack of one of our divisions at Cantigny. This was followed early in June by the entrance into battle of the two divisions that stopped the German advance on Paris near Château-Thierry, and by three others that were put in the defensive line. In July two American divisions, with one Moroccan division, formed the spearhead of the counterattack against the Château-Thierry salient, in which nine of our divisions participated. There was a total of approximately 300,000 American troops engaged in this Second Battle of the Marne, which involved very severe fighting, and was not completed until the Germans were driven beyond the Vesle in August. In the middle of September an army of 550,000 Americans reduced the St. Mihiel salient. The latter part of September our great battle of the Meuse-Argonne was begun, lasting through forty-seven days of intense fighting and ending brilliantly for our First and Second Armies on November 11th, after more than 1,200,000 American soldiers had participated.

It was a time to forget the hardships and the difficulties, except to record them with the glorious history of our achievements. In praise and thanks for the decisive victories of our armies and in guidance for the future, the following order was issued:

"G. H. Q.

"American Expeditionary Forces.

"General Orders }
     "No. 203. }   "France, Nov. 12, 1918.

"The enemy has capitulated. It is fitting that I address myself in thanks directly to the officers and soldiers of the American Expeditionary Forces who by their heroic efforts have made possible this glorious result. Our armies, hurriedly raised and hastily trained, met a veteran enemy, and by courage, discipline and skill always defeated him. Without complaint you have endured incessant toil, privation and danger. You have seen many of your comrades make the supreme sacrifice that freedom may live. I thank you for the patience and courage with which you have endured. I congratulate you upon the splendid fruits of victory which your heroism and the blood of our gallant dead are now presenting to our nation. Your deeds will live forever on the most glorious pages of America's history.

"These things you have done. There remains now a harder task which will test your soldierly qualities to the utmost. Succeed in this and little note will be taken and few praises will be sung; fail, and the light of your glorious achievements of the past will sadly be dimmed. But you will not fail. Every natural tendency may urge towards relaxation in discipline, in conduct, in appearance, in everything that marks the soldier. Yet you will remember that each officer and each soldier is the representative in Europe of his people and that his brilliant deeds of yesterday permit no action of to-day to pass unnoticed by friend or by foe. You will meet this test as gallantly as you have met the tests of the battlefield. Sustained by your high ideals and inspired by the heroic part you have played, you will carry back to our people the proud consciousness of a new Americanism born of sacrifice. Whether you stand on hostile territory or on the friendly soil of France, you will so bear yourself in discipline, appearance and respect for all civil rights that you will confirm for all time the pride and love which every American feels for your uniform and for you.

"JOHN J. PERSHING,
"General, Commander-in-Chief.
"Official:
"ROBERT C. DAVIS,
"Adjutant General."

The experience of the World War only confirmed the lessons of the past. The divisions with little training, while aggressive and courageous, were lacking in the ready skill of habit. They were capable of powerful blows, but their blows were apt to be awkward—teamwork was often not well understood. Flexible and resourceful divisions cannot be created by a few maneuvers or by a few months' association of their elements. On the other hand, without the keen intelligence, the endurance, the willingness, and the enthusiasm displayed in the training areas and on the battlefields, the decisive results obtained would have been impossible.

The Meuse-Argonne battle presented numerous difficulties, seemingly insurmountable. The success stands out as one of the great achievements in the history of American arms. Suddenly conceived and hurried in plan and preparation; complicated by close association with a preceding major operation; directed against stubborn defense of the vital point of the Western Front; attended by cold and inclement weather; and fought largely by partially trained troops; this battle was prosecuted with an unselfish and heroic spirit of courage and fortitude which demanded eventual victory. Physically strong, virile, and aggressive, the morale of the American soldier during this most trying period was superb.

Upon the young commanders of platoons, companies, and battalions fell the heaviest burden. They not only suffered all the dangers and rigors of battle but carried the responsibility of caring for and directing their men, often newly arrived and with but little training. Where these leaders lacked practical knowledge of tactics, they supplied the deficiency by fearless onslaughts

392 MY EXPERIENCES IN THE WORLD WAR

against the enemy's line. Yet, quick to learn, they soon developed on the field into skilled leaders who inspired their men with increasing confidence.

To the higher commanders and their staffs great credit is due for the successful performance of an exceptionally complicated and arduous task. The problems born of inexperience multiply with each increase of strength, and the division, corps, and particularly the army headquarters were confronted by questions of superlative difficulty. The importance of their work is rarely realized or appreciated. The army staff at one time was involved in serving a front of ninety-four miles and a force of approximately one million men. With typical American directness of action and intensity of purpose, each member carried out his duties despite all obstacles.

Deeds of daring were legion. It is not intended to discriminate in favor of those whose heroic services have been recognized. There were thousands of others who bore themselves with equal gallantry but whose deeds are known only by the victorious results they helped to achieve. However, as typifying the spirit of the rank and file of our great army, I would mention Lieutenant Samuel Woodfill, 5th Division, who attacked single-handed a series of German machine gun nests near Cunel and dispatched the crews of each in turn until reduced to the necessity of assaulting the last detachment with a pick; Sergeant Alvin C. York, of the 82d Division, who stood off and captured 132 Germans after his patrol was literally surrounded and outnumbered ten to one; and Major Charles W. Whittlesey and his men of the 77th Division, who, when their battalion was cut off in the Argonne, refused to surrender and held out until finally relieved.

There is little to add in praise of the spirit of determination that stimulated each individual soldier to overcome the hardships and difficulties that fell to his lot. With fortitude and perseverance he gave his every energy to the accomplishment of his task, whether it required him to charge the enemy's guns or play the less conspicuous rôle of forwarding supplies. In their devotion, their valor, and in the loyal fulfillment of their obligations, the officers and men of the American Expeditionary Forces have left a heritage of which those who follow may ever be proud.

While we extol the virtues of the men who had the privilege of serving America in the ranks of her armies, it must be remembered that they received their inspiration of loyalty and of devotion to the country's cause from those at home. They were but the chosen representatives of the American people, whose resolute spirit they transformed into victory on the field of honor.

We who were in France were conscious always of the indefatigable efforts made to supply us with the men and materials necessary for our success. Individual officers and men, no matter what their position or their duty, were inspired by patriotic determination to respond to the fullest extent possible to our calls. We became, in fact, a nation in arms, a nation imbued with and expressing the will to victory.

(Diary) Paris, Tuesday, November 12, 1918.   Arrived in Paris this morning. Colonel Mott was here with instructions from Marshal Foch about following up the Germans. Held brief conference on subject with McAndrew and Harbord, and left immediately with Boyd and Quekemeyer for Marshal Foch's headquarters at Senlis. Met Marshal Foch for the first time since victory and the meeting was one to be remembered. By direction of the President, bestowed on him the Distinguished Service Medal. We returned to Paris in the afternoon to find pandemonium.

When I saw Marshal Foch he was in high spirits and said a great many complimentary things about the splendid work of the American Army, my cordial coöperation, and how he appreciated my straightforward methods. He said that he had always known my attitude on every question, because I stated it frankly and clearly and then lived up to it. I was equally enthusiastic in praise of his leadership. What was said and the realization that the victory was won and the war actually over affected us both deeply and for some moments we were speechless. Both of us were rather overcome by emotion as we embraced and each gave the other the time-honored French "accolade."

We pulled ourselves together shortly, as one of the objects of my visit was to decorate him with the Distinguished Service Medal, this being the first to be presented to any officer other than an American. He had directed a small guard of some fifteen or twenty territorial orderlies, under the command of a sergeant, to be formed in the yard in rear of his quarters, with two trumpeters to furnish the music. Standing in front of this command and facing him, I made a short speech in French and pinned on his blouse the token of our country's esteem and appreciation of his distinguished services. My aide handed one of his aides a signed copy of what I said. The Marshal spoke somewhat at length on how he valued the honor and how brilliantly the Americans had fought beside the Allies and was so moved that he could hardly finish what he had to say. He shook hands with me very cordially and stood holding my hand with both of his as he ordered the flourish of trumpets to close the ceremony.

I had luncheon with him, during which Weygand gave a brief account of the conference with the German delegates regarding the terms of the Armistice. He said that the Germans came across the line by automobile on the afternoon of November 7th and boarded a special railway coach sent by the French to meet them. During the night this car and the Marshal's were placed side by side in the forest between Compiègne and Soissons. The emissaries were ushered into the Marshal's presence and after producing their credentials were asked the object of their visit. They replied that they had come to discuss the terms of an armistice. The Marshal then made it clear that he, himself, was not requesting an armistice and *did not care to have one*. When asked if they wished an armistice, they replied that they did. The Marshal said if that was the case, here were the terms, a copy of which he handed them. The severity of the demands seemed to surprise them and they appeared very much depressed. They had no power to sign an armistice, they said, without the consent of the Chancellor, and after some little discussion they started an officer to the German capital with the terms.

They did not seem to object to turning over 5,000 cannon, but deplored the condition which required them to surrender 30,000 machine guns. They finally succeeded in getting this reduced to 25,000 machine guns on the ground that they might have some left for riot duty. In speaking of the danger of riots, the delegates were asked why they did not send some of their reserve divisions to maintain order in the interior. Their reply was that they had no divisions in reserve, as *every division that they had was actually in line*. Then they complained about the short time allowed for evacuation, stating that the German Army was in no condition to move, either forward or backward.

During the 9th and 10th, while waiting for instructions from their Government, the delegates talked very freely with Weygand about conditions in Germany and spoke particularly of the lack of food and the fear that there would be famine in places because of the bad transportation service.

A wireless message from the German Government authorizing the delegates to sign the Armistice was received about 11:00 P.M. on the 10th. It took until 5:00 A.M. the 11th to decode the message, complete the discussion and draw up the terms in the rough. In order to stop bloodshed, the last page of the conditions was written first, and this was signed a few minutes after 5:00 A.M. on the 11th. At that hour word was sent out to the armies that fighting would cease at 11:00 A.M.

After luncheon we drove back to Paris and everybody was still celebrating. It looked as though the whole population had gone entirely out of their minds. The city was turned into pandemonium. The streets and boulevards were packed with people singing and dancing and wearing all sorts of odd costumes. The crowds were doing the most clownish things. One could hardly hear his own voice, it was such a bedlam.

It was next to impossible for our automobile to make any headway through the mass of humanity. We were two hours in crossing the Place de la Concorde, the crowd was so dense and so riotous. It happened that I was recognized before we had gone very far and French men and women boarded the car, climbed on top of it and got inside, and no amount of persuasion would prevail upon them to let us pass. Finally a group of American soldiers, who were enjoying the hilarity, came along and seeing our helpless condition took charge and succeeded in making an opening sufficiently large to permit the car to be moved a yard or so at a time until we got free. If all the ridiculous things done during those two or three days by dignified American and French men and women were recorded the reader would scarcely believe the story. But this was Paris and the war was over.

(Diary) Paris, Thursday, November 14, 1918. Yesterday conferred the Distinguished Service Medal on Marshal Joffre and on General Pétain. Saw Mr. House, Stettinius, Atterbury and several others on variety of subjects.

To-day at Cambrai I decorated Marshal Haig. Saw Lord Derby, who always speaks warmly of the relations between our two Governments. Called on M. Clemenceau.

I went to the Ecole de Guerre, where Marshal Joffre had his quarters, and in a very simple ceremony that took place in his office I pinned our Distinguished Service Medal on his breast. Only a few staff officers were present, among them the Marshal's faithful Chief of Staff, Colonel Fabre, while the officers who accompanied me were Harbord, Boyd, and Quekemeyer. This grand old French Commander-in-Chief was very proud of this recognition by our Government, but expressed himself in few words. It gave me the greatest pleasure to make this presentation.

We next motored to Provins to confer the same decoration on General Pétain. After luncheon, together with several of his generals and staff officers, we repaired to the front court, where a guard of about twenty soldiers was already formed. Facing General Pétain, who stood in front of the command, I spoke a few words regarding his exceptional service to his country and thanked him for his uniform consideration and great assistance to our armies, and pinned on the medal. It was especially gratifying to me to decorate Pétain, as my relations with him were always closer than with any of the other Allied officers and we had become fast friends. He made some complimentary remarks about our Army and seemed much pleased and deeply appreciative of the recognition shown by our Government of his great abilities.

At Cambrai, where I went to decorate Field Marshal Sir Douglas Haig, a brigade of Highlanders, which included some of the most distinguished units of the British Army, was assembled for the occasion. The ceremony was very impressive. Marshal Haig stood opposite the center of the line, the very picture of the ideal soldier that he was. The band of bagpipes swung down the line playing a medley of Scottish airs in thrilling fashion. As the command stood at "Present Arms," I approached the Field Marshal and after a few words pinned our decoration on him. The march-past of the troops completed a memorable event.

Upon my arrival in Paris that afternoon, I hastened over to call on M. Clemenceau. To my mind, he was the greatest of French civil officials. Though some seventy-six years of age, he had the vigor, the fire, and the determination of a man of fifty. He will live long in history. I had not seen him since the cessation of hostilities and when we met he was much affected, and indeed demonstrative. We fell into each other's arms, choked up and had to wipe our eyes. We had no differences to discuss that day.

APPENDIX

GENERAL ORGANIZATION OF THE AMERICAN
EXPEDITIONARY FORCES NOVEMBER 1, 1918

APPENDIX

GENERAL ORGANIZATION OF THE AMERICAN
EXPEDITIONARY FORCES NOVEMBER 1, 1918

GENERAL HEADQUARTERS

Commander-in-Chief:
GEN. JOHN J. PERSHING
Chief of Staff:
MAJ. GEN. JAMES W. MCANDREW
Deputy Chief of Staff:
BRIG. GEN. LEROY ELTINGE
Asst. Chief of Staff, G-1 (Administrative):
BRIG. GEN. AVERY D. ANDREWS
Asst. Chief of Staff, G-2 (Intelligence):
BRIG. GEN. DENNIS E. NOLAN
Asst. Chief of Staff, G-4 (Coördination):
BRIG. GEN. GEORGE V. H. MOSELEY
Secretary, General Staff:
LT. COL. ALBERT S. KUEGLE
Judge Advocate General:
BRIG. GEN. WALTER A. BETHEL
Chief of Artillery:
MAJ. GEN. ERNEST HINDS

Aides-de-Camp:
COL. CARL BOYD
COL. JOHN G. QUEKEMEYER
COL. EDWARD BOWDITCH, JR.
CAPT. JOHN C. HUGHES
COL. ADELBERT DE CHAMBRUN (French)
CAPT. CHARLES DE MARENCHES (French)
Asst. Chief of Staff, G-3 (Operations):
BRIG. GEN. FOX CONNER
Asst. Chief of Staff, G-5 (Training):
BRIG. GEN. HAROLD B. FISKE
Adjutant General:
BRIG. GEN. ROBERT C. DAVIS
Inspector General:
MAJ. GEN. ANDRÉ W. BREWSTER
Chief of Tank Corps:
BRIG. GEN. SAMUEL D. ROCKENBACH

SERVICES OF SUPPLY

Commander:
MAJ. GEN. JAMES G. HARBORD
Deputy Chief of Staff:
COL. JOHN P. MCADAMS
Asst. Chief of Staff, G-2:
LT. COL. CABOT WARD
Adjutant General:
COL. LOUIS H. BASH
Inspector General:
BRIG. GEN. THOMAS Q. DONALDSON
Chief Surgeon:
COL. WALTER D. MCCAW
Chief Engineer Officer:
MAJ. GEN. WILLIAM C. LANGFITT
Chief of Air Service:
MAJ. GEN. MASON M. PATRICK
Provost Marshal General:
BRIG. GEN. HARRY H. BANDHOLTZ
Director General of Transportation:
BRIG. GEN. WILLIAM W. ATTERBURY
Director Construction and Forestry:
BRIG. GEN. EDGAR JADWIN
*Director Military Engineering and Engineer
Supplies:*
BRIG. GEN. JAMES F. MCINDOE

Chief of Staff:
BRIG. GEN. JOHSON HAGOOD
Asst. Chief of Staff, G-1:
COL. JAMES B. CAVANAUGH
Asst. Chief of Staff, G-4:
COL. HENRY C. SMITHER
Judge Advocate General:
COL. JOHN A. HULL
Chief Quartermaster:
MAJ. GEN. HARRY L. ROGERS
Chief Ordnance Officer:
BRIG. GEN. JOHN H. RICE
Chief Signal Officer:
BRIG. GEN. EDGAR RUSSEL
Chief of Chemical Warfare Service:
BRIG. GEN. AMOS A. FRIES
General Purchasing Agent:
BRIG. GEN. CHARLES G. DAWES
Director Motor Transport Corps:
BRIG. GEN. MERIWETHER L. WALKER
Director Light Railways:
BRIG. GEN. CHARLES H. MCKINSTRY
*Director Renting, Requisition and Claims
Service:*
COL. JOHN A. HULL

402 APPENDIX

SERVICES OF SUPPLY (*Continued*)

Director Army Service Corps:
 Col. Douglas Settle
Base Section No. 1:
 Col. John S. Sewell
Base Section No. 3:
 Maj. Gen. John Biddle
Base Section No. 5:
 Brig. Gen. George H. Harries
Base Section No. 7:
 Col. William Kelly
Intermediate Section:
 Brig. Gen. Arthur Johnson

Chief War Risk Insurance Section:
 Col. Henry D. Lindsley
Base Section No. 2:
 Brig. Gen. William D. Connor
Base Section No. 4:
 Brig. Gen. Richard Coulter, Jr.
Base Section No. 6:
 Col. Melvin W. Rowell
Base Section No. 8:
 Brig. Gen. Charles G. Treat
Advance Section:
 Brig. Gen. William R. Sample

District of Paris: Brig. Gen. William W. Harts

FIRST ARMY

Commander:
 Lt. Gen. Hunter Liggett
Deputy Chief of Staff:
 Col. Walter S. Grant
Asst. Chief of Staff, G-2:
 Col. Willey Howell
Asst. Chief of Staff, G-4:
 Col. John L. DeWitt
 Lt. Col. Edward G. McCleave
 (Acting)
Chief of Air Service:
 Col. Thomas DeW. Milling
Chief Signal Officer:
 Col. Parker Hitt
Chief of Chemical Warfare Service:
 Col. John W. N. Schulz

Chief of Staff:
 Brig. Gen. Hugh A. Drum
Asst. Chief of Staff, G-1:
 Col. Leon B. Kromer
Asst. Chief of Staff, G-3:
 Col. George C. Marshall, Jr.
Asst. Chief of Staff, G-5:
 Col. Lewis H. Watkins
Chief of Artillery:
 Maj. Gen. Edward F. McGlachlin, Jr.
Chief Engineer Officer:
 Col. George R. Spalding
Chief Surgeon:
 Col. Alexander N. Stark

SECOND ARMY

Commander:
 Lt. Gen. Robert L. Bullard
Deputy Chief of Staff:
 Col. David L. Stone
Asst. Chief of Staff, G-2:
 Lt. Col. Charles F. Thompson
Asst. Chief of Staff, G-4:
 Col. George P. Tyner
Chief of Artillery:
 Maj. Gen. William Lassiter
Chief of Air Service:
 Col. Frank P. Lahm
Chief Surgeon:
 Col. Charles R. Reynolds

Chief of Staff:
 Brig. Gen. Stuart Heintzelman
Asst. Chief of Staff, G-1:
 Col. George K. Wilson
Asst. Chief of Staff, G-3:
 Col. William N. Haskell
Asst. Chief of Staff, G-5:
 Col. James E. Bell
Chief Engineer Officer:
 Brig. Gen. Herbert Deakyne
Chief Signal Officer:
 Col. Hanson B. Black
Chief of Chemical Warfare Service:
 Lt. Col. Byron C. Goss

THIRD ARMY

(Organized after the Armistice; Commander, Maj. Gen. Joseph T. Dickman.)

I CORPS

Commander:
   MAJ. GEN. JOSEPH T. DICKMAN
Asst. Chief of Staff, G-1:
   LT. COL. GEORGE GRUNERT
Asst. Chief of Staff, G-3:
   COL. JOHN C. MONTGOMERY

Chief of Staff:
   BRIG. GEN. MALIN CRAIG
Asst. Chief of Staff, G-2:
   COL. RICHARD H. WILLIAMS
Chief of Artillery:
   MAJ. GEN. WILLIAM S. McNAIR (From Nov. 7)

II CORPS

Commander:
   MAJ. GEN. GEORGE W. READ
Asst. Chief of Staff, G-1:
   LT. COL. RICHARD K. HALE
Asst. Chief of Staff, G-3:
   COL. FRED E. BUCHAN
   LT. COL. LAWRENCE E. HOHL (Acting)

Chief of Staff:
   BRIG. GEN. GEORGE S. SIMONDS
Asst. Chief of Staff, G-2:
   LT. COL. KERR T. RIGGS
Asst. Chief of Staff, G-4:
   LT. COL. JOHN P. TERRELL

III CORPS

Commander:
   MAJ. GEN. JOHN L. HINES
Asst. Chief of Staff, G-1:
   LT. COL. MARTIN C. SHALLENBERGER
Asst. Chief of Staff, G-3:
   COL. ADNA R. CHAFFEE

Chief of Staff:
   BRIG. GEN. CAMPBELL KING
Asst. Chief of Staff, G-2:
   LT. COL. HORACE C. STEBBINS
Chief of Artillery:
   MAJ. GEN. CLEMENT A. F. FLAGLER

IV CORPS

Commander:
   MAJ. GEN. CHARLES H. MUIR
Asst. Chief of Staff, G-1:
   LT. COL. JAMES A. ULIO
Asst. Chief of Staff, G-3:
   COL. BERKELEY ENOCHS

Chief of Staff:
   BRIG. GEN. BRIANT H. WELLS
Asst. Chief of Staff, G-2:
   LT. COL. JOSEPH W. STILWELL
Chief of Artillery:
   BRIG. GEN. WILLIAM M. CRUIKSHANK

V CORPS

Commander:
   MAJ. GEN. CHARLES P. SUMMERALL
Asst. Chief of Staff, G-1:
   COL. ALBERT W. FOREMAN
Asst. Chief of Staff, G-3:
   COL. THOMAS H. EMERSON

Chief of Staff:
   BRIG. GEN. WILSON B. BURTT
Asst. Chief of Staff, G-2:
   LT. COL. GEORGE M. RUSSELL
Chief of Artillery:
   BRIG. GEN. DWIGHT E. AULTMAN

VI CORPS

Commander:
   MAJ. GEN. CHARLES C. BALLOU
Asst. Chief of Staff, G-1:
   COL. CHARLES H. BRIDGES
Asst. Chief of Staff, G-3:
   COL. GEORGE F. BALTZELL

Chief of Staff:
   COL. EDGAR T. COLLINS
Asst. Chief of Staff, G-2:
   LT. COL. SAMUEL T. MACKALL
Chief of Artillery:
   BRIG. GEN. ALBERT J. BOWLEY (From Nov. 7)

VII CORPS

Commander:
   (Chief of Staff, Acting)
Asst. Chief of Staff, G-1:
   COL. CLYFFARD GAME

Chief of Staff:
   COL. HERBERT J. BREES
Asst. Chief of Staff, G-2:
   COL. GEORGE A. HERBST

   Asst. Chief of Staff, G-3: MAJ. DAVID E. CAIN (Acting)

1ST DIVISION

Commander:
BRIG. GEN. FRANK PARKER
1st Infantry Brigade:
COL. HJALMER ERICKSON (*Ad interim*)

Chief of Staff:
COL. JOHN N. GREELY
2d Infantry Brigade:
BRIG. GEN. FRANCIS C. MARSHALL

1st Field Artillery Brigade: BRIG. GEN. HENRY W. BUTNER

2D DIVISION

Commander:
MAJ. GEN. JOHN A. LEJEUNE, U.S.M.C.
3d Infantry Brigade:
COL. ROBERT O. VAN HORN

Chief of Staff:
COL. JAMES C. RHEA
4th Infantry Brigade:
BRIG. GEN. WENDELL C. NEVILLE, U.S.M.C.

2d Field Artillery Brigade: BRIG. GEN. ALBERT J. BOWLEY

3D DIVISION

Commander:
BRIG. GEN. PRESTON BROWN
5th Infantry Brigade:
BRIG. GEN. FRED W. SLADEN

Chief of Staff:
COL. ROBERT McCLEAVE
6th Infantry Brigade:
BRIG. GEN. ORA E. HUNT

3d Field Artillery Brigade: BRIG. GEN. HARRY G. BISHOP

4TH DIVISION

Commander:
MAJ. GEN. MARK L. HERSEY
7th Infantry Brigade:
BRIG. GEN. BENJAMIN A. POORE

Chief of Staff:
COL. CHRISTIAN A. BACH
8th Infantry Brigade:
BRIG. GEN. EWING E. BOOTH

4th Field Artillery Brigade: BRIG. GEN. EDWIN B. BABBITT

5TH DIVISION

Commander:
MAJOR GEN HANSON E. ELY
9th Infantry Brigade:
BRIG. JOSEPH C. CASTNER

Chief of Staff:
COL. CLEMENT A. TROTT
10th Infantry Brigade:
BRIG. GEN. PAUL B. MALONE

5th Field Artillery Brigade: BRIG. GEN. WILLIAM C. RIVERS

6TH DIVISION

Commander:
MAJ. GEN. WALTER H. GORDON
11th Infantry Brigade:
BRIG. GEN. WILLIAM R. DASHIELL

Chief of Staff:
COL. JOSEPH W. BEACHAM, JR.
12th Infantry Brigade:
BRIG. GEN. JAMES B. ERWIN

6th Field Artillery Brigade: BRIG. GEN. EDWARD A. MILLAR
LT. COL. BALLARD LYERLY (*Ad interim*)

7TH DIVISION

Commander:
MAJ. GEN. EDMUND WITTENMYER
13th Infantry Brigade:
BRIG. GEN. ALFRED W. BJORNSTAD

Chief of Staff:
LT. COL. WILLIAM W. TAYLOR, JR.
14th Infantry Brigade:
BRIG. GEN. LUTZ WAHL

7th Field Artillery Brigade: BRIG. GEN. TIEMANN N. HORN

26TH DIVISION

Commander:
BRIG. GEN. FRANK E. BAMFORD
51st Infantry Brigade:
BRIG. GEN. GEORGE H. SHELTON

Chief of Staff:
COL. DUNCAN K. MAJOR, JR.
52d Infantry Brigade:
BRIG. GEN. CHARLES H. COLE

51st Field Artillery Brigade: COL. OTHO W. B. FARR

27TH DIVISION

Commander:
MAJ. GEN. JOHN F. O'RYAN
53d Infantry Brigade:
BRIG. GEN. CHARLES I. DeBEVOISE

Chief of Staff:
COL. STANLEY H. FORD
54th Infantry Brigade:
BRIG. GEN. PALMER E. PIERCE
COL. EDGAR S. JENNINGS (*Ad Interim*)

52d Field Artillery Brigade: BRIG. GEN. GEORGE A. WINGATE

28TH DIVISION

Commander:
MAJ. GEN. WILLIAM H. HAY
55th Infantry Brigade:
BRIG. GEN. FREDERICK D. EVANS

Chief of Staff:
COL. WALTER C. SWEENEY
56th Infantry Brigade:
BRIG. GEN. FRANK H. ALBRIGHT

53d Field Artillery Brigade: BRIG. GEN. WILLIAM G. PRICE, JR.

29TH DIVISION

Commander:
MAJ. GEN. CHARLES G. MORTON
57th Infantry Brigade:
BRIG. GEN. LaRoy S. UPTON

Chief of Staff:
COL. SYDNEY A. CLOMAN
58th Infantry Brigade:
COL. JOHN McA. PALMER

54th Field Artillery Brigade: BRIG. GEN. LUCIUS R. HOLBROOK

30TH DIVISION

Commander:
MAJ. GEN. EDWARD M. LEWIS
59th Infantry Brigade:
BRIG. GEN. LAWRENCE D. TYSON

Chief of Staff:
COL. JOHN K. HERR
60th Infantry Brigade:
BRIG. GEN. SAMSON L. FAISON

55th Field Artillery Brigade: BRIG. GEN. JOHN W. KILBRETH, JR.

31ST DIVISION (Depot)

Commander:
BRIG. GEN. WALTER A. HARRIS
62d Infantry Brigade:
BRIG. GEN. ROBERT E. STEINER

61st Infantry Brigade:
DIVISION COMMANDER
56th Field Artillery Brigade:
BRIG. GEN. JOHN L. HAYDEN

32D DIVISION

Commander:
MAJ. GEN. WILLIAM G. HAAN
63d Infantry Brigade:
BRIG. GEN. FRANK R. McCOY

Chief of Staff:
COL. ROBERT McC. BECK, JR.
64th Infantry Brigade:
BRIG. GEN. EDWIN B. WINANS

57th Field Artillery Brigade: BRIG. GEN. GEORGE LeR. IRWIN

33D DIVISION

Commander:
MAJ. GEN. GEORGE BELL, JR.
65th Infantry Brigade:
BRIG. GEN. EDWARD L. KING

Chief of Staff:
BRIG. GEN. WILLIAM K. NAYLOR
66th Infantry Brigade:
BRIG. GEN. PAUL A. WOLF

58th Field Artillery Brigade: BRIG. GEN. HENRY D. TODD, JR.
BRIG. GEN. EDWARD A. MILLAR (*Ad interim*)

34TH DIVISION (Replacement)

Commander:
BRIG. GEN. JOHN A. JOHNSTON
67th Infantry Brigade:
BRIG. GEN. HUBERT A. ALLEN

Chief of Staff:
COL. WILLIAM H. RAYMOND
68th Infantry Brigade:
COL. WILLIAM T. MOLLISON

59th Field Artillery Brigade: COL. THOMAS W. HOLLYDAY

406 APPENDIX

35TH DIVISION

Commander:
MAJ. GEN. PETER E. TRAUB
BRIG. GEN. THOMAS B. DUGAN (*Ad interim*)
69th Infantry Brigade:
BRIG. GEN. LOUIS M. NUTTMAN

Chief of Staff:
COL. HAMILTON S. HAWKINS
70th Infantry Brigade:
BRIG. GEN. THOMAS B. DUGAN
BRIG. GEN. CHARLES GERHARDT (*Ad interim*)

60th Field Artillery Brigade: BRIG. GEN. LUCIEN G. BERRY

36TH DIVISION

Commander:
MAJ. GEN. WILLIAM R. SMITH
71st Infantry Brigade:
BRIG. GEN. PEGRAM WHITWORTH

Chief of Staff:
COL. EZEKIAL J. WILLIAMS
72d Infantry Brigade:
BRIG. GEN. JOHN A. HULEN

61st Field Artillery Brigade: BRIG. GEN. JOHN E. STEPHENS

37TH DIVISION

Commander:
MAJ. GEN. CHARLES S. FARNSWORTH
73d Infantry Brigade:
BRIG. GEN. WILLIAM M. FASSETT

Chief of Staff:
COL. DANA T. MERRILL
74th Infantry Brigade:
BRIG. GEN. WILLIAM P. JACKSON

62d Field Artillery Brigade: BRIG. GEN. EDWIN BURR

38TH DIVISION (Replacement)

Commander:
MAJ. GEN. ROBERT L. HOWZE
75th Infantry Brigade:
BRIG. GEN. FRANK M. CALDWELL
COL. GEORGE T. SMITH (*Ad interim*)

Chief of Staff:
COL. JAMES B. GOWEN
76th Infantry Brigade:
COL. GEORGE H. HEALEY

63d Field Artillery Brigade: BRIG. GEN. AUGUSTINE MCINTYRE

39TH DIVISION (Depot)

Commander:
MAJ. GEN. HENRY C. HODGES, JR.
77th Infantry Brigade:
BRIG. GEN. LUCIUS L. DURFEE

Chief of Staff:
COL. HENRY H. SHEEN (Acting)
78th Infantry Brigade:
BRIG. GEN. WILDS P. RICHARDSON
COL. GEORGE C. HOSKINS (*Ad interim*)

64th Field Artillery Brigade: BRIG. GEN. IRA A. HAYNES

40TH DIVISION (Depot)

Commander:
MAJ. GEN. FREDERICK S. STRONG
79th Infantry Brigade:
BRIG. GEN. ALEXANDER M. TUTHILL

Chief of Staff:
LT. COL. FRANCIS H. FARNUM (acting)
80th Infantry Brigade:
COL. CHARLES F. HUTCHINS (*Ad interim*)

65th Field Artillery Brigade: BRIG. GEN. RICHARD W. YOUNG

41ST DIVISION (Depot)

Commander:
BRIG. GEN. ELI K. COLE, U.S.M.C.
81st Infantry Brigade:
(Replacement)

Chief of Staff:
COL. OREN B. MEYER (Acting)
82d Infantry Brigade:
BRIG. GEN. EDWARD VOLLRATH

66th Field Artillery Brigade: COL. ERNEST D. SCOTT

42D DIVISION

Commander:
MAJ. GEN. CHARLES T. MENOHER
83d Infantry Brigade:
COL. HENRY J. REILLY

Chief of Staff:
COL. WILLIAM N. HUGHES, JR.
84th Infantry Brigade:
BRIG. GEN. DOUGLAS MACARTHUR

67th Field Artillery Brigade: BRIG. GEN. GEORGE G. GATLEY

76TH DIVISION (Depot)

Commander:
MAJ. GEN. HARRY F. HODGES
151st Infantry Brigade:
COL. PERCY W. ARNOLD

Chief of Staff:
LT. COL. GEORGE M. PEEK
152d Infantry Brigade:
COL. JOHN F. PRESTON

151st Field Artillery Brigade: BRIG. GEN. RICHMOND P. DAVIS

77TH DIVISION

Commander:
MAJ. GEN. ROBERT ALEXANDER
153d Infantry Brigade:
BRIG. GEN. WILLIAM R. SMEDBERG, JR.

Chief of Staff:
COL. CLARENCE O. SHERRILL
154th Infantry Brigade:
BRIG. GEN. HARRISON J. PRICE

152d Field Artillery Brigade: BRIG. GEN. MANUS McCLOSKEY

78TH DIVISION

Commander:
MAJ. GEN. JAMES H. McRAE
155th Infantry Brigade:
BRIG. GEN. SANFORD B. STANBERY

Chief of Staff:
COL. CHARLES D. HERRON
156th Infantry Brigade:
BRIG. GEN. JAMES T. DEAN

153d Field Artillery Brigade: BRIG. GEN. CLINT C. HEARN

79TH DIVISION

Commander:
MAJ. GEN. JOSEPH E. KUHN
157th Infantry Brigade:
BRIG. GEN. WILLIAM J. NICHOLSON

Chief of Staff:
COL. TENNEY ROSS
158th Infantry Brigade:
BRIG. GEN. EVAN M. JOHNSON

154th Field Artillery Brigade: BRIG. GEN. ANDREW HERO, JR.

80TH DIVISION

Commander:
MAJ. GEN. ADELBERT CRONKHITE
159th Infantry Brigade:
BRIG. GEN. GEORGE H. JAMERSON
MAJ. GEN. ADELBERT CRONKHITE (*Ad interim*)

Chief of Staff:
COL. WILLIAM H. WALDRON
160th Infantry Brigade:
BRIG. GEN. LLOYD M. BRETT

155th Field Artillery Brigade: COL. ROBERT S. WELSH

81ST DIVISION

Commander:
MAJ. GEN. CHARLES J. BAILEY
161st Infantry Brigade:
BRIG. GEN. GEORGE W. McIVER

Chief of Staff:
COL. CHARLES D. ROBERTS
162d Infantry Brigade:
BRIG. GEN. MUNROE McFARLAND

156th Field Artillery Brigade: BRIG. GEN. ANDREW MOSES

82D DIVISION

Commander:
MAJ. GEN. GEORGE B. DUNCAN
163d Infantry Brigade:
BRIG. GEN. MARCUS D. CRONIN

Chief of Staff:
COL. GORDON JOHNSTON
164th Infantry Brigade:
BRIG. GEN. JULIAN R. LINDSEY

157th Field Artillery Brigade: COL. EARLE D'A. PEARCE (*Ad interim*)

83D DIVISION (Depot)

Commander:
MAJ. GEN. EDWIN F. GLENN
165th Infantry Brigade:
BRIG. GEN. LOUIS C. COVELL

Chief of Staff:
COL. KENYON A. JOYCE
166th Infantry Brigade:
COL. WILLIAM H. ALLAIRE

158th Field Artillery Brigade: BRIG. GEN. ADRIAN S. FLEMING

84TH DIVISION (Replacement)

Commander:
MAJ. GEN. HARRY C. HALE
167th Infantry Brigade:
BRIG. GEN. DANIEL B. DEVORE

Chief of Staff:
COL. LAURENCE HALSTEAD
168th Infantry Brigade:
BRIG. GEN. WILBER E. WILDER

159th Field Artillery Brigade: COL. CHARLES M. BUNDEL

85TH DIVISION (Depot)

Commander:
MAJ. GEN. CHASE W. KENNEDY
169th Infantry Brigade:
COL. BENJAMIN W. ATKINSON *(Ad interim)*

Chief of Staff:
COL. JAMES M. KIMBROUGH, JR.
170th Infantry Brigade:
COL. GEORGE E. BALL *(Ad interim)*

160th Field Artillery Brigade: BRIG. GEN. GUY H. PRESTON

86TH DIVISION (Replacement)

Commander:
COL. GUY G. PALMER *(Ad interim)*
171st Infantry Brigade:
COL. GUY G. PALMER *(Ad interim)*

Chief of Staff:
LT. COL. CHARLES E. T. LULL (Acting)
172d Infantry Brigade:
COL. CHARLES R. HOWLAND *(Ad interim)*

161st Field Artillery Brigade: BRIG. GEN. OLIVER L. SPAULDING, JR.

87TH DIVISION

Commander:
MAJ. GEN. SAMUEL D. STURGIS
173d Infantry Brigade:
COL. JOHN O'SHEA *(Ad interim)*

Chief of Staff:
COL. HENRY R. RICHMOND
174th Infantry Brigade:
BRIG. GEN. WILLIAM F. MARTIN

162d Field Artillery Brigade: LT. COL. ROBERT R. LOVE *(Ad interim)*

88TH DIVISION

Commander:
MAJ. GEN. WILLIAM WEIGEL
175th Infantry Brigade:
BRIG. GEN. MERCH B. STEWART

Chief of Staff:
LT. COL. FAY W. BRABSON (Acting)
176th Infantry Brigade:
BRIG. GEN. WILLIAM D. BEACH

163d Field Artillery Brigade: BRIG. GEN. STEPHEN M. FOOTE

89TH DIVISION

Commander:
MAJ. GEN. WILLIAM M. WRIGHT
177th Infantry Brigade:
MAJ. GEN. FRANK L. WINN

Chief of Staff:
COL. JOHN C. H. LEE
178th Infantry Brigade:
BRIG. GEN. THOMAS G. HANSON

164th Field Artillery Brigade: BRIG. GEN. EDWARD T. DONNELLY

90TH DIVISION

Commander:
MAJ. GEN. HENRY T. ALLEN
179th Infantry Brigade:
BRIG. GEN. JOSEPH P. O'NEIL

Chief of Staff:
COL. JOHN J. KINGMAN
180th Infantry Brigade:
BRIG. GEN. ULYSSES G. McALEXANDER

165th Field Artillery Brigade: MAJ. RALPH B. FAIRCHILD *(Ad interim)*

91ST DIVISION

Commander:
MAJ. GEN. WILLIAM H. JOHNSTON
181st Infantry Brigade:
BRIG. GEN. JOHN B. McDONALD

Chief of Staff:
COL. HENRY C. JEWETT
182d Infantry Brigade:
BRIG. GEN. VERNON A. CALDWELL

166th Field Artillery Brigade: BRIG. GEN. BEVERLY F. BROWN
COL. LOUIS E. BENNETT *(Ad interim)*

92D DIVISION

Commander:
MAJ. GEN. CHARLES C. BALLOU
183d Infantry Brigade:
BRIG. GEN. MALVERN-HILL BARNUM

Chief of Staff:
COL. ALLEN J. GREER
184th Infantry Brigade:
COL. FRED R. BROWN *(Ad interim)*

167th Field Artillery Brigade: BRIG. GEN. JOHN H. SHERBURNE

INDEX

INDEX

ABAINVILLE, i. 126.
Abaucourt, capture of, ii. 385.
Abbeville, ii. 20-34.
Adamson, Lieut. George E., i. 381, ii. 5, 192.
Address to First Division A.E.F., i. 393.
Adinkerke, i. 269.
Adjutant General; branch office, Tours, ii. 194.
Aërial photography, i. 347.
Agreement, the Abbeville, ii. 49; the Rapallo, i. 215.
Ailette, the, i. 203.
Aincreville, capture of, ii. 353.
Aire River, ii. 282, 296, 324, 329, 340.
Airplane manufacture, plans for coöperation, ii. 18.
Airplane pilots, training, i. 161.
Airplanes, 5,000 ordered from France, i. 161; exaggerated newspaper reports, i. 334; French contract abrogated, i. 285; order placed in Italy, i. 325.
Air Service, condition on entry into the war, i. 27; efficiency of, ii. 125; organization and equipment, i. 161.
Air Service School, Issoudun, i. 346.
Aisne River, i. 203, ii. 61, 241, 244, 251, 326, 375.
Albert, King of Belgium, i. 268, 270.
Alexander, Gen. Robert, ii. 17, 291, 323, 339, 373.
Allaire, Col. William H., i. 126, 133.
Allen, Gen. Henry T., ii. 129, 145, 265, 290, 372, 384.
Allen, Gov. Henry J., i. 164.
Allenby, Field Marshal, i. 46, 258.
Allery hospital center, ii. 202.
Allied armies, mutual support, i. 300; replacement problems, ii. 122; strength of in May, 1917, i. 8.
Allied Maritime Transport Council, i. 333, 336, ii. 9, 13, 15, 38.
Allies, morale of in 1917, i. 94; in June, 1918, ii. 105; requests for American troops, ii. 83, 106, 112; strength in Nov. 1917, i. 233, in spring of 1918, i. 233; urge larger shipments of men, ii. 72-80.
Alvord, Gen. Benjamin, i. 20, 50, 111, 193, 196, ii. 38.
Amalgamation, French and British pro-

posals, i. 159, 165, 254, 269, 273, 288, ii. 6; Foch's plea for, ii. 99, 219; Joffre's views, i. 305; Lloyd George's complaint, ii. 315.
Ambulance sections borrowed from Italy, ii. 308.
American agencies in British Isles, ii. 201.
American Chamber of Commerce, Paris, i. 93.
American characteristics, as reported by French Mission, ii. 66.
AMERICAN EXPEDITIONARY FORCES:
First American Army, A.E.F., order creating, ii. 175; organized, ii. 212; Gen. Pershing takes command, ii. 212; organization completed, ii. 260; total strength in St. Mihiel drive, ii. 261; order of battle, St. Mihiel, ii. 265; order of battle in Meuse-Argonne attack, ii. 290; Gen. Liggett placed in command, ii. 350; orders for general attack, Oct. 21st, ii. 356; order for Briey-Longwy drive, ii. 378; total strength in Meuse-Argonne, ii. 389.
Second American Army, A.E.F., order to organize, ii. 329; organization completed, ii. 335; order for the Briey-Longwy drive, ii. 378; composition of, ii. 383.
I Corps, i. 357, 369, 395, ii. 17, 94, 126, 143, 153, 164, 175, 208, 210, 265, 266, 269, 289, 291, 292, 294, 296, 297, 302, 322, 323, 329, 336, 339, 351, 373, 375, 376, 380, 381, 383.
II Corps, ii. 1, 127, 129, 137, 220, 294, 304, 353.
III Corps, ii. 113, 127, 151, 158, 167, 175, 210, 289, 290, 292, 294, 295, 297, 322, 323, 333, 336, 338, 339, 352, 353, 372, 375, 376, 379, 384, 386.
IV Corps, ii. 127, 239, 265, 266, 269, 290, 336, 353.
V Corps, ii. 151, 265, 266, 269, 289, 290, 292, 296, 297, 322, 323, 329, 332, 336, 338, 339, 352, 353, 372, 373, 375, 376, 380, 381, 383.
VI Corps, ii. 383.
1st Division, i. 3, 196, 239, 323, 338,

AMERICAN EXPEDITIONARY FORCES—*Continued*

42d Div., i. 337, 338, 369, 395, ii. 17, 46, 47, 91, 95, 96, 104, 113, 153, 226, 236, 259, 336; origin of, i. 25; arrival in France, i. 252; at Lafauche, i. 264; Badonviller raid by Germans, i. 339; in German offensive, July 15, ii. 151; at Soissons, ii. 208; in St. Mihiel drive, ii. 265, 268, 286; in Meuse-Argonne battle, ii. 290, 323, 338-340, 373, 380, 381.

76th Div., ii. 192.

77th Div., i. 343, ii. 1, 3, 20, 46, 61, 104, 113, 145, 323, 333, 339, 373, 392; in Second Battle of the Marne, ii. 210; in Meuse-Argonne battle, ii. 291, 297, 299, 323, 340, 376, 380-385; "Lost Battalion," ii. 324, 330, 331.

78th Div., ii. 20, 129, 226, 290, 373; in St. Mihiel drive, ii. 266; in Meuse-Argonne battle, ii. 340, 352, 375, 376, 380.

79th Div., ii. 192, 302; in Meuse-Argonne battle, ii. 291, 294, 296, 297, 298, 379, 385.

80th Div., i. 343, ii. 20, 70, 129, 226, 290, 323, 373; in St. Mihiel drive, ii. 266, 269; in Meuse-Argonne battle, ii. 295, 297, 333, 375, 380.

81st Div., ii. 241, 379, 380, 385, 386.

82d Div., i. 343; ii. 20, 46, 60, 70, 104, 145, 226, 392; in St. Mihiel drive, ii. 265, 266, 268, 270; in Meuse-Argonne battle, ii. 291, 323, 330, 333, 340.

83d Div., ii. 94, 118, 129.

84th Div., ii. 306.

85th Div., ii. 241.

86th Div., ii. 306.

87th Div., ii. 306.

88th Div., ii. 241, 383.

89th Div., ii. 145, 226, 259, 290, 336, 373; in St. Mihiel drive, ii. 265, 266; in Meuse-Argonne battle, 353, 376, 380, 383, 385.

90th Div., ii. 129, 145, 226, 259, 265, 290, 372, 383; in St. Mihiel drive, ii. 266, 270; in Meuse-Argonne battle, 376, 384, 386.

91st Div., ii. 192, 226, 266, 291, 323, 329; in Meuse-Argonne battle, ii. 296, 298, 302; in Flanders, at Audenarde, ii. 385.

92d Div., ii. 45, 115, 129, 145, 225, 228; in Meuse-Argonne battle, ii. 291, 302, 323, 383, 384, 386.

93d Div., i. 268, 291, ii. 46, 97, 115.

3d Brigade, ii. 376.

7th Brigade, ii. 147.

8th Brigade, i. 4.

51st Brigade, ii. 269.

57th Brigade, ii. 332.

64th Brigade, ii. 340.

84th Brigade, ii. 340.

Infantry

9th Regt., i. 321.

15th Regt., ii. 90.

16th Regt., i. 3, 91, 126, 217.

17th Regt., ii. 90.

18th Regt., i. 3, 126, ii. 60.

23d Regt., i. 321.

26th Regt., i. 3, 126, ii. 60.

28th Regt., i. 3, 126; ii. 59.

30th Regt., ii. 153.

38th Regt., ii. 153.

101st Regt., i. 197.

131st Regt., ii. 215.

165th Regt., i. 338.

166th Regt., i. 338.

168th Regt., i. 338.

332d Regt., ii. 94.

339th Regt., sent to Russia, ii. 176.

369th Regt., i. 268, ii. 97.

Cavalry

3d Regt., i. 323.

10th Regt., ii. 117.

Marine

5th Regt., i. 321, ii. 143, 326.

6th Regt., i. 321.

Engineer

6th Regt., i. 355, 397.

11th Regt., i. 252.

19th Regt., ii. 199.

35th Regt., ii. 198.

30th Gas and Flame Regt., ii. 46.

Artillery

6th Field, i. 3.

151st Field, i. 339.

Machine Gun

7th Battalion, at Château-Thierry, ii. 62.

American Expeditionary Forces, preliminary plans on the *Baltic*, i. 43; organizing in France, i. 71; school system adopted, i. 150-156; civil jurisdiction question, i. 182; official newspaper *Stars and Stripes*, i. 318; résumé of strength, May 10, 1918, ii. 46; discipline in, ii. 97; minimum force of 3,000,000 fixed, ii. 107; campaign of 1919 discussed, ii. 232; combat strength, Oct. 23, 1918, ii. 357; total strength, June 30, 1917, i. 90; July 31, 1917, i. 127; Aug. 31, 1917, i. 156; Sept. 30, 1917, i. 188; Oct. 31, 1917, i. 213; Nov. 30, 1917, i. 252; Dec. 31, 1917, i. 268; Jan. 31, 1918, i. 310; Feb. 28, 1918, i. 338; Mar. 31,

414

AMERICAN EXPEDITIONARY FORCES—Con-
tinued
1918, i. 373; April 30, 1918, ii, 20;
May 31, 1918, ii. 70; June 30, 1918, ii.
129; July 31, 1918, ii. 192; Aug. 31,
1918, ii. 241; Sept. 30, 1918, ii. 306;
Oct. 31, 1918, ii. 370.
American Library Ass'n, i. 108.
American sector, selection of, i. 84.
American troops, first appearance in Paris,
i. 92; offered to General Foch, i. 364;
to General Pétain, i. 357.
Ames, Winthrop, i. 320.
Amiens, i. 355, 362, ii. 34, 91, 280.
Ammunition, manufacturing capacity in
1916, i. 27; problems, i. 221.
Amundsen, Capt. Roald, i. 308.
Ancemont, ii. 48.
Anderson, Col. E. D., i. 100.
Anderson, Lieut. M. H., ii. 219.
Andrews, Col. Avery D., i. 333, 337, ii.
138, 192, 229, 235.
Angers, i. 174, ii. 200.
Ansauville, i. 323.
Anthoine, Gen., i. 299, 356.
Antilles, the, torpedoed, i. 201.
Apremont, ii. 330; capture of, ii. 299.
Arbe Guernon, ii. 354.
Arcachon, i. 211.
Archangel, ii. 149.
Archbishop of Canterbury, i. 49, ii. 42, 43.
Archbishop of Chaumont, i. 264.
Archbishop of Langres, i. 264.
Arches, ii. 113.
Ardennes, the, ii. 147.
Argonne Forest, i. 83, ii. 246, 247, 281,
282, 291-297, 307, 322, 329, 331, 388.
Arietal Farm, taken, ii. 324.
Armentières, i. 396.
Armistice, General Orders concerning, ii.
390.
Armistice proposal discussed by Allied
Conference, ii. 359-363; terms proposed,
ii. 366; announcement of, ii. 388.
Armistice Conference, German delegates at,
ii. 394.
Arras, i. 353.
Arras-Argonne Front discussed, ii. 147.
Arras sector, British advance in, i. 69.
Arras Offensive, i. 113.
Artillery, British, July, 1917, i. 113.
Artillery in Meuse-Argonne battle, ii. 285,
373; in St. Mihiel drive, ii. 260; short-
age and needs, i. 105, ii. 64, 173.
Artillery School, Camp Mailly, i. 208; Le
Valdahon, i. 173.
Artillery schools, i. 173, 174, 344.
Artillery training camp, Meucon, ii. 200;
at Souge, ii. 197.

Artillerymen requested by British, ii. 41.
Asser, Sir John, i. 310.
Astor, Lady, i. 50.
Astor, Lord, ii. 5.
Atterbury, Gen. William W., i. 107, 108,
135, 156, 170, 201, 252, 258, 263, 283,
287, 288, 292, 308, 326, 340, 352, 391,
ii. 138, 177, 192.
Attigny, ii. 281.
Aubréville, ii. 286.
Audenarde, capture of, ii. 385.
Aultman, Col. Dwight E., i. 100.
Australian 5th Division, ii. 304.
Austria, i. 4, 5, 172.
Austrian offensive at Caporetto, ii. 206.
Austrian repulse in Italy, ii. 98.
Austro-Hungarian divisions, distribution
of, Nov., 1917, i. 235.
Austro-Hungary, ii. 141.
Autreville, occupied, ii. 385.
Aviation, British, in 1917, i. 115; con-
ditions Aug. 1, 1918, ii. 194; condi-
tions in America in 1917, i. 27; first all-
American squadron, ii. 208; in St.
Mihiel drive, ii. 260; organization diffi-
culties, i. 333; prior to the war, i. 159;
problems, i. 285, 389, ii. 50; in the
Meuse-Argonne battle, ii. 337; shortage
of planes and material, i. 325.
Aviation Instruction Center for Observers,
ii. 195.
Aviation School, Issoudun, i. 207, 211, ii.
109, 202.
Aviation stations, French, i. 326.
Aviators, increase in, ii. 125; training, ii.
51; training in England, i. 286.
Avocourt, ii. 284.

BAÂLON, ii. 384, 386.
Baccarat, i. 339, ii. 17, 104, 113.
Bacon, Col. Robert H., i. 23, 59, 283, ii.
60, 129, 169.
Badonviller, i. 339.
Bailey, Gen. Charles J., ii. 241, 379,
385.
Baker, Col. Chauncey B., i. 100.
Baker, Newton D., i. 17, 18, 257, 284,
293, 313, 330, 352, 357, ii. 6, 8, 33,
34, 110, 177, 235, 311, 377; instructions to General Pershing, i. 38; writes
of problems of war, i. 223; arrives in
Paris, i. 342; inspects American organization in France, i. 343-350; goes to
London, i. 358; confers on attitude of
Allies, i. 358-367; visits Italy, i. 371,
372; discusses training with British
troops, i. 383-384; letter to the A.E.F.,
i. 385; instructions for Liberty Day, i.

Jadwin, Gen. Edgar, ii. 108, 193.
James, Col., i. 54.
Jametz, capture of, ii. 384.
Japan, military development of, i. 4; aid to the Allies, i. 237.
Jaulgonne, ii. 152; capture of, ii. 165.
Jaulny, ii. 270.
Jay, Capt. Dean, i. 317.
Jellicoe, Adm., i. 52.
Jerusalem, British advance on, i. 247; captured by British, i. 258.
Jewish Welfare Board, i. 108.
Joffre, Marshal Joseph J., i. 30, 57, 62, 91, 198, 342, ii. 53; first meeting with, i. 34; meets Pershing on arrival in Paris, i. 58; heads liaison group, i. 72; at American Chamber of Commerce lunch, i. 93; visits A.E.F. Headquarters, i. 196; disapproves amalgamation, i. 305-307; receives Distinguished Service Medal, ii. 396.
Joffre Mission to U.S.A., i. 78.
Johnson, Col. A., i. 347.
Johnson, Congressman A., i. 208.
Johnson, Gen. Evan M., ii. 3, 20.
Johnston, Gen. John A., ii. 266, 291, 302, 306, 323, 385.
Joint Army and Navy Aviation Committee, ii. 50.
Joint Note 18 of Supreme War Council, i. 360, 382, 383, ii. 6, 7, 21, 34.
Jonchery ammunition depot, i. 346.
Jones, Col. Percy, ii. 9.
Jordan, Col. H. B., ii. 16.
Joyce, Maj. Kenyon A., i. 308.
Judge Advocate General's office, European branch established, ii. 40.
Jugo-Slavs, ii. 141.
July 14th declared a holiday, ii. 133; celebration of, ii. 150.
Jusserand, Ambassador, i. 36.
Juvigny, capture of, ii. 242.

KAHN, Otto, ii. 88.
Kean, Col. Jefferson R., i. 181.
Kemmel Hill, i. 397.
Kendrick, Senator, i. 232.
Kenly, Gen. William L., i. 161, 184, 248.
Kennedy, Gen. Chase W., ii. 241.
Kenyon, Senator, i. 232.
Keppel, F. P., ii. 388.
Kerensky, Alexander F., i. 117, 233, ii. 148.
Kernan, Gen. Francis J., i. 193, 221, 248, 308, 345, 388, ii. 55, 107, 177, 193.
Kersey, Maj. Maitland, i. 46, 54.
Kiggell, Gen. Sir L. E., i. 243.
Kilbourne, Col. Charles E., i. 308.
Kilner, Col. W. G., i. 159, 346.

King, Col. Campbell, ii. 60, 167.
Kitchener, Lord, i. 166.
Knight, Ridgeway, i. 147.
Knights of Columbus, i. 108.
Knoll, the, capture of, ii. 305.
Krauthoff, Col. Charles R., i. 207.
Kreger, Gen. Edward A., ii. 38.
Kuhn, Gen. Joseph E., i. 26, ii. 192, 291, 379, 385.

LA BESACE, ii. 380.
Labor procurement bureau established, i. 319.
Laborers, shortage of, i. 186, 318, ii. 39, 193.
Lacaze, M., i. 62.
La Croix Rouge Farm, ii. 208, 209.
Lafauche, i. 264.
Lafayette Escadrille, the, i. 162.
"Lafayette, we are here," i. 93.
Lafayette, tomb of, i. 92.
La Fère, i. 353.
La Ferté-sous-Jouarre, ii. 147, 175, 212.
La Guardia, Capt. F. H., i. 317.
La Houssière, ii. 148.
Laking, Sir Guy, i. 54.
"Landes de la Lanvaux," i. 208.
Landres-et-St. Georges, ii. 338, 340, 371.
Lane, Franklin K., i. 314.
Langfitt, Gen. William C., i. 340, ii. 107, 108, 129, 192.
Langres, i. 337.
Langres General Staff School, i. 259, 347.
Langres War College, i. 155.
Lansing, Robert, Secretary of State, i. 36, ii. 342.
Laon, ii. 92.
La Pallice, i. 81, 109, 328, 343, ii. 198.
La Rochelle, i. 343, 344, ii. 198.
Lassiter, Gen. William, i. 52, 54, 164, 208.
La Tuilerie Farm, ii. 376.
Laughlin, Irwin, i. 48, 52.
Lawrence, Gen., i. 299, ii. 20-34, 169, 171.
Le Bourget, i. 62.
Le Charmel, ii. 165, 209.
Le Chesne, ii. 281, 292.
Le Chêne Tondu, ii. 299, 324.
Le Courneau, i. 174, ii. 196.
Le Courneau detention camp, i. 207, 211.
Lee, Col. H. R., ii. 202.
Leeds, Mrs. William, i. 50.
Legion of Honor, Grand Cross of, bestowed on General Pershing, ii. 213.
Le Havre, i. 269.
Lejeune, Gen. John A., ii. 97, 265, 325, 373.
Lenihan, Gen. Michael J., i. 338.
Lenin, Nikolai V. U., i. 233, ii. 149.

THE END

Help Us Help You

So that we can better provide you with the practical information you need, please take a moment to complete and return this card.

1. **I am interested in books on the following subjects:**
- ☐ architecture & design
- ☐ automotive
- ☐ aviation
- ☐ business & finance
- ☐ computer, mini & mainframe
- ☐ computer, micros
- ☐ other_____
- ☐ electronics
- ☐ engineering
- ☐ hobbies & crafts
- ☐ how-to, do-it-yourself
- ☐ military history
- ☐ nautical

2. **I own/use a computer:**
- ☐ Apple/Macintosh_____
- ☐ Commodore_____
- ☐ IBM_____
- ☐ Other_____

3. **This card came from TAB book (no. or title):**

_____

4. **I purchase books from/by:**
- ☐ general bookstores
- ☐ technical bookstores
- ☐ college bookstores
- ☐ mail
- ☐ telephone
- ☐ electronic mail
- ☐ hobby stores
- ☐ art materials stores

Comments _____

_____

_____

Name _____

Address _____

City _____

State/Zip _____

TAB BOOKS Inc.